Contributions to Management Science

More information about this series at http://www.springer.com/series/1505

Andrea S. Funk

Crowdfunding in China

A New Institutional Economics Approach

Springer

Andrea S. Funk
University of Würzburg
Würzburg, Germany

a.t.: Würzburg, Univ., Diss., 2018

ISSN 1431-1941 ISSN 2197-716X (electronic)
Contributions to Management Science
ISBN 978-3-319-97252-7 ISBN 978-3-319-97253-4 (eBook)
https://doi.org/10.1007/978-3-319-97253-4

Library of Congress Control Number: 2018954487

This Springer imprint is published by the registered company Springer Nature Switzerland AG
The registered company address is: Gewerbestrasse 11, 6330 Cham, Switzerland

To my dad who has enabled me to realise all my dreams.

Acknowledgements

I would like to thank all the people who have supported me over the last few years to realise this project. First and foremost, I would like to thank my supervisor Prof. Dr. Doris Fischer, who has always encouraged me to follow my interests and who enabled me to realise my own research project and simultaneously develop my personality. Secondly, I would like to thank Prof. Dr. Peter Bofinger for his openness on China-related topics and his readiness to assess my thesis. Thirdly, I would like to thank the University of Wuerzburg and my colleagues at the Institute of East and South Asian Cultural Studies for providing me a welcoming working atmosphere. Amongst these, I am particularly grateful to Maximilian Dullo, who served as my sparring partner for all kinds of issues. Fourthly, I thank Rune Steenberg, who introduced me to the theory of financialisation.

Besides, I would like to thank my research peers and interview partners, who have shared my passion for crowdfunding and provided me with valuable insights. Amongst these, I would like to highlight the *German Crowdfunding Network* and the *European Crowdfunding Network*, who enabled me to exchange views with other scholars and also practitioners from the field of crowdfunding. My field research would not have been possible without Feng He, the pioneer of crowdfunding in China, who promptly replied to my LinkedIn request and who introduced me to Du Mengjie. The latter proved to become my most valuable contact in Beijing. I was not just impressed by the information he provided me, but also by his personality and entrepreneurial spirit at a young age. Next to these two gentlemen, I am grateful for knowing Fabienne Frauendorfer, who has introduced me to Grace, a tough lady who patiently taught me a lot about crowdfunding in China. Moreover, I would like to thank Sean and his wife for valuable insights into China's changing crowdfunding landscape, for offering me free accommodation in Guangdong without knowing me in person, and for being heart-warming hosts.

Furthermore, I thank my brother, Joseph Funk, for convincing me of the benefits of the software LaTeX. In addition, my thanks go to Florian Thünken for assisting me with any technical questions and to Thiago Peixoto who shared long hours with me sitting at the desk whenever I was searching for hidden errors. Thanks also go to Katharina Höhendinger for proofreading my draft.

I would also like to thank my friends, who helped me to overcome struggle and supported me with scientific and non-scientific talks. Above all, I would like to thank Isabell Dettmer, Sabrina Weithmann, Laura Böhnlein, and last but not least Lena Ulmer. My family has always been the greatest support, for which I am deeply grateful.

This dissertation was financially and ideationally supported by a doctoral scholarship of *Hanns-Seidel-Stiftung*. I further thank the *Bayerisches Hochschulzentrum für China*, which has funded one of my field studies in China.

Contents

List of Abbreviations

3C	Computer, communications, and consumer electronics
A	Agent
ABC	Agricultural Bank of China
ADBC	Agricultural Development Bank of China
AMC	Asset management company
AON	All-or-nothing crowdfunding
app	Application
ATM	Automatic teller machine
B2B	Business-to-business
B2C	Business-to-consumer
BA	Business angel
BaFin	Bundesanstalt für Finanzdienstleistungsaufsicht
BAT	Baidu Alibaba Tencent
bn	Billion
BOC	Bank of China
BOCOM	Bank of Communications
C2C	Consumer-to-consumer
CBRC	China Banking Regulatory Commission
CCP	Chinese Communist Party
CCTV	China Central Television
CDB	China Development Bank
CEB	China Exim Bank
CF	Crowdfunding
CFP	Crowdfunding platform
CIC	China Investment Corporation
CMB	China Minsheng Bank
CN	China
CNNIC	China Internet Network Information Center
COD	Cash on delivery
CSRC	China Securities Regulatory Commission
e-	Electronic-based

EC	Equity crowdfunding
ECN	European Crowdfunding Network
e.g.	For example
etc.	Et cetera
excl.	Excluding
FinTech	Financial Technology
GCN	German Crowdfunding Network
GDP	Gross domestic product
GMV	Gross merchandise value
Huijin	Central Huijin Investment Company
ibid.	Ibidem
ICBC	Industrial and Commercial Bank of China
ICT	Information and communication technologies
ID	Identification
i.e.	That is
incl.	Including
IP	Intellectual property
IPO	Initial public offering
IT	Information technology
JOBS Act	Jumpstart Our Business Startups Act
KIA	Keep-It-All crowdfunding
LSE	Life-style entrepreneur
m-	Mobile-based
MAU	Monthly active user
MOF	Ministry of Finance
N/A	Not available
n.a.	No author provided
NCFG	Net Credit Finance Group
n.d.	No date provided
NFC	Near-Field Communication
NIE	New Institutional Economics
n.p.	No page provided
NPL	Non-performing loan
n.y.	No year provided
O2O	Online-to-offline
OCF	Original crowdfunding
P	Principal
P2B	Peer-to-business lending
P2P	Peer-to-peer lending
PBOC	People's Bank of China
PC	Personal computer
PCBC	People's Construction Bank of China
PDA	Personal digital assistant
PE	Private equity
PI	Project initiator

PKU	Peking University
PME	Profit-maximising entrepreneur
POE	Privately owned enterprise
PR	Public relations
PRC	People's Republic of China
QR	Quick response
RCC	Rural credit cooperative
ROSCA	Rotating Savings and Credit Association
SAC	Securities Association of China
SAFE	State Administration of Foreign Exchange
SCMP	South China Morning Post
SE	Serial entrepreneur
SEC	Securities and Exchange Commission
SME	Small and medium-sized enterprise
SMS	Short message service
SOB	State-owned bank
SOE	State-owned enterprise
TA	Transactions
TCE	Transaction cost economics
TIF	Traditional informal finance
TK	Transaction costs
tn	Trillion
UCF	Unified Compliance Framework
UK	United Kingdom
US	United States
USA	United States of America
VC	Venture capitalist
VPN	Virtual private network
vs.	Versus
WCC	World Crowdfunding Conference
WTO	World Trade Organization

List of Figures

List of Tables

Chapter 1
The Matter of Crowdfunding in China

1.1 Motivation

Crowdfunding (CF) is becoming an increasingly important financial tool. In 2010, the global crowdfunding market accounted for only USD 880 million.[1] According to the recent Crowdfunding Industry Report, the crowdfunding volume in 2014 totalled USD 16.2 billion.[2] By 2016, crowdfunding is expected to surpass the market value of classical venture capital funding.[3] Whilst some years ago, crowdfunding was predominantly applied by charities and actors of the creative industry, it has turned into an alternative financial tool for start-ups, entrepreneurs and Small and medium-sized enterprises (SMEs) across all sectors. Crowdfunding's global growth rate is mainly driven by the Asian crowdfunding market, which grew by 320% between 2013 and 2014, putting it slightly ahead of Europe as the second-biggest crowdfunding region, right after North America. Within Asia, the People's Republic of China (PRC) has been identified as the key market for CF's growth.[4] Despite its growing popularity, research on crowdfunding, particularly on crowdfunding in China, is still scarce. This work aims at closing this research gap.

According to a recent World Bank report, China holds the greatest potential for crowdfunding's future. By 2025, the PRC could account for more than half of the global crowdfunding volume potentially totalling up to USD 50 billion.[5] Even though crowdfunding was non-existent in China before 2011, its exponential growth rates reflect this potential. In 2014, Chinese citizens had contributed a total of USD 436 million (RMB 2.82 billion) to domestic crowdfunding projects; this figure

[1]Emmerson (2015).

[2]Massolution (2015, p. 13).

[3]Emmerson (2015).

[4]Massolution (2015, p. 52).

[5]infoDev (2013, p. 10).

A. S. Funk, *Crowdfunding in China*, Contributions to Management Science,
https://doi.org/10.1007/978-3-319-97253-4_1

rose to USD 864 million (RMB 5.585 billion) in the first half of 2015. Particularly since China's government has passed draft regulations on equity crowdfunding in December 2014, the number of Chinese Crowdfunding platforms (CFPs) has been increasing, from 142 in 2014 to 235[6] by the end of June 2015.[7] As the PRC's crowdfunding industry is still quite young, and its growth rates are expected to rise even further, China could indeed become the largest crowdfunding market in the world in the near future.

The approximated figures in the World Bank report seem plausible, yet, the results are based on questionable parameters. Some of the key variables are not applicable to China and thus probably have biased the findings.[8] In addition, the report contains some errors and contradictions.[9] On the other hand, China's crowdfunding features some characteristics that have been neglected by the World Bank and which eventually could justify the estimated growth rates.

In my opinion the World Bank's findings could even fall short of the actual future development as China holds a unique environment for crowdfunding. Certain external factors favour the development of crowdfunding and have provided China a beneficial initial position which eventually led to those exponential growth rates. These features are rooted in China's history and therefore cannot be assimilated by other countries. In particular, I expect a growing potential for crowdfunding in China due to the following three reasons:

First of all, crowdfunding's rise in China can be traced back to its established informal finance sector. As China's formal finance sector is underdeveloped and cannot serve the entire market, Chinese are used to employing alternative sources of finance. Therefore, the Chinese population is relatively open to new forms of finance. In the end, the existing informal finance structures could contribute to a faster and more comprehensive acceptance of crowdfunding in China.

Secondly, crowdfunding in China is promoted by its agile internet sector, driven by e-commerce giants and social media providers. Next to their core businesses, these companies also provide online payment systems and financial services like crowdfunding. As a consequence, banks and other traditional financial institutions have to face additional competition.

Thirdly, the Chinese government welcomes and promotes this development. Whilst the PRC is struggling to alter its traditional formal financial sector, internet finance per se is considered to be a motor for financial reform. China's premier minister, Li Keqiang, in particular set the development of internet finance as a

[6]This number is likely to include only donation-, rewards-, and equity-based CFPs as China is said to have about 1000 debt-based P2P CFPs. See Ren (2015).

[7]Research and Markets (2015, n.p.).

[8]E.g. the number of a country's *Facebook* users is utilised as a proxy for social media engagement. However, *Facebook* is officially banned from China. Yet, the PRC has a very high social media engagement; although the majority of Chinese use domestic social media.

[9]Funk (2016).

policy priority in 2014.[10] In China's *Financial Stability Report* of 2014, financial innovation is stressed and a special chapter has been dedicated to the *Development and Oversight of Internet Finance*. Therein internet finance was officially defined for the first time as comprising of the following six categories: *Internet payment, P2P online lending, non-P2P online micro loans, internet-based mutual fund sales, innovative online platforms of financial institutions*, and *crowdfunding*.[11] The report also states that "[i]nternet finance and traditional finance compete and cooperate with each other".[12] Internet finance in particular challenges the hegemony of state-owned financial corporates, which are forced to innovate in order to become more competitive. For example, China's big state-owned banks nowadays also offer mobile banking to improve customer experience.[13] Ultimately, crowdfunding and other forms of internet finance could accelerate the reformation of China's formal financial sector.

Not least, crowdfunding and other sources of internet finance can bridge the gap between formal and informal finance in China and probably therefore are promoted by the Chinese government. As Chinese formal banks only serve a certain clientele, a substantial part of the Chinese society relies on informal financial sources. However, informal finance is comparably expensive and rather opaque. The internet, on the other hand, provides transparency and is able to reduce transaction costs. Consequently, financial services become affordable to a broader customer base. According to the People's Bank of China (PBOC), the invention of "internet finance has promoted inclusive finance and filled in the gap in traditional financial services".[14] This statement hints at the role that tools like crowdfunding are intended to fill: Aiding the underserved market participants, replacing less transparent forms of traditional informal finance (TIF) and thereby integrating both alternative forms of finance and marginal market actors into the formal finance sector.

In the end, the triad of an underdeveloped formal financial sector, an established informal finance sector, and a dynamic internet finance sector provides a unique setting for crowdfunding in China.

This work aims to investigate crowdfunding's role in China and particularly its potential to change the Chinese informal finance sector. In order to evaluate crowdfunding's function within China, I discuss the features that crowdfunding provides for all respective stakeholders who are affected by this new form of finance. First, crowdfunding is a financial tool for individual founders, start-ups, ventures and entrepreneurs, which I subsume under the term *project initiators (PIs)*. Secondly, crowdfunding is also an alternative investment tool for savers and other capital providers. Whilst investments in TIF commonly are face-to-face, offline, and geographically restricted, crowdfunding eliminates physical investment boundaries

[10] Xie et al. (2016, p. i).

[11] People's Bank of China (2014, pp. 173–176).

[12] People's Bank of China (2014, p. 172).

[13] Xie et al. (2016, p. 30).

[14] People's Bank of China (2014, p. 188).

and thereby provides an attractive alternative for formal and informal creditors. All potential depositors or crowdfunding investors respectively are subsumed under *the crowd*, which I use as a synonym for *crowdfunders*. Thirdly, the Chinese *crowdfunding platforms* (*CFPs*), their influence and motivation for providing crowdfunding services are also analysed in order to identify their role and crowdfunding's overall function in China. Last but not least, the Chinese government is another important stakeholder for crowdfunding's development. By contrasting its attitude towards TIF and crowdfunding and analysing where these attitudes stem from, I appraise where crowdfunding's future will lead to. In the end, by comparing TIF and crowdfunding in China, and their role for their respective stakeholders—PIs, crowdfunders, CFPs, and the Chinese government—I can estimate to what extent crowdfunding could become a game changer for informal finance in China.

From the context outlined above, the following research questions are derived:

- Which role does crowdfunding take in the spectrum of China's financial sector?
- Which features does crowdfunding in China hold in comparison to the Original crowdfunding (OCF) (i.e. Western crowdfunding) *concept* and in the context of China's internet industry, particularly its social media and e-commerce sector?
- Which function does crowdfunding fulfil in China in contrast to Traditional informal finance?

Crowdfunding in China started out as a form of informal finance. Whilst (equity) crowdfunding belonged to the grey or rather informal area of finance, it was officially included in the formal financial sector with the introduction of draft regulations in December 2014. These draft regulations particularly serve a certain form of crowdfunding, which I denominate as *e-commerce crowdfunding*. Crowdfunding in China is highly integrated into e-commerce and social media, and thereby becomes more seizable for Chinese authorities. With the support of established e-commerce corporates and advanced social media providers, financial transactions can be more easily monitored, which amongst others is one reason for the authorisation of crowdfunding by the government. As *e-commerce crowdfunding* is not just the dominant form of crowdfunding in China, but at the same time quite unique in the world, it is the focus of this thesis. Yet, other forms of crowdfunding in China are also elaborated.

Prior to identifying crowdfunding's role in China and evaluating whether it could indeed replace traditional forms of informal finance, the general role of financial institutions is depicted. Furthermore, parameters which start-ups and entrepreneurs base their financial decisions on are illustrated. Finally, the underlying reasons, why Chinese private enterprises utilise informal finance are analysed. In particular, the preceding questions of this research are:

- What is the function of financial mediators and of formal versus informal institutions?
- Which factors do entrepreneurs base their financial decisions on?
- Why do Chinese entrepreneurs prefer informal finance?
- Why could they choose crowdfunding in the future?

1.2 Theory

In order to approach the above mentioned research questions, a theoretical framework is used to locate crowdfunding in China within the range of formal and informal finance. Specifically, I intend to understand how and why institutions evolve, why they change over time and what their underlying function is, both in general (for all kinds of financial institutions worldwide) and for Chinese financiers in particular. This research is therefore based on findings of New Institutional Economics (NIE). In contrast to neoclassical economics, NIE assume imperfect economic actors with bounded rationality and ethics. The focus of interest in NIE are institutions, which are "expectations that may be socially disciplined and which refer to behaviour patterns of one or several individuals".[15] Scholars of NIE analyse interactions between entities, organisations, companies, and individuals; they see institutions as instruments compensating for the bounded rationality of human beings. Moreover, they evaluate the impacts of institutions on human behaviour.[16]

> Institutions provide the structure for exchange that (together with the technology employed) determines the cost of transacting and the cost of transformation. How well institutions solve the problems of coordination and production is determined by the motivation of the players (their utility function), the complexity of the environment, and the ability of the players to decipher and order the environment (measurement and enforcement[17]).[18]

Economic actors typically need to balance risks and transaction costs. The former can be reduced by spending resources ex ante and ex post of a transaction in order to decrease information asymmetries. However, such measures can be very costly and can reduce the attractiveness of a transaction. Yet, alternatively, they have to face higher risks. Institutions create stability and reduce overall uncertainty by providing a framework to our daily life.[19] With the instalment of institutions, transaction costs and therefore risks can be diminished. In this thesis, the NIE perspective is used to evaluate the pros and cons of crowdfunding for its respective Chinese stakeholders and eventually explain crowdfunding's rise in China.

As crowdfunding is progressively accepted by Chinese market players, i.e. PIs, crowdfunders, CFPs, and the Chinese government, I assume that this financial instrument is capable of reducing uncertainties and providing the actors with some benefits. Yet, in order to make a profound judgement, the underlying motivations of the respective actors need to be analysed as well as the environment in which crowdfunding is embedded in China, the transaction costs which each player needs to face, and also the capabilities each stakeholder has, which enable them to deal

[15] Own translation from Picot et al. (2002, p. 57): "sozial sanktionierbare Erwartungen, die sich auf die Handlungs- und Verhaltensweisen eines oder mehrerer Individuen beziehen".

[16] Picot et al. (2002, pp. 43–57).

[17] According to North (1990), measurement (i.e. information research) and enforcement (i.e. monitoring) are those actions which afford transaction costs.

[18] North (1990, p. 34).

[19] North (1990, p. 3).

with the complexities of the environment. This is because a single institution unfolds within its institutional context, but never as an isolated entity.[20] Even though North (1990) states that institutions provide "a stable (but not necessarily [an] efficient) structure"[21] for transactions, I argue that institutions eventually evolve to those specifications which include the least transaction costs; and this in turn can be equalised with highest efficiency. In this context, Aoki (2007) claims that institutional change derives from situations of crises that lead to an equilibrium shift. These situations can be evoked through "changes in the activated sets of individual choices due to the accumulation and development of skills, learning, innovation-induced new action possibilities [...] [or through] changes in technological and environmental conditions that result in different physical consequences for the same action choices [...], [or through] new laws or fiats which are enacted as consequences of the game in the political domains".[22] In fact, with the advent of crowdfunding in China, a PI's choice of finance has been expanded, and with the publication of draft regulations on equity crowdfunding the entire situation further has been altered. In the end, crowdfunding and its features could evoke some institutional change in China.

This work builds upon several strands of NIE, foremost on transaction cost and principal agent theory. Moreover, I apply the concept of transaction cost economics to classify crowdfunding within China's financial spectrum. Besides, this research further relies on findings of behavioural economics, informal finance and specific crowdfunding literature. Insights from literature on entrepreneurs' choice of finance help me to locate crowdfunding within the broad range of financial alternatives. Additionally, by analysing literature on informal finance, particularly on informal finance in China, crowdfunding and its features are contrasted to TIF in China. Furthermore, earlier findings on crowdfunding[23] are used to assess the outcomes of this research and make statements on crowdfunding in China. Based on the theoretical framework of NIE, behavioural finance, informal finance, and crowdfunding literature, I try to draw a comprehensive picture of crowdfunding in China.

1.3 Research Design and Methodology

As research on crowdfunding, particularly on crowdfunding in China, is still scarce, this work uses a qualitative approach, which aims to provide insight into the scope of crowdfunding in China and its relation to TIF. In addition to an evaluation of existing literature on crowdfunding, including scientific but also non-academic

---

20 Picot et al. (2002, p. 12).

21 North (1990, p. 6).

22 Aoki (2007, p. 19 ff.).

23 These are predominantly findings on crowdfunding in the West.

sources like blogs, periodicals and internet websites, this research mainly relies on expert interviews and participatory observation. The original research design also incorporated a quantitative analysis based on a survey among PIs and crowdfunders; however, the achieved sample size of this survey was too small and therefore the results could only be analysed in qualitative terms. Still, in the end, the data collected from various sources provide a first detailed overview of the multifaceted picture of crowdfunding in China.

The literature analysis was based on scientific and non-scientific sources in English, Chinese and German. Western sources were predominantly obtained from online databases and libraries as well as from conferences like e.g. *the Crowddialog*.[24] Chinese sources, on the other hand, were obtained from the database *China academic journals* through *CrossAsia*,[25] collected from book stores on-sight in China or provided from Chinese research institutes. As scientific works, particularly Chinese sources, were hardly existing before 2014, this work also relies on blogs, newspaper articles, guide books and other non-academic sources.

This work further refers to data gathered during conferences in Europe and China, which I either attended personally or from which I received first hand reports from a peer. Personally, I participated in several fora like the *German Crowdfunding Network (GCN)* and the *European Crowdfunding Network (ECN)* in order to also grasp the developments of crowdfunding outside of China. As crowdfunding is becoming popular amongst practitioners, but also amongst scholars, the number of conferences on crowdfunding or related topics is simultaneously increasing. Institutions like the *GCN* and the *ECN* have been established in order to bundle common interests, to represent these in front of politicians and other interest groups, to distribute knowledge and to promote the development of crowdfunding. At the *2015 ECN Crowdfunding Convention* in Paris I exchanged views with several Chinese participants, who had earlier also attended the *2015 World Crowdfunding Conference (WCC)* in Guiyang, China. These second-hand information were very valuable because, as a non-Chinese participant, I would not have been entitled to follow the main sessions of the *WCC*, even if I had visited the conference in person. Thus, for this work and the overall understanding of the concept of crowdfunding in China, informal information derived from Chinese crowdfunding actors was crucial.

Furthermore, this work is based on a field study during which I conducted semi-structured expert interviews with Chinese PIs as well as with founders and employees of Chinese CFPs. In total, this field research comprised of 5 months in China, separated into three research sequences: In August/September 2013, I spent 7 weeks in Beijing and 1 week in Tibet; in April/May 2015, I interviewed probands in Beijing, Shanghai, Shenzhen, and Guangzhou; in September 2015, I made follow-up interviews in Beijing. Some follow-up conversations were also conducted

[24]For more information on this conference see http://www.crowddialog.de/.

[25]For more information see http://crossasia.org/.

via email, *WeChat*[26] and *Skype*. The first Chinese probands were contacted via *Sina Weibo*,[27] and thereafter most interview partners were introduced to me via previous contacts. Overall, the interviewees were quite cooperative and ready to share sensitive information in their mother-tongue. In the end, the success of the field research relied, amongst others, on my language skills as the majority of the semi-structured interviews were conducted in Chinese.

In order to get a better idea of the actual processes of a Chinese crowdfunding campaign, I additionally set up my own crowdfunding campaign on a Chinese CFP and emulated the role of a PI. Thereby, I learned the prerequisites for a setup of such a campaign, how a Chinese CFP can support PIs, and which dynamics eventually can lead to a successful crowdfunding in China. Although this experiment has been far from representative for a typical crowdfunding campaign in China as variables like the project category, the nationality of the PI, the pre-set target sum etc. were not controlled and thus may have led to several biases, it provided a good insight into the perspective of PIs in China and the daily work of a Chinese CFP. Eventually, by setting up my own crowdfunding campaign on a Chinese CFP, I gained a better idea of the crowdfunding dynamics in China.

The original research design also included a regression analysis based on the quantitative evaluation of a questionnaire, which should have given more insight into the motivational drivers of PIs and crowdfunders for applying crowdfunding. This questionnaire has been formulated on the basis of literature research. During my second research stay in China, I distributed a sample questionnaire to PIs, which thereafter was further amended, and which I intended to distribute on a larger scale via Chinese CFPs. However, as only few CFPs were willing to distribute the questionnaire via their channels and therefore the overall return rate stayed below expectations, the questionnaire was only evaluated on a qualitative basis. As a result, the research design of this dissertation is a mixture of theoretical and empirical analysis, relying on literature research, semi-structured expert interviews, participatory observation, and the qualitative evaluation of a questionnaire.

Crowdfunding and in particular crowdfunding in China is a very dynamic phenomenon which is still in a state of constant change. When I started my research, in 2013, there were hardly any publications on crowdfunding in China. By 2015, crowdfunding has become a topic of interest for PIs, crowdfunders, CFPs and also the Chinese government. Yet, at that time Chinese crowdfunding still relied on draft regulations, its stakeholders waited for their official implementation and further regulations were expected—not least due to the developments of Peer-to-peer lending (P2P) in China.

---

[26] *WeChat*, or its Chinese equivalent *Weixin [微信]*, is an Application (app) invented by the Chinese internet company *Tencent*. Amongst many other functions, this app includes an instant messenger. *WeChat* is further analysed in Sects. 4.4.2.2 and 5.3.4.

[27] *Sina Weibo*, or its Chinese equivalent *Xinlang Weibo [新浪微薄]* is one of China's most popular micro blogs.

Whilst in 2013, P2P was non-existent in China and consequently not relevant at all, it has become a huge topic by 2015. By then, P2P platforms have mushroomed and absorbed large amounts of capital. At the same time, there have been already several cases of fraud of tremendous scale. Against this background, my research on crowdfunding in China, which intentionally excluded P2P from the very beginning, appears of less weight. However, these developments could not be foreseen in 2013. Moreover, the relevance ranking of crowdfunding and P2P in China is likely to shift again if P2P fails in the long run.

Ultimately, crowdfunding in China (like P2P) has been and is still under continuing change. As it is hard to hit a moving target, this thesis focusses on the evolution of crowdfunding in China from 2011 until the end of 2015. Yet, I have used some sources from beyond that time (e.g. with regard to e-commerce and social media in China) in order to stress my findings and make statements on the potential future development of crowdfunding in China.

1.4 Structure of This Work

Following this introduction, which has depicted the motivational background and the methodological approach of this work, Chap. 2 sets the theoretical foundation of this research. It presents a detailed discussion of NIE and the benefits of applying such an approach to crowdfunding. Furthermore, it illustrates the range of entrepreneurial finance and locates crowdfunding within the financial spectrum. Moreover, different types of entrepreneurs are highlighted. In addition, it discusses the role of classic financial intermediaries and introduces the theory of financialisation, which explains the changing role of formal financial intermediaries. The chapter further analyses informal financial intermediaries and introduces *ROSCAs* as a benchmark for formal and informal financial institutions. Finally, it refers to the FinTech industry and the evolution of internet finance, of which crowdfunding is a subcategory.

Chapter 3 deals with the *Original concept of crowdfunding (OCF)*, which has been established in the West. A definition of crowdfunding is provided, and its origins but also its modifications are elaborated. Furthermore, this chapter includes a literature review of both Western and Chinese sources. Subsequently, the phenomenon of crowdfunding is embedded within the theoretical context. Crowdfunding is analysed in terms of its principal-agent-relationships, the involved transactions and transaction costs. It is evaluated in terms of transaction cost economics and contrasted to other financial institutions, particularly to a commercial bank and a ROSCA. Ultimately, the choice for crowdfunding is de-constructed in terms of its underlying features.

The following Chap. 4 focusses on China's institutional, societal and economic environment for crowdfunding. In a first step it analyses China's financial sectors, i.e. the formal and informal one, and also its FinTech sector; it secondly illustrates China's internet industry. Therein, the role of the Chinese government is stressed.

Moreover, the ecosystem of China's major internet corporates is depicted, and the business models of *Alibaba* and *Tencent* are elaborated. In addition, the relevance of mobile internet, e-commerce and online payments in China, is pointed out. These strands build the foundation for the understanding of crowdfunding's evolution in China.

Chapter 5 describes China's crowdfunding market, its origins and unique features. Following a discussion of current crowdfunding education and regulation, this chapter specifically explains the Chinese understanding of crowdfunding and includes a preliminary categorisation of different types of Chinese CFPs. By means of three case studies, the dynamics and procedures of different crowdfunding campaigns in China are illustrated. Finally, this chapter embeds Chinese crowdfunding in the theoretical context, and highlights the idiosyncrasies, similarities and distinctions of crowdfunding in China in comparison to the Original crowdfunding concept.

The penultimate chapter contrasts China's traditional informal finance with the different types of crowdfunding and elucidates implications for the major stakeholders of crowdfunding in China. Not only project initiators (PIs) but also the Chinese government, the crowdfunders and the crowdfunding platforms (CFPs) are affected by crowdfunding's rise in China. In an approach to address the main question of this dissertation, I deduce how crowdfunding eventually could become a game changer of informal finance in China.

The seventh and final chapter concludes this work and provides a summary of the major findings. It gives an outlook of potential developments of the Chinese and global crowdfunding sector and suggests questions for future research.

Chapter 2
Crowdfunding in the Context of New Institutional Economics

2.1 Theories of New Institutional Economics

New Institutional Economics can help explain why new institutions (like crowdfunding) arise.[1] Scholars associated with this strand of theories argue that economic actors aim at minimising transaction costs rather than at maximising profits, which is the credo of *neoclassical economists*.[2] Reality holds many cases which are not driven by "pure wealth-maximizing behavior, but of altruism and of self-imposed constraints".[3] Yet, in contrast to *old institutional economists*, representatives of NIE do not reject neoclassical economic perspectives per se; they rather see NIE as an evolutional strand to neoclassical theories.[4] Both, NIE and the neoclassical school, anticipate scarcity and competitive markets. However, whilst neoclassical axioms hold up for perfect markets without frictions, in reality market actors typically face imperfect conditions: "[P]roperty rights are [not] perfectly and costlessly specified and information is likewise [not] costless to acquire".[5] According to North (1990), neoclassical economists lack "an understanding of the nature of human coordination and cooperation".[6] Moreover, whilst neoclassical theory has contributed a lot to the understanding of markets in developed countries, NIE can help to explain more idiosyncratic phenomenons in developing countries,[7] such as crowdfunding in China.

---

[1] Picot et al. (2002, p. 36).

[2] Williamson (1986, p. 178 ff).

[3] North (1990, p. 20).

[4] Rutherford (1989).

[5] North (1990, p. 11).

[6] Ibid.

[7] Ibid.

A. S. Funk, *Crowdfunding in China*, Contributions to Management Science,
https://doi.org/10.1007/978-3-319-97253-4_2

The term NIE has been significantly coined by Oliver Williamson. It is foremost a microeconomic concept which integrates theories of law, politics and economics, and examines the impact of institutions on economic entities. NIE scholars see the cause for difficulties in transactions and the reason for market failure in the combination of individuals' *bounded rationality*, their *opportunistic behaviour*, and overall *uncertainties*.[8] For the analysis of this work, I rely on a subcategory of institutional theory, on financial theory, particularly on the role of formal and informal financial intermediaries. The existence of financial institutions can be explained by the concepts of transaction costs and principal-agent-relationships, which are two essential strands of NIE theory. According to Williamson (1990), "agency theory focuses on ex ante incentive alignments, [whereas] transaction cost economics emphasizes ex post governance".[9] However, I will follow the position of Picot et al. (2002) which implies that transaction costs as well as agency problems can arise at any point during the course of transaction—before, during and after the accomplishment of an interaction.[10]

2.1.1 Institutions, Transaction Costs and Principal-Agent-Relations

2.1.1.1 Institutions

North (1990) specified institutions as "the rules of the game in a society or [...] the humanly devised constraints that shape human interaction."[11] The author clearly differentiates between *institutions* (i.e. the rules) and *organisations* (i.e. the players), whereas both are mutually shaped.[12] Several years later, Hodgson (2006) has defined institutions as "systems of established and prevalent social rules that structure social interactions".[13] Whilst Hodgson (2006) distinguishes between *structures* and *agents*,[14] he contemplates organisations and agents not as separate entities but just as special sub-categories of institutions. Likewise, the Oxford Dictionary (2011) defines institutions as *organisations* and *social institutions*.[15] For the analysis part of this work, I do not distinguish between the players (i.e.

[8]Williamson (1975, p. 7).

[9]Williamson (1990, p. 69).

[10]Picot et al. (2002, p. 70).

[11]North (1990, p. 3).

[12]North (1990, p. 4 ff).

[13]Hodgson (2006, p. 2).

[14]Hodgson (2006, p. 9).

[15]*Social institutions* "refer to established ways of behaving [...] which organize the primary social practices, roles, and relationships within a culture". (Chandler and Munday 2011, n.p.).

organisations and agents) and the structures (i.e. rules), but consider both as coequal institutions.

Institutions can be formal or informal; however, the definition of these terms is also open to interpretation. Some scholars equalise *formal* with *legal* and *informal* with *non-legal* or *illegal*; others regard *explicit* institutions as *formal*, and *tacit* rules as *informal* institutions.[16] According to North (1990), formal rules incorporate "constitutional [law], statute law, common law",[17] i.e. written formal law. By contrast, he defines informal constraints as "reputation, broadly accepted standards of conduct (effective to the extent that the conduct of the other parties is readily observable), and conventions that emerge from repetitive interactions."[18] Both, informal and formal institutions shape everyday life and are of equal importance. Even if a country has explicit regulations on certain issues, informal institutions like conventions can influence people to defer from these rules. Or as North put it, "[a]lthough formal rules may change overnight as the result of political or judicial decisions, informal constraints embodied in customs, traditions, and codes of conduct are much more impervious to deliberate policies."[19] Consequently, formal institutions are not necessarily people's first choice; rather, people choose those institutions which suit their respective circumstances best, i.e. those which minimise their transaction costs to the lowest level. For this work, I follow North's definition of informal institutions, including all rules, values, norms, and codes of behaviour which are common habits but not explicitly accredited, regulated or promulgated by official authorities. Formal institutions, on the other hand, are defined as authorised rules and laws within the context of this work.

Irrespective of their constitution and status, institutions receive their legitimacy from the necessity to restrict and organise transactions and social behaviour. Under the assumption of imperfect markets, the Coase Theorem[20] does not hold. Information asymmetries and information searches create considerable uncertainties, which, in return, make transaction costs likewise prohibitive. In this context, institutions can reduce uncertainties and optimize transactions; they "offer [...] predictability and stability",[21] which is reflected by their nature of durability.[22] Yet, institutions only become manifest and sustained if they are "exercised with sufficient frequency".[23] In addition, even though institutions can be socially and

[16]Hodgson (2006, p. 11).

[17]North (1990, p. 61).

[18]North (1990, p. 61). The author explicitly distinguishes between *formal rules* and *informal constraints*; however, as informal institutions can likewise enable and formal institutions simultaneously can restrict, the terms *rules* and *constraints* are used as synonyms in this work.

[19]North (1990, p. 6).

[20]The Coase Theorem proposes that market participants can solve market problems that arose from externalities themselves as long as there are no transactions costs (Coase 1960).

[21]Chandler and Munday (2011, n.p.).

[22]Hodgson (2006, p. 2).

[23]Hodgson (2006, p. 3).

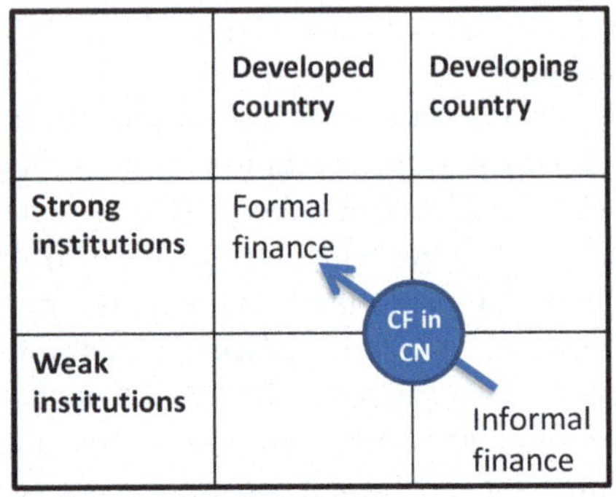

Fig. 2.1 Common path of institutional change

culturally transmitted,[24] "institutions and patterns of behaviour are always in the process of formation, transformation, and decline".[25] In return, institutions also have an impact on the social behaviour of players. Within this context, Hodgson (2006) distinguishes between *agent-sensitive* and *agent-insensitive* institutions, of which the latter have little influence on players' attitudes. In the end, as mentioned in Chap. 1.2, institutions always need to be regarded in their receptive environmental context.[26]

Characteristically, developed countries have stronger institutions and their citizens primarily rely on formal institutions. Empirical research has revealed a correlation between innovativeness and effective formal institutions.[27] Therefore, developing countries tend to strengthen their institutional environment during the transition process towards becoming a developed country. Likewise, people who previously relied on forms of informal finance start to opt for formal finance once appropriate institutions become available. Although exception proves the rule, Fig. 2.1 demonstrates the usual path from a developing towards a developed country, from the lower right field towards the upper left corner. Per definition and as of today, the PRC is still a developing or at least a transition country.[28] Yet, the Chinese government is promoting the formalisation of its institutions, moving the country towards the upper right corner of the chart. However, in terms of its financial sector, China is struggling to accelerate reforms, the majority of its population still relies on informal finance as formal institutions do not meet their demand for finance. Thus, regarded in isolation, China's financial sector would position the country in

[24]Hodgson (2006, p. 3 ff).

[25]Chandler and Munday (2011, n.p.).

[26]North (1990, p. 34).

[27]Granville and Leonard (2010).

[28]Depending on the eye of the beholder, China is either categorised as a developing or a transitory country. Each definition includes certain advantages and disadvantages, depending on the respective situation. For example, a developing status may be supportive to obtain subsidies, whilst a transitory status, for instance, may ease international trade. Thus, the PRC or other actors deliberately using one or the other definition are likely to pursue a certain end.

the lower right corner of the chart.[29] This dissertation will argue that crowdfunding has the potential to bridge informal and formal financial institutions in China and eventually support the country's move to the upper right corner of the chart.

2.1.1.2 Transaction Costs

Whilst neoclassical economists have focussed on production costs, NIE scholars focus on transaction costs, which are the "costs of running the economic system".[30] The foundation for the theory of transaction costs has been laid in the 1930s by Ronald Coase,[31] and was later expanded by Williamson. Whilst classical economists stress the role of markets ruled by price mechanism, Coase analysed *the nature of the firm* and explained the reasons why firms exist. In fact, the author claims that "the distinguishing mark of the firm is the supersession of the price mechanism"[32] as the application of the latter would incur certain costs. He thereby refers to efforts which arise from e.g. information collection in order to discover the correct or justifiable prices. If transactions are costly, then institutions are relevant[33] and "[o]nce created, institutions determine the costs of acting".[34] Williamson further indicates that "[t]he social context in which transactions are embedded—the customs, mores, habits and so on—[...] need to be taken into account",[35] which refers to the importance of the respective institutional environment.[36]

Originally, the theory of transaction costs has been applied to study industrial organisations and has put contracts in the focus of analysis. Contracts are carried out with varying degrees of efficiency, depending on the institutional setting and the organisations involved. Transaction cost theory tries to explain this variety and therefore takes transactions as the basic units of investigation.[37] Williamson referred to Macneil (1978)[38] and distinguished between three kinds of contracts: *Classical contracts*, *neoclassical contracts*, and *relational contracts*. In *classical contracts* the identities of the participating actors are irrelevant, the nature of the contract is rather standardised or "ideal", it is short-termed, and the transaction is based on legal rules and formalised processes. An example for a classical contract would be

[29]In this context, Hall and Soskice (2001) have discussed *varieties of capitalism*. Depending on the criteria and sector in perspective, China can be located in different categories of capitalism.

[30]Arrow (1969, p. 1).

[31]Coase (1937).

[32]Coase (1937, p. 389).

[33]North (1990, p. 12).

[34]North (1990, p. vi).

[35]Williamson (1985, p. 22).

[36]North (1990, p. 34).

[37]Williamson (1986, p. 175).

[38]Macneil (1978).

Table 2.1 Categories of transaction costs

	Williamson (1985)	Dahlmann (1979)	Furubotn and Richter (1991)
Ex ante	Agreement drafting	Information search	Preparing contracts
Ex post	Agreement negotiating, maladaption, haggling, dispute solving, bonding costs	Bargaining, decision making, policing and enforcement	Concluding contracts, monitoring

a purchase agreement. *Neoclassical contracts* are typically longer termed and do not contain all specifications of the respective cooperation ex ante; the involved parties rather anticipate ex post adjustments of the contract like in a joint-venture or an alliance. *Relational contracts* are the most complex ones as they include social interaction; their duration and complexity are steadily increasing, and thus much more adjustments are necessary as compared to *neoclassical contracts*.[39] Ultimately, it is assumed that economic players would always choose an institutional setting and respective contracts which incur the least transaction costs for them.

Transaction costs should not be underestimated, though they are not easy to measure. Wallis and North (1986) have calculated for the US economy that the country in 1970 dedicated more than 50% of its national income to the transaction sector.[40] The actual level of costs of a transaction is inherently influenced by three dimensions, which are *frequency*, *uncertainty,* and *asset specificity*. Williamson claims that innovative institutions and organisational variety foremost evolve from the aspiration to cope with these dimensions and to reduce overall transaction costs. The variety of existing institutions is very large, whereas non-standard forms dominate. It is difficult, however, to measure factors like uncertainty, therefore, instead of calculating transaction costs for single processes, respective analyses commonly rely on comparisons of processes across different institutions.[41] As a result, transaction cost theory is a comparative approach.

Williamson (1985) distinguished between *ex ante* and *ex post* transaction costs (cf. Table 2.1 (Williamson 1985; Dahlmann 1979; Furubotn and Richter 1991)). The former comprise of "costs of drafting, negotiating, and safeguarding an agreement",[42] which include information gathering. *Ex post* transaction costs encompass negotiating, maladaption and haggling costs, and the latter occur once a transaction needs to be corrected after its accomplishment. Furthermore, these include costs which ensue from dispute solving; and finally "*bonding costs* of effecting secure commitments".[43] Dahlmann (1979), on the other hand, subsumed

[39] Williamson (1985, p. 69 ff).

[40] Wallis and North (1986, p. 120).

[41] Williamson (1985, p. 17 ff, p. 387).

[42] Williamson (1985, p. 20).

[43] Williamson (1985, p. 21).

transaction costs under "search and information costs, bargaining and decision costs, policing and enforcement costs".[44] By further contrast, Furubotn and Richter (1991) have categorised transaction costs in terms of their time of occurrence or their function respectively: "(a) the cost of preparing contracts, (b) the cost of concluding contracts, and (c) the cost of monitoring and enforcing the performance of a contract".[45] This thesis is predominantly based on the classifications by Dahlmann (1979), and Furubotn and Richter (1991).

2.1.1.3 Principal-Agent-Relations

Like transaction cost theory the principal-agent theory also analyses contracts, particularly ones between an instructing entity (the principal) and an executing person (the agent). The contract characterises the agency relationship, under which the principal delegates a task to the agent, who thereby gains some authority. However, the agent can misuse this authority and act against the principal's interest in order to increase his own utility. Thus, the principal needs to install mechanisms, which either incentivise the agent to comply or which enable the principal to monitor the agent's activities. Both kinds of arrangements involve specific transaction costs, which are denominated as *agency costs*. Consequently, agency costs are a subcategory of transaction costs. Jensen and Meckling (1976) define the following three different categories of agency costs: "(1) the monitoring expenditures by the principal, (2) the bonding expenditures by the agent, [and] (3) the residual loss".[46] Ultimately, a large share of transaction costs constitutes of agency costs.

The underlying problems that incur agency as well as transaction costs are information asymmetries that are a product of bounded rationality,[47] opportunism[48] and uncertainties between the involved parties, and which can lead to (ex ante) *adverse selection*, (ex post) *moral hazard*, and (ex post) *hidden action*. The following paragraphs explain these dangers and further provide solutions to minimise the respective information asymmetries.

Akerlof (1970) has explained *adverse selection* by means of *the markets for lemons*. For example, in the case of medical insurance, the insurance price level should reflect the risk of the client to become sick. However, if the price level increases, the risk to exclusively address risky clients will rise accordingly. Consequently, the insurance company runs in danger to choose the wrong clients. In order

---

[44] Dahlmann (1979, p. 148).

[45] Furubotn and Richter (1991, p. 9).

[46] Jensen and Meckling (1976, p. 308).

[47] "[H]uman agents are intendedly rational but only limitedly so. That is manifestly true and massively influences the manner in which the subject of contract is conceived". (Williamson 1985, p. 388).

[48] According to Williamson, opportunism "is a condition of self-interest seeking with guile". (Williamson 1985, p. 30).

to avoid this *adverse selection*, the company would rather set its prices to a lower level and thereby simultaneously address people who will not need the insurance due to their lower risk level.[49] Literature further suggest two other measures for reducing adverse selection, that derives from ex ante information asymmetries and quality uncertainty: *self-selection* and *signalling*. By designing a contract with long-term incentives, the insurance company can enforce that clients pre-select themselves for a win-win transaction. For example, the company (principal) could proclaim that it provides its services only from a certain time period after completion of the contract onwards. Thereby, risky clients (i.e. those, who need the insurance instantaneously) automatically exude themselves. Alternatively, an agent can obviously signal her credibility. For instance, by attending sports classes and verifying her attendance to the insurance company, she signals an overall lower risk level. In sum, an incentivised self-selection and a proactive signalling by the agent can reduce the risk of *adverse selection*.

Situations of *moral hazard* appear, if the agent holds more information than the principal (*hidden information*) at a time after the agency relationship has already been enforced. *Hidden action*, on the other hand, literally encompasses an action or decision by the agent, which the principal is not aware of and consequently cannot oversee. These two dangers are related as in both cases the agent holds a surplus of information, which he can misuse in order to maximise his profits. For example, a renter of a flat (agent) could sublet the flat to another person without the landlord's (principal's) permission (*hidden action*). The renter could further withhold information, for example, confidential information on his credit rating (*hidden information*). In order to incentivise the agent's moral behaviour, a contract could encourage compliant performance. For example, the landlord could claim some collateral from the client (e.g. in form of some deposit). Alternatively, ex post information asymmetries can also be reduced through re-occurring cooperation (or in the renting case through a long-term lease). Hereby, reputation plays a crucial role. Similar to collateral, reputation can serve as a form of security as the agent runs in danger to lose his reputation, if he defaults. For example, once the landlord searches for a new renter, he could prefer renters who were recommended by his friends. Ultimately, risks of *moral hazard* can be reduced by collateral, reputation and contracts which ensure the agent's compliance.[50]

All in all, information asymmetries as a product of *bounded rationality*, *opportunism* and *uncertainties* bear the dangers of *adverse selection*, *moral hazard* and *hidden action*. In order to cope with these dangers and reduce overall risks, economic actors need to dedicate resources like time and capital: principals need to prepare and oversee transactions, while agents have to engage in installations like signalling and collateral. All these actions and incorporated efforts are subsumed

---

[49] Akerlof (1970, p. 492 ff).

[50] Goebel (2002, p. 278 ff).

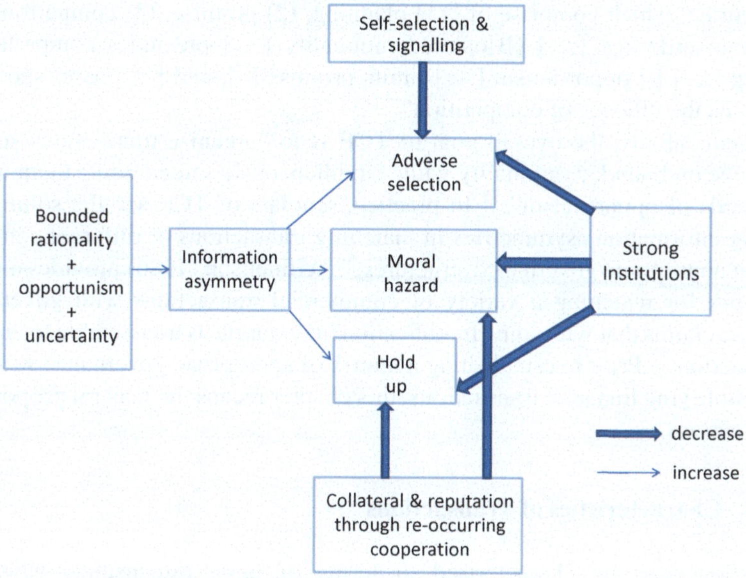

Fig. 2.2 Sources of information asymmetry and transaction costs and potential countermeasures

under transaction costs, including agency costs. Figure 2.2 (Williamson 1985, 1986) summarises the interrelations of information asymmetries, their corresponding dangers and respective countermeasures.

2.1.1.4 Transaction Cost Economics

Transaction cost economics (TCE) "maintain[...] that any issue that can be formulated as a contracting problem can be investigated to advantage in transaction economizing terms."[51] Whilst NIE are commonly applied to macroeconomic issues, TCE theory as part of NIE is suitable for microeconomic analyses.[52] Yet, in line with NIE, TCE theory also ascribes all market actors three distinct behavioural assumptions, which are *bounded rationality*, *opportunism*, and *risk neutrality*. Although Williamson himself concedes that the latter assumption is rather disputable, risk neutrality is implicated as a matter of simplicity of the theory.[53] The above mentioned three preconditions directly affect the essentials

[51] Williamson (1986, p. 174).

[52] Ibid.

[53] Williamson (1985, p. 388 ff).

of a contract, which comprise of "(1) planning, (2) promise, (3) competition, and (4) private ordering. [...] [B]ounded rationality [...] precludes comprehensive planning [...] [,] opportunism [...] limits promise [..], and [...] asset specificity [...] limits the efficacy of competition".[54]

Consequentially, the overall goal of TCE is to "organize transactions so as to economize on bounded rationality while simultaneously safeguarding them against the hazards of opportunism".[55] In practice, scholars of TCE see the solution for reducing information asymmetries in matching transactions of different complexities with appropriate governance structures.[56] Williamson (1986) provides a matrix framework for matching a variety of commercial transactions with governance, though he claims that with some modification his example is transferable to any kind of transaction.[57] Prior to establishing a matrix of appropriate governance structures for exemplifying financial transactions, this chapter recaps the general propositions of transactions.

2.1.1.5 Characteristics of Transactions

Transactions can be characterised in terms of three dimensions, which are "(1) uncertainty, (2) the frequency with which transactions recur, and (3) the degree to which durable transaction-specific investments are incurred"[58] (see also Sect. 2.1.1.2 and Fig. 2.2). Whilst uncertainty is not further elaborated by Williamson (1986), but presumably differs in terms of the level of information asymmetry, the author provides three nuances for each of the other two dimensions. Hence, a transaction can occur either once, or occasionally, or frequently. Williamson subsumes once and occasionally simply under the latter. Investments, on the other hand, can be generally classified as either non-specific, mixed, or idiosyncratic.[59] Considering capital market transactions, however, Williamson suggests to substitute the dimension of asset specificity with *ease of verification*.[60] In the end, a combination of those three characteristics—the degree of uncertainty, frequency and ease of verification—shape the constituency of financial transactions. Like Williamson, I only distinguish between two types of frequency, i.e. occasional and frequent transactions, which eventually results in Fig. 2.3 (Williamson 1986, pp. 112, 117), a matrix of six different forms of financial transactions, which is explained in more detail below.

[54]Williamson (1986, p. 181).
[55]Williamson (1986, p. 178).
[56]Williamson (1986, p. 187).
[57]Williamson (1986, p. 118).
[58]Williamson (1986, p. 105).
[59]Williamson (1986, p. 111).
[60]Williamson (1986, p. 122).

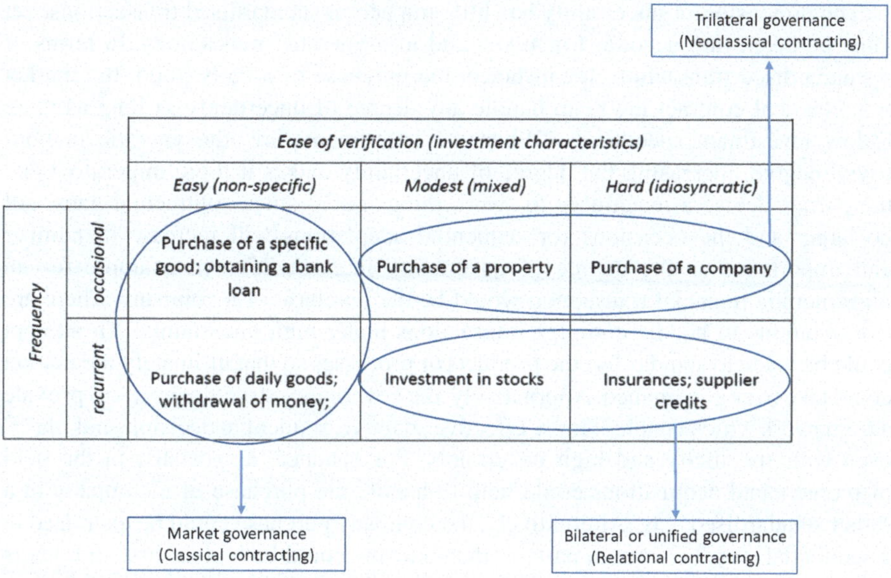

Fig. 2.3 Categorisation of different financial transactions and respective appropriate governance structures

2.1.1.6 Governance Structures

Different forms of financial transactions demand different forms of contracts or governance structures. Like transactions, governance structures can also be classed in three different types, namely "non-transaction-specific, semi-specific and highly specific".[61] "Macneil's three-way discussion of contracts [. . .] suggests that governance structures—the institutional matrix within which transactions are negotiated and executed—vary with the nature of the transaction."[62] First, all transactions which do not demand specific governance due to their high standardisation can rely on governance by the market, irrespective of their frequency. Secondly, non-standardised transactions with high frequency demand relational contracts (i.e. highly-specific governance). Such transactions are often accomplished on a bilateral basis; alternatively, companies try to internalise these transactions, which Williamson (1986) frames as *unified governance*. Thirdly, transactions of non-standardised nature which occur occasionally are governed best by neoclassical or semi-specific contracts. However, as the costs for supervising occasional transactions are rather high and the relative high specificity precludes market governance, such transactions are often supported by third-party entities.[63]

[61] Williamson (1986, p. 112).

[62] Williamson (1986, p. 105).

[63] Williamson (1986, pp. 112–114).

The dimension of uncertainty has little impact on standardised transactions, yet must be taken into account for mixed and idiosyncratic transactions. In terms of a standardised transaction, for instance, the purchase of a daily good, the market (i.e. classical contract law) can handle any degree of uncertainty as long as there is low investment specificity. "Whenever investments are idiosyncratic in non-trivial degree, increasing the degree of uncertainty makes it more imperative that the parties devise a machinery to 'work things out'—since contractual gaps will be larger and the occasions for sequential adaptations will increase in number and importance as the degree of uncertainty increases".[64] An example for an idiosyncratic financial transaction would be the purchase of a company. There are two solutions to handle complex transactions under high uncertainty. An attempt could be made to standardise the products or processes so that ultimately the market could take over governance. Alternatively, the governance structure needs to provide a framework which enables "more effective adaptive, sequential decision-making"[65] even with specificity and high uncertainty. For instance, a specialist in the field of mergers and acquisitions could help to handle the purchase of a company in a rather standardised way. Alternatively, the company purchase could be exercised in a sequential way, i.e. certain parts of the company could be bought first and others at a later stage, which enables an adaptive decision-making. As mentioned before, depending on the frequency of mixed or idiosyncratic transactions, one should rather opt for a trilateral or bilateral/unified governance structure.[66] Figure 2.3 provides examples of financial transactions with different characteristics and matches them with appropriate governance structures.

2.2 Choice of Finance

> The theory of choice usually treats the choice of an optimal consumption or production plan in the context of a given institutional structure. [...] Choice of institutions, though, seems problematic because the set of possible institutional alternatives is open ended and evolving over time.[67]

Any enterprise or individual demanding capital has to choose its, his or her optimal source of funding. There is a large variety of different forms of finance, which leads to the question of which parameters influence the choice of finance. One could expect that start-ups and PIs act thoroughly rational; yet, people in fact sometimes decide against the most obvious financial tool. Such deviations from classical theory have created a new branch of research, namely *behavioural finance*. Previous studies have revealed that the choice of finance depends on both, the

[64] Williamson (1986, p. 117 ff).

[65] Williamson (1986, p. 118).

[66] Williamson (1986, p. 118).

[67] Furubotn and Richter (1991, p. 14).

Table 2.2 Examples of internal and external finance

Internal finance	External finance
Own sources	Venture capitalist (VC)
Sources from family and friends	
Cash flows	Private equity (PE)
	Leasing
	Public funding/subsidies
	Bank loan
	Crowdfunding
	Initial public offering (IPO)
Bootstrapping	

features of the respective financial tools, the entrepreneur's personal characteristics and also the purpose for which the financial tool is intended to be used. Before contemplating personal factors which influence an entrepreneur's financial decision, the financial spectrum for PIs is illustrated.

2.2.1 Categories of Finance

Sources of finance can be categorised in several ways. First, authors distinguish between internal and external finance, i.e. whether a PI taps his own financial resources, or rather invests capital from external providers. Internal capital could also include financial support from family and friends, depending on the eye of the beholder. Table 2.2 provides examples for internal and external finance. With regard to internal finance, Lambert and Schwienbacher (2010) refer to the term of *bootstrap finance* which focusses on the liquidity of an enterprise.[68] Winborg (2009) has identified four different categories of bootstrapping, "namely: minimizing outflow, eliminating outflow, delaying outflow, and speeding up inflow of financial means."[69] Belleflamme et al. (2014) see parallels between crowdfunding and bootstrapping.[70] By contrast, Schwienbacher and Larralde (2012) draw a clear line between the two. "In both cases, founders use creative ways to finance their investments, while avoiding traditional investors. At the same time, crowdfunding differs from bootstrapping in many ways; most importantly, founders relying on crowdfunding do seek to attract external investors, unlike bootstrappers who primarily rely on internal resources and active cash management techniques".[71] However, I argue that bootstrapping can also include the management of external cash.

[68]Lambert and Schwienbacher (2010, p. 7).

[69]Winborg (2009, p. 72).

[70]Belleflamme et al. (2014, p. 590).

[71]Schwienbacher and Larralde (2012, p. 377).

Secondly, a distinction is drawn between formal and informal or illegal finance respectively. However, some forms of finance are difficult to classify; those rather belong to a grey area of finance. Sometimes the classification of a financial tool depends on the location of its implementation, the judgement of the beholder (see also Sect. 2.4.1), or the point in time. For instance, crowdfunding in Germany has only been officially regulated by the *Bundesanstalt für Finanzdienstleistungs-aufsicht (BaFin)* since 2012. CFPs that ran crowdfunding campaigns prior to this regulation had been operating in a rather grey area as there were neither guidelines for such a phenomenon like crowdfunding nor was crowdfunding explicitly prohibited. Another example for grey finance is the virtual currency *Bitcoins*, which was invented in 2009. Whilst this digital money can legitimately be used for financial transactions in most European countries, in December 2013 the PBOC prohibited Chinese financial and payment institutions to conduct business with *Bitcoins*.[72] Ultimately, not all forms of finance can easily be categorised as formal or informal finance.

Thirdly, finance can be further divided into the spheres of equity and debt. If an entrepreneur chooses equity finance, he transfers shares of his enterprise in exchange for capital; jointly with the share, the creditor also obtains chances and risks of the enterprise. By contrast, with debt the entrepreneur receives capital from e.g. a bank in exchange for the payment of interest at a certain rate on top of the payback amount; the debtee, on the other hand, has neither a voting right nor any right of participation in the entrepreneur's venture. Moreover, debt can be subdivided into short-term and long-term debt, whereas equity finance is commonly a tool for long-term investments.

Utilising these three categories, a classification like the one in Fig. 2.4 can be formulated. Within this chart, crowdfunding could be put in any of the four lowest categories. Foremost, its legality status (formal versus informal) depends on a location's progress in regulation. Moreover, there are different kinds of crowdfunding, including debt- and equity-based crowdfunding (see also Sect. 3.1). Thus, a PI applying a certain form of crowdfunding simultaneously chooses between debt versus equity, and formal versus informal finance.

Fourthly, funding options can be classified into early and late(r) sources of finance depending on the time of their implementation during a company's or a project's life cycle. Different forms of finance fulfil different tasks in line with different demands of enterprises in different stages of their life cycle. A newly founded company, for example, first needs seed capital in order to create a prototype of its core product. By contrast, a more mature company is likely to demand ample funding in order to increase its market presence through marketing activities. Figure 2.5 (Fueglistaller 2012, p. 259) schematically incorporates not just the funding stages of an entity, but also the recommended funding sources for these

[72]People's Bank of China (2014, p. 135). However, private Chinese citizens are allowed to trade with Bitcoins. In fact, "China has become the world's largest bitcoin trading market." (Cryptocoinsnews.com n.d., n.p.).

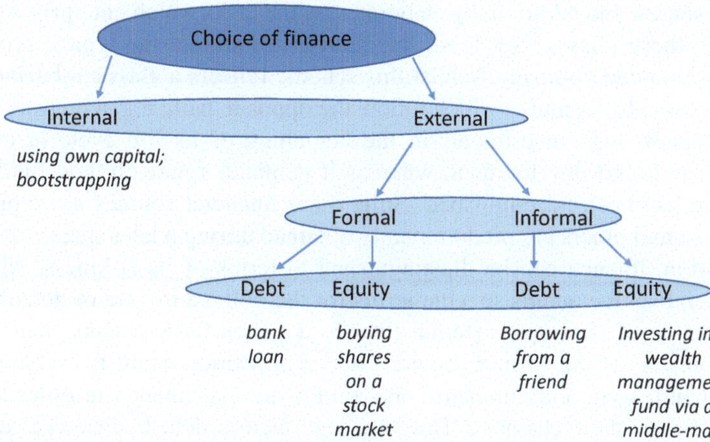

Fig. 2.4 Categories of finance including examples

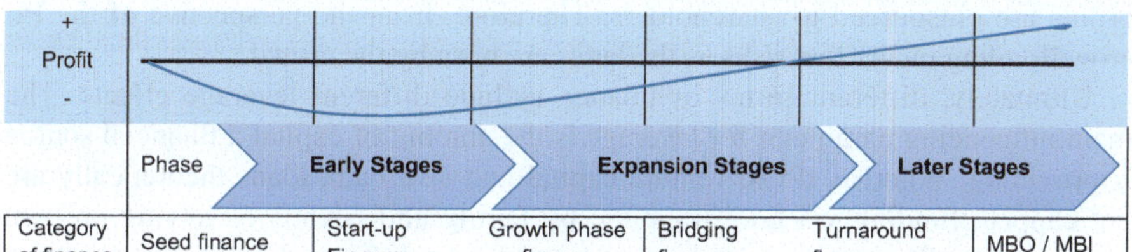

Fig. 2.5 Classification of different forms of finance according to the time of their implementation

respective stages, and additionally elaborates on the tasks which enterprises usually face during these phases. Not least, the chart also includes the typical profit line of a newly founded company. Whilst this scheme reflects a classical business life cycle, there are also ventures which follow the opposite path; e.g. a high-tech start-up rather needs huge investments in the beginning of its life cycle in order to realise research and development, whereas it demands relatively low funds once prototyping has been accomplished. Still, some financial sources are typical for early finance and others are predominantly obtained during a later stage.

In addition, finance can be dinstinguished in terms of its riskiness. Although each financial source entails specific terms for the obligee in case of default, from the perspective of start-ups, external finance is generally less risky than relying on own sources, as the former provides better protection against insolvency. On the other hand, some entrepreneurs may prefer internal finance in order to keep full control over their business. Thus, for such actors debt finance (i.e. external finance without giving out shares and any right of co-determination) is a good alternative. Crowdfunding, and in particular equity crowdfunding, counts as risk capital.[73] Yet, as mentioned above, with equity finance, risks as well as potential profits are outsourced to shareholders. Therefore, from the perspective of the PI, crowdfunding incurs low risks as the latter are born by the crowd.

Ultimately, different forms of finance include different leverage effects. The main influencing parameter for leverage is the amount of capital a financial source is providing. Whereas IPOs, venture capital and also bank loans theoretically are not capped, funding via bootstrapping, by family and friends or relying on own sources typically encompasses lower sums of capital. Thus, I argue that start-ups which intend to scale their business within a short time period should rather opt for external financial sources than relying on internal funding. With crowdfunding, PIs can collect small but also larger amounts of capital. Typically, donation- and reward-based campaigns collect smaller sums, whereas PIs with a higher capital demand commonly utilise debt- or equity-based crowdfunding.[74] In the end, crowdfunding provides a solution for different PIs with different leverage demands.

In conclusion and as can be seen from the charts and analyses above, crowdfunding belongs to early stage external financing, and can be assigned to both debt and equity finance. From the perspective of the PI, crowdfunding incurs low risks and can have a low as well as a great leverage effect, depending on the amount of capital that has been raised. The choice of finance, however, depends not only on the features of the financial tools, but also on the personal characteristics of the individuals that apply those tools.

[73]Harrison (2013).

[74]The differences of donation-, reward-, debt-, and equity-based crowdfunding are explained in Sect. 3.1.

2.2.2 *Personal Parameters Influencing the Choice of Finance*

Research on choice of finance has revealed that there are not only different forms of finance, but also certain criteria which entrepreneurs base their financial choices on. Some scholars have focussed on the characteristics of the respective financial categories; others claim that the choice of finance depends on typical personal characteristics of the entrepreneurs and also on the kind of their businesses.

According to Donaldson's (1965) *pecking order theory*, companies prefer internal funding to debt funding. Equity, by contrast, rarely is a company's first choice, but is rather applied at a later stage of the funding cycle and sometimes an option of last resort.[75] As Fig. 2.5 illustrates, start-ups and entrepreneurs typically start their business by investing the founders' own money as seed capital, unless they can rely on public sources like subsidies or the expertise and sources of a Business angel (BA). Once these resources are exhausted, ventures commonly approach external options in order to secure liquidity.

Yet, Schwienbacher (2007) argues that "[t]here is not one type of entrepreneur populating the economy, but many [...] [and] they may take different strategic and financial decisions in given situations".[76] He refers to works by Woo et al. (1991)[77] who have identified two entrepreneur types, *craftsmen* and *opportunists.* "[O]pportunists are motivated by financial success and the chance to build a successful enterprise. Craftsmen, in direct contrast, pursue independence and the chance to work in a problem area of personal interest."[78] Miner et al. (1992) described a third type, the *inventor-entrepreneurs*, who "use their firms as a vehicle for invention and producing the product invented, rather than growth".[79] Thus, the *inventor-entrepreneur* is like the *craftsman*, though he does not mind about dependent firm structures in order to reach higher ends. However, neither Woo et al. (1991) nor Miner et al. (1992) have investigated whether these three types differ in terms of their financial choices. I assume that craftsmen tend to rely on internal finance in order to ensure their independence, whereas opportunists and inventors rather strive for external funding in order to advance their business or invention.

Westhead and Wright (1998) have analysed a sample of *novice*,[80] *portfolio*,[81] and *serial founders*[82] and concluded that these types of entrepreneurs not just

[75]Donaldson (1965).

[76]Schwienbacher (2007, p. 755).

[77]Woo et al. (1991).

[78]Woo et al. (1991, p. 107).

[79]Miner et al. (1992, p. 112).

[80]"Novice founders are those that have no prior entrepreneurial experience as either a founder, an inheritor, or a purchaser of a business." (Westhead and Wright 1998, p. 173).

[81]"Portfolio founders retain their original business and inherit, establish, and/or purchase another business." (Westhead and Wright 1998, p. 173).

[82]"Serial founders are those who sell their original business but at a later date inherit, establish, and/or purchase another business." (Westhead and Wright 1998, p. 173).

differ in terms of their personal and parental backgrounds, regarding demographics, work experience and motivation, but also in respect to which funds they choose in order to set up their businesses.[83] The authors have subsumed serial and portfolio entrepreneurs under the term "*habitual entrepreneurs* who are founders, inheritors, or purchasers of businesses or who have undertaken multiple actions as corporate entrepreneurs."[84] In general, *habitual founders*, in contrast to *novice entrepreneurs*, can rely on "more resourceful backgrounds [as] they are more likely to have developed contacts and networks with potential partners and sources of resources (such as financiers, suppliers, customers, etc.)".[85] This implies that they can more easily obtain external formal funding. However, the *serial founders* in that study in fact were the ones, who relied most on own savings or funding from peers and friends, which also supports the estimation of Westhead and Wright that serial entrepreneurs finance their existing businesses with refunds from the sale of previous ones. The investigated *portfolio founders*, in contrast, often relied on bank loans; presumably as their track record easily proved their creditworthiness.[86] Still the majority of all founders in that survey across the three groups stated that they do rely on internal capital.[87] Moreover both types of *habitual founders*, "particularly serial founders, used significantly more sources of finance than novice founders".[88] Notably, more than half of all entrepreneurs interviewed in the survey had also relied on bank loans[89]; yet, the authors of the paper did not discuss these findings further.

Schwienbacher (2007) distinguished three types of entrepreneurs and two different types of financing strategy: The *Serial entrepreneur (SE)*, the *Life-style entrepreneur (LSE)* and the pure *Profit-maximising entrepreneur (PME)*, all of whom can either follow the rather conservative *wait-and-see strategy*, i.e. start their business only after they have collected sufficient funding, or opt for the *just-do-it strategy*, and start without exhaustive funding.[90] In his work, the author focusses on capital-constrained entrepreneurs with similar goals and took the *PME* as a benchmark. However, Schwienbacher (2007) exclusively considered an entrepreneur's choice for/against VC or BA funding, and did not include debt finance in his consideration. He discovered that *LSEs* rather follow the *just-do-it* approach and exclusively rely on own funding (or additionally on funding from BAs) in the earlier stages, in order to stay in control of their venture. More often than

[83]Westhead and Wright (1998, p. 174).

[84]Westhead and Wright (1998, p. 177).

[85]Westhead and Wright (1998, p. 179).

[86]Westhead and Wright (1998, p. 191).

[87]80.5% of novice founders, 73.3% of portfolio founders, and 87.9% of serial founders stated that they relied on personal savings and capital from friends and family in order to start-up their venture. (Westhead and Wright 1998, p. 191).

[88]Westhead and Wright (1998, p. 190). The authors discovered that novice, portfolio and serial founders on average applied a number of 1.6, 1.7, and 1.8 sources respectively for their start-up phase. (Westhead and Wright 1998, p. 187).

[89]Westhead and Wright (1998, p. 190 ff).

[90]Schwienbacher (2007, p. 754).

not, a *LSE* intends to start a single business and run this as a life-time occupation. By contrast, *SEs* care less about control but more about the renewal of previous successes and the recognition of their businesses.[91] Therefore, *SEs* in contrast to *LSEs* would rather opt for the *wait-and-see* financial strategy.[92] Entrepreneurs need to weigh the two mentioned funding strategies and decide which one is more suitable to their needs. Business processes can be accelerated by additional external (equity-based) funds.[93] On the other hand, entrepreneurs who first utilise their own funds and thereby reach a certain milestone, and only thereupon approach a VC appear to be more trustworthy as they can demonstrate some proof of concept, and also some proof of commitment by investing their personal savings. Consequently, a *wait-and-see* approach provides a better standing in front of a VC, once a milestone has been reached.

The trade-off between the two financial strategies has been called "*equity gap*, because venture capitalists only invest in larger projects".[94] Entrepreneurs therefore have to decide which uncertainty they intend to resolve first, the technological or the financial one. Ultimately, Schwienbacher (2007) concludes that entrepreneurs with the most profitable businesses would rather follow a *just-do-it* strategy and use their own funds for the first milestone, before approaching a VC. In order to close the equity gap, they are also likely to contact a BA first.[95] Yet, the question remains how entrepreneurs know when to start their business. Schwienbacher also remains silent as to whether the *LSE* or rather the *SE* is more likely to choose this *just-do-it + BA + VC approach.*

Although any financial decision has its individual features and is influenced by external factors like the availability of debt or equity finance, there seem to be some unifying traits for each particular founder type, which explain tendencies of financial choice. To my best knowledge, to date there has been no research investigating the typical features of a PI choosing to apply crowdfunding as a means of finance nor a study that contemplates those factors which influence an entrepreneur's choice for crowdfunding. Therefore, by considering literature on crowdfunding and incorporating common crowdfunding practice, in Sect. 3.4.4 I draw a picture of a typical PI, and further identify aspects which promote his choice for different forms of crowdfunding.

---

[91] According to (Schwienbacher 2007, p. 759), in terms of financial decisions "portfolio entrepreneurs and opportunistic entrepreneurs share some similarities with serial entrepreneurs, while craftsman entrepreneurs and inventor entrepreneurs resemble life-style entrepreneurs."

[92] Schwienbacher (2007, p. 756).

[93] Schwienbacher (2007, p. 755 ff).

[94] Schwienbacher (2007, p. 755).

[95] Schwienbacher (2007, p. 755 ff).

2.3 The Role of Financial Intermediaries

2.3.1 The Original Function of Financial Intermediaries

"[I]n a perfect market, a market with no frictions such as transaction costs, information costs, or indivisibilities, financial intermediaries would not exist."[96] As the real world diverges from the general equilibrium theory,[97] market actors need to rely on financial intermediaries. Predominantly, as information is not distributed equally amongst market actors, there are information asymmetries, which can lead to moral hazard and adverse selection problems. In order to prevent such situations and reduce information asymmetries, market actors need to spend substantial resources before, during and after transactions. Whereas transaction costs are absent in general equilibrium theory, their existence is the *raison d'être* for financial intermediaries.[98]

By relying on institutions like financial intermediaries, market actors can save transaction costs. Commonly, financial intermediaries fulfil one or several of the following three tasks: "(1) acquiring information about economic entities; (2) processing information about economic entities; and (3) packaging or repackaging the financial claims of these economic entities."[99] The latter further implies that information can be traded like a commodity at a certain price.[100] Commonly, the comparative advantage of financial intermediaries derives from the following three factors. First, they can exploit economies of scale and thereby reduce transaction costs as financial intermediaries often specialise in a certain field of operation.[101] Particularly, they can offer the services of "documentation, information and monitoring [that] reduce frauds, litigation, and misunderstandings which are expected to be [...] costly."[102] Secondly, in comparison to individual market actors, financial institutions can obtain sensitive information more easily due to their reputation and expected discretion. Thirdly, as financial institutions act as a platform for capital providers and capital demanders, their overall searching and matching costs are lower compared to individual market actors.[103] All in all, market actors can reduce their overall transaction costs with the support of financial intermediaries.

Financial intermediaries can be differentiated into *commercial banks* (which provide indirect finance) and *securities markets* (which provide direct finance).[104] Xie et al. (2016) argue that with *internet finance* a third type of financial interme-

---

[96]Benston and Smith (1976, p. 217).

[97]See e.g. Mas-Colell (2016).

[98]Benston and Smith (1976, p. 215).

[99]Draper and Hoag (1978, p. 595).

[100]Benston and Smith (1976, p. 215 ff).

[101]Benston and Smith (1976, p. 222).

[102]Ibid.

[103]Benston and Smith (1976, p. 223).

[104]This dissertation will not further analyse securities markets.

diation emerges, which appears to be a perfect form of direct finance and therefore eventually will evoke a paradigm shift.[105]

> Under Internet finance, mobile payments of individuals will be efficiently integrated with central payments systems managed by central banks. Information processing and risk assessment will be conducted on the Internet, and information will be highly transparent. Costs of maturity matching and risk sharing will be so low that financial intermediaries will be unnecessary, and the issuance and trading of stocks, bonds, and loans will be carried out smoothly. Markets will be so efficient that they highly resemble the world without financial intermediaries described by general equilibrium theory. Furthermore, Internet finance will be able to achieve the same allocative efficiency while greatly reducing transaction costs.[106]

Consequently, the authors predict that with internet finance financial intermediaries will eventually become obsolete. Whether internet finance has the potential to create a general equilibrium status or not, is yet to be determined. However, internet technologies are able to reduce transaction costs as will further be elaborated in Chaps. 4–6. In the following, the analysis of the role of financial intermediaries will focus on features of commercial banks.

The main task of banks is to intermediate between potential borrowers and existing creditors; they effectively match financial demand with supply. Thereby, banks fulfil the following three functions: (1) financial coordination; (2) capital allocation; and (3) the rating of a borrower's creditworthiness.[107] By providing an institutional platform, banks coordinate deposits and loans. They regulate supply and demand with the interest level and thereby should be able to allocate capital effectively. However, as Akerlof (1970) has demonstrated with *the market for lemons* (and as elaborated in Sect. 2.1.1), a bank rather chooses lower interest rates than the ones which meet demand in order to address a variety of debtors including credit-worthy ones. Moreover, financial intermediaries need to prove the creditworthiness of a potential borrower through the gathering and evaluation of information. Due to their expertise and typical specialisation, banks can reduce information asymmetries more easily compared to individual actors of the market, and due to economies of scale, they can monitor borrowers at lower costs. In sum, commercial banks prevent adverse selection and moral hazard situations at lower costs and therefore can effectively intermediate between capital providers and capital demanders.

Besides the above-mentioned roles, a financial intermediary should further fulfil three transformational functions, i.e. *lot-size transformation*, *term transformation*, and *risk transformation*. Even though financial intermediaries try to match financial demand with financial supply, it is rather unlikely that they find two counterparts that request for and provide the same amounts of capital. Therefore, banks need to balance the requests with deposits and allocate available capital accordingly. This process is called *lot-size transformation*. Secondly, debtors and creditors

---

[105] Xie et al. (2016, p. 10).

[106] Ibid.

[107] Hartmann-Wendels et al. (2007, p. 4 ff).

hardly request for the same length of time for their loan or credit respectively. Whereas this incongruence would easily lead to failure in an ordinary market, financial intermediaries can rely on primary and secondary financial markets. This combination enables them to cope with term discrepancies and to ensure term transformation. Thirdly, financial transactions usually come along with a certain level of risk. Moreover, each market actor has a certain level of risk aversion. Again, there are hardly two counterparts with the same level or readiness of risk assumption; thus, creditors and debtors rely on an entity, which balances their differences in risk aversion. A bank, for example, can cope with such discrepancies more easily as it holds a portfolio of projects with different risk levels, which eventually reduces overall risks.[108]

2.3.2 The Theory of Financialisation

In the wake of the recent financial crisis of 2007–2009, the role of commercial banks has been scrutinised. Once scholars had analysed the underlying reasons for the systemic failure of the global financial sector, they came up with a new term to characterise recent developments, i.e. *financialisation*. In essence, financialisation describes the reverted role of commercial banks. According to this theory, over the last few decades banks have transformed from lenders for corporates to speculators and providers of a variety of (erstwhile public) services. Financialisation is said to have its roots in neo-liberalism, and eventually could change capitalism fundamentally.

Financialisation can be illustrated by means of three groups of actors, i.e. big corporates, banks, and households, plus the state. According to Lapavitsas (2013a) financialisation originated in the non-financial sector, more specifically in the fact that large enterprises have increasingly become independent from banks as they can rely on retained profits to finance themselves. Although these companies still maintain relationships with financial intermediaries, the former in fact could do without credit from the latter. Hence, banks have lost their key customers and therefore increasingly shift their focus towards SMEs and households. Moreover, as they no longer can live on net-returns from interest earnings, banks also revised their business models. Besides financial services, banks nowadays also provide services like insurances and housing, or strategies for different schemes of life. At the same time, households are progressively drawn into the financial system, which according to Lapavitsas has two interrelated reasons. First, public provision of services like education, transportation, health and housing is in retreat. Thus, households have to pay for these kinds of services on a private basis and, consequently, accumulate debts. Secondly, the service gap is closed by financial intermediaries. Today, households are not only holding more debts, but also more

[108] Hartmann-Wendels et al. (2007, p. 5 ff).

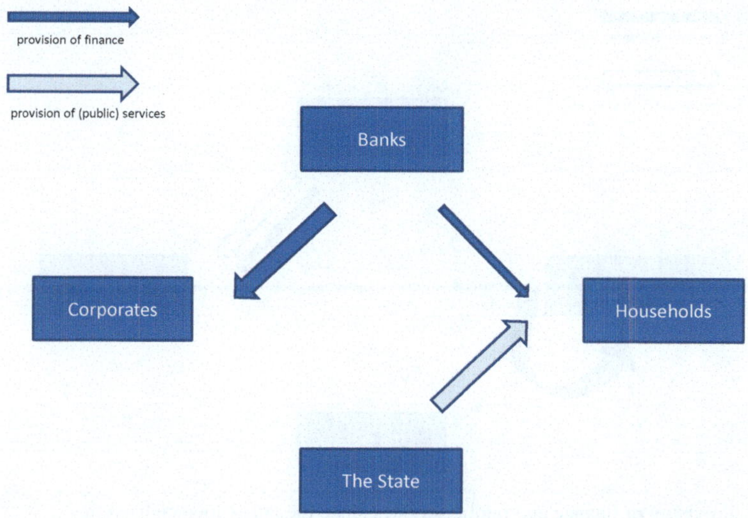

Fig. 2.6 Provision of finance and public services in the West before the era of financialisation

assets as they increasingly invest into things like insurances, pension funds, etc. Therefore, households are becoming more intertwined with the financial sector. In the end, the combination of increasingly independent corporates, a change in banks' business model and the progressive integration of households in the financial system leads towards financialisation of a society.[109]

Financialisation evokes a new interplay between the involved four actors, i.e. banks, corporates, households and the state. Whereas hitherto banks served predominantly corporates and secondarily households with credit, and the state provided public services to households (see Fig. 2.6 (Lapavitsas 2013a)), in the course of financialisation corporates are becoming financially independent and banks increasingly concentrate their efforts on households. Simultaneously, the state is withdrawing from its original function as social gatekeeper. The new system (see Fig. 2.7 (Lapavitsas 2013a)) looks rather fragmented and unstable, and evokes "a profound change in social structure".[110] This change is also reflected in the following three issues. First and foremost, financial profits of non-financial institutions have become a substantial proportion of total profits. Moreover, only a small share of the society benefits from this development, and often these financial profits come in the form of bonuses, which overall looks like a new form of rentier system. Ultimately, Lapavitsas claims that neo-liberalism has been penetrating many spheres of society, which supports the development of financialisation.

---

[109] Lapavitsas (2013a).

[110] Boston University (2014, 35:25).

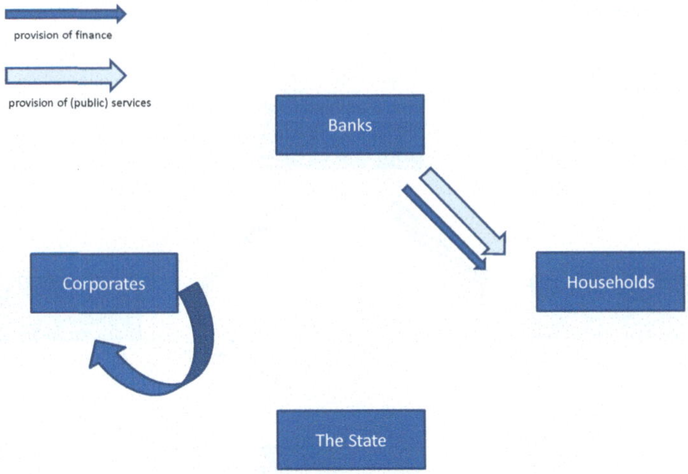

Fig. 2.7 Provision of finance and public services since the era of financialisation

However, according to Lapavitsas, financialisation "is not really a spontaneous development [...] but would have been impossible without the state."[111] Contrary to the ideas of neo-liberalism and the theory of free markets, the "state has retained and actually strengthened its monopoly command over the final means of payment".[112] This first can be seen from the central bank's power to create liquidity, which is based on the state's monopoly on money, and ultimately supports the banks. Secondly, the state has supported financialisation by means of regulation. Contrary to expectations, the past three to four decades were not marked by deregulation, but in fact, by re-regulation. Yet, this regulation is "semi-public, [...] operated by institutions that are and are not public, focussing on the individual activities of financial institutions and above all aiming to protect the profit making capabilities of these institutions. This kind of regulation is captured most clearly in the Basel agreements, Basel I and II, and now Basel III".[113] According to Lapavitsas, this regulation is just in line with the interests of financial institutions. Thirdly, in the wake of the financial crisis the state has obtained the role of the lender of last resort, it has furthermore ensured deposits, and all of a sudden there are banks which are too big to fail—"[three] key ways in which the state has supported and sustained and *created* financialisation".[114] Therefore, the question is not about more market versus more state, but in fact a question of regulation *pro* versus *of* the market.

[111]Boston University (2014, 45:18).

[112]Boston University (2014, 46:05).

[113]Boston University (2014, 49:33).

[114]Boston University (2014, 51:42).

Lapavitsas further puts financialisation into the context of three larger phenomenons. First, since the initiation of the era of financialisation, producing companies have been struggling to increase profitability and productivity, despite the evolution of digitalisation. Secondly, financialisation went along with "a fundamental rise in inequality [. . .] in terms of income [. . .] but also [in terms of] function[. . .]. Capital has won against labor, or labor has lost against capital."[115] In this context, Piketty (2014) remarks that this rise in inequality will eventually lead to severe economic issues and political tensions.[116] However, the author was criticised for the empirical data he had based his analysis on.[117] Thirdly, financialisation goes hand in hand with deregulation,[118] with regard to both the labour and the financial market. These three developments are symptoms as well as drivers of financialisation.[119]

According to Lapavitsas, financialisation is predominantly a Western phenomenon, which started out in the wake of the oil crisis of the 1970s and since then has been observed almost exclusively in the US and Europe. Some middle income countries like Brazil, Turkey and Mexico have been drawn into financialisation due to international cash flows and the presence of banks from mature countries in developing countries. Having been asked whether financialisation has already reached China, in 2014, the economist negated this question and justified his opinion with the following arguments: First, China's currency is not international. Second, there are capital controls in China. Third, most banks are publicly owned and non-financial companies do not finance themselves.[120] Yet, I argue that, in particular since 2014, financialisation in China is on the rise, even though its roots lie elsewhere. Moreover, the extent of financialisation in China could reach a unique magnitude. At least in this respect, Lapavitsas agrees with me.

> If [the Chinese government] lift[s regulation] and China begins to financialise, then the nature of crisis that we're gonna see in the future will make what we've lived through[121] *seem like a little insignificant episode.*[122]

In Chap. 6 and by means of the example of crowdfunding, I will demonstrate that, in fact, in China financialisation has already reached a new and unique dimension.

---

[115]Boston University (2014, 24:36–25:30).

[116]Piketty (2014).

[117]Bofinger and Scheuermeyer (2015).

[118]Lapavitsas used the term "re-regulation", see above.

[119]Lapavitsas (2013b).

[120]Boston University (2014, 1:18:50).

[121]Lapavitsas refers to the global financial crisis of 2007–2009.

[122]Boston University (2014, 1:21:40).

2.4 Informal Finance as a Complement to the Formal Finance Sector

2.4.1 Research on Informal Finance

"Informal finance refers to a kind of direct private credit relation that takes the form of a loan in currency or goods".[123] It pertains to "all financial transactions, loans and deposits, occurring outside the regulation of a central monetary or financial market authority".[124] Studies on informal finance agree upon the fact that there is no single method of informal finance dominating; rather, there is a wide range of informal financing tools, owing to the heterogeneity of individuals and enterprises in low income countries.[125]

Informal finance is usually addressed as a phenomenon of developing countries as there are no studies on informal finance in high income countries. First assessments of informal finance date back to the late 1950s, when e.g. Wai (1957) conducted a survey on the nature of informal markets focussing on interest rates.[126] Another pioneer of studies on nonbank financial institutions has been the *Agency for International Development*.[127] While the early researchers of informal finance mostly were anthropologists and sociologists, by the 1980s economists started to pay attention to it as they recognised its importance for resource mobilisation and resource allocation.[128] The majority of early economic studies focussed on Asian developing countries,[129] some studies concentrated on Latin America.[130] Few authors like Begashaw,[131] Graham and Cuevas[132] and Shipton[133] have evaluated informal finance in African countries.

More recent studies searched for plausible reasons why people still apply informal finance despite access to formal institutions. Scholars concluded that informal finance just better meets people's demand for financial services,[134] and that informal tools can be very productive in terms of capital accumulation.[135] The

---

[123] Jiang (2009a, p. 12).

[124] Adams and Fitchett (1992b, p. 2).

[125] Adams (1992, p. 18).

[126] Wai (1957).

[127] Hsu (2009, p. 4).

[128] Callier (1990, p. 273).

[129] See e.g. Maloney and Ahmed (1988) directing at Bangladesh; Bell (1990) contemplating India; Lamberte (1992) concentrating on the Philippines; amongst others.

[130] See e.g. Larson and Urquidi (1987), Adams and Canavesi (1992).

[131] Begashaw (1978).

[132] Graham and Cuevas (1990).

[133] Shipton (1992).

[134] Baydas et al. (1995).

[135] Besley and Levenson (1996).

concurrent existence of formal and informal finance is a prevailing phenomenon[136]; and notably, the application of informal finance does not disproportionally decrease with the expansion of formal financial institutions.[137] "Many households participate in both sectors, since the two sectors serve differing credit demands. The formal sector services loans for investment purposes, while the informal sector provides smaller loans for bridging or consumption smoothing purposes".[138] Even though authors distinguish between so-called *production loans* and *consumption loans*,[139] the assumption that informal finance solely serves consumption ends is questionable.[140] Nevertheless, informal finance traditionally plays an essential role for the development of poor areas and disadvantaged people, specifically for "small farmers, landless people, operators of microenterprises, and women".[141]

Compared to the impression of early investigations in the 1950s, the image of informal finance has changed. Previously, informal finance was associated with evil moneylenders and monopolies, high interest rates and exploitation.[142] Accordingly, terms with rather negative connotations emerged, including *underground finance*, *unorganised finance*, *non-institutional finance*, and also *finance for curb markets*.[143] With regard to *underground finance*, sometimes *grey finance* is discriminated from *black finance*. The former is likely to be tolerated by the authorities as it serves the progress of the economy and could eventually be formalised and transformed into formal finance with respective regulation. On the contrary, *black finance* serves illegal and criminal ends. It is perceived as rather pernicious for the economy and therefore should be banned.[144] Nowadays, most authors simply subsume all kinds of non-formal financial transactions under *informal finance*. This change in terminology tries to include a wide range of different kinds of informal tools that cannot be easily categorised.[145] Bouman and Moll (1992) in this regard use the terms *hybrid* or *semi-formal institutions*.[146]

Moreover, the evolution of informal finance reflects its innovativeness, which goes in line with its claim to reduce transaction costs of savers and borrowers to a minimum.[147] In contrast to formal banking, informal finance is more customised and thus provides a wider variety in financial solutions. Whereas some forms of informal finance have prevailed for a long time (e.g. pawnshops), others are the

[136] Madestam (2014).
[137] Adams and Fitchett (1992b, p. 3).
[138] Mohieldin and Wright (2000, p. 658).
[139] Wai (1992, p. 344).
[140] Wai (1992, p. 339 ff).
[141] Adams and Fitchett (1992a, p. xi).
[142] Adams (1992, p. 7).
[143] Adams and Fitchett (1992b, p. 2).
[144] Jiang (2009a).
[145] Wai (1992, p. 338).
[146] Bouman and Moll (1992, p. 211).
[147] Adams (1992, p. 20).

results of more recent socio-economic developments and therefore rather new. Wai (1992) in this context explicitly mentions the evolution of Rotating Savings and Credit Associations (ROSCAs), which are widespread in most low-income countries but whose specific shape and features vary according to their specific environment.[148] In Sect. 2.4.3, I will further illustrate the generalised concept of a ROSCA and introduce it as a benchmark for informal and formal finance.

Whilst early research almost exclusively focussed on rural areas, since the 1990s, scientists have included urban regions in their analysis. In fact, informal finance can also be found in established sectors. For instance, India's film industry and Philippines' shoes industry have to a wide extent been financed by informal channels.[149] Furthermore, according to Wai (1992) scholars had to rewrite their association of informal finance with penniless people on the rural curb as, in fact, informal finance is popular amongst all social classes.[150] Yet, it could be that Wai in this context rather refered to *shadow banking* instead of informal finance as the former is rather a phenomenon of urban regions[151] and utilised by people who are better off.

Shadow banking is a term coined by Paul McCulley.[152] Like formal banking *shadow banking* encompasses the provision of credit. However, whilst in the formal system deposits and loans commonly are processed within the same entity, *shadow banking* includes several entities that transform "opaque, risky, long-term assets into money-like, short-term liabilities."[153] By further contrast, *shadow banks* do not have access to a central bank or other public sources of liquidity, but exclusively rely on the private sector and thus enjoy no credit guarantees. Statistics demonstrate that *shadow banking* is prospering, despite its instability. The Federal Reserve Bank of New York has estimated for the US that from the 1990s until 2009 shadow bank liabilities have always outreached formal bank liabilities. With the financial crisis of 2007–2009, a large share of the shadow banking system collapsed.[154] Still, the global scale and scope of *shadow banking* remains large. For more information on the setup and processes of the shadow banking system see Pozsar et al. (2012).

Although the borders between *shadow banking* and informal finance are rather blurred, there are some features which distinguish them. *Shadow banking* has its origins in the US[155]; yet, it is also omnipresent in emerging economies like China.[156] Informal finance is a phenomenon of developing countries (see above). In contrast to informal finance, *shadow banking* is based on complex structures

[148] Wai (1992, p. 343).
[149] Wai (1992, p. 339).
[150] Ibid.
[151] Acharya et al. (2013).
[152] McCulley (2007).
[153] Pozsar et al. (2012, p. 1).
[154] Pozsar et al. (2012, p. 7 ff).
[155] Pozsar et al. (2012, p. 13).
[156] See e.g. Wei and Burns (2016).

and often involves several levels of credit distribution. Moreover, it is organised "around securitization and wholesale funding. [...] [L]oans, leases, and mortgages are securitized and thus become tradeable instruments."[157] In comparison, informal financial transactions involve less entities, and assets are commonly not subject to several transformation processes. Whilst *shadow banking* is considered a threat to financial stability as it is "non-transparent and has few formal safety backstops",[158] informal finance includes specific mechanisms to prevent fraud and default (see Sect. 2.4.2). Finally, I argue that informal finance is rather similar to formal finance than to *shadow banking* as in both informal and formal finance deposits and credit are commonly processed by the same intermediary. In sum, as long as the formal financial sector shows defects and *shadow banking* is no safe alternative, new forms of informal finance will continue to emerge spontaneously.[159]

2.4.2 Features of Informal Finance

As of today, most stereotypes regarding informal finance have been disproved and literature stresses the potential benefits of informal financial organisations.[160] "The existence of these institutions has served to fill a specific need and/or complement the socioeconomic culture in which economic transaction[s] take place".[161] A common feature of such transactions is the relatively small size of capital involved, usually borrowed or lent for a short term, without the premise of tangible collateral.[162] Many authors stress the importance of informal institutions as last resort for people without access to formal institutions.[163] As Adams (1992) has depicted, informal lenders are like hospitals serving a "difficult set of clients [...]. Many of the patients who go there are physically (financially) stressed. They lack sufficient knowledge (funds) to heal themselves. As a result of their visit, some of these patients are cured and never return to the hospital. [...] A few patients may perish (default) after coming to the hospital because their illnesses were too far advanced".[164]

Lending rates in informal finance are usually quite high, a fact that has been attributed to the rather high risks that informal lenders have to bear and to the lenders monopoly power. According to surveys conducted by Li (2009) in 2004 and 2006, the average informal interest level in China then has been 16.4%, with the

157 Pozsar et al. (2012, p. 10).

158 Wei and Burns (2016, p. 2).

159 Jiang (2009a, p. 26).

160 See e.g. Besley and Levenson (1996); Tsai (2002); Madestam (2014); amongst others.

161 Hsu (2009, p. 4).

162 Adams (1992, p. 6).

163 Tsai (2002), Adams and Fitchett (1992a), amongst others.

164 Adams (1992, p. 19 ff).

rate for deposits usually being lower than the one for loans.[165] Yet, high borrowing rates are less a result of lenders' monopoly power and exploitation, but rather reflect the shortage in funds and the high opportunity costs related to informal finance.[166] Another argument against the existence of lenders' monopoly is the relatively low entry barrier for additional lenders. Anyone who holds resources can access informal finance and become a lender.[167]

In addition, informal institutions also serve a savings function. In a survey by Adams and Canavesi (1992), 91% of 470 interviewees stated that their intention to save was the main reason for participating in an informal credit association.[168] "The large amounts of savings that surface in informal financial markets are an indication of substantial propensities to save voluntarily and also show the failure of most formal financial systems to provide attractive deposit services".[169] In addition to shorter retention periods, informal institutions are likely to offer higher interest rates compared to formal institutions. In January 2016, the average deposit rate of Chinese banks stood at 1.75%,[170] whilst China's average inflation rate of 2015 was 1.54%.[171] Against such a background, informal investments are interesting as they often promise much higher returns.

Although informal financial institutions are often said to be *unorganised*,[172] they are in general quite disciplined and efficient. Lenders require sufficient information on potential clients in order to avoid bad loans, while borrowers strive to demonstrate their creditworthiness to fellow borrowers and lenders in order to qualify for future loans.[173] Borrowers and lenders usually know each other personally, they share some communality like their place of residence, and thereby often know about each other's reputation. Typically, informal finance is organised in interest groups, comprising of e.g. migrants who all originate from the same village or people who all follow the same profession. Shared backgrounds or interests create some form of *trust*. Conversely, group binding prevents fraud and also default. If a borrower, for example, did not meet his repayment obligations, he would not just run the risk of being excluded from the informal finance group, but also of being socially stigmatised. Thus, despite its non-institutionalised character, informal finance works quite effectively as social ties compensate for a lack of collateral and formal institutions.

On the one hand, informal finance resembles formal finance, on the other hand, it clearly differs from formal finance. In terms of financial scope, informal

[165] Li (2009, p. 53).

[166] Wai (1992, p. 337 ff).

[167] Adams (1992, p. 16).

[168] Adams and Canavesi (1992, p. 320).

[169] Adams and Canavesi (1992, p. 19).

[170] Deposits.org (2016).

[171] Inflation.eu (n.d.).

[172] See Sect. 2.4.1.

[173] Adams (1992, p. 19).

finance is by no means inferior to formal financial services. However, in contrast to formal institutions, informal finance occurs less planned, and rather happens spontaneously[174] and often at high speed. Informal financial transactions can emerge between all kinds of individuals and entities. There are no regulations and therefore no strict and comprehensive rules, but rather specific codes of conduct for each transaction, which all actors involved agree upon. Furthermore, informal finance provides no standardised but individually customised solutions for creditors and capital seekers.[175]

Private enterprises specifically benefit from informal financial services as Baydas et al. (1995) have discovered during their research on informal finance in Egypt.[176] Jiang (2009a) goes even further to state that "the better developed the private economy is, the greater the demand for informal finance and the greater the supply of private capital, and therefore the more numerous the categories of informal finance".[177] Thus, the private economy and informal finance promote each other. Funds are often channelled from formal to informal banking institutions. Similarly, capital can be channelled the other way round. Some "savings group[s] deposit their joint funds in banks, thus reducing the banking costs [i.e. the transaction costs of the banks] of mobilizing small individual deposits."[178] Therefore, many forms of informal finance are interrelated with formal institutions and thus complement, rather than substitute, formal finance.[179] Thereby, the private sector indirectly has access to formal finance.

In the end, actors switch between informal to formal institutions depending on their external environment and their personal conditions. For example, for borrowers living in a remote village borrowing from friends is more direct, less time-consuming and less bureaucratic than obtaining a bank loan. Informal lenders usually do not demand that borrowers provide collateral or a certain level of income. If there is no bank affiliate in the borrowers' village, the latters' expected transaction costs would further increase. Thus, for the average rural borrower in a developing country, informal finance is a convenient choice. In contrast, citizens in a developed country probably feel reluctant to borrow from friends and rather choose the private bank of their trust in the city they live in. For them, it could be very stressful to set up contracts with several neighbours to define the re-payment procedures. They would rather opt for a standard offer from their bank, which guarantees fixed interest rates and relatively anonymous debts. Still, the perspective of the rural borrowers is likely to change, if a bank opens a branch in their village or if they suddenly lose their friends. Then their preference could shift towards the formal institution, or, in reference to Fig. 2.1, from the lower right to one of the upper corners. As

[174]This characteristic of informal finance reflects its *unorganised* connotation.

[175]Li (2009, p. 43).

[176]Baydas et al. (1995, p. 652).

[177]Jiang (2009b, p. 60).

[178]Wai (1992, p. 343).

[179]Adams and Fitchett 1992b, p. 3 ff; Wai (1992, p. 342 ff).

these examples demonstrate, such a movement is dependent on both personal and environmental circumstances of the actors. Not least, an individual's choice for informal or formal institutions depends on the involved transaction cost.

Informal financial institutions manage to reduce overall transaction costs. People who are less wealthy typically conduct small, but numerous financial transactions. Moreover, any individual is organised in several groups like the family, the village, guilds etc. The interdependencies within such social structures evoke many responsibilities. Mutual assistance is necessary as there are always friends or relatives in financial need; thereby reciprocity is a matter of course. Not least due to the overall lack of resources, borrowers often obtain credit from several obligees; likewise, savers often provide their money to more than one debtee. As a consequence, the number of transactions is rather high and overall transaction costs and accumulated risks are equally high for all involved actors.

Yet, transaction costs can be minimised as the informal lender and the borrower know each other personally. Usually, they have interacted over a longer time period and maintain close relations alongside the financial deal. They rely on each other's reputation, which reduces the dangers of adverse selection, moral hazard and hidden action. In addition, social ties lower the costs for information search, bargaining, decision making and monitoring, which in turn decrease overall transaction costs (see Fig. 2.2). Whilst informal financial institutions are generally characterised as transaction cost saving entities, within informal finance, there are institutions which involve more or less transaction costs. A prime example for economising on transaction costs is a Rotating Savings and Credit Association.

2.4.3 Rotating Savings and Credit Associations: A Benchmark for (Formal and Informal) Finance

Rotating Savings and Credit Associations (ROSCAs) are a typical form of informal finance and often used as ideal models by scholars analysing informal finance.[180] Wai (1992) came to the conclusion that there are hardly any low-income countries that do not have such savings and credit groups. On a cumulative basis, these groups collect large amounts of funds and thus are an important source of finance for people in developing countries.[181]

Presumably, as ROSCAs comprise of a group of people like the *crowd*, Alijani et al. (2016) have contrasted ROSCAs to the concept of crowdfunding with regard to "group compliance, collaboration and cooperation".[182] The authors reason that ROSCAs and crowdfunding share some similarity as in both cases "[t]rust, engagement, transparency and accountability reduce the transaction costs

[180] See e.g. Callier (1990); Besley and Levenson (1996).

[181] Wai (1992, p. 343).

[182] Alijani et al. (2016, p. 210).

of carrying out business transactions."[183] Not least due to these facts, this chapter illustrates the phenomenon of ROSCAs. First of all, their concept is described, and secondly, ROSCAs are analysed in terms of transaction costs and principal-agent-relationships.

> The classic ROSCA consists of not more than several dozen members who know each other, usually as a result of social, employment, or locational bonds; who have little or no access to formal finance; and who agree to contribute a fixed sum periodically to a pool or "hand" that is assembled and distributed by a lot at meetings on agreed dates. One member receives the hand at each meeting. When each member has received a hand the cycle is completed, and the ROSCA disbands or reorganizes. Classic ROSCAs are typically established by an organizer who presides over meetings and takes the first hand.[184]

Pischke (1992) sees in ROSCAs a benchmark for other forms of finance, formal as well as informal ones, as they demonstrate some distinctive reoccurring features, which strengthen their sustainability. The author attributes their uniqueness to the three adjectives *ubiquitous*, *intermediate* and *collective*. First, as mentioned above, ROSCAs can be found in every developing country, though their denomination varies. This means that such associations are not just quite common and accessible by many people, but also that this financial concept is applicable to a variety of cultures. Secondly, ROSCAs effectively intermediate between borrowers and savers, or rather, between "saver-borrower[s]"[185] as each member of an association is both, debtor and creditor, though not at the same time. ROSCAs provide a "state-of-the-art intermediation"[186] as they "transform[...] future payments into immediate hands and accumulat[e] small payments into larger pools".[187] Thirdly, ROSCAs operate on a collective, private and voluntary basis, and each member agrees with the underlying norms and conditions that such an association is subject to.[188] There are no other forms of informal finance which show a similar combination of ubiquitous access, smooth intermediation and collective action.

ROSCAs not least are popular for their savings function. As mentioned in Sect. 2.4.2, actors in informal finance are usually subject to reciprocity and mutual assistance. Yet, the obligations to an association are given priority over supporting other social peers. Thus, as a member of a ROSCA, an individual can eventually save for a certain purpose, without the external pressure to support others in need for capital. Gugerty (2007) called it the "protection of funds from family demands".[189] Not least due to this fact, membership in a ROSCA is valued. In addition, Levenson and Besley (1996) revealed that in Taiwan ROSCA participation increases with

[183] Alijani et al. (2016, p. 222).
[184] Pischke (1992, p. 327).
[185] Pischke (1992, p. 334).
[186] Pischke (1992, p. 330).
[187] Pischke (1992, p. 329).
[188] Pischke (1992, p. 326 ff).
[189] Gugerty (2007, p. 278).

the level of income.[190] Similarly, Donoso et al. (2011) discovered that in Bolivia, ROSCAs are predominantly applied by citizens with middle income.[191] These findings further indicate that a membership in a ROSCA is valued for its savings function.

However, ROSCAs are more than just a financial tool. Benda (2013) claims from his research on ROSCAs in Rwanda that, above all, such associations are inclusive tools and promoters of certain values. By only contributing small payments, savers can become a member of a ROSCA. This membership can increase not just the image of these savours but also the latters' self-esteem. Thus, ROSCAs manage to integrate marginalised people and effectively contribute to more equality within the society. Moreover, "RoSCAs [...] warrant appraisal beyond the immediate financial opportunities they generate, because of their production and reproduction of values such as democracy, reciprocity, and solidarity, and thus their significant contribution to community development and human well-being."[192] In sum, ROSCAs are effective beyond their financial function.

Yet, primarily, ROSCAs stand out due to their financial performance. Particularly, "they economize transaction costs, they lengthen term structures, and they manage risks effectively."[193] These features are further discussed below by means of illustrative examples.

First, ROSCAs save time and other resources. Commonly, all members meet on a regular basis. Thereby, the payments are collected and disbursed on-site, which makes any written documentation obsolete.[194] Additionally, this coordination of savings and borrowing at one point in time reduces capital management cost to zero. Usually, terms are clear, straightforward and limited to a manageable set of rules. Most members know each other personally and a ROSCA even can be set up for a shared purpose. Consequently, costs of information gathering are also low. The simple but strict set of terms and conditions leaves little room for bargaining and decision making. As mentioned above, social pressure replaces monitoring. The organisation of a ROSCA forces its members to be disciplined and deposit on a regular basis. If a member defaults on a payment, he gets stigmatised, not only by his peer members but also beyond the ROSCA (see also Sect. 2.4.2). Therefore, the "[m]embership is generally taken very seriously. [...] Reported cases of ROSCA failure are infrequent, and suicides by defaulters have been recorded."[195] Yet, a study by Guha and Gupta (2005) revealed that the most sustainable associations are

[190] Levenson and Besley (1996).

[191] Donoso et al. (2011, p. 191).

[192] Benda (2013, p. 232).

[193] Pischke (1992, p. 327).

[194] However, in fact, the members do not have to meet all in person in order to form a group; it is sufficient if the organiser approaches each member, collects the deposits and finally disburses it to the one who is entitled to receive the hand. (Pischke 1992, p. 328).

[195] Pischke (1992, p. 328).

Table 2.3 Transaction costs involved in a typical ROSCA

Type of transaction costs	Level of transaction costs
Information searching	Low
Bargaining and preparing	Low to modest
Decision making	Low to modest
Policing and enforcement	Low

those with "decremental social sanction[s]",[196] which implies that ROSCAs work without the threat of harsh penalties. All in all, contrasting these findings to the identified types of transaction cost by Dahlmann (1979), and Furubotn and Richter (1991) (see Table 2.1), it becomes clear that a ROSCA incurs relatively low costs for all participating actors.[197] Table 2.3 depicts these findings.

Secondly, ROSCAs support people to make long-term financial decisions. "[A]ll members except the recipient of the final hand receive the cumulative contractual amount of their contributions in the form of a hand before they could have accumulated it by acting alone, by saving the amount of their contribution each period."[198] Indeed, the fact that members can obtain the entire lump sum earlier than if they saved it on their own, amongst others, is a strong motivation for such a long-term commitment.[199] On the other hand, some members might not be able to save such a large amount of capital on their own and over such a long period without peer pressure. In the end, long-term oriented structures provide more security and planning reliability, not just on the micro level but also from a macro perspective.

ROSCAs, thirdly, are effective risk managing tools. As Pischke described it, "[t]he major credit risk is that a winner of an early hand may fail to make subsequent contributions."[200] Yet, as already mentioned above, defaulting members become socially stigmatised as all members are interrelated beyond the credit association. A typical ROSCA is a closed circle of people who either know each other personally or via a third party (commonly the organiser). Every participant therefore is able to evaluate his peers' background, their motives, efforts and corresponding achievements. Additionally, the current status of each member can be observed at the regular meetings of the association. Risk can be further steered by the actual size of the group. Moreover, the selection of appropriate members is essential as well as

[196]Guha and Gupta (2005, p. 1473).

[197]In contrast to ordinary members of a ROSCA, the organiser commonly bears a larger share of the overall transaction costs. Yet, she is often compensated for the latter by receiving the first hand of the cycle (Pischke 1992, p. 327).

[198]Pischke (1992, p. 329).

[199]"Inflation of course skews the benefits of ROSCAs when the hand consists of a fixed amount of currency. This may be accommodated by distributing the hand by auction, by shortening the life of the ROSCA, by specifying that ROSCA payments [are] made in kind, by requiring payment in dollars, or by reversing the order or rotation in subsequent cycles" (Pischke 1992, p. 332).

[200]Pischke (1992, p. 330).

the length of the cycle, the frequency of deposits and the amount for each deposit. Usually, the organiser cares for all these issues; he is also likely to help out in case of a default. In sum, the structure and procedures of ROSCAs keep risks and therefore transaction costs at a relatively low level. Of the residual costs, the major share is born by the organiser of the cycle.

The popularity of ROSCAs is not least driven by the ease of its setup. Anyone who has steady cash inflows and a good network of people with similar income and potentially congenial interests can form a ROSCA. Whenever the fixed cycle has ended, people can easily exit and new members can apply to enter the association.

> ROSCAs require no tangible collateral and are purely cash flow lending operations that do not require supervision of members' use of the hands they receive. ROSCAs work entirely on promise, trust, and consent, before other members as witnesses having intimate knowledge of each other. They create or confirm relationships among members that permit the application of certain sanctions. Participants clearly recognize that their relations with other members are the basis for transactions, and that their worth in the eyes of others depends significantly upon their performance under their shared promise.[201]

The importance of cohesiveness is further expressed by a shared meal or drinks whenever the hand is disbursed. Typically, the member who receives the hand invites the other members on that day. Although this institution increases the transaction costs for each receiving member, it strengthens the group spirit and payment behaviour of the members. Moreover, during such face-to-face meetings, members have the opportunity to get a feeling for their peers' overall constitution, their "health and moods, and [...] each others' [sic!] current financial status".[202] In the end, ROSCA meetings can be entertaining and therefore function as social events.

Figure 2.8 depicts the formation of a typical ROSCA. As can be seen, within the closed circle of the association each member holds an equal status, except from the organiser, who holds a slightly highlighted position since he has more duties and responsibilities. The members' equality is demonstrated by the reverse arrows in the chart, which show that each member is principal (P) and agent (A) at the same time. Everyone is responsible for the others' compliance, and at the same time each member is observed by his peers. Moreover, the multiple interrelation arrows indicate that all members outside the ROSCA have further linkages. This tight and interrelated network in the end guarantees smooth financial transactions; it diminishes risks and default and enhances overall trust and performance.

As mentioned in Sect. 2.1.1 and illustrated in Fig. 2.2, the level of transaction costs (including agency costs) is influenced by the three dimensions of frequency, uncertainty and ease of verification. ROSCAs are based on frequent and regular meetings and often the members interact beyond the association. Frequent interaction likewise reduces uncertainties between the involved actors. Moreover, informal information, personal meeting and knowledge about each other's back-

[201]Pischke (1992, p. 331).

[202]Ibid.

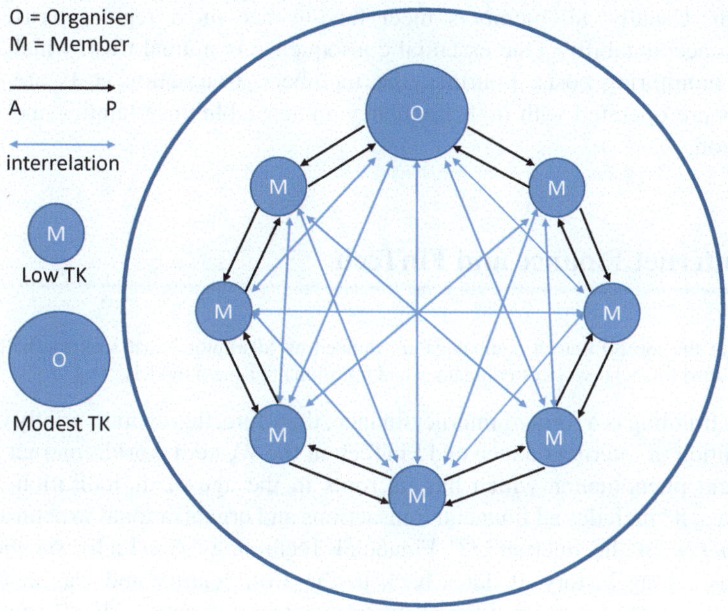

Fig. 2.8 Relationships between members of a ROSCA

ground further minimises uncertainties. Last but not least, the personal character of ROSCAs together with the potential utilisation of social ties enable members to easily verify peers and transactions.[203] Finally, high frequency, manageable uncertainties and ease of verification within a ROSCA keep overall transaction costs at a low level and lead to the results in Table 2.3.

To sum up, the main findings of this chapter are restated. ROSCAs are established institutions in developing countries. They incorporate many features, which can be taken as a benchmark for other (formal and informal) financial institutions. First, ROSCAs work self-sufficiently and without external governance by a superior institution. Participation is voluntary, easy and independent of tangible collateral. Rules and standards are flexible and an individual matter of each ROSCA. Secondly, ROSCAs provide savings-based loans and encourage long-term planning. They perfectly match debts with savings as all deposits and each hand are based on cash flows and not on capital assets. In fact, participating members only require liquidity but no additional assets in order to be eligible to participate. Thereby, ROSCAs include many people into the financial market, who have no other access to finance. Thirdly, ROSCAs manage risk through the evaluation of informal information, which is available as all members directly or indirectly know each other. Impending sanctions go beyond the association and therefore support discipline and compliant

[203]"Ease" of verification is a synonym for "convenience and speed" of verification. (Arner et al. 2015, p. 38).

behaviour. Usually, all members meet face-to-face on a regular basis, which promotes accountability. One essential consequence is mutual trust, which further reduces monitoring costs. Fourthly, the members' transaction costs are low as ROSCAs are operated with high frequency, manageable uncertainties and ease of verification.

2.5 Internet Finance and FinTech

> Most of the top 50 fintech companies are dubbed as 'disruptors' that seek to challenge established financial services companies and traditional business models.[204]

Crowdfunding is a form of internet finance, therefore, this chapter briefly outlines the evolution of internet finance and FinTech in the Western world. Internet finance is a recent phenomenon which has its roots in the age of digitalisation. As the term states, it "includes all financial transactions and organizational structures under the influence of the internet".[205] Financial Technology (FinTech), on the other hand, has a long history. It dates back to the 19th century and was in the first instance promoted by the traditional finance sector. In essence, "FinTech refers to the application of technology to finance."[206] In recent literature, FinTech is often used as a synonym for internet finance,[207] although FinTech is the generic term and internet finance rather one of its sub-categories. More often than not, FinTech is associated with tech-savvy, non-financial start-ups which provide different types of financial services. However, with regard to its origin, FinTech is rather a "[n]ew [t]erm for an [o]ld [r]elationship".[208]

Since the commercial use of the telegraph (in 1838) and the first transatlantic cables (in 1866), people have utilised technology to deliver financial solutions;[209] yet, since these beginnings, FinTech has changed essentially. Scholars distinguish between three phases of financial technology. FinTech 1.0 relied on analogue technologies which later were replaced by digital solutions. In 1967, the introduction of the first Automatic teller machine (ATM) marked a change and the initiation of FinTech 2.0. Representative for this stage are innovations brought forward by regulated financial institutions which capitalised on innovative Information technology (IT) products and services. Electronic-based (e-)payments evolved as well as electronic marketplaces for the trade of securities in the 1970s. During this phase, banks and other institutions started to shift from paper-based processes

[204]Dunkley (2016, n.p.).

[205]Xie et al. (2016, p. 1).

[206]Arner et al. (2015, p. 4).

[207]Yang (2016).

[208]Arner et al. (2015, p. 4).

[209]Ibid.

to digital mechanisms. The advent of the internet, and internet finance, further promoted the evolution of FinTech; it enabled customers to enjoy online banking services and further set the stage for the first direct banks.[210] The turning point and commencement of FinTech 3.0 correlated with the aftermath of the global financial crisis of 2007–2009. Since then "[n]ew start-ups and established technology companies have begun to deliver financial products and services directly to businesses and the general public."[211] Essentially, FinTech 3.0 companies are non-financial institutions providing financial services.

In fact, the global financial crisis catalysed the development of FinTech 3.0 through the following two issues. First, the image of traditional banks suffered tremendously as they were held responsible for the crisis. Therefore, customers were relatively open to alternative providers of financial services. Second, the financial crisis led to an economic crisis and many workers, amongst them many financial professionals, lost their jobs. This under-utilised human capital together with dissatisfied employees of the traditional financial industry who longed for a new challenge built the foundation of many FinTech 3.0 companies. Founders of such start-ups are commonly well-educated, often young and tech oriented. The most distinguishing feature of such non-financial FinTech institutions is that they successfully compete with FinTech 2.0 companies, i.e. traditional financial institutions.[212]

Already with the advent of internet finance, i.e. prior to the advent of FinTech 3.0, regulators saw the danger of credit risks as, first, increased competition amongst financial institutions can lead to financial instability, and as secondly, online (i.e. impersonal) financial services impede direct assessment of borrowers' creditworthiness. However, concerns then were rather low as FinTech was the domain of regulated financial institutions. This situation has changed since more and more non-financial FinTech providers have successfully entered the market. Although FinTech 3.0 companies could bring some innovation to the financial sector, not everyone welcomes this development. Calls for more regulation of the FinTech sector not only stem from customers who fear default and fraud, but also from actors of the traditional finance sector (i.e. FinTech 2.0), who dread unfair competition. For example, post-crisis reforms like Basel III have forced banks to keep higher capital reserves, in order to reduce insolvency risk and overall market instability. This regulation is said to decrease the banks' scope of operations and thus their competitiveness, in particular, to FinTech 3.0 companies, which are not subject to Basel III.[213] Individual countries have started to regulate non-financial financial service providers. Yet, scholars postulate that "regulators should remain technologically neutral and focus on the outcome of the technology. [They should follow a] wait-and-see approach [...] to learn whether the market will adopt

---

[210]Direct banks are "banks without physical branches" (Arner et al. 2015, p. 11).

[211]Arner et al. (2015, p. 6).

[212]Arner et al. (2015, p. 15 ff).

[213]Arner et al. (2015, p. 17).

the technology, and draw on historical data as to the risks a specific technology creates."[214] Otherwise, they run in danger to kill innovation in its infancy.

Governments seem to appreciate the rise of non-financial FinTech companies for at least two reasons. First, FinTech 3.0 firms predominantly serve households and SMEs, which commonly are the first ones to suffer from credit shortage; and secondly, FinTech start-up companies also create jobs.[215] It therefore is no miracle that, in 2012, the US passed the so-called *Jump Start Our Business Startups (JOBS) Act*, which addresses these issues of credit shortage and unemployment. In fact, the Act promulgates "[t]o increase American job creation and economic growth by improving access to the public capital markets for emerging growth companies."[216] The JOBS Act de facto legalised equity crowdfunding in the US. Yet, it entailed criticism and raised questions regarding protection of investors.[217]

FinTech 3.0 can be categorised in several ways. According to Arner et al. (2015), FinTech covers the following six areas: "(1) finance and investment, (2) operations and risk management, (3) payments and infrastructure, (4) data security and monetization, [...] (5) customer interface, [...] [and (6)] the use of technology in regulation itself."[218] For this thesis, on first sight, only category (1) seems to be relevant as crowdfunding belongs to the field of finance and investment. However, as will be shown in Sect. 4.3, crowdfunding in China is in fact also interrelated with payments (in particular mobile payments), customer interface and risk management.

In a nutshell, whilst internet finance is a more recent phenomenon, FinTech, which is the integration of finance and technology, has a long history. FinTech 1.0 was characterised by analogue financial services which were later on replaced by digital solutions. During the FinTech 2.0 era, the sector was dominated by regulated financial service providers. Since recently, tech-savvy start-ups and established technology companies have been disrupting the financial market, which marks the advent of FinTech 3.0. With these non-financial companies, traditional financial institutions face fierce competition, not least as tech-firms are typically not subject to regulations like Basel III. Although FinTech 3.0 companies are watched with suspicion, governments generally appreciate their innovations as they are likely to stimulate job creation and increase the supply of credit to SMEs and households. Internet finance and FinTech per definition differ, yet, in literature *FinTech 3.0* and *internet finance* are often used as synonyms.

[214] Arner et al. (2015, p. 33).

[215] Arner et al. (2015, p. 17).

[216] Jumpstart Our Business Startups: H.R.3606 (2012, p. 1).

[217] See also Sect. 3.3.1.

[218] Arner et al. (2015, p. 18).

Chapter 3
The Concept of Crowdfunding in the West Versus in China

3.1 Definition and Origins of Crowdfunding

The term *crowdfunding* is based on the concept of *crowdsourcing*, which was coined by Jeff Howe in 2006.[1] Kleemann and Voß (2008) draw on several authors and define *crowdsourcing* as "the act of taking a job traditionally performed by a designated agent (usually an employee) and outsourcing it to an undefined, generally large group of people".[2] Consequently, *crowdfunding* is the outsourcing of finance from the designated agent (e.g. a bank) to a large group of people (the crowd). As an extension, Belleflamme et al. (2010) state that "[c]rowdfunding involves an open call, essentially through the Internet, for the provision of financial resources either in form of donation or in exchange for some form of reward and/or voting rights".[3] In a later work, the authors have re-framed their definition to include "all entrepreneurs who use the Web 2.0 to generate funds for their investments via a large number of internet users".[4]

As a concept, crowdfunding is anything but new. For example, the basement of the *Statue of Liberty* has also been financed through a form of (offline) crowdfunding. As the constructors lacked the money to accomplish the monument, Joseph Pulitzer, the then editor of the newspaper *The New York World*, in 1885 initiated a public call searching for donators. He rewarded all investors by releasing their names in the newspaper. Likewise, public buildings such as cathedrals have occasionally been established by means of funds collected from citizens. Yet, "[t]he Statue of Liberty campaign resembles a modern online crowdfunding effort in several impressive ways: the speed with which the money was raised, the number of

[1] Howe (2006).

[2] Kleemann and Voß (2008, p. 5).

[3] Belleflamme et al. (2010, p. 5).

[4] Belleflamme et al. (2013, p. 5).

A. S. Funk, *Crowdfunding in China*, Contributions to Management Science,
https://doi.org/10.1007/978-3-319-97253-4_3

small donations, and the fact that the whole process was managed by one agent—the newspaper."[5] In the end, more than USD 100,000 were collected from more than 160,000 donors within just 5 months.[6] Pulitzer utilised the circulation of his outlet to boost his campaign. Similarly, by employing functions of the World Wide Web, crowdfunding enables a fast and extensive outreach to potential funders.

The boundaries between crowdfunding and similar forms of finance are sometimes blurred, yet most authors agree upon at least four different types of crowdfunding, referring to the nature of return that the capital providers (i.e. crowdfunders) receive in exchange for their investment:

- *donation-based crowdfunding* (i.e. the crowdfunder does not receive any return)
- *reward-based crowdfunding* (i.e. the crowdfunder obtains a material or immaterial compensation)
- *debt-based crowdfunding*, which is a synonym for *crowdlending* and *Peer-to-peer lending (P2P)* (i.e. the crowdfunder gives a loan which will be paid back by the PI with or without a certain interest rate)
- *equity-based crowdfunding* (i.e. the crowdfunder receives shares of a company in exchange for her investment).[7]

A more detailed classification is provided by de Buysere et al. (2012) who distinguish between *donations, rewards, pre-sales, lending, social lending, P2P* and *Peer-to-business lending (P2B), equity crowdfunding, revenue sharing* and several *hybrid models*.[8]

Some scholars debate on whether crowdfunding is a form of *microfinance*, or whether microfinance can be subsumed under the concept of crowdfunding. Whilst de Buysere et al. exclude microfinance from their listing, infoDev (2013) claims that "[c]rowdfunding draws inspiration from concepts like microfinance [. . .] but [. . .] represents a unique category of fundraising, with different vehicles, processes, and goals".[9] One could argue that microfinance usually is undertaken by a bank and the financing is thus not outsourced to a group of people. Following this logic, microfinance is not a subcategory of crowdfunding.[10] Fink (2015) frames it differently and states that "[c]rowdfunding represents the natural convergence of *microfinance* and *crowdsourcing*",[11] which I totally agree with.

---

[5]BBC News Magazine (2013, n.p.).

[6]This amount would equal to about USD 2.52 million today (BBC News Magazine 2013).

[7]Equity- and debt-based crowdfunding sometimes are further subsumed under the term *crowdinvesting*.

[8]de Buysere et al. (2012, p. 10 ff).

[9]infoDev (2013, p. 17).

[10]However, I argue that P2P also not necessarily meets all features of crowdfunding. If a project is realised by one singular person, then finance is also not outsourced to the crowd, but just to one single external peer. Yet, most Western scholars regard P2P as a sub-category of crowdfunding.

[11]Fink (2015, p. 4).

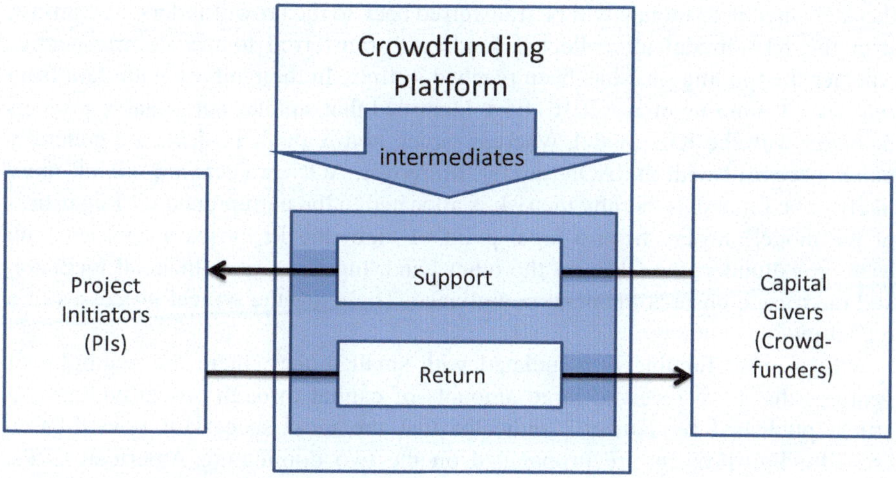

Fig. 3.1 The Original crowdfunding concept

The Original crowdfunding (OCF) concept[12] involves three or four parties respectively: the Project initiator (PI), the investors (i.e. crowdfunders), a Crowdfunding platform (CFP), and sometimes a trustee, in case the CFP is not allowed or willing to administer the invested capital itself. The CFP lists a PI's project on its online platform and thereby mediates between the PI and potential crowdfunders. The PI introduces his project on the platform with a project description and commonly a project video, which visualises the purpose of his campaign; therein, the PI states his desired crowdfunding target sum and also specifies what exactly a crowdfunder would get in return for her investment. Figure 3.1 (Haas et al. 2014, p. 6) illustrates the Original crowdfunding principle.

Crowdfunding platforms either follow the *All-or-nothing crowdfunding (AON)* or the *Keep-It-All crowdfunding (KIA)* concept.[13] Usually, a crowdfunding project call runs for 30–60 days, and with the AON concept a campaign is only successful if a beforehand set target sum can be reached within a pre-settled time period. During the campaign's runtime, crowdfunders can contribute to a project by transferring money via the CFP. Commonly, this money is not directly sent to the recipient, neither the CFP nor the PI, but instead held in trust by a fourth party until the end of the campaign. If the target sum is reached or even outreached in time, all money is transferred to the PI after the campaign's closure; alternatively, it is agreed that the crowdfunders' bank account or credit card will only be charged once a project has been successfully funded. In return for the payment, all rewards/shares/debt certificates must be handed over to the investors. However, if a project fails, with

[12] I.e. the Western crowdfunding model.

[13] Cumming et al. (2016, p. 2). Some platforms like the American *Indigogo* in fact offer both models, KIA and AON.

the AON model all money will be transferred back to the crowdfunders. In contrast, with the KIA model all collected funds are transferred to the PI, irrespective whether the funding goal has been reached in time. In their survey with data from *Indigogo*, Cumming et al. (2016) have identified that smaller but scalable projects do better with the KIA model, whereas larger, non-scalable projects are generally more successful with the AON model. Moreover, AON projects are overall more likely to be funded as thereby the risk is allocated to the entrepreneur.[14] Regardless of the model chosen, from a legal point of view, the PI closes a contract with each crowdfunder; the CFP, on the other hand, functions as a financial mediator, and the trustee ensures financial compliance. These are the typical processes of a crowdfunding campaign.

Whilst crowdfunding is associated with small money, there are examples of ventures that have received large amounts of capital through crowdfunding. An article published by *Forbes*[15] indicates that the most successful reward-based crowdfunding projects are propagated on the two dominating American CFPs, *Kickstarter* and *Indigogo*. Amongst these projects, there is one which offered a product called *Coolest Cooler*, an innovative product for leisure activities in summer. It is a portable cooling box with an integrated ice crushing blender, a USB charger and a waterproof Bluetooth speaker. In total, 62,642 individuals contributed to this project on *Kickstarter*, investing a total amount of USD 13,285,226. The *Pepple Watch* has been equally successful and arguably even reached greater prominence. For the production of this e-paper smartwatch, which is compatible with an iPhone and also Android smartphones, the investors collected USD 10,266,845 via *Kickstarter* and thereby *pre-bought* a sophisticated device. Nevertheless, high funding sums are not reserved for high tech products but can also be reached with social ventures. An outstanding example is the campaign called *An Hour of Code for Every Student* by the non-profit organisation *Code.org*. The initiators' vision is to teach children all over the world how to code and in doing so, supplement the schools' curricula with computer science classes. About 2,800 contributors provided USD 5,022,041 via *Indigogo* and thereby kick-started the project.[16] Yet, many other ventures could be realised with far less crowdfunding capital. Some scholars have investigated how to apply crowdfunding to civic projects.[17] Notably, academics have already contemplated crowdfunding as a funding source for science and discussed its utility in contrast to traditional sources. They conclude that crowdfunding encompasses more than just funds; it additionally enables "public outreach and science education".[18]

Likewise, Belleflamme et al. (2013) claim that "there is more to crowdfunding than just funding [...]. [C]rowdfunding may also help firms in testing, promoting

[14]Cumming et al. (2016, p. 1).

[15]Press (2015).

[16]Ibid.

[17]E.g. Stiver et al. (2015); Davies (2014); Hainzer et al. (2014).

[18]Wheat et al. (2013, p. 2).

Table 3.1 Fictional crowdfunding campaign of a music album

Investment in EUR	Offered reward
10	Signed postcard + personal message from artist
30	Recorded CD
50	Recorded CD + signed t-shirt
100	Recorded CD + signed t-shirt + personal phone call from artist
1000	Concert in your living room

and marketing their products, in gaining a better knowledge of their consumers' tastes, or in creating new products or services altogether".[19] In fact, *pre-testing* and *pre-selling* contribute to a number of marketing functions that can be provided by crowdfunding.

First of all, crowdfunding can function as a market survey. Whenever a PI sets up a crowdfunding campaign and presents his business idea to the crowd, he practically conducts a market test and thereby gains customer insight. If the project convinces a critical mass to invest in the campaign, it demonstrates market potential. Moreover, a successful crowdfunding campaign is in itself a valuable marketing tool and further promotes a subject via Public relations (PR). On the other hand, a failed crowdfunding campaign demonstrates certain shortcomings. It either implies a lack of demand by the crowd or low quality of the product/service. A failed campaign could further refer to the PI's insufficient communication skills. In any case, a crowdfunding campaign tests a project's soundness and coherence.

Secondly, crowdfunding can encompass the *pre-selling*[20] of a product before it actually has been produced. Some people equate reward-based crowdfunding with the *pre-selling* of a certain product. In fact, once a PI applies reward-based crowdfunding and intends to use the generated funds for producing some kind of product, she is likely to offer an example of that product among a range of other give-aways from which the funders can choose. Commonly, reward-based campaigns provide about four to eight different rewards in return for different amounts of investment; these rewards are typically ranked from lowest to highest value of investment. Table 3.1 illustrates an example of a PI, who is a musician and who intends to finance her new music album via crowdfunding. In total, her costs (including the recording and the platform's commission) could add up to EUR 7000; therefore, she sets the target sum accordingly. Moreover, she offers five different categories of rewards for five respective investments, ranging from EUR 10, over EUR 30, EUR 50, and EUR 100 to EUR 1000. In this fictional example, if an investor is willing to contribute EUR 10 to the project, the PI offers him a signed postcard including a personal message as reward; in return for a EUR 30 investment, the crowdfunder receives the recorded CD; a contribution of EUR 50 yields the recorded CD plus a signed t-shirt; for EUR 100, the PI offers her CD plus

[19]Belleflamme et al. (2010, p. 3).

[20]From the crowdfunders' perspective it is in fact *pre-ordering*; see also further below.

the t-shirt plus a personal phone call; and for a EUR 1000 investment, the musician offers a small concert in the crowdfunder's living room. This example demonstrates that reward-based crowdfunding indeed can involve some sort of *pre-selling* or *pre-ordering*[21]—in this case, the PI *pre-sells* her future CD for EUR 30, EUR 50 and respectively EUR 100. Presumably, the expected CD is also the main motivation for the crowdfunders to contribute to this project. However, the more creative a PI is in terms of her offerings, the more likely it is that her project will become a success. Most Western CFPs stress that they do not support pure *pre-selling*; they rather urge PIs to creatively think about their rewards and to offer more than just the finished product.

The chance of *pre-testing* and *pre-selling* can both be subsumed under crowdfunding's huge *marketing* potential. First of all, the CFP provides a stage for the project and thereby makes it visible to potential crowdfunders. The latter can actively search on the platform by using filters that reflect their personal interests. To attract the attention of the crowdfunders, projects further are staged with a story of the venture, either within the project description or in a crowdfunding video. Whilst these efforts are all time consuming and demand further resources from the PI,[22] the content produced for the crowdfunding campaign can be used severalfold; e.g. a crowdfunding video can be further distributed via the PI's social media channels and attract people for the campaign and the entire venture. People who have already contributed to the project are asked to spread the word by, for example, sharing such social media content, demonstrating their support and by asking their friends and acquaintances to also become crowdfunders. Thus, crowdfunding and its features can function as a kick-off for viral marketing.

In order to employ crowdfunding's marketing power, a PI highly depends on active *communication* and *transparency*. Commonly, a campaign is related to a PI or a team of initiators, who present(s) his/their full name(s), contact details and his/their face(s) on a CFP. Such a presence creates *trust* as the crowdfunders are able to see who in fact would get their money. Crowdfunders typically register on a CFP and also leave their contact details, though these data are kept anonymous by the platform and only provided to the PI after the successful accomplishment of his campaign. PIs are required to frequently provide information and updates during the project's runtime via the CFP to all involved investors. If the latter do not agree with the project's course or the PI's decisions, they can directly reply to the PI. The initiator, on the other hand, though independent, could wisely take the crowd's advice into account and amend his product/service according to the crowdfunders' ideas. Crowdfunding therefore provides an integrated communication tool. Ultimately, in order to evoke trust and run a successful campaign, a PI

[21]In this specific example of the musician, crowdfunding relies on what Scott has called *fan-ancing* as often such a project is realised by the contribution of fans (Scott 2015, p. 167 ff.).

[22]In order to cover all costs for the preparation of the campaign, the recording of the video, the production of the rewards, etc. usually the target sum is set higher than the actual funding demand.

needs to have distinct communication skills and should be willing to openly share information.

The marketing function of crowdfunding is also stressed by Kleemann and Voß (2008), who claim that crowdsourcing and, in consequence, crowdfunding are "evidence of historically significant change in the relations between firms and their customers".[23] Whilst in the past, customers were rather passive consumers who received finished products, the authors see current customers as *co-workers* taking part in the production processes. These kind of actors are so-called *prosumers*,[24] which are customers who are consuming what they have (co-)created themselves before. For example, a customer buying a t-shirt on an internet platform could be able to choose or even provide the motive on her shirt herself. Thus, the customer directly contributes to the creation of her individualised product. Her involvement would further intensify if the realisation of her order relied on a financial contribution to the manufacuring company, i.e. if she first had to *crowdfund*[25] the start-up, which afterwards would manufacture her desired product. Belleflamme et al. (2014) have dedicated one paper to the specific crowdfunding aspect of *pre-ordering*, i.e. customers pre-fund products, which have not yet been produced at the time of ordering.[26] In this case, the entire business can only be realised, production only starts and all orders can only be delivered, if there are sufficient pre-orders.

In a similar context, Leadbeater and Miller (2004) have created the term "*Pro-Am*, [for] amateurs who work to professional standards".[27] Whereas in the past, it was rather difficult to follow one's own profession, the internet and digital solutions have lowered overall transaction costs, and thereby enable many hobby entrepreneurs and artists to follow their passion. For example, an amateur web designer nowadays can easily provide his service via the internet to a worldwide potential customer base. He neither demands an office nor sophisticated networks; the internet functions as his workplace and stage for self-made marketing. Moreover, emails and social media enable smooth, boundless and quick communication. Even though the designer could follow another profession as his main occupation, he can still act out his hobby as a layman on a professional level. Such changes in the collaboration between service providers and customers are the foundation of phenomena like crowdfunding. The latter not only enables laymen to realise their passion, but also to eventually transform the characteristics of an established investor. In theory, crowdfunding allows anybody to set up a company and become an investor, or even do both at the same time.

---

[23]Kleemann and Voß (2008, p. 5).

[24]The term *prosumer* was first mentioned by Toffler (1980).

[25]The verb *crowdfund* refers to the act of funding a project through small contributions by many investors, usually via a CFP.

[26]Belleflamme et al. (2014).

[27]Leadbeater and Miller (2004, p. 12).

These changes can be mainly ascribed to the rise of the Web 2.0,[28] which "is a Web-as-participation-platform that facilitates interaction between users."[29] The Web 2.0 enables two essential aspects, which are crucial for crowdfunding: The creation of networks and the realisation of communication. Web 2.0 can also be seen as "a shorthand term for new internet applications that make two-way communication easier to manage".[30]

Summing up the findings above, I provide my own definition of crowdfunding as follows:

> Crowdfunding is a scalable online tool for venture financing and marketing. It is highly dependent on networks and good communication, yet, can be applied by any individual or entity, who/which understands to employ the power of the crowd.

3.2 The Evolution and Modifications of Crowdfunding

Crowdfunding can be traced back to the US in 2003, when *ArtistShare*, the first known CFP, started to support musicians with funding from music fans.[31] Back then, *ArtistShare* did not denominate its business model as crowdfunding, though the platform de facto provided crowdfunding for musicians. Only later, in 2006, the term *crowdfunding* was coined (see Sect. 3.1). In the aftermath of the global financial crisis, crowdfunding gained momentum, presumably because the creative industry suffered most under the shortage of credit. Banks were curbing their credit allocation, and consequently, people without any collateral or any financial records—predominantly artisans and inexperienced entrepreneurs—were least likely to obtain a formal loan. However, like in more traditional informal finance, once official channels were capped, borrowers turned to their immediate environment.

> Crowdfunding began as an online extension of financing by friends and family: communities pool[ed] money to fund members with business ideas. During crowdfunding's early stages, capital came in the form of donations, but increasingly it takes the form of debt or equity investments targeting high-growth entrepreneurs—only one of many ways the model is evolving as awareness spreads.[32]

---

[28]"Web 2.0 has been the term used to describe the social Web, where social networking sites hold a prominent place in users' online activities. The shift to this more interactive Web from Web 1.0 generally occurred as a result of technological changes that made the Internet—and the ability to develop content—more accessible. [...] In Web 2.0, applications are also more likely to be open source, providing users with a greater ability to influence the Web." (Techopedia n.d.).

[29]Lambert and Schwienbacher (2010, p. 5).

[30]Kleemann and Voß (2008, p. 6).

[31]Freedman and Nutting (2015, p. 1).

[32]infoDev (2013, p. 14).

Crowdfunding originated as start-up finance, yet in the meantime has undergone some change. Moreover, crowdfunding in China differs substantially from the Original (Western) concept (see Chap. 5). In order to highlight the linkages and differences between crowdfunding in China and in the West and to identify their possible future trajectories, this sub-chapter deals with modifications of crowdfunding in the Western world. In particular, with the example of *BMW*, I will first demonstrate how crowdfunding is used as a market test. Secondly, I will analyse the progressive commercialisation of crowdfunding by means of the film industry and the example of a politician. Thirdly, I will refer to the question whether crowdfunding should be reserved for the start-up industry. Ultimately, in Sect. 6.4, I will demonstrate that Chinese *e-commerce CFPs* in fact utilise crowdfunding for market tests and commercial ends, which in China has raised critical voices. In a nutshell, all examples will demonstrate that crowdfunding in the West like in China is under constant change.

Whilst crowdfunding was once considered to be an idealistic tool for no-names and self-made entrepreneurs, established companies like *BMW* and *Procter & Gamble* have more recently recognised the advantages of crowdfunding and crowdsourcing and started to apply these tools for specific projects. Their crowdfunding campaigns do not differ from those of start-ups, however, it is unlikely that these large companies require the capital of the crowd. Rather, they use crowdfunding to actively integrate consumers into product development and thereby create products of definite demand. Kleemann and Voß (2008) explain this change of crowdfunding purpose with the transformation of Web 2.0 applications. "The initial impetus for Web 2.0 programming came from the anti-commercial 'open source' movement, but the corporate world has since discovered it as a platform for its own goals".[33]

For example, *BMW*'s Innovation Team in 2014 collaborated with *Startnext*, Germany's largest reward-based CFP, to jointly launch a so-called *Mobility Experience Challenge*.[34] In fact, *BMW* started a crowdfunding competition in order to come up with a new app for their high-end car models. Start-ups were asked to set up independent crowdfunding campaigns for their app ideas and the projects were displayed on the *Startnext* platform. Just like with other crowdfunding projects, crowdfunders could invest into these ideas and get some reward for their contribution. In addition, the teams of the ten apps that received the highest amount of funding were invited to present their ideas in front of the *BMW App jury*, which then finally decided on the three winners of the challenge.[35] *BMW* promised a modest prize money of USD 1,500 for the first and USD 500 each for the second and third winner, and pointed out that these apps eventually had a chance to become *BMW*'s next release.

[33] Kleemann and Voß (2008, p. 10).

[34] Startnext (2014).

[35] I assume that all projects which received sufficient funding were eventually realised, irrespective of *BMW*'s choice. However, the crowdfunders' ranking was not said to have any impact on *BMW*'s final choice.

Indeed, *BMW*'s approach was a combination of crowdfunding and marketing. By inviting ideas for the app, *BMW* practically outsourced its R&D via crowdsourcing. Instead of directly selecting among the generated ideas, *BMW* utilised crowdfunding to *pre-test* them. This was based on the assumption that people would only invest in apps they eventually liked to use themselves. By this means, *BMW* actually did not only outsource the idea generation, but also the selection process to the crowd, and therefore turned crowdfunding into a market test device. Eventually, the company needed a comparably small budget as it paid neither for the staff (i.e. the start-ups developing the apps), nor for the research and development. In the end, *BMW* could choose from a range of innovative, pre-tested, and merchantable apps. By applying a combination of crowdsourcing and crowdfunding, the company not just minimised its costs, but also its risks.

Besides, crowdfunding has become increasingly commercialised, which can be seen from cases of famous film-makers. Early on, the combination of finance and marketing did produce some self-made celebrities, who had been no-names prior to their crowdfunding campaign. Today, however, crowdfunding is increasingly utilised by celebrities who in fact do not need the capital of the crowd in order to realise a movie. For instance, the actor *Zack Braff* applied crowdfunding in order to fund the production of a Hollywood movie.[36] *Braff*'s campaign on *Kickstarter*, the most renowned American CFP, raised more than USD 3 million, collected from about 40,000 crowdfunders. As *Braff* had access to other financial sources, he presumably used crowdfunding because of the marketing effect in advance of the movie's release.

Critics argue that corporates like *BMW* and celebrities like *Braff* misuse the model of crowdfunding and thereby harm the entire crowdfunding sector. One could indeed argue that those start-ups providing their app ideas for small money to *BMW* were exploited as cheap labour. On the other hand, they were given the unique opportunity to partner with an established company. Therefore, crowdfunding can be seen as a mutual supportive tool for start-ups to raise awareness for their products or services, and for established enterprises to extend their research and development approach. With regard to celebrities, critics probably distinguish between different industries or maybe even between individuals. A famous example for a politician utilising the crowd is *Barack Obama*, who raised about USD 750 million for his presidential campaign in 2008[37] with a kind of donation-based crowdfunding. Back then, however, nobody accused him of misusing crowdfunding.

Whether the use of crowdfunding should be limited to non-celebrities or self-made celebrities, start-ups and entrepreneurs or be open for anyone and any purpose is still under debate. The most essential characteristic of crowdfunding is the fact that it theoretically—just like other internet tools—can be applied by any person or entity, regardless of status, gender, age, ethnicity, preliminary networks or other attributes. There are numerous examples of individuals with restricted access to

[36] Kühl (2013).

[37] Bradley (2008).

finance, early-stage start-ups, teenagers as well as grandmas becoming successful PIs. Crowdfunding also enjoys great popularity amongst social entrepreneurs and not-for-profit enterprises, which is demonstrated by the relatively large number of CFPs specialising in social projects. Ultimately, crowdfunding per se can be applied for any venture, regardless of reasonability, profitability or accountability—as long as there is a CFP willing to list the project and as long as there is a crowd eager to fund the idea. Consequently, crowdfunding and its specifications could even be misused for criminal purposes such as the financing of terrorism. There has been evidence by Australian investigators that e.g. the terror militia of the Islamic State have used social media as CFPs in order to collect funds from the crowd.[38]

3.3 Crowdfunding Research

3.3.1 Western Literature on Crowdfunding

Due to the novelty of crowdfunding, literature on this research field, especially academic literature, is still limited. Practitioners, professionals and laymen have published numerous guidebooks on how to run a successful crowdfunding campaign.[39] Some of these handbooks give explicit advice on projects within specific industries like food,[40] culture[41] or independent video games.[42] All manuals and scientific papers on the proper implementation of crowdfunding share the understanding that any campaign, regardless of the industry, needs to be thoroughly planned and demands resources like time and manpower. Moreover, preparation should start long before a campaign's implementation. Ultimately, the inspiration of and communication with the crowd are essential for a project's success.

To date four literature reviews on crowdfunding have been published. Bachmann et al. (2011) exclusively contemplated works on P2P lending and identified 43 scientific articles, of which the majority focuses either on success factors of campaigns or on the interest rates paid for the loans. The authors point out that future research should "identify similarities and differences between the traditional banking and the P2P lending market".[43] Lehner[44] has conducted a literature research specialising on the financing of social ventures and crowdfunding. Feller et al. (2013) have

[38]McDonald (2015).

[39]See e.g. Young (2013); Lawton and Marom (2013); Spirer (2014); Schramm and Carstens (2014).

[40]E.g. Wallhäuser (2014).

[41]E.g. Junge and Eidinger (2013).

[42]E.g. Koch Ramos (2014).

[43]Bachmann et al. (2011, p. 13).

[44]Lehner (2012).

compiled literature on the four most popular forms of crowdfunding[45]; however, their intention was rather to quantify the research on crowdfunding than analysing the content of the respective scientific works. One of their findings was that existing literature on crowdfunding is dominated by research on crowdlending.[46] Moreover, half of their literature corpus comprised of studies that apply an economic approach, followed by social (25%), legal (13%), and technical (12%) contemplations.[47] Furthermore, they concluded that about three quarters of all scientific designs are empirical studies on crowdfunding.[48] Moritz and Block (2016) reviewed the crowdfunding literature in terms of the crowdfunding actors, who are in the focus of the respective works, and defined the following three categories: capital seekers, capital providers, and intermediaries (i.e. CFPs). They identified 127 scientific articles and working papers, of which 41 were related to capital seekers, 53 ones to capital providers, and 12 to intermediaries.[49] However, I do not entirely agree with this classification as some articles subsumed under the category of capital seekers (e.g. Agrawal et al. 2011; Agrawal et al. 2015; Burtch et al. 2014[50]) in fact focus on capital providers.

3.3.1.1 Motivation for Applying Crowdfunding

Many academic works concentrate on the motivation of PIs for utilising crowdfunding. Presumably, raising money is a strong extrinsic driver for applying crowdfunding, which has been confirmed by several studies.[51] However, Belleflamme et al. (2013) have discovered "that crowdfunding is preferred to traditional funding [only] as long as the capital requirement stays below some upper bound".[52] Therefore, they conclude that crowdfunding is more suitable for non-profit organisations and social entrepreneurs. Besides the importance of funding, their survey has revealed that public attention raised via crowdfunding and the corresponding feedback on a project by backers are also important drivers.[53] Likewise, Gerber et al. (2012)

---

[45]They explicitly mention *peer-to-peer lending at interest* (i.e. debt-based crowdfunding), *peer-to-peer investing in return for equity/future income* (i.e. equity-based crowdfunding), *peer-to-peer funding given without expectation of return or with expectation of token return* (i.e. donation- and reward-based crowdfunding respectively) (Feller et al. (2013, p. 5).

[46]I.e. debt-based or P2P crowdfunding.

[47]Feller et al. (2013, p. 11).

[48]Feller et al. (2013, p. 14).

[49]Presumably, some of the identified papers could not be assigned to any category as the sum of the three categories is less than 127.

[50]Moritz and Block (2016) in their article referred to the working paper of Burtch et al. 2014; this paper was thereafter published in a journal in 2014.

[51]This has been confirmed by e.g. Belleflamme et al. (2013); Gerber et al. (2012); Schwienbacher and Larralde (2012).

[52]Belleflamme et al. (2013, p. 325).

[53]Belleflamme et al. (2010, 2014).

have discovered that PIs particularly value the anticipated long term relationship and mutual interaction with the crowd, which also goes beyond funding.[54] By contrast, most forms of debt like a bank loan are associated with "stupid money",[55] since they include neither advice nor any other non-financial support from the capital provider. Furthermore, PIs long for awareness and appreciation of their work. A successfully funded project demonstrates online validation and evokes a feeling of satisfaction.[56] Ultimately, academic works have verified that PIs are not solely driven by monetary motives when they apply crowdfunding.

In addition, capital seekers no longer have to scout for one single suitable capital provider but can instead market their project to a wide range of potential investors, namely the crowd.[57] Thereby, overall search costs are reduced. Moreover, whereas debt finance often requires collateral, and therefore excludes fundless entrepreneurs, crowdfunding can be applied without physical security assets. Kim and Hann (2016) claim that "web-enabled crowdfunding has the potential to democratize access to capital"[58] as anyone could become a PI or a crowdfunder. Notably, Arner, Barberis and Buckley (2015) in the context of FinTech 3.0 also spoke of the democratisation of financial services.[59] In another context, Lapavitsas (2013a) used the term *democratisation of finance* in order to describe the real-estate bubble in the US, which had been created by the poors' access to initially cheap mortgage loans.[60] Therefore, *democratisation of finance* is not per se positively connoted. With regard to crowdfunding, Agrawal et al. (2013) further state that this financial tool incurs "a lower cost of capital"[61] as PIs and investors are better matched on a global scale based on mutual exchange of information. Particularly, the benefits for entrepreneurs based in smaller cities and those who have difficulties in obtaining formal credit are relatively high.[62] In conclusion, web-based crowdfunding demands few prerequisites and reduces overall transaction costs.

With crowdfunding, PIs bear relatively low risks, which could be another motivational driver. In particular, with the *KIA*, all risks are born by the crowd as a PI receives all collected funds irrespective of whether his funding goal is reached. Once the *AON* is applied, a PI's mere risk is that the campaign might fail and he would end up without any funds.[63] Schwienbacher and Larralde (2012) have compared crowdfunding with classical debt finance and claim that—especially with equity-based crowdfunding—risk is spread amongst the crowd, whereas with debt

---

[54] Gerber et al. (2012).

[55] Schwienbacher and Larralde (2012, p. 378).

[56] Gerber et al. (2012, p. 5 ff).

[57] Dorfleitner et al. (2014, p. 32).

[58] Kim and Hann (2016, p. 1).

[59] Arner et al. (2015, p. 15).

[60] Lapavitsas (2013a, p. 18).

[61] Agrawal et al. (2013, p. 11).

[62] Kim and Hann (2016, p. 4).

[63] Cumming et al. (2016).

finance, risk is concentrated and entirely held by the entrepreneur[64] or the bank respectively. Equally important is the fact that—at least with donation-, debt- and reward-based crowdfunding—a PI can obtain financial resources without the risk of losing ownership of his project.[65]

Mollick (2014) has identified further motivational drivers for applying crowdfunding, above all the access to potential customers and additional external funders.[66] Therefore, crowdfunding can also be seen as a tool for proof of concept: a successful campaign could encourage people to become customers and attract financiers like BAs or VCs to invest in the project. Table A.2 in the appendix summarises the academic findings on motivational drivers for PIs to utilise crowdfunding.

However, there are also dissuading arguments against crowdfunding. Some projects are only suited for certain forms of crowdfunding; others should better opt for other financial sources. For instance, in order to fund a *high-quality invention*, entrepreneurs should refrain from equity crowdfunding but rather opt for reward-based crowdfunding as the former affords the dilution of more information to potential investors and thereby incurs higher risks of losing Intellectual property (IP).[67] Indeed, there are evident cases of business ideas which were stolen from CFPs and realised (or rather replicated) and brought on the market, before the original inventor had finished his crowdfunding campaign.[68] Therefore, a PI needs to decide wisely, which information he releases on the CFP. Another reason why PIs may hesitate to apply crowdfunding are the relatively high *investor management costs*. In fact, investor relations with the crowd are more time-consuming than relations with one single VC. In the end, a PI also cannot choose his investors via crowdfunding and consequently could have to deal with difficult characters.[69] Thus, crowdfunding also incurs certain costs and potential issues. Gerber et al. (2012) suggest that future research should consider whether a PI's motivation to apply crowdfunding is influenced by the entrepreneur's personal characteristics like his length of profession and level of expertise, the size of his social network, his online presence and also his project type.[70]

Some authors have analysed the motivation of capital providers for contributing to a project. Gerber et al. (2012) discovered that *sympathy*, *empathy*, an *identification with the PI* and corresponding *happiness* play a role, but that *guilt* or an *obligation* can also motivate a person to become a crowdfunder.[71] Funders apparently are also eager to obtain the offered reward and like the idea of contributing to

[64]Schwienbacher and Larralde (2012, p. 379).

[65]Hui et al. (2012, p. 2).

[66]Mollick (2014, p. 3).

[67]Agrawal et al. (2013, p. 7).

[68]Horwitz (2016).

[69]Agrawal et al. (2013, p. 18).

[70]Gerber et al. (2012, p. 8).

[71]Gerber et al. (2012, p. 3).

a respectable community.[72] This is in line with Schwienbacher and Larralde (2012), who came to the conclusion that investors are not solely driven by financial motives, but rather the desire to participate in an innovative project. Conjoint contribution apparently evokes recognition[73] and eventually also satisfaction.[74] Agrawal et al. (2013) have also identified community participation as an essential motivation to become a crowdfunder. However, they also stress that some crowdfunders, particularly equity investors, in fact want to seize an investment opportunity.[75] Yet, others could support a project out of philanthropic motives. Burtch et al. (2014) also stress "group-specific altruism"[76] as a key driver to participate in crowdfunding, which is also mentioned in the crowdfunding study by Blohm et al. (2013). The latter distinguish three categories of crowdfunding projects with reference to the funders' motivation, namely *hedonistic*, *altruistic* and *profit-oriented* projects.[77] With crowdfunding, capital providers could also gain earlier access to innovative products as some PIs exclusively offer a new product as reward (like in the case of the Pebble Watch). Last but not least, it should not be neglected that crowdfunding offers formalised contracts. This can be an aspect that encourages friends and family members, who are often amongst the very first investors of a venture, to financially contribute to a project. Such investments become institutionalised if crowdfunded via a CFP, whereas lending amongst friends commonly has informal character.[78]

Besides, there are also potential disincentives for capital providers to get involved in crowdfunding, above all "creator incompetence, fraud and project risk".[79] Even though CFPs pre-select crowdfunding campaigns or PIs respectively, the platforms are not obliged to conduct a due diligence of the projects or the founders. Moreover, projects on a CFP are not differentiated in terms of their risk level. CFPs, in fact, also not necessarily state which parameters their choice of projects is based on. At the same time, platforms do not act as a warrantor, neither for the reliability of the PIs nor for the feasibility of the projects, and thus cannot be held responsible in case of fraud or the PIs' default. In the end, investors could be discouraged to utilise crowdfunding, if their expected returns fall short of the anticipated risks and uncertainties.

---

[72]Gerber et al. (2012, p. 6 ff).

[73]Schwienbacher and Larralde explicitly mentioned *recognition* as an *intrinsic motivation* to contribute to a CF campaign, though recognition per se is not an intrinsic phenomenon. I suppose that the authors in this context rather meant *self-esteem*.

[74]Schwienbacher and Larralde (2012, p. 386).

[75]Agrawal et al. (2013, p. 15).

[76]Burtch et al. (2014, p. 779).

[77]Blohm et al. (2013).

[78]Agrawal et al. (2013, p. 16).

[79]Agrawal et al. (2013, p. 19).

3.3.1.2 Success of Crowdfunding

The motivation to fund a crowdfunding campaign obviously is also linked to the anticipated success of a project. While investors can never be sure about the success of a project, there are indicators and factors that influence the perception of the crowd.

Thereby the concept of signalling and particularly the signalling of a company's (or a project's) value,[80] a project's legitimacy[81] and a project's quality[82] play a crucial role. Legitimacy can be transmitted through appropriate target sums and shorter duration periods. Frydrych et al. (2014) claim that projects with "lower funding targets"[83] tend to be more successful, which has also been statistically identified by Kuppuswamy and Bayus.[84] In this context, it seems plausible that non-profit ventures—ceteris paribus—are more likely to succeed with crowdfunding[85] as such projects generally pursue less capital. A PI's legitimacy can also be reflected by outside endorsements, a high number of *Facebook* friends, an approved and appropriate background and a presence on the most successful CFP.[86] Moreover, a project's narrative[87] and the provision of a convincing video[88] can support a project's image and thus its potential success. Regarding equity crowdfunding, Ahlers et al. (2012) have revealed that an enterprise's financial planning strategy (e.g. whether it aims at an IPO), its internal governance as well as potential risk factors influence investors' decision and are therefore crucial for a campaign's success.[89] Likewise, the provision of "social information (i.e. others' funding decisions)"[90] determines the dynamics of the crowd. Potential crowdfunders are influenced by the investment decisions of their peers and also of strangers who have already contributed to a project; therefore it is beneficial for a PI and his project to continuously update and publish its level of support.[91]

Furthermore, crowdfunding relies on social interaction and a PI's social capital, which is the "sum of the actual and potential resources embedded within, available through, and derived from the network of relationships possessed by an individual

[80]Ahlers et al. (2012, p. 1).

[81]Frydrych et al. (2014).

[82]Mollick (2014, p. 1).

[83]Frydrych et al. (2014, p. 247).

[84]Kuppuswamy and Bayus (2016, p. 18).

[85]Lambert and Schwienbacher (2010); Belleflamme et al. (2013, 2014); Saxton and Wang (2014).

[86]Mollick and Kuppuswamy (2015, p. 2).

[87]Frydrych et al. (2014, p. 247).

[88]Kuppuswamy and Bayus (2016, p. 18).

[89]Ahlers et al. (2012, Abstract).

[90]Kuppuswamy and Bayus (2016, p. 1).

[91]Although the CFP provides the infrastructure for continuous updates, in fact, the PI is responsible for all contents of his campaign. Moreover, it is his task to regularly inform the crowd about news and the campaign's progress.

or social unit".[92] Giudici et al. (2013) in their study on crowdfunding further distinguish between *individual (exclusive)* and *territorial (locally shared) social capital*. Specifically, they have investigated, whether a crowdfunding project's success can be explained by the individual social capital of a PI or the geographic social capital of the area where a PI is located. As for the former, the authors have utilised the number of a PI's *Facebook* contacts as a proxy. As for the latter, the authors "refer to the municipality of residence of each proponent and resort to the traditional measure of localized social capital used in the literature".[93] Eventually, their survey revealed that a project's success indeed correlates with a PI's *individual social capital*; yet, *territorial social capital* rather diminishes the probability of a campaign's success.[94] Moreover, there is evidence that projects that receive more funds within the early stages of a campaign's running period are typically more likely to be entirely funded. In this context, Colombo et al. (2015) have analysed the influence of a PI's *internal social capital* on the amount of early contributions. They utilised the number of projects that a PI had contributed to until the time of his own campaign start and concluded that social capital within the community of a CFP is essential for early contributions of a crowdfunding campaign.[95] Therefore, a PI could increase the success rate of his own campaign by investing in other crowdfunding campaigns. Lehner (2012) in this respect refers to a transformation of *social capital* into *economic capital*.[96] Ultimately, social capital is crucial for a successful crowdfunding project.

A PI's social capital of course is not fully reflected by his *Facebook* contacts. Personal networks between founders and funders are also helpful. As mentioned above, relatives and friends are often amongst the first people who invest in a crowdfunding campaign.[97] Commonly, personal relations also arise from geographic proximity of individuals. Earlier studies on VCs and BAs have revealed that capital providers prefer syndicating investments and rather contribute to geographically proximate ventures.[98] In doing so, they can more easily rely on informal information which often form the foundation for a project's due diligence. In line with this are the results of a study by Burtch et al. (2014) who have analysed the cultural and geographical dimensions of lending-based crowdfunding. According to their findings, capital providers prefer projects which are culturally and physically proximate.[99] On the other hand, Agrawal et al.[100] claim that physical distance plays a minor role since the start of the digital age. The authors have specifically analysed

[92] Nahapiet and Sumantra (1998, p. 243).

[93] Giudici et al. (2013, p. 2).

[94] Ibid.

[95] Colombo et al. (2015, p. 75).

[96] Lehner (2012, p. 478).

[97] Agrawal et al. (2011, p. 2).

[98] Wong et al. (2009).

[99] Burtch et al. (2014, p. 773).

[100] Agrawal et al. (2011, 2013, 2015).

early-stage investment decisions and claim that the internet and particularly the online platform is capable "to eliminate most distance-related economic frictions but not the social-related frictions".[101] This means that in terms of information search pre-existing social networks indeed accelerate processes.[102]

In a first cross-cultural study on the impact of an entrepreneur's social networks on crowdfunding, Zheng et al. (2014) compared data from China and the US and applied the three-dimensional view on social capital of Nahapiet and Sumantra (1998). This concept refers to the *structural dimension* (i.e. the range of network ties), the *relational dimension* (i.e. the quality of those ties evaluated by e.g. obligations and trust), and the *cognitive dimension* (i.e. shared meaning, e.g. via shared language and a clear project description).[103] Zheng et al. expanded the model to include *culture* as a "moderator"[104] because values can differ across countries. The authors reason that Chinese people due to their collectivist culture feel more obliged to contribute to a peer's crowdfunding campaign, in comparison to US citizens. Zheng et al. explicitly refer to the reciprocal characteristic of *guanxi*.[105] Eventually, their regression analysis demonstrates that social capital in both countries correlates with the success of crowdfunding campaigns; yet, their model is significantly more predictive for projects in China.[106] Thus, I conclude that social capital is essential for crowdfunding, and in particular for crowdfunding in China.

Still, there are complementary factors which can compensate for an absence of such personal relationships and eventually explain the rise of crowdfunding. Agrawal et al. (2013) explicitly mention "transaction costs, reputation, and market design".[107] Crowdfunding platforms and their features reduce overall transaction costs, particularly in terms of information search and monitoring. Secondly, by a solid online presence, a PI is able to increase his reputation. Thirdly, the interplay of different institutions and entities—e.g. the PI and the CFP with several social media—can provide a positive investment culture. Ultimately, this framework creates trust, compensates for a lack of social capital and eventually motivates a stranger to become a crowdfunder. I will further discuss these aspects in Chap. 6. Table A.3 in the appendix summarises the identified methods and features of a successful crowdfunding campaign.

---

[101] Agrawal et al. (2011, p. 1).

[102] Agrawal et al. (2011, p. 15).

[103] Nahapiet and Sumantra (1998).

[104] Zheng et al. (2014, p. 490).

[105] *Guanxi* are "personalized connections and related social networks characterized by relations of reciprocity, i.e. the giving and receiving of favours. [. . .] [One can] note the significance of such personal relationships in the supposedly impersonal world of business networks" (Castree et al. 2013, n.p.).

[106] Zheng et al. (2014, p. 493).

[107] Agrawal et al. (2013, abstract).

Hui et al.[108] have investigated whether raising money via crowdfunding demands less efforts than obtaining traditional forms of finance. Thereby they have identified the following six steps of work, which are essential for conducting a crowdfunding campaign:

> (1) understanding the opportunities and responsibilities of crowdfunding, (2) preparing campaign content and initial prototypes, (3) testing the campaign content and initial prototypes, (4) marketing the crowdfunding project to potential supporters, (5) executing the project by following through with campaign goals, and (6) contributing to the crowdfunding community with advice and mentorship.[109]

The authors conclude that crowdfunding is anything but "quick and easy funding [; that] [. . .] many people underestimate the work involved and [rather] find themselves overwhelmed with tasks that are time consuming and outside their skillset."[110] Therefore, even though crowdfunding reduces transaction costs, the setup of a crowdfunding campaign still affords a lot of tasks that consume resources and require specific skills.

In addition, crowdfunding, especially equity based crowdfunding, raises many legal questions. Although, more recently governments have started to implement regulations, by 2015 few countries provided an established legal framework for crowdfunding. Authors analysing legal issues of crowdfunding primarily refer to the *Jumpstart Our Business Startups Act (JOBS Act)* of 2012, which laid the foundation for legal equity investment by private citizens in the US.[111] The law raised many concerns as it, for example, "exempt[s] a new class of filter—emerging growth companies (EGC)—from certain [. . .] rules."[112] Critics see investor protection in danger and predict potential fraud and investment failure, which would increase with a loosened regulation.[113] Indeed, investor protection was loosened for the sake of increased access to capital for start-ups.

Nevertheless, from the perspective of PIs and CFPs, it is still difficult to operate internationally because regulations often differ substantially across borders. A comparison of different implementations of crowdfunding regulation has been conducted by Gabison (2015), who contrasts the US to Australia, Italy, UK and France.[114] Hooghiemstra and Buysere (2016) have studied the fragmented

---

[108] Hui et al. (2012, 2015).

[109] Hui et al. (2012, p. 4).

[110] Hui et al. (2012, p. 10).

[111] "The JOBS Act works to increase access to capital by scaling back new regulations and modifying old regulations through three main mechanisms: the initial public offerings (IPO) 'on-ramp,' crowdfunding, and mini-public offerings. It affects an extensive list of laws, including the Securities Act of 1933, the Securities Exchange Act of 1934, Regulation FD (Fair Disclosure), the Sarbanes-Oxley Act of 2002 (SOX), and the Dodd-Frank Wall Street Reform and Consumer Protection Act of 2010." (Salzsieder and Cornell 2013, p. 18).

[112] Salzsieder and Cornell (2013, p. 18).

[113] See e.g. Fink (2015); Salzsieder and Cornell (2013); Stemler (2013).

[114] Gabison (2015).

crowdfunding legislation in Europe, specifically in Finland, France, Germany, Italy, Spain, and the UK, and developed a detailed suggestion for a harmonized legislation across Europe. They conclude that "[c]rowdfunding regulation needs to be based upon the balancing of two conflicting goals: fostering capital formation and investor protection".[115]

The majority of Western academic literature concentrates on crowdfunding in Western countries, though Asia records the highest growth rates in crowdfunding (see Chap. 1.1). In the recently published World Bank Report on *Crowdfunding's Potential for the Developing World* the authors stress the "important role that academia must play in building deeper, more robust bodies of knowledge"[116] on crowdfunding. Particularly, there is little understanding amongst Western scientists on crowdfunding in Asia and other developing areas. While one could assume that e.g. the motivation of Asian PIs and crowdfunders is similar to the one of Western actors, Zheng et al. (2014), however, suggest that there are alterations due to differences in culture, geography, history and mentality. In addition, the fact that the structure of the financial sectors differs across countries, also leads to the assumption that the features of crowdfunding and the characteristics of the people using it probably differ accordingly. Thus, the following chapter deals specifically with Chinese literature on crowdfunding.

3.3.2 Chinese Literature on Crowdfunding

Chinese literature on crowdfunding is growing fast. However, to my best knowledge, to date no review of Chinese literature on the topic of crowdfunding exists. There is only one Chinese review by Xia et al. (2015), who contemplate respective Western literature.[117] Crowdfunding or its Chinese equivalent, *zhongchou (众筹)*, is embedded in Chinese literature on internet finance which recently has gained much attention by Chinese academics and practitioners. In order to get an idea about the prominence of *internet finance* and its Chinese pendant *hulianwang jinrong (互联网金融)*, two keyword searches[118] were conducted on *Google* and the Chinese search engine *Baidu* respectively. Whilst Western netizens predominantly use *Google*, *Baidu* is the most popular search engine amongst Chinese.[119] *Internet finance* on *Google* provided 166,000 results, which was far behind the 7,720,000 records related to *hulianwang jinrong (互联网金融)* on *Baidu*, and which demonstrates that *internet finance* is much more prominent in the Asian discourse than in the

[115] Hooghiemstra and Buysere (2016, p. 146).

[116] infoDev (2013, p. 5).

[117] Xia et al. (2015).

[118] The keyword search was conducted on November 12, 2015.

[119] One reason for *Baidu*'s prominence in China, amongst others, is that *Google* is officially banned there.

Western. A further search with *Google Scholar* (searching for *internet finance*) and within the database *Chinese Academic Journals*[120] (searching for *hulianwang jinrong (互联网金融)*) has reflected a similar discrepancy of 1,090 versus 9,381 records.[121] Whilst there were hardly any Chinese academic publications on crowdfunding/*zhongchou* before 2013, crowdfunding recently has become a topic of high interest. Correspondingly, bookshelves in Chinese metropolises are filling with manuals and guidebooks on *zhongchou*. Moreover, crowdfunding has become an object of research interest for Chinese academics. A database search in *Chinese Academic Journals* identified a total of 2200 articles with the term *zhongchou* in their titles.[122]

The Chinese terminology of crowdfunding differs in some respect from the Western understanding. Many works, especially those focussing on a pure description or explanation of crowdfunding, have simply adopted the established quadripartite classification of crowdfunding from the West. Sheng et al. (2014) refer to *guquanxing zhongchou (股权型众筹)* for equity-based crowdfunding，to *zhaiwuxing zhongchou (债务型众筹)* for crowdlending *mujuanxing zhongchou (募捐型众筹)* for donation-based crowdfunding，and *huibaoxing zhongchou (回报型众筹)* for reward-based projects.[123] The latter is commonly better known as *jianglizhi zhongchou (奖励制众筹)*.[124] Donation-based crowdfunding is also translated with *juanzengshi zhongchou (捐赠式众筹)*,[125] *gongyi zhongchou(公益众筹)* and *cishan zhongchou (慈善众筹)*.[126] Crowdlending is further described as *jiedaizhi zhongchou (借贷制众筹)*.[127] In contrast to Western academics, the majority of Chinese scholars clearly distinguishes between P2P (i.e. crowdlending / debt-based

---

[120]This database was provided by *CrossAsia.org*.

[121]As internet finance is a subcategory of FinTech, two further keyword searches were conducted with *FinTech* and its Chinese equivalent *jinrong keji (金融科技)* on October 30, 2016. These searches produced 33,900,000 results on *Google*, and 18,400,000 records on *Baidu*. From my own observations, I assume that in the West the term *FinTech* is more prominent than *internet finance*, whereas Chinese rather use *hulianwang jinrong (互联网金融)* (i.e. internet finance) than *jinrong keji (金融科技)* (i.e. FinTech). However, as mentioned in Sect. 2.5 despite their difference in definition, *internet finance* and *FinTech* are often used as synonyms. In order to get an idea of the prominence of crowdfunding, two further keyword searches were conducted on *Google* (with *crowdfunding*) and on *Baidu* (with *zhongchou (众筹)*) respectively as of October 30, 2016. *Crowdfunding* on *Google* provided 31,300,000 results, which was less than half of the 69,600,000 records related to *zhongchou (众筹)* on *Baidu*.

[122]The keyword search was conducted on November 12, 2015.

[123]Sheng et al. (2014, pp. 5–13).

[124]See e.g. Tu [涂涛] (2014); Liu [刘文献] (2015a); Yang [杨东] et al. (2015); amongst others.

[125]Yang [杨东] et al. (2015, p. 55); Yin (2015, p. 58).

[126]Wen (2015, p. 75).

[127]Tu [涂涛] (2014, p. 103).

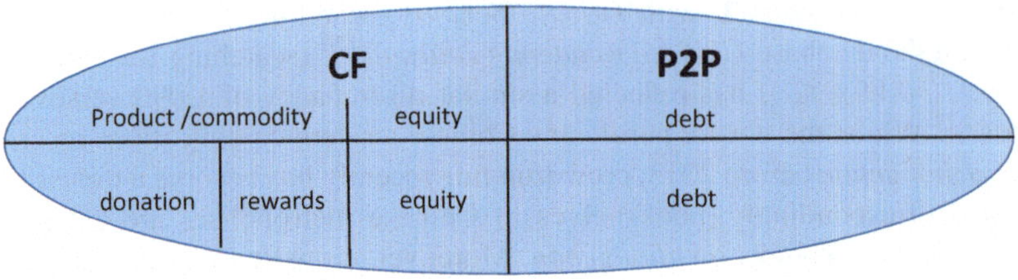

Fig. 3.2 The Chinese categorisation of crowdfunding versus P2P

crowdfunding) and other categories of crowdfunding,[128] presumably because P2P is overseen by a different Chinese regulatory body.[129]

By contrast, those Chinese publications, which do not rely on Western sources predominantly, distinguish only between two forms of crowdfunding, namely equity crowdfunding (*guquan zhongchou (股权众筹)*) and commodity/product crowdfunding. As for the latter, literature again provides two synonyms, namely *chanpin zhongchou (产品众筹)*,[130] and *shangpin zhongchou (商品众筹)*.[131] Ding (2015) distinguishes between equity crowdfunding and the term *yugoushi zhongchou (预购式众筹)*,[132] which can be translated as *pre-order* or *pre-sales crowdfunding*, and which in fact is a sub-category of reward-based crowdfunding.[133] Yu (2015b) further distinguishes between investment models of crowdfunding, including debt- and equity-based crowdfunding, and non-investment models which do not yield any financial return for the investors. The latter comprise of donation- and reward-based crowdfunding as well as pre-purchasing.[134] Finally, from Chinese literature it can be seen that Chinese crowdfunding terminology is rich in nuances; the most striking difference from the West though is its clear distinction between P2P and other forms of crowdfunding (see also Fig. 3.2).

So far, Chinese scholars study crowdfunding from a variety of angles and with mixed views. Foremost, they see crowdfunding as a promotional tool for grassroots' innovation[135] and micro self-employment.[136] Moreover, crowdfunding is believed

---

[128]E.g. Yu et al. (2015, pp. 124–140); Luo et al. (2012, p. 100 ff; p. 179 ff); Yao (2014, p. 38 ff); Hu (2014, p. 43 ff); Huang and Deng (2014, p. 20 ff); amongst others.

[129]P2P is overseen by the China Banking Regulatory Commission (CBRC), whereas (equity-based) crowdfunding in China is regulated by the China Securities Regulatory Commission (CSRC). Donation- and reward-based crowdfunding do not demand any supervision. (Interview with Du Mengjie, 2015-04-16.)

[130]See e.g. Zheng et al. (2015).

[131]Sun (2015, p. 32).

[132]Ding (2015, p. 51).

[133]See Sect. 3.1.

[134]Yu (2015a, p. 12).

[135]Sun (2015).

[136]Fan (2013).

to have an enduring impact on the Chinese start-up industry[137] as it could reduce the lack of finance for young entrepreneurs.[138] However, Chinese academics also mention the dangers that crowdfunding could incorporate.[139] Like Western scholars (see Sect. 3.3.1), they stress that crowdfunding raises IP issues[140]; whenever a project is published on a CFP, it can be easily copied by some viewer. Legal risks are also in the focus of scientists.[141] Notably, some authors have put crowdfunding in relation to illegal finance,[142] which reflects that until recently crowdfunding belonged to the grey area of finance. Correspondingly, Chinese practitioners as well as scientists have analysed crowdfunding's legal status in the US and Europe[143] and thereupon made suggestions for crowdfunding regulation in China.[144] In line with this, a number of academic comparisons of Chinese CFPs with their foreign counterparts has been published.[145] Other works focus on specific sectors like e.g. (illegal) *real estate crowdfunding*,[146] which has experienced great popularity in China.[147] Eventually, Chinese literature on crowdfunding is quite diverse in terms of topics and notions; yet, far from being mature, it leaves much scale and scope for further research.

Whilst many authors stress the chances and potential benefits crowdfunding holds for the Chinese entrepreneurial sphere, more recent publications have raised questions on whether crowdfunding in China evolves to its best. According to Tan (2015)[148] crowdfunding originally has been a financial tool for idealists to include the community of the crowd into their projects. Yet, this tool of inclusion has transformed to a means of a purely capitalistic end. In the past, crowdfunding was associated with *zhongchou wan (众筹玩)*, which can be translated as *crowdfunding + play/fun*; today it rather aligns with *chou qian (筹钱)*, which means *raising money*. The point in time when this change occurred is said to closely correlate with the time when big Chinese corporates, which actually have their core business in another industry, have entered the crowdfunding market in China. Initially, crowdfunding

137 Meng et al. (2014).

138 Jiang (2015).

139 See e.g. Shao (2012).

140 Sun (2015).

141 See e.g. Cai and Wang (2014); Hu (2015).

142 See e.g. Yu (2015c); Ye and Wu (2015).

143 See e.g. Chai (2014); Zhang (2014); Liu (2015b).

144 see e.g. Zhong and Wang (2015).

145 See e.g. Wen (2015); Lin (2015); Fan (2015).

146 See e.g. Li (2015a); Luo and Cheng (2015).

147 The evolvement of real estate crowdfunding correlates with the creation of China's recent real estate bubble, of which analysts in 2016 feared that it could burst in the near future (Sands (2016)).

148 Tan (2015).

grew out of the share-economy,[149] however, more recently *JD.com*,[150] *Alibaba*[151] and their companions have demolished this spirit.[152] Correspondingly, the language of crowdfunding research has also transformed. Whereas earlier studies on crowdfunding investigated success factors of crowdfunding projects, more recent studies analyse the *purchasing behaviour of customers* in terms of crowdfunding.[153] This discourse reminds of the situation in the West, where crowdfunding is also increasingly commercialised (see Sect. 3.2).

To date, there are few academic works and reports including quantitative data on crowdfunding in China. Zero2IPO (2014) has accomplished a study which compares data from nine Chinese CFPs with data from the two dominating American CFPs.[154] In the first half of the year 2014, the authors identified 5,513 American projects and 1,423 projects in China, attracting 2,805,553 and 109,174 investors respectively, and summing up to USD 215 million and USD 29 million respectively.[155] Thus, on average, American projects generated much more funds.[156] Whilst this probably still holds true today, the comparison contains some pitfalls which could lead to biased conclusions. First, the Chinese data included rewards-, donation- and also equity-based crowdfunding projects, whereas the American sample only included reward- and donation-based campaigns. Secondly, due to the dynamics of China's crowdfunding market, the study can only be taken as a snap-shot of the Chinese crowdfunding industry in Q2 2014; some of those platforms included in the research no longer exist or have changed their business model[157]; on the other hand, there are other players which have recently gained some great prominence and become market leaders but which were not considered in the report.[158] In August 2014, Li (2014) counted more than 90 Chinese CFPs, comprising of 63 product-based/pre-purchase-platforms, and 23 equity-based platforms; this number further included nine platforms which provided both product and equity crowdfunding. Yet, the author does not make any statement about the nature of the remaining four platforms,[159] which raises doubts about the accuracy of this source. Zero2IPO has published a second crowdfunding report in 2015, which is much more comprehensive than the first one and refers to data of the entire year 2014. Therein, the authors base their data on 13 Chinese CFPs, four equity-based

[149]n.a. (2014, p. 43).

[150]JD.com is "China's largest online direct sales company." (JD.com n.d.).

[151]For more information on *Alibaba* see Sect. 4.4.2.1.

[152]Tan (2015, p. 74 ff).

[153]Huang et al. (2015).

[154]I.e. *Kickstarter* and *Indigogo*.

[155]Zero2IPO (2014, p. 9).

[156]USD 509 versus USD 77.

[157]The platform *Demohour*, for instance, no longer counts as CFP.

[158]E.g. *Jingdong zhongchou* and *Taobao zhongchou*.

[159]Li (2014, p. 50).

ones and nine rewards-/product-based ones.[160] Although these CFPs appear to have been the most influential ones by 2014, the data probably covers only a certain share of the entire Chinese crowdfunding market at that point in time as iResearch[161] in 2014 identified at least 75 rewards-based crowdfunding platforms in China.[162] In their report, the authors put China's crowdfunding evolution into an international and economic perspective, and also extrapolated the market's development for the coming years.

Another report by the *China Impact Fund* from 2014 intended to evaluate the acceptance rate of crowdfunding by investors and entrepreneurs. In total, 126 investors and 45 entrepreneurs from China, and another 60 overseas Chinese participated in this survey. However, few of them had applied or even heard of crowdfunding before and correspondingly the number of answers varied enormously within the range of questions. Crowdfunding's "innovative financing mechanism"[163] and the creativeness of the offered products were identified as the major drivers for the Chinese respondents to become crowdfunders (29.9% each), followed by their interest in the offered projects/activities (24.7%). Yet, more than 20% of the investors indicated insufficient information on the provided projects and desired more stability in terms of platform operation.[164] The entrepreneurs, on the other hand, longed for more services and would appreciate if the CFPs provided more assistance with communication and payments processing (62.5%). They also criticised the amount of information which is available on the projects (54.2%), though it is not clear whether they wished more or less information to be disclosed. Moreover, they saw some improvement in the impact of the CFPs, but again the report provides no hint whether the entrepreneurs would prefer more or less engagement of the platforms. I assume that they wish more service provision by the platforms. None of the interviewed overseas Chinese in that study, however, has ever utilised a Chinese CFP due to a lack of credibility (46.0%), the potential of committing something illegal (24.3%) and a lack of trust in crowdfunding as a venture finance tool (21.6%).[165]

Currently, several reports on the topic of *Crowdfunding in China* or *Crowdfunding in Asia* respectively are in progress.[166] Domestic and an increasing number of international authorities are interested in the Chinese crowdfunding market. Yet, so far only few Chinese CFPs have been willing to share quantitative data.[167] In

---

[160] Zero2IPO (2015).

[161] iResearch is a Chinese analytics and consulting company focussing on online consumption in China.

[162] iResearch (2016a).

[163] Zhang et al. (2014, p. 42).

[164] Ibid.

[165] Zhang et al. (2014, p. 43 ff).

[166] Both, from Western and also Asian researchers.

[167] Interview with Luke Deer, one of the editors of *The Asia-Pacific Alternative Finance Benchmarking Report*, 2016-01-21.

order to evaluate the Chinese crowdfunding market, academics need to rely on both, Western and Chinese literature, and also on primary sources as literature on crowdfunding, particularly on crowdfunding in China, is still limited.

3.4 Crowdfunding and New Institutional Economics

3.4.1 Crowdfunding as an Institution that Rules Principal-Agent-Relations and Economises Transaction Costs

3.4.1.1 Principal-Agent-Relations Within a Crowdfunding Campaign

Crowdfunding constitutes a set of rules which guide transactions between a PI and crowdfunders via a CFP, optionally supported by a trustee.[168] The CFP functions as (financial) intermediary between the PI and the crowd. Consequently, there appear up to six agency relationships amongst these three players. On the one hand, these dependencies enable a smooth and secure handling of the transactions, on the other hand, they also bear potential conflicts. Due to information asymmetries, dangers like adverse selection, moral hazard and hold up can arise. Figure 3.3 (Kortleben and Vollmar 2012) demonstrates that each player can obtain both roles, the one of the principal but also the one of the agent, depending on the situation in perspective. The principal (P) commonly has less knowledge and "tries to suppress the agent's (A) opportunistic behaviour".[169] In the following paragraphs, the six relationships are elaborated.

The first relationship characterises the agency relationship between a PI as agent and the crowd as principal. Hereby, all three dangers can arise as the PI holds more knowledge on his venture than the crowd, before and also after the accomplishment of the contract. Therefore, a misleading project description or a lack of information may lead to adverse selection by the crowd. Moreover, if the crowd cannot monitor the PI adequately, the latter could deliberately act contrary to the crowd's interest (moral hazard). Last but not least, the PI could run away with the crowd's capital instead of investing it in the intended project (i.e. hold up). Still, both parties can counteract these threats (see also Fig. 2.2). The PI, for example, can provide the crowd with sufficient information in advance and frequent updates during the crowdfunding's running time (i.e. signalling). The crowd, on the other hand, could ask for more details on the project, e.g. a business plan,

---

[168]As both, the PI and the crowd only indirectly cooperate with the trustee, I do not analyse the relationships between the trustee and the PI and the trustee and the crowd respectively. Still the trustee can be relevant as in some countries CFPs are not allowed to manage the investments of the crowd themselves.

[169]Kortleben and Vollmar (2012, p. 3).

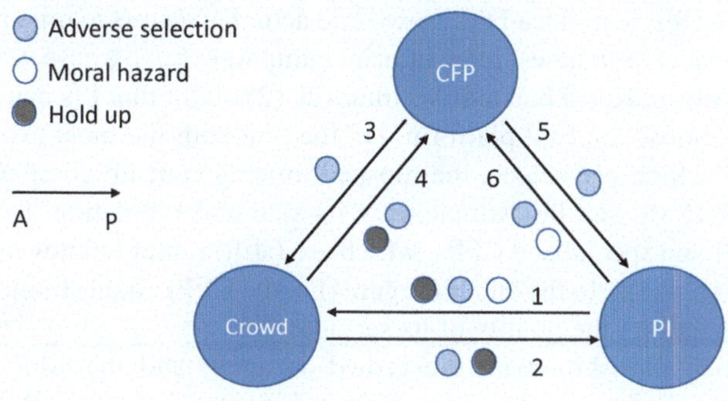

Fig. 3.3 Triangular relationship and potential threats of a crowdfunding campaign

and check the latter on its reliability (i.e. screening). If the PI previously had concluded another crowdfunding campaign, the crowd could further take this as an indicator (i.e. reputation). However, crowdfunding usually is based on non-recurring contracts, unless the PI has already initiated another project in the past to which the crowdfunder also has contributed to.

The second relationship indicates that the PI is not only an agent, but in part also a principal in his relationship towards the crowd and therefore faces the problems of adverse selection and hold up. First, the PI cannot choose his crowdfunders. While he can address his intended crowd with the release of respective data (i.e. a form of self-signalling), he can neither be sure to attract reliable investors, nor oversee why his investors have been attracted.[170] In addition, he faces the danger of an undesired or unsuitable representation. As crowdfunders are associated with the projects they invest in and vice versa, the PI could find his project represented by people whom he cannot identify with, who could harm his campaign or even endanger the whole project. Secondly, the crowd could potentially steal the PI's project idea. Once a crowdfunder has contributed to a certain project, she is privileged to obtain regular updates and potential insider information on the project. Consequently, the PI has to face the danger of hold up from competitors or other people, who could have an interest to sabotage the campaign. Therefore, the PI has to decide on the appropriate degree of information disclosure. Alternatively, he could force his crowdfunders to disclose their identity before they receive any sensible information,[171] yet, the danger of hold up still remains.

Relationship three describes the principal-agent-relationship between the crowd (P) and the CFP (A). As the latter pre-selects the projects, the platform in fact decides the range of campaigns that the crowd is able to contribute to. False pre-

[170] Kortleben and Vollmar (2012, p. 3) in this regard also state that PIs cannot ensure the solvency of interested crowdfunders. The authors exclusively refer to equity-based crowdfunders (i.e. *crowd-investors*). Whilst for donation-/rewards-/debt-based crowdfunders, this danger can be neglected, for equity-based crowdfunding insolvency indeed is relevant.

[171] Kortleben and Vollmar (2012, p. 5).

selection by the CFP would lead the crowd and actual investors to miss an interesting or profitable project or to invest in an inferior campaign. Such a case would be a case of adverse selection. Kortleben and Vollmar (2012) claim that PIs can prevent such cases if they "choose the best platform, i.e. the one with the most experienced and qualified staff, which pre-selects the most promising start-up companies".[172] The quality of a platform can be estimated by its size and reputation. However, there are many small and specialised CFPs, which are (still) rather unknown, though their work could be valuable. In the end, the agent (i.e. the CFP) could countervail adverse selection by signalling the quality of its services.[173]

The fourth relationship, with the crowd as agent and the CFP as principal, incorporates the same dangers as in relationship two. Like the PI also the CFP cannot assure that it addresses suitable investors. The latter could potentially harm the CFP's reputation, e.g. by spying on the CFP's projects. Therefore, the platform should wisely deal with the disclosure of sensitive information and potentially also conduct a due diligence on interested investors.

Relationship five depicts the PI as principal with the platform as agent. Before preparing the campaign, the initiator has to decide on a suitable CFP, which supports the funding aim. Specifically, the platform should be able to generate sufficient investors to reach the funding goal. Thereby, previous (successful and also failed) campaigns could provide a reference point, and information on these could be either provided by the CFP (i.e. signalling) or researched by the PI (i.e. screening). Still, the relationship bears the danger of adverse selection.

Last but not least, in relationship six, the CFP as principal runs in danger to choose the wrong projects or PIs (i.e. agents) respectively. For example, the PI could provide only extenuated information on his business idea and thereby mislead the CFP in its decision-making. In the end, it depends on the skills of the platform's staff and the available evaluation tools, whether the CFP chooses appropriate projects and reliable PIs. Besides adverse selection, the CFP also has to face potential moral hazard from the PI. Although the PI probably also wants to reach as many investors as possible, the CFP cannot be sure whether the PI is able or willing to follow the recommended measures (like e.g. frequently updating his crowd) for a successful crowdfunding campaign. Moreover, there is no guarantee that the PI keeps the project's risks to a minimum, once he has obtained funds via the CFP or from the crowd respectively. For both of the above mentioned cases, the CFP can monitor the PI only to a certain degree.[174]

This analysis demonstrates that crowdfunding heavily relies on principal-agent-relations and therefore incurs many risks. The latter mainly result from the fact that all involved actors of a crowdfunding campaign typically do not know each other in advance (like e.g. in TIF), and relations are initially characterised by anonymity.

[172]Ibid.

[173]Platforms can demonstrate the quality of their services by e.g. stating the number of successfully funded projects in relation to the overall number of listed projects.

[174]Kortleben and Vollmar (2012).

Some of the stated risks can be avoided by self-selection and signalling, others can be minimised by information search and monitoring. Yet, all of these efforts demand transaction costs which eventually need to be traded off against expected returns.

3.4.1.2 Transaction Costs of Crowdfunding

Although PIs and crowdfunders are subject to the regulation of their respective country and the rules of their chosen CFP, a campaign following the Original crowdfunding (OCF) concept incorporates typical processes and each of the involved players has to fulfil certain tasks so that the crowdfunding system runs smoothly. In order to identify the transaction costs that a typical OCF campaign incurs, Fig. 3.4 (Hui et al. 2012, p. 4; Sciencestarter n.d., n.p.) illustrates the six stages of a crowdfunding campaign according to Hui et al. (2012) (see also Sect. 3.3.1), which reveals the precise tasks at each stage from the perspectives of the PI and the crowdfunders. Moreover, Fig. 3.5 classifies these tasks in terms of transaction costs according to Dahlmann (1979), and Furubotn and Richter (1991).

Initially, the PI has to spend resources on the collection of information. Throughout the other five stages, she continuously has to prepare content for the crowdfunding project, first for the testing, secondly for the marketing of the campaign, and finally for the continuous updates during and after the campaign. Moreover, she has to make several decisions, first on the appropriate CFP, then on the outline of the campaign including the range of rewards,[175] and also on the channels, content and timing for her marketing actions. All these activities demand constant monitoring and potential amendments. If it was only in return for the funding, the transaction costs for the PI would be quite high. However, the calculation needs to incorporate the marketing effects of a successful crowdfunding campaign (including pre-testing, PR, etc., see also Sect. 3.2), which counterbalance the involved costs.

From the perspective of a crowdfunder, transaction costs are manageable. If he was proactively asked to contribute to a certain crowdfunding campaign, his entire transaction costs would comprise of the effort to decide whether he wants to invest and regarding the intended amount or the aspired compensation respectively. On the other hand, if no PI or CFP had directly contacted him, but the idea to invest was grown by the crowdfunder himself, he additionally would have to face search costs for identifying a suitable investment opportunity. Moreover, the crowdfunder has to bear monitoring costs during the execution stage; however, the crowdfunder's ability to monitor the PI is limited. The investor could expect the CFP to care for the monitoring of the PI, yet, as mentioned above, the platform commonly does not take responsibility for any potential frauds or default cases. Thus, despite the crowdfunder's relatively modest transaction costs,[176] he has to face rather high

[175]This only refers to reward-based CF; in case of equity CF, the PI has to think of the number of shares and the value per share.

[176]E.g. in comparison to the PI.

A typical crowdfunding process						
Actors	Understanding	Preparing	Testing	Marketing	Executing	Contributing
PI	Information gathering (e.g. on best practice models) decide on a CFP	Establish a project description, a video and pictures; decide on project span, budget and rewards; create communication plan	Collect fans within a certain time period and include their feedback into the campaigns outline	Activate one's community; marketing efforts like news, blog posts, updates; constant communication; advertising	Launch crowdfunding project	Inform community about progress of project; send rewards to all supporters; continue conversation with the crowd; keep your network of supporters
Crowd-funders	Search for appropriate investment opportunities	Search for appropriate investment opportunities	Search for appropriate investment opportunities	Search for appropriate investment opportunities; answer to crowdfunding request; (due diligence)	Decide on a project; Choose reward and respective amount of investment; transfer money to CFP or trustee respectively; monitoring the PI	Monitoring of PI

Fig. 3.4 Tasks of a typical crowdfunding campaign (OCF type)

Transaction costs of a typical crowdfunding process

Actors	Understanding	Preparing	Testing	Marketing	Executing	Contributing
PI	Information search costs; decision making costs	Costs for preparing content and contracts; decision making costs	Preparing costs; decision making costs; monitoring costs (how does pre-test work out?)	Preparing costs; decision making costs; costs for monitoring of marketing activities	Preparing costs	Preparing costs
Crowd-funders	Information search costs	Information search costs	Information search costs	Information search costs	Decision making costs; monitoring costs	Monitoring costs

Fig. 3.5 Transaction costs of a typical crowdfunding campaign (OCF type)

risks. In particular, the crowd has to face the dangers of moral hazard and hidden action. As indicated in Fig. 2.2, these risks could be lowered by collateral and the PI's reputation. However, crowdfunding per se does not include any collateral, and as the OCF concept is based on anonymity, and contributions to a single PI are usually non-recurring, the crowd cannot rely on any reference points from previous interactions with the PI either.

Yet, I argue that some features of crowdfunding, in particular its integration into social media and other online channels, can partly compensate for such missing institutions; these mechanisms lower the risk of potential fraud and also help the investors to better evaluate a project's overall risk. First of all, a PI is likely to have at least one more online profile, besides her presence on the CFP, e.g. on *Facebook*, *Xing* or *LinkedIn*. Thereby, interested crowdfunders have the chance to gather additional information on the PI, on her social environment and her other activities. Simultaneously, a PI should have an interest to provide as much information on her person as possible and interlink her online profiles, in order to become tangible, even for strangers. Secondly, the internet and its channels allow for a direct, instantaneous and mutual communication. Whilst in the past, communication was often restricted to one's immediate or indirect contacts, the online presence of individuals facilitates a direct interaction with previously unattainable people. Moreover, instant messaging has accelerated the speed of communication; digital technologies bridge geographical distances and enable a smooth conversation with short reaction times over thousands of miles. In the end, the PI becomes more transparent through the features of the internet. Likewise, a PI can easily lose her (online) reputation in case of default or fraud, if dissatisfied investors express their resentment, for instance, via social media. Thus, the online embedding of crowdfunding at least partly compensates for a PI's lack of physical collateral and history of records, and therefore reduces overall transaction costs.

3.4.1.3 The Governance of Crowdfunding Transactions

In line with the concept of transaction cost economics by Williamson (1986), I conclude that crowdfunding demands neoclassical governance. As discussed in Sect. 2.1.1.2, the level of transaction costs in financial transactions is influenced by the dimensions of *frequency*, *uncertainty* and *ease of verification*. Within a single crowdfunding campaign, transactions are typically non-recurring, or at most occasional.[177] Uncertainties increase with the level of information asymmetries, and as crowdfunding is based on anonymous relations, information is typically unequally distributed among the involved actors. Although standardised, such transactions are not trivial as monitoring and ease of verification are limited. For both actors, the PI and the crowdfunders, it is hard to verify each other's reliability.

[177]CF transactions can be occasional, if a PI starts another project or if a crowdfunder invests in several projects.

Finally, crowdfunding transactions are characterised by low frequency, substantial uncertainties and difficulties in verification. Therefore, I locate crowdfunding in the upper right corner of the financial transaction matrix depicted in Fig. 2.3.

Crowdfunding transactions are best governed by a third-party regulation. Consequently, PIs and crowdfunders should rather rely on an external intermediary, instead of conducting the crowdfunding themselves. Although there have been successful examples of individual projects, which were presented on an own website, instead of on a CFP, I argue that such projects demand a well-targeted and pre-existing fan base as well as a well-connected PI in order to reach their funding goals. For the average PI with a network of an average size and a project of average interest, governance via a third party like a CFP incurs the least transaction costs.

Indeed, a CFP and its services help to reduce overall information asymmetries. Both, the PI and the crowd can collect data on existing and previous projects from the platform, which could decrease information search and decision making costs. For example, PIs can learn which kind of rewards their peers have successfully offered, and thereupon base their own range of compensations. Potential crowdfunders, on the other hand, can choose from a broad scope of different projects. Many CFPs provide a filter mechanism, which shows projects according to one's chosen branch and geography. Thereby, the crowdfunders' choice can be optimised and their search costs reduced.

Moreover, the CFP provides an established infrastructure, which does not only facilitate capital transfers, but also data collection on the project, communication between all involved parties, and additional marketing for crowdfunding campaigns. First, the collection, management and (re-)distribution of capital is outsourced to the CFP (or a trustee respectively). The investments are commonly transferred via *PayPal*, credit card or direct debit from the crowdfunders to the CFP (or trustee respectively), and neither the crowd nor the PIs need to care for the financial transactions. Secondly, the platform collects data not just on the projects and the PIs, but likewise on all crowdfunders. On Western platforms, the latter usually need to register and thereby disclose their identity, at least towards the platform. During the funding process, the PI only obtains limited data on his investors. Once a funding has been accomplished, the PI obtains all contact details of the crowdfunders in order to be able to send out the rewards. Besides the qualitative data and details on the crowdfunders, the PI also receives quantitative data, e.g. the number of interested people (i.e. fans) of his project, and the actual number of investors. These data are all provided by the CFP's infrastructure and save the PI resources. Thirdly, the platform provides communication tools like a project blog, which enables a direct information flow from the PI to all of his investors. Additionally, all contributors can directly reply to a PI's updates or address comments to the entire project community. With these tools, PIs and crowdfunders can concentrate on the contents of their communication, whilst the CFP cares for the exchange environment. Fourthly, the CFP literally provides a platform to all listed projects which often extends beyond the CFP's website. For example, a CFP commonly also communicates its activities on (social) media channels. Thereby, the projects' visibility can be enforced. A renowned CFP can increase the likelihood of successful funding.[178] However, as popular CFPs are likely to list more projects than less established ones, projects need to differentiate themselves in order to stick out from the mass. All in all, a crowdfunding platform can support PIs and (potential) crowdfunders in several ways, foremost with additional marketing and a reduction in search costs due to the provision of information.

3.4.2 Crowdfunding Platforms Versus Classic Financial Intermediaries

A comparison of a CFP with a commercial bank regarding the dimensions of capital transformation, shows that a platform following the OCF type cannot fulfil either of three tasks. *Lot-size transformation* is not the mission of a CFP as the latter allocates certain amounts of capital to a specific project selected by the investors, and not to those projects with the highest efficiency. The investors' capital is never scattered on several projects, unless they decide to contribute to several campaigns. Likewise, *term transformation* is not a function of the CFP. Each PI starts his crowdfunding campaign according to his demand schedule; from the starting point, he has to take into account the running time of the campaign until the collected money is disbursed (if the project has been successful). The crowdfunders simultaneously invest just at that point of time, when they have chosen an appropriate project and decided to contribute. Moreover, a CFP neither takes care of *risk transformation*. Each crowdfunder has to decide himself, which level of risk he is willing to take. He further has to evaluate the risk level of the offered projects, and thereupon come to a concluding choice which he has to live with until the end of the respective campaign. Likewise, a PI cannot choose a well-adjusted crowd of investors with a broad range of risk aversion. She is only able to address her intended crowd by presenting the project accordingly.

Indeed, in terms of risk distribution, crowdfunding differs a lot from banking. Even though a CFP pre-selects the PIs according to certain criteria and in some cases also checks the investors' liquidity, it takes no responsibility in case of the project's failure or the investors' insolvency. By contrast, a bank typically has to cope with a borrower's default, whereas the savers' deposits are relatively safe. With crowdfunding, on the other hand, the risk of a project's default is entirely held by the crowdfunders. Even though, with the *AON* model, risks before a campaign's completion are relatively low, there are no guarantees for the crowdfunders after a successful funding. It could happen that they never receive the promised rewards

[178]See Mollick and Kuppuswamy (2015, p. 2), who have discovered that a listing on *Kickstarter* correlates with a successful funding.

or that the intended project will actually not be implemented. Moreover, the CFP's ability to rate PIs is limited and not very specific at all. The former only distinguishes between accepted and non-accepted projects; however, accepted projects are not further classified into e.g. low, modest and high risk categories. Eventually, the risks of a crowdfunding project could be underestimated by the crowd, which justifies calls for more investor protection.[179] Ultimately, if *lot-size transformation*, *term transformation* and *risk transformation* are essential features of a financial intermediary, then we may not count the classical CFP a financial intermediary.

Still, a CFP shares some commonalities with a commercial bank. First and foremost, a CFP fulfils the role of a financial coordinator between PIs and crowdfunders. It further acquires and processes information on all involved players, although a CFP usually does not repackage these information nor sell it to another entity. CFPs, like banks, often specialise in a certain field of operation, for example a specific branch (like electronic devices) or a certain mode of crowdfunding (like equity-based crowdfunding), and thereby can create economies of scale. Depending on their reputation, CFPs, like banks, can more easily obtain sensitive information (for instance on the solvency of an investor) compared to individuals, although this often depends on the willingness of the involved actors to disclose this information. Moreover, as supply and demand are located at one single platform, CFPs like banks can reduce overall searching and matching costs. In terms of credit rating, both a bank's and a CFP's abilities to rate the involved actors depend on their respective pool of data and their capabilities in data analysing. In the end, the features of a CFP still resemble some functions of a typical commercial bank.

In the context of financialisation, the OCF model to a certain extent contributes to a transformation of capitalism. Crowdfunding indeed draws the consumer (or the households respectively) closer towards the financial sector, as suggested by Lapavitsas and his view on financialisation. In particular, *civic crowdfunding*[180] finances public projects and thereby the crowd alleviates the government's financial pressure. Corporates, on the other hand, are hardly affected by crowdfunding, though they are increasingly utilising crowdfunding as marketing tool. Yet, crowdfunding platforms in fact substitute or complement banks through the provision of finance for PIs, i.e. SMEs, start-ups and entrepreneurs, and also by offering an alternative investment opportunity for savers. As a consequence, banks face competition, unless they manage to integrate crowdfunding into commercial banking (see Sect. 3.4.3 for an example). However, so far, Western banks do not perceive crowdfunding as a challenge to their current business model.[181]

---

[179] See e.g. Stemler (2013); Carni (2014).

[180] *Civic crowdfunding* describes the funding of a public good financed by the crowd via crowdfunding.

[181] See e.g. Dapp (2013).

3.4.3 Crowdfunding Versus Rotating Savings and Credit Associations and Other Forms of Traditional informal finance

Following the analysis of Traditional informal finance (see Sect. 4.2), of ROSCAs (see Sect. 2.4.3) and Original crowdfunding (OCF) (see Sect. 3.2) respectively, this chapter contrasts the characteristics of these financial tools and highlights commonalities and discrepancies. Table 3.2 lists the most crucial features, which eventually tell the distinctive story about each institution.

Crowdfunding started out in industrialised countries; it is concentrated in urban areas with good internet infrastructure and is only gradually expanding to the developing world. On the other hand, TIF and ROSCAs are predominantly present in rural areas. Whilst online based crowdfunding is a recent phenomenon, TIF and the concept of a ROSCA have a long tradition. Although, all three institutions per se are ubiquitous and nowadays can be found in all kinds of areas, TIF and

Table 3.2 Contrasting TIF to ROSCAs and the OCF[a]

Features	TIF	ROSCAs	OCF
Networks	Personal	Personal	Anonymous
Communication	Face to face	Face to face	Virtual
Transparency	Low	Low	High
Location	Rural and urban, local	Predominantly rural, local	Everywhere
Durability	Short and long	Long	30–60 days
Frequency of transactions	Non-recurring to frequent	Frequent	Non-recurring
Trust through	Informal information	Informal information	*AON* model and online information
Size of financial transactions	Small	Small payments are accumulated into larger pools	Small payments are accumulated into larger pools
Feasibility	Rather spontaneous	Rather spontaneous	Demands planning
Addressees	All kinds	All kinds	All kinds
Including reciprocity	Yes	Yes	No
Interest rates	High	Zero	Low (just commission)
Savings function	High	High	Only in terms of equity CF

[a]Note to interest rates: With donation-, rewards- and equity-based crowdfunding, in case of a successful crowdfunding, the PI has to pay the CFP a commission, which is a certain percentage of the target sum. P2P (i.e. debt-based crowdfunding) next to the commission further could include some interest, which the PI has to pay back to his crowdfunders on top of the collected funds

ROSCAs are limited in terms of their geographical scope as borrowers and lenders commonly live in the same area. By contrast, crowdfunding due to its online character theoretically faces no borders; it is rather a global tool which can bridge huge distances.[182]

Crowdfunding and ROSCAs, in contrast to TIF, enjoy a rather positive public image. One explanation for this may be the fact that both ROSCAs and crowdfunding do not incur interest rates,[183] although with crowdfunding, the PI has to pay commission to the CFP in case of a successful crowdfunding campaign. The level of that commission varies amongst CFPs, but is usually lower than the average interest of most informal financial institutions.[184] Moreover, ROSCAs are known for their savings function, whilst TIF is said to be used for consumption purposes. Notably, with regard to crowdfunding, equity-based CF is rather seen as an investment tool which promotes entrepreneurship, whilst P2P often serves consumption or even illegal ends like cash laundry.[185]

Irrespective of their reputation, all three financial tools are appreciated because they are easy to setup, they do not demand any tangible collateral and funds are collected and disbursed relatively quickly. Within a ROSCA and other forms of TIF, collateral is compensated by social ties and informal information, which further enable a sanctioning in case of a default. If a member of a credit association, for instance, does not meet her liabilities (i.e. regularly contribute to the cycle), then she gets socially stigmatised, not just within the ROSCA, but in fact beyond the association. In contrast, the crowdfunding framework, theoretically incorporates neither informal information nor social ties, but relies on rather anonymous transactions between strangers instead. Partly, the internet and its features compensate for the lack of information. Moreover, regulations by governments and CFPs can encourage compliance. Yet, the question remains how these two players enforce sanctions in case of defaults.

TIF, OCF and ROSCAs differ in terms of the involved amounts of capital, their formation and duration. First of all, TIF is associated with small scale finance, whereas ROSCAs are distinct as they accumulate small payments into larger pools. Crowdfunding, on the other hand, can incorporate both, small and larger sums of capital, which are simultaneously accumulated from many small contributions. Secondly, ROSCAs commonly evolve around interest groups, and sometimes are even set up for shared purposes. Likewise, a crowd forms out of a shared interest for a certain campaign. By contrast, informal lenders and borrowers do not necessarily have common interests as long as they share some other commonalities and informal

---

[182]However, as noted in Sect. 3.3.1, different regulations across countries still impede cross-country crowdfunding projects.

[183]Sometimes the disbursements of a credit association are adjusted to inflation; however, commonly members of a ROSCA do not pay any interest on their loans.

[184]*Kickstarter* e.g. as of May 2016 charged a commission of 5%, whereas the average interest rate for informal finance in China in 2004 and 2006 was estimated to be at 16.4% (Li 2009, p. 53; see also Sect. 2.4.2).

[185]Interview with Conor Roche, 2015-05-06.

information, which are the basement for the financial transaction. In terms of duration, TIF typically is short term oriented, whilst the length of a ROSCA depends on the cycle and consequently the number of participants. The tenure of interactions between PIs and the crowd depends on the mode of crowdfunding in place; equity- and debt-based campaigns tend to aim at a long-term investment, whereas donation- and reward-based crowdfunding projects are rather short-term oriented. Simultaneously, the retention periods of all financial tools are different, and accordingly short or long, parallel to the respective duration.

Moreover, all three financial institutions differ in terms of their organisation and regulation. Regarding organisation, TIF and credit associations are operated on a private basis, whereas crowdfunding usually involves an incorporated platform. Furthermore, both, ROSCAs and campaigns corresponding the OCF concept, differ from TIF as they demand certain preparation and therefore cannot be implemented as immediate as TIF. One explanation for the spontaneity of TIF amongst others is the fact that it is purely based on customised solutions; there are no other arrangements, but just those norms which all involved actors agree upon. Crowdfunding, in contrast, relies on country- and platform-specific regulations, and PIs and crowdfunders need to obey to these, regardless of their status. Compared to TIF and OCF, regulation of ROSCAs is settled somewhere in between. There are no authorised rules but rather codes of conduct within a credit association, which restrict the scope for bargaining and decision making. In the end, this characteristic in combination with their private organisation lowers overall transaction costs of ROSCAs to a minimum. TIF leaves more room for bargaining and decision making, depending on the bargaining power of the debtor; therefore, transaction costs are slightly higher than within a ROSCA. In pure contrast, the OCF commonly involves more documentation and capital management (by the CFP or the trustee respectively). Thus, compared to TIF and ROSCAs, efforts (or transaction costs) for organisation and regulation are relatively high.

Besides, the three financial tools differ in terms of their beneficiaries. As mentioned above, the private sector, and in particular SMEs, profit most from instalments like informal finance, ROSCAs and crowdfunding; yet, the latter can also be utilised in order to fund public projects. For example, in the Netherlands, one example for a civic crowdfunding campaign is the *Luchtsingel pedestrian bridge*, a public infrastructure project which has been realised with contributions of more than 8,000 crowdfunders.[186] Thereby, public finances were relieved as citizens financed the bridge privately. Apart from the government, financial corporates also profit from crowdfunding and its innovative image. Since recently, crowdfunding is increasingly integrated into established financial institutions. For instance, German *Volksbanken Raiffeisenbanken* have discovered *social crowdfunding* as an extension of their business scope.[187] Thus, crowdfunding just like informal finance (see Sect. 2.4.2) maintains connections to established financial institutions; although in

[186]Frearson (2015).

[187]Volksbanken Raiffeisenbanken (n.d).

the case of crowdfunding, these interlinkages are much more transparent. Moreover, in contrast to TIF, these relations do not serve a reduction in transaction costs for the borrowers and depositors, but rather provide a diversification of a bank's business model, an extension to borrowers' choice of finance and an alternative investment opportunity for lenders.

Further differentiating aspects are the requirements regarding the use of the capital, the means necessary to run those institutions and also the features that help to manage the involved risks. Whilst members of a ROSCA face no specifications on how to use the hand they receive (unless the association was set up for a common purpose), PIs applying crowdfunding need to pre-define their intended investment object. In terms of TIF, the requirements are dependent on the attitude of the lender. Finally, the three financial institutions are based on different foundations. Informal information and personal relationships are the grease for both, TIF and ROSCAs; they eventually create trust, and consequently transactions are carried out with promise and consent. Moreover, they ensure compliance as all involved players usually have an interest to uphold these relationships. Close social ties further mitigate risks and reduce default, whilst in a ROSCA the residual risks are born by the organiser of the association (see also Sect. 2.4.3). Crowdfunding, however, apparently lacks such social institutions that could sanction in cases of fraud or default and manage overall risk.

Informal finance is said to be a means of last resort (see Sect. 2.4.2). Likewise, for many PIs, crowdfunding often constitutes the only chance to get recognition and financing for their projects. Yet, I argue that both, the membership in a ROSCA and the successful initiation of a crowdfunding campaign are reserved to people with pre-existing social networks or at least sufficient networking skills. If one's reputation is damaged or if a person has neither friends nor acquaintances who could speak in favour of her, she is very unlikely to enter a selected circle of a ROSCA. Similarly, a PI without the initial support of his family, friends and fools[188] is very unlikely to succeed with his crowdfunding campaign. On the contrary, anyone who is willing to pay high interest rates, could get a loan from an informal moneylender or a pawnshop. This example demonstrates that ROSCAs are special vehicles amongst common forms of informal finance.

Crowdfunding and ROSCAs are both collective funding tools to realise a venture. However, this feature is even more distinct for a ROSCA as it includes collective saving and borrowing at the same time. In fact, ROSCAs excel as they transform future payments into immediate hands by purely relying on cash flow lending. As mentioned in Sect. 2.4.3, ROSCAs are given priority over other liabilities, thus people can save money over a long period as they may subordinate other obligations. With regard to crowdfunding, the savings function so far has been neglected by scholars; rather, the PI and his access to finance have been put forward. Yet, particularly in times of low savings rates, depositors search for alternative investment opportunities. Whilst donation-based crowdfunding can be excluded

[188] See e.g. Agrawal et al. (2011).

from this contemplation, and rewards-based crowdfunding only qualifies to a limited extend, debt- and equity-based crowdfunding could be true alternatives to unprofitable bank deposits. However, the degree to which a crowdfunding campaign can fulfil a savings function depends on the propensity of the investors to take risk.

Ultimately, there are some idiosyncratic characteristics of each financial institution, which make them somehow unique. ROSCAs manage to establish tight communities, not least through the regular, personal meetings of all members and their shared meal and drinks during such events. TIF (and partly also ROSCAs) proceeds rather invisible, despite its omnipresence, and thus is difficult to be traced by authorities. Crowdfunding stands out due to its online nature, which first of all makes it independent from time and place restrictions, and secondly enables a matching of PIs and crowdfunders on a global scale. The integration of a platform reduces overall search costs for both, entrepreneurs and investors. Moreover, with crowdfunding, a PI can raise public attention and awareness, which is not the mission of TIF. Furthermore, a campaign of a PI is likely to receive feedback from the crowd. Thus, crowdfunding contributions can be declared clever money[189]; the result of the campaign is like an online validation for the respective project or service. However, the question remains, whether and how these idiosyncrasies influence the choice of finance of a PI and also a crowdfunder.

From the contrasting analysis above, it is obvious that OCF demonstrates several drawbacks. Above all, it is not clear how exactly the PI or the CFP can evoke trust. Secondly, the OCF concept provides no standardised solution for cases of default and fraud. Common CFPs typically have neither the reputation nor the capabilities to ensure trust, compliance and punishment. I argue that not least for these reasons, Chinese have created new versions of crowdfunding, in particular, *WeChat crowdfunding* and *e-commerce crowdfunding*, which are able to better cope with information asymmetries and uncertainties.

3.4.4 The Choice for Crowdfunding

An entrepreneur's choice for or against crowdfunding is likely to depend on the features of crowdfunding, the actor's personal characteristics as well as external factors which influence an entrepreneur's individual situation. As depicted in Sect. 2.2, crowdfunding per categorisation belongs to early stage external financing, and either appears in the form of debt, equity, reward or donation. Whilst *equity finance*, according to Fueglistaller's categorisation of finance and Donaldson's pecking order theory, is predominantly chosen at a later stage of a venture, *equity crowdfunding*, in contrast, like the other three forms of crowdfunding counts as seed finance. However, the four types of crowdfunding differ in terms of several features,

[189]By contrast, Schwienbacher and Larralde (2012, p. 378) regard a bank loan as "stupid money".

and thus the choice of crowdfunding needs to be further distinguished. Therefore, this chapter deals not only with the general choice for or against crowdfunding, but also with the choice between the different types of crowdfunding.

One aspect that influences a PI's and an investor's choice for crowdfunding is the incorporation of contracts. Whilst it is quite common that entrepreneurs obtain financial support from family members, friends or acquaintances, often such financial transactions lack formalisation. If crowdfunding via a CFP is legalised by authorities, then it belongs to formal finance. The CFP not only processes all transactions, but also documents all obligations. Furthermore, the transactions are subject to pre-defined rules and potential disputes are precluded. For example, previously, a person probably has asked his friends for financial support (e.g. for an interest-free loan for a certain time period) for his business idea, and all agreements were based on oral contracts. Nowadays, he can start a crowdfunding campaign on a rewards- or debt-based CFP and ask his friends to contribute via that platform. Each friend decides herself on the size of her contribution; and each one gets some reward or interest in exchange. Moreover, the disbursement of the rewards or the repayment-schedule (including potential interest rates) are pre-set, and the entrepreneur is subject to the CFP's rules and the respective country's crowdfunding regulations. Whilst bargaining about financial issues amongst friends could lead to a distraction of a friendship, with the integration of a CFP, all conditions are pre-defined.

Moreover, the choice for crowdfunding and the selection of the specific crowdfunding type could also depend on the level of risk and potential leverage that a project incorporates. Depending on the mode of crowdfunding, risks are either concentrated on the side of the PI (with the *AON* model) or on the side of the crowd (with the *KIA* model). With the former, each crowdfunder gets her money back if the target sum is not entirely reached, whereas the PI may keep all of the contributions regardless of the final funding sum with the *KIA* model. Additionally, the level of risk and leverage also varies with the amounts of investment and with the type of crowdfunding. On average, donation- and rewards-based projects collect lower sums of capital.[190] Thus, risk-averse PIs and investors are likely to opt for a donation-/rewards-based crowdfunding, whereas risk-friendly actors are more likely to choose debt- and/or equity-based crowdfunding. Still, all categories of crowdfunding, except donation-based CF,[191] are forms of venture capital and therefore must be seen as risk capital.

Once a PI has decided to apply crowdfunding, his choice of the specific crowdfunding category is likely to be influenced by his personal background. I assume that craftsmen and life-style entrepreneurs would rather choose a donation- or rewards-

[190] For instance, in 2014, the average project on the German donation-/rewards-based CFP *Startnext* achieved EUR 8415 (own calculation based on Startnext n.p.). Projects on *Seedmatch*, a German equity-based CFP, on average collected EUR 312,213 (own calculation based on Seedmatch n.d.).

[191] Donation-based crowdfunding is an exception as crowdfunders of donation-based campaigns deliberately contribute funds without expecting any returns.

Table 3.3 Likely choices of crowdfunding by different types of entrepreneurs

	Categories of crowdfunding		
Types of entrepreneurs	Donations and rewards	Debt	Equity
Craftsman	x		
Opportunist		x	x
Inventor	x	x	x
Life-style	x		
Serial		x	x

based crowdfunding in order to stay independent from the crowd. Except for the rewards, there are no further obligations which they have to bear in exchange for the crowdfunders' investment. However, as donation- and reward-based projects yield comparably low sums, opportunists and serial entrepreneurs are likely to opt for equity- or debt-based crowdfunding in order to leverage their business. Finally, as the inventor entrepreneur cares less about 100% ownership of his venture, I assume he would choose whatever form of crowdfunding enables him best to realise his invention. Table 3.3 illustrates the different types of entrepreneurs and their likely favoured type of crowdfunding.

Still, the question remains whether crowdfunding rather suits for novice or habitual entrepreneurs. On the one hand, crowdfunding is said to be open for any individual and entity. PIs do not require any prerequisites and therefore crowdfunding is a great alternative for novice founders without any contacts and business experience. On the other hand, pre-existing (online and offline) networks are certainly advantageous for the success of a crowdfunding campaign. Habitual founders who opt for crowdfunding can profit from their social capital, i.e. previous contacts, if these contacts (again) become crowdfunders and eventually leverage the campaign. By contrast, novice founders still need to establish their crowd before they can actually start their campaign. Therefore, novice entrepreneurs seem to need more time for their entire crowdfunding. They first need to gather social capital in order to translate it into economic capital. In the end, I argue that both, habitual and novice entrepreneurs, can successfully apply crowdfunding, however, the former have an easier initial position.

Yet, the choice for or against crowdfunding depends on more than just the above mentioned financial, legal, or personal aspects. Once crowdfunding is considered a marketing as much as a financial tool, the actors' motivation changes accordingly. In this case an opportunist or serial entrepreneur could likewise opt for a donation- or rewards-based crowdfunding, if it ensures her respective recognition for her campaign. Thereby, cases like that of *BMW* (see Sect. 3.2) can be explained; *BMW* certainly employed a rewards-based crowdfunding campaign for larger ends than pure finance. Likewise, there are PIs who utilise crowdfunding in order to realise a certain milestone, i.e. they first follow a *just-do-it strategy* in order to obtain funds to realise parts of a business idea, e.g. the development of a prototype.[192] Once a start-up has accomplished a successful campaign, it can approach a bank, a VC or another external investor for further funding. A successful crowdfunding not least is great PR and a representable proof of concept. Ultimately, the marketing and after-effects of a crowdfunding campaign should not be underestimated.

It is yet to be determined what a typical (Western) PI looks like. However, from the findings of successful crowdfunding campaigns, I can induce the characteristics of a succesful PI. Even though crowdfunding is applicable by individuals and entities without any networks, scholars found evidence that social capital is beneficial for crowdfunding.[193] Whilst it is not important where the PI is located (i.e. his level of *territorial social capital*) as the internet bridges distances, his personal contacts (i.e. *individual social capital*) do matter a lot and can eventually make the difference for his crowdfunding.[194] In particular, as the first contributors to a campaign often are friends, family and fools[195] and as those projects, which initially pass the threshold of 40% funding within a short time period, are likely to be fully funded,[196] a successful PI commonly has sound social networks. These networks should excel in their range as well as in quality, and also in terms of shared meaning. Additionally, a successful PI is likely to have sufficient capabilities and resources in order to manage the challenging and time-consuming tasks of preparing a crowdfunding campaign. Besides, a successful PI usually has great communication skills for interaction with the crowd before, during and after the campaign. He is creative and eloquent, which enables him to accomplish a fascinating crowdfunding project (including the creation of a crowdfunding video); he also evokes trust via his confidential appearance, which further enables him to signal the project's quality and legitimacy. The latter can be further stressed by a modest target sum and a relatively short running period of the campaign. Moreover, external endorsements and a high number of *Facebook* friends[197] make the PI even more convincing. Finally, a successful PI is not reluctant to share personal information via social media and other channels as, in fact, crowdfunders not least depend their investment decision on the availability and reliability of information on the project and the PI respectively.

---

[192] Klein (2014); and own observation.

[193] See e.g. Giudici et al. (2013); Zheng et al. (2014).

[194] Giudici et al. (2013).

[195] Agrawal et al. (2011).

[196] Artmorpheus, (2012).

[197] This refers to countries where *Facebook* is the dominant social medium. For other countries (like China) other social media (like *WeChat*) would be a better indicator.

Chapter 4
From Informal Finance to Internet Finance in China

As described in Sect. 2.1.1, commonly a developing country follows the path from informal to formal institutions during its evolution towards a developed country. Likewise, individuals and enterprises shift their finances from informal to formal financial institutions. In China, however, the formal financial sector lags far behind the development of other industries. Due to a lack of formal sources, Chinese ever since have utilised informal forms of finance. They thereby have chosen those financial institutions which provided them with the lowest transaction costs. However, the central government regards informal finance with suspicion. As formal finance cannot meet financial demand and informal finance is not the most favoured institution to fill this gap, the Chinese government has started to promote internet finance or FinTech. The latter has rapidly evolved in China, and in fact has the potential to challenge both, informal and formal finance.

Even though, FinTech 3.0 (including internet finance) started later in China than in the West, by 2016, "China is leading the world in its embrace of financial technology, or fintech".[1] However, in contrast to the West, FinTech 3.0 in China not only started from a different point of departure, the market is also dominated by different actors, namely Chinese e-commerce and social media providers. Thus, in order to understand crowdfunding's embeddedness in China's FinTech 3.0 sector, this chapter starts with an overview of formal and informal finance and proceeds with an analysis of FinTech evolution in China. In addition, it draws a concise picture of China's internet industry. In particular, it first illustrates the ecosystem of China's internet giants, exemplified by the businesses of *Alibaba* and *Tencent*. Secondly, it depicts China's mobile internet market. Thirdly, it explains the success and challenges of China's e-commerce market, and fourthly, it analyses China's payments market. Eventually, China's shift from informal to internet finance will become more plausible.

[1] Linnane (2016, n.p).

A. S. Funk, *Crowdfunding in China*, Contributions to Management Science,
https://doi.org/10.1007/978-3-319-97253-4_4

4.1 China's Formal Finance Sector

According to Walter and Howie (2012), "banks are China's [formal] financial system".[2] Even though China's formal finance sector also includes other players like investment funds, insurance or real estate companies, banks indeed have dominated the Chinese market, and therefore, this chapter focusses on the banking sector.

4.1.1 Historical Development of China's Banking Sector

> [T]he banking sector shouldered and accumulated the systemic costs of reforms in other sectors and thus increasingly became the Achilles' heel of the overall economy, the weakest link in an otherwise rapid growth model.[3]

Since its establishment in 1949, the PRC has experienced several banking reforms. Still, the country is far from having a banking sector, which serves the needs of all its entities, individuals as well as enterprises. The market is dominated by State-owned banks (SOBs), which like State-owned enterprises (SOEs) are a legacy of the planned economy. With the foundation of the PRC, all banks had been nationalised and subordinated under the People's Bank of China (PBOC). Until the initiation of the opening and reform era, in the late 1980s, China's finance sector predominantly served the interests of the centrally planned economy. The PBOC then was the controlling instance, which oversaw not just functions of a central bank but also ruled over commercial activities and the treasury of the state, although the bank officially was under the administration of the Ministry of Finance (MOF). In the 1980s, the PBOC was transformed into a real central bank, reporting to the State Council,[4] which marked the beginning of the banking reforms.

According to Bell and Feng (2013), China's banking reform is accompanied by a continued struggle between the PBOC and the MOF. The latter is rather associated with a traditional socialist institution that refuses profound change, whereas the PBOC is seen as the major driver for financial reforms.[5] Most works on China's banking reform only refer to three phases of reform,[6] yet, Bell and Feng follow a more differentiated approach and distinguish between five phases of reform: (1) the period from the 1980s until the early 1990s; (2) the phase between 1990 and 1997; (3) the time during and after the Asian financial crisis until 2002; (4) the period between 2002 and 2005; and (5) the time since 2005.

[2] Walter and Howie (2012, p. 29).

[3] Bell and Feng (2013, p. 267).

[4] "The State Council is the highest executive organ in the [Chinese] state administration. Under the State Council are ministries, commissions and bureaus. It is further represented through government authorities at the provincial and local levels." (Cousin 2011, p. 271).

[5] Walter and Howie (2012, p. 219).

[6] See e.g. Hsu (2009, p. 8), Cousin (2011, p. 4).

During the first phase, the banking sector was transformed from a monobank system into a two-tiered system. The PBOC's commercial banking tasks were transferred to the "four newly established or reestablished specialized SOBs, the Agricultural Bank of China (ABC), the Bank of China (BOC), the People's Construction Bank (later renamed the China Construction Bank, CCB), and the Industrial and Commercial Bank of China (ICBC.) The four SOBs have since dominated China's banking and financial system and are collectively called the Big Four."[7] Despite their designated commercial banking function, however, the Big Four mainly fulfilled a fiscal function by "providing directed credit and subsidized capital to state-owned enterprises (SOEs) and to projects of political priority."[8] Moreover, overall competition for the SOBs was low. Although some regional banks, non-financial institutions and, to a limited extent, also foreign banks were allowed to enter the Chinese market, there were few incentives for the SOBs to become profitable or base their credit allocation on market principles as the lion's share of the financial market was still owned by the state. Competition among the SOBs was also limited as they all served different industry sectors. As neither the SOBs nor the SOEs, which were financed by the former, had incentives to operate profitably, the Big Four started to accumulate large amounts of Non-performing loans (NPLs).

The second phase of reform, from 1990 to 1997, brought several new laws and again new institutions as a reaction to "the economic chaos [prevailing in the late 1980s and early 1990s, which was] represented by gigantic flows of banking funds channelled into speculative real estate ventures, the newly opened stock market, and the prevalence of an active black interbank market, built upon rapid monetary expansion and high inflation."[9] The Central Bank Law and the Commercial Bank Law were implemented, which strengthened the PBOC's standing and regulatory power. Moreover, loan quotas were abolished.[10] Furthermore, three specialised policy banks were created in 1994, which henceforth should take over all policy lending operations from the SOBs.[11] The latter should fulfil their original function as commercial banks and operate more market-oriented. In order to enhance competition, the first Chinese private bank, China Minsheng Bank (CMB), was established in 1995; entry barriers for foreign banks were lowered, and urban credit cooperatives were transformed into urban cooperative banks. Still, the dominance of the Big Four and their under-performance prevailed.[12]

Even though China was hardly affected by the Asian financial crisis of 1997 thanks to its closed financial markets, the crisis induced Chinese authorities to promote banking reforms, which marked the third phase of reforms. In particular,

[7] Bell and Feng (2013, p. 267).

[8] Ibid.

[9] Bell and Feng (2013, p. 268).

[10] Hsu (2009, p. 8).

[11] Cousin (2011, p. 4 ff).

[12] Bell and Feng (2013, p. 268).

the central government adopted a recapitalisation program to address the SOBs' NPLs and to increase their capital adequacy ratio to the Basel level of 8%. Moreover, four Asset management companys (AMCs) were created, to which the existing NPLs were transferred. In fact, "the [...] AMCs issued 1.4 trillion yuan in financial bonds to the Big Four and used the funds to purchase 1.4 trillion in NPLs from the same banks at face value."[13] Bell and Feng regard the recapitalisation as "short-sighted"[14] and the measurements only as delay of the problem: instead of implementing a fiscal solution to wipe out the bad loans, the NPLs were only hidden within AMCs bonds. By contrast, a more positive event during this phase was the PBOC's membership of the Bank of International Settlements, which enhanced the central bank's aspiration to foster regulation in order to comply with international standards.[15]

Phase four of China's banking reform was marked by China's accession to the World Trade Organization (WTO) in 2001. In order to accelerate negotiations on its membership, Chinese authorities accepted extensive requirements from the international community and used accession pressure for far-reaching reforms of the domestic banking sector. Besides the opening of the financial sector for foreign banks, a major step was the structural reform of major state banks in the form of an *equitisation*[16] with the help of foreign investment.[17] This shareholding reform was implemented in three stages. "The first step was to replenish the [banks'] capital to internationally accepted levels and turn [them] into shareholding enterprises. After cleaning their balance sheets, the banks would [secondly] engage in attracting foreign financial institutions [...] for equity investment so that the domestic banks could gain management expertise and market confidence. The [third] step was to list the banks in an overseas stock market."[18] Although the first step further increased the amount of NPLs that in this connection were again transferred from the Big Four to the AMCs, the equitisation as a whole brought more financial stability and above all foreign expertise and international standards to Chinese state-owned banks. The shareholding reform was accomplished by the PBOC and the *Central*

[13]Bell and Feng (2013, p. 270).

[14]Ibid.

[15]Bell and Feng (2013, p. 271).

[16]Martin (2012) defines "equitization" as "a process of transforming [state-owned banks] into joint-stock commercial banks" (Martin 2012, p. 12).

[17]"Alternatively, inviting in domestic private capital [would have been] financially viable, given China's high savings ratio and the rapid development of the private sector in the 1990s. Nevertheless, liberalizing domestic private investment in the financial sector could be politically risky for the Communist Party since this meant that the regime could lose control of key financial resources. Thus, foreign investment in a supervised partnership with domestic institutions was instead put on the table." (Bell and Feng 2013, p. 273)

[18]Bell and Feng (2013, p. 274).

Huijin Investment Company (Huijin), "a special policy vehicle [and] effectively a proxy of the [PBOC]."[19]

Walter and Howie (2012) argue that China's banking reform came to an end in 2005, as then, the PBOC lost power towards the MOF. Although China's central bank indeed lost influence on the financial sector to the MOF,[20] "2005 did not mark the death of financial reform in China; rather, it initiated a new phase of reform, one in which the [PBOC] remains a major player but deliberates through a more inclusive, consensus-seeking process, compared with its previous unilateralism."[21] With the advent and sudden rise of internet finance in China, a sixths phase of reform could be added. Yet, since then transformations of the banking sector rather can be traced back to external pressures rather than to developments from within the established banking sector.

In conclusion, China's banking reform followed a gradual and sequential path. Despite the PBOC's achievement regarding the recapitalisation and equitisation of the state-owned banks, some short-sighted measurements by career driven actors of the past have created the challenges of China's current banking system. "Because of the critical significance of financial resources as a component of political capital in China, the financial system was always a highly politicized and contested area in domestic politics."[22]

4.1.2 Current Structure of China's Banking Sector

There are currently four key entities, which are responsible for the regulation of China's formal finance sector. (1) The People's Bank of China (PBOC), which is China's central bank and which formulates and implements China's monetary policy. (2) The China Banking Regulatory Commission (CBRC), created after the Asian financial crisis in 1997, which together with the PBOC oversees the operations of all banking institutions in the PRC and enforces banking regulation. (3) the Ministry of Finance (MOF), responsible for China's fiscal policies and the budget of the central government, and (4) the State Administration of Foreign Exchange (SAFE), which supervises and monitors all foreign exchange transactions in China and also manages the government's foreign exchange reserves.[23]

---

[19]Bell and Feng (2013, p. 280). For further information on the *Huijin*, see Bell and Feng (2013, pp. 279–284).

[20]The PBOC's loss in impact on the financial sector for instance can be seen from the fact that it lost the Huijin to the MOF. "[I]n September 2007, the MOF managed to convince the State Council to establish a sovereign wealth fund, the China Investment Corporation (CIC), under its control, and to merge Huijin into the CIC."(Bell and Feng 2013, p. 287)

[21]Bell and Feng (2013, p. 288).

[22]Bell and Feng (2013, p. 266).

[23]Martin (2012, p. 11).

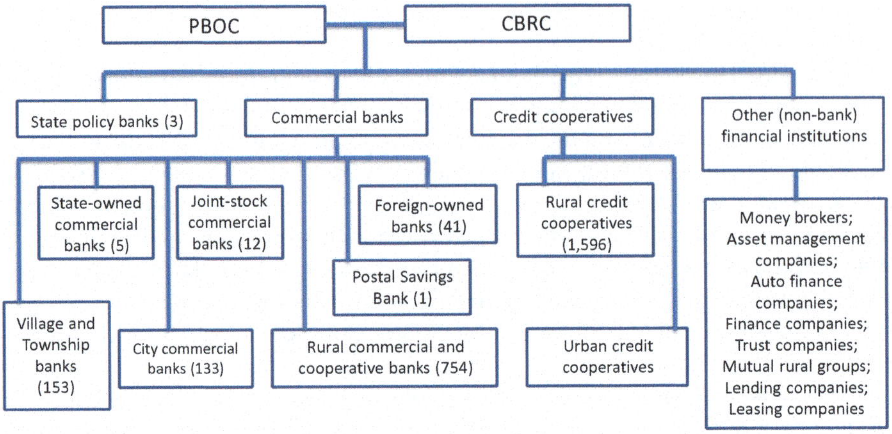

Fig. 4.1 Structure of China's banking sector as of 2014

In line with Fig. 4.1 (Cousin 2011, p. 5; CBRC, p. 23 ff), China's banking institutions can be divided into four categories, namely state policy banks, commercial banks, credit cooperatives and other (non-bank) financial institutions. As mentioned above, in 1994 three specialised policy banks were installed, the *Agricultural Development Bank of China (ADBC)*, the *China Development Bank (CDB)*[24] and the *China Exim Bank (CEB)*.[25] As suggested by its name, *ADBC* serves the development of agricultural and predominantly rural areas, whereas *CDB* rather finances large infrastructure projects. Last but not least, *CEB* serves China as institution for international transactions and investments, promoting imports and exports. All three policy banks are under the authority of the State Council and implement the latter's directives.[26]

In terms of subcategories and also the number of institutions, commercial banks make the largest share of Chinese banks. Thereunder, the state-owned commercial banks comprise of the Big Four plus the Bank of Communications (BOCOM).[27] The number of joint-stock commercial banks and foreign-owned banks has stayed relative constant over the past few years, whereas the number of rural commercial banks has increased a lot, from 43 in 2009 to 665 in 2013. During the same period, the number of rural credit cooperatives has almost halved, from 3056

[24]"China Development Bank is reportedly to be equitized sometime in the near future, but plans for its initial public offering (IPO) have been on hold" (Martin 2012, p. 5). Yet, Bloomberg in 2015 announced the IPO of two of CDB's subsidiaries in Hong Kong (Bloomberg 2015).

[25]Notably, in the CBRC 2011 Annual Report, the authorities counted "two policy banks and China Development Bank (CDB)" (CBRC 2011, p. 24), whereas the CBRC 2014 Report counted "three policy banks" (CBRC 2014, p. 23).

[26]Martin (2012, p. 5).

[27]Chapman and Marshall (2012, p. 55).

in 2009 to 1596 in 2014.[28] Since 2004, China's government has promoted the transformation of rural credit cooperatives into joint-stock companies. Furthermore, it has encouraged domestic banks (and even private and foreign investors) to buy (limited) shares of rural credit cooperatives. Moreover, the CBRC in 2009 announced the opening of more than 1000 new rural financial institutions within 2 years.[29] This demonstrates the government's awareness of financial demand, especially amongst China's rural population. Due to their smaller size, local banks are less competitive compared to state-owned commercial banks. However, as the former are (geographically and psychically) closer to local debtors, they are better equipped to estimate the creditworthiness of potential customers.[30]

Many local banks have been established by provincial and municipal governments, including city commercial banks serving regional interests like the development of local infrastructure projects. Whereas previously, these kinds of banks used to be wholly-owned by local authorities, most of them in the meantime have been transformed into joint-stock banks; still, government entities often hold the majority of the shares.[31] The range of local banks is complemented with a variety of further institutions, e.g. village and township banks, microfinance banks, and of course non-financial institutions.

In summary,

> [a]s of end-2014, China's banking sector consisted [of] three policy banks, five large commercial banks, 12 joint-stock commercial banks, 133 city commercial banks, 665 rural commercial banks, 89 rural cooperative banks, 1596 rural credit cooperatives (RCCs), one postal savings bank, four banking assets management companies, 41 locally incorporated foreign banking institutions, one China-German Bausparkasse, 68 trust companies, 196 finance companies of corporate groups, six consumer finance companies, 1153 village or township banks, 14 lending companies and 49 rural mutual cooperatives. In 2014, the establishment of five private banks[32] was approved with one opening business; one guarantee trust fund compan[y] was established. Overall, the number of [formal] incorporated banking institutions in China's banking sector amounted to 4091 with 3.76 million employees."[33]

4.1.3 *Challenges of China's Banking Sector*

Despite banking reforms and an overall large number of financial institutions, China's banking sector is facing several challenges. First and foremost, the banking sector is biased towards SOEs and thus non-SOEs have difficulties to receive formal

---

[28] CBRC (2009, p. 30), CBRC (2014, p. 23 ff).

[29] Martin (2012, p. 7).

[30] Martin (2012, p. 27 ff).

[31] Ibid.

[32] See Sects. 4.4.2.1 and 4.4.2.2.

[33] CBRC (2014, p. 23 ff).

credit. Secondly, the industry suffers from large amounts of accumulated NPLs. Thirdly, the system is based on financial repression.

Although, China's formal banking landscape is manifold and the above mentioned institutions seem to address a broad spectrum of potential customers, the banking sector is biased towards SOEs. A major reason behind this is that SOEs are employers of millions of Chinese, which care for wages and social benefits. Against the backdrop of impending mass unemployment, SOEs and their projects are supported with cheap funding.[34] Even though China's SOEs have experienced some reforms,[35] Lardy (1998) argues that these reforms are unfinished. Despite their unprofitability, there are still many SOEs which preferably receive loans from Chinese banks. Tsai (2009) claims that state banks need to fulfil quotas and are therefore under pressure to predominantly provide their loans to SOEs. Moreover, these banks lack experience of lending towards Privately owned enterprises (POEs) and therefore prefer SOEs as debtors. In addition, state banks hardly have budget constraints and thus few incentives to choose creditworthy and profitable clients. Ultimately, POEs' image is still negatively connoted.[36] "Since the banking system is designed to support the state-owned sector of the economy, private companies only have very limited access to credit. Non-state companies are thus heavily dependent on alternative financing channels".[37]

Closely related to the SOE issue is the second challenge, China's large amounts of NPLs. As mentioned before, China's SOBs over a long period fulfilled fiscal functions and provided subsidised loans to SOEs. SOBs and SOEs "are both legacies of the socialist system that suffer from soft budget constraints, by which an organization expects that financial difficulties will lead to a bailout rather than liquidation or closure".[38] In the end, "[t]his tied the bank's balance sheets to the fate of the state sector"[39] and consequently the SOBs accumulated large amounts of NPLs. However, SOBs and in particular the Big Four "are institutions too big to fail."[40] In fact, the de facto insolvent banks could only sustain due to the large amounts of Chinese household savings.[41] The authorities established AMCs to wipe the NPLs from the SOBs' balance sheets. Yet, this was rather a postponement of the problem rather than a true solution. In 2001, NPLs reached their peak with a share of 29.8% of China's GDP.[42] In the course of the recapitalisation and shareholding reform of major state-owned banks, further NPLs were transferred to the AMCs. The ratio of NPLs has declined over the last 15 years to below 2% of GDP, however,

[34]Lardy (1998, p. 3).

[35]For a detailed analysis of China's enterprise reform see You (1998).

[36]Tsai (2009, p. 99).

[37]Heep (2014, p. 38).

[38]Bell and Feng (2013, p. 269).

[39]Bell and Feng (2013, p. 267).

[40]Walter and Howie (2012, p. 33).

[41]Lardy (1998, p. 5).

[42]The World Bank (2016).

only because China's GDP grew much faster than the NPL rate. As SOEs are still advantaged in terms of credit allocation, and as a large share of Chinese SOEs is unprofitable,[43] the issue of NPLs will remain until the transformation of SOEs is accomplished.

Thirdly, China's banking sector is characterised by financial repression in the form of low interest rates.[44] In fact, interest rates on household savings deposits have progressively stayed below the rate of consumer price inflation. "In February 2002 the [PBOC] fixed the maximum interest rate banks could pay on demand deposits at 0.72% [...]. But inflation, as measured by the consumer price index, ticked up by almost 9% points—from −0.8% in 2002 to 4.8% in 2007 and then to 8% in the first quarter of 2008. Thus the real rate of return on demand deposits went from 1.52 to −4.08% and then to −7.28%."[45] In 2015, China's deposit interest rate stood at 1.5%,[46] which just equalled the average inflation rate of that year.[47] The main beneficiary of this implicit tax on households is the government.[48] In sum, the challenges of China's formal financial sector—the bias towards SOEs, the burden of NPLs, and financial repression of households—are the foundation of its established informal sector.

4.2 Informal Finance in China

China has a long history of informal finance, which dates back to the Western Zhou dynasty.[49] Until the foundation of the PRC, institutions like pawnshops and money houses were omnipresent. Whilst the latter were banned and persecuted during the Mao era, many forms of informal finance have re-emerged since the reform and opening era starting in 1978.[50] "Informal finance has played an increasing role in China's transition from a planned economy to a market economy[51] [...] and has since been a major factor in China's economic success in the last 30 years".[52] However, informal finance is officially banned in China, individuals and private organisations are prohibited to operate financial institutions or handle informal transactions; still, informal finance is tolerated and sometimes even promoted

[43]Lardy (1998, p. 3).

[44]Lardy (2008), Heep (2014).

[45]Lardy (2008, p. 1 ff).

[46]Trading Economics (n.d.).

[47]Inflation.eu (n.d.).

[48]For more information on this financial repression see Lardy (2008) and Heep (2014, pp. 37–41).

[49]Western Zhou, i.e. *Xi Zhou [西周]*, 1046–770 BC.

[50]Jiang (2009a, pp. 17–20).

[51]However, it is debatable whether China in fact is already a market economy or still an *economy in transition*.

[52]Hsu (2009, p. 6).

depending on the circumstances. One explanation for this ambivalent status is provided by Jiang (2009a):

> [The government's] attitude toward informal finance has been changing all the time. When informal finance is considered to favour the development of the economy, the government will turn a blind eye; when informal finance is considered a threat to the monopolistic position of state-owned financial institutions, or a source of disorder in financial markets or a disturbance to monetary policy, it will be resisted or banned. [Notably, d]ifferent local governments, even different departments of local governments, have different attitudes toward informal finance.[53]

Irrespective of its level of legality, informal finance has spread far beyond the government's expectations, and thus in fact does challenge the monopoly of China's state-owned formal financial institutions. Hence, in order to prevent persecution, informal finance rather stays underground; therefore, data on informal finance in China is limited.[54] Neither the central government nor local authorities collect official data on this sector, though it affects both, the macroeconomic and microeconomic sphere in China. Still, according to Hsu (2009), there are some surveys on informal finance in China, which focus on narrow geographic areas. Jiang (1996)[55] and Jiang and Ding (2004)[56] have contemplated the cities of Jinan, Qingdao and Weifang; Jiang (2000)[57] has analysed the situation in Fuzhou, Xiamen, Beijing and Shanghai; Tsai (2002)[58] has focussed on the city of Wenzhou; Liao et al. (2003)[59] have described informal finance in Wuhan.[60]

Even though official data is hard to come by and I could not obtain any recent calculations, there are some older estimations for the entire informal finance sector in China, which at least provide an indication of its dimensions. For the first quarter of 2006, scholars extrapolated that there were informal deposits between RMB 1.556 and 2.955 trillion, and loans between RMB 472.6 and 897.7 billion being channelled through informal finance.[61] Projected to the entire year, the sum of informal loans accounted for nine to 17% of China's GDP in 2006.[62] From these figures and the high ratio of deposits to loans, it becomes obvious that informal finance is more than just small credit to people without access to formal finance.

[53] Jiang (2009a, p. 35).

[54] Jiang (2009a, p. 20).

[55] Jiang (1996).

[56] Jiang and Ding (2004).

[57] Jiang (2000).

[58] Tsai (2002).

[59] Liao et al. (2003).

[60] As Hsu (2009, p. 6) in her citation only provides the Pinyin of the authors' names and the English titles of the sources, and as she did not reply to my request via email, in some cases I could not identify the primary (Chinese) sources.

[61] Li (2009, p. 56).

[62] Own calculation based on National Bureau of Statistics of China (2007, p. 57).

In fact, many Chinese apply informal finance as an alternative way for savings and investment.[63]

Although Adams and Fitchett (1992a) claim that informal finance is particularly spread in urban areas,[64] in China it is rather a phenomenon of rural areas.[65] Rural citizens mainly rely on small-scale and frequent loans, and usually lack collateral. Such transactions are less attractive for formal institutions as the profits to expected transaction costs are disproportionately low. Moreover, the entire density of formal finance is much lower in rural areas. "Due to the absence of formal financial institutions, informal finance with its advantages of reducing transactions costs, uncertainty, and risk, is one of the important sources of capital flowing into rural areas".[66] Thus, I assume that particularly creditors in rural areas are pulled towards informal finance.

Notably, some formerly informal institutions in Chinese rural areas have mutated into authorised entities. For example, *Rural credit cooperatives (RCCs)* in China used to informally serve the financial needs of farmers and people in agricultural areas. "After 1958, RCCs became semi-state-owned financial organizations, whose ownership and risk all belonged to the central government rather than to an informal financial organization".[67] Since then, RCCs have become one of the main formal sources for rural finance. Similarly, *village and township banks* have been legalised and their establishment has been eased since 2006.[68] As mentioned in Sect. 4.1, by 2014, China had 1596 RCCs and 1153 village and township banks,[69] which demonstrates the dimension of the institutional change.

4.2.1 Informal Finance in China: In Line with the Emergence of Private Entrepreneurship

Over the last 70 years, the number of Chinese POEs has decreased and increased tremendously. At the time of the foundation of the PRC, in 1949, there were about nine million private businesses in China. However, they all vanished with the introduction of the planned economy and the so-called *socialist reconstruction*, from 1953 to 1956. Later on, during the 1960s, "some individual business households were established, but until the end of 1978, only about 150,000 existed in the whole country".[70] The Third Plenum of the Chinese Communist Party (CCP),

[63] Hsu (2009, p. 7).

[64] Adams and Fitchett (1992b, p. 3).

[65] Tsai (2002), Jiang (2009a).

[66] Jiang (2009a, p. 14).

[67] Jiang (2009a, p. 18).

[68] Jiang (2009a, p. 34).

[69] CBRC (2014, p. 24).

[70] Liu (2003, p. 1).

in 1978, marked a turning point for the reputation of private enterprises and individual business operations, which until then were considered "the root of evil behavior—the so-called 'Capitalistic tail'".[71] A second milestone was set by Deng Xiaoping's *journey to the South*, in 1992, which further encouraged private business development. From 1992 to 1993, private firm development increased by more than 70%, leading to a number of 238,000 POEs. For 2010, Liu extrapolated a figure of 1.76 million POEs.[72] Yet, according to Wang (2013), by 2010 there were more than 430 million POEs in China.[73]

Comparing data on privately-owned enterprises, one needs to be aware of the underlying categorisations that the respective statistics are based upon. In line with most Chinese statistics since the late 1980s, Wang (2013) distinguishes between so-called *small-scale private enterprises* (*geti qiye [个体企业]*), *regular private enterprises* (*siying qiye [私营企业]*) and *non-state-owned enterprises* (*minying qiye [民营企业]*). *Geti qiye* describes privately-owned enterprises of up to eight employees, whereas *siying qiye* refers to private businesses with more than eight employees. *Minying qiye* literally means "enterprise run by the people", and besides private enterprises also includes collective enterprises.[74] Besides, some statistics further differentiate *minying* companies with a "narrow", "inner" and "broad" definition. The category of "narrow minying" (*xia minying [狭民营]*) only includes small-scale and regular private enterprises; "inner minying" (*nei minying [内民营]*) further includes collective businesses and joint stock companies; and "broad minying" (*guang minying [广民营]*) further includes private companies with foreign investment. Figure 4.2 (Wang 2013, p. 70; Fischer 2006, p. 311) depicts this classification of Chinese companies. Data on the finances of POEs reveal that their access to formal finance decreases with their degree of privatisation. Although the situation has slightly improved over the last years, *small-scale* and *regular private enterprises* only to a small share rely on bank loans (see Table 4.1 (Wang 2013, p. 70)).

According to the *2013 Annual report on China's non-state-owned economy*, the number of Chinese *small-scale private enterprises* and *regular private enterprises* has increased by a multiple from 2002 to 2012 (see Table 4.2 (Wang 2013, pp. 25–30)). At the same time, the total amounts of registered capital of both groups of enterprises increased only moderately. Still, Chinese POEs, in comparison to SOEs, have disproportionally contributed more to China's GDP. For instance, in 2011, China's *minying qiye* generated 54% of the countries GDP, whilst obtaining only 10% of overall bank loans.[75] As mentioned above, Chinese POEs compete with SOEs for credit. More often than not, they are discriminated against the latter

[71] Liu (2003, p. 2).

[72] Liu (2003, p. 3).

[73] Wang (2013, pp. 25; 30).

[74] A clear categorisation of Chinese enterprises is provided by Fischer (2006).

[75] Wang [王思惟] (2015b, p. 304).

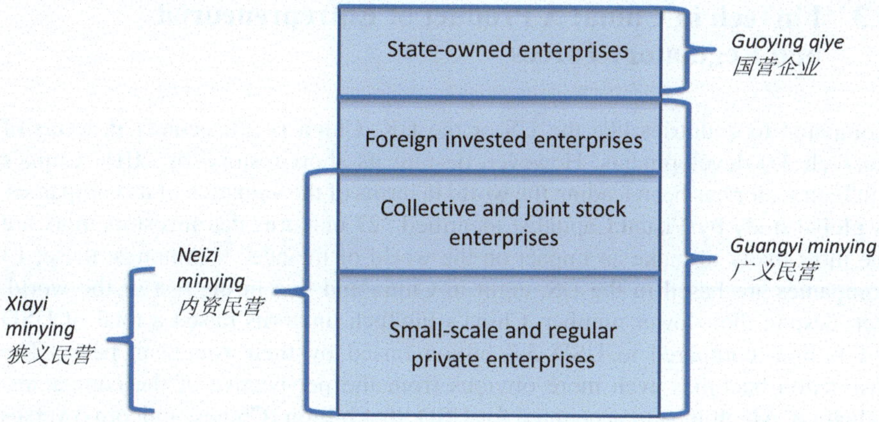

Fig. 4.2 Classification of Chinese state-owned enterprises and privately-owned enterprises

Table 4.1 Share of bank loans of total capitalisation of Chinese POEs

Classification of POEs	2007	2008	2009	2010	2011	2012
Xiayi minying	13.5	13.0	13.7	14.8	16.6	17.5
Neizi minying	49.8	53.0	53.1	55.9	48.0	48.9
Guangyi minying	59.2	61.1	57.7	60.7	65.7	65.7

Table 4.2 Numbers of small-scale private enterprises and regular private enterprises and their capitalisation

Corporate form	Factor	2002	2012
Small-scale POEs	Number of enterprises (in mn)	37.82	197.67
Geti qiye	Total registered capital (in bn RMB)	237.78	405.93
Regular POEs	Number of enterprises (in mn)	2.48	31.10
Siying qiye	Total registered capital (in bn RMB)	26.38	108.57

as "70% of all financial resources are under the control of state-owned banks".[76] As the number of these companies and their capitalisation has increased substantially from 2002 to 2012 (see Table 4.2) despite financial discrimination, *small-scale* and *regular private enterprises* apparently have financed their businesses with other funds than formal bank loans. Thus, they either have lived on retained profits or relied on informal financial sources. Besides, with the advent of internet finance, Chinese POEs have further (i.e. online) funding options.

[76]Jiang (2009a, p. 33).

4.3 FinTech in China: A Product of Entrepreneurial and Regulatory Forces

Compared to countries like the US or the UK, China is a latecomer in terms of FinTech 3.0 developments. However, despite its short history, by 2016, China's FinTech sector has been leading the world in terms of the valuation of its companies. A global study by Visual Capitalist identified "27 unicorns that investors think are the most likely to make an impact on the world of finance".[77] Amongst these, 14 companies are based in the US, eight in China and five in the rest of the world. Yet, despite their lower number, China's FinTech unicorns raised a total of USD 9.4 billion, compared to USD 5.7 billion raised by their American peers. The distinction becomes even more obvious from the perspective of the companies' valuation, which in sum accounted for USD 96.4 billion (Chinese unicorns) versus USD 31 billion (American unicorns).[78] Thus, in the long run, global developments in FinTech are likely to be shaped by Chinese players.

That FinTech in China in fact has already leapfrogged Western countries, can be ascribed to the underlying drivers of this industry. Whilst in the West, recent developments were catalysed by the global financial crisis (see Sect. 2.5), modern FinTech in China is not a post-crisis phenomenon. It is rather a product of entrepreneurial and regulatory forces. On the one hand, Chinese internet corporates are aggressively entering the financial market. On the other hand, China's government supports their endeavours for several reasons. First, it knows about the lack of finance for SMEs and households. Secondly, internet corporates like *Alibaba*[79] have more experience with consumers compared to domestic banks. Thus, Arner et al. (2015) even claim that China like some other emerging markets has already approached the era of FinTech 3.5.[80]

Economic development usually is accompanied by financial development, yet, in China the latter lags behind overall development. Some authors argue that "[t]he lack of financial infrastructure is the driving force behind [China's] fintech innovation."[81] Infrastructure first of all refers to the availability of financial services. According to the World Bank, China's ratio of commercial bank branches per 100,000 people is far lower than in Germany or the US. Likewise, relative to its population also the number of bank ATMs is comparably low (see Table 4.3 (World Bank n.d.)).[82] Until recently, only few Chinese held a bank account. Although since 2011, this number has been increasing a lot, by 2014 there were still "234 million

[77] Desjardins (2016, n.p).

[78] Ibid.

[79] *Alibaba* is China's largest e-commerce provider.

[80] Arner et al. (2015, p. 20).

[81] Moon (2016, n.p).

[82] World Bank (n.d.).

Table 4.3 Indicators of financial infrastructure in China versus the US and Germany[a]

Indicator	China	US	Germany
Commercial bank branch per 100,000 people	8.1	32.4	14.5
Bank ATM per 100,000 people	55.0	173.0	118.2

[a]The figures of commercial bank branches are from 2014 (China and the US) and 2013 (Germany) respectively. The figures of bank ATMs were from 2014 (China), 2009 (the US) and 2013 (Germany) respectively

unbanked Chinese adults".[83] China is unlikely to catch up in the traditional financial service sector, including credit cards, universal investment products and savings accounts. However, according to Moon (2016), "the absence of these products is [. . .] the root of innovation in China".[84] Moreover, for unbanked people, compared to people who are used to relying on formal means, alternative financial services include less transaction costs as they incur no costs that derive from a change in existing habits. Thus, in the end, China's underdeveloped financial sector in fact has emerged as promoter for the FinTech sector.

In addition, FinTech development in China is boosted by active government support and the dominance of its informal finance sector. As illustrated in Sect. 4.2, informal finance in China seems to be a sufficiently well-performing system. It therefore is an essential resource for entrepreneurs and an important institution for the economy. However, the central government regards informal finance with suspicion. One underlying reason for this is the fact that formal finance is often channelled to the informal sector and vice versa, threatening financial stability.[85] In addition, from the outside, informal finance is rather opaque. This undermines the state's aspiration to control the financial sector. Therefore, as the formal financial sector cannot meet overall financial demand and informal finance seems to be not the most favoured solution to fill this gap, the Chinese government has started to push internet finance or FinTech respectively.

As mentioned above, China's FinTech sector is dominated by established internet corporates, rather than by tech-savvy start-ups.[86] Above all, *Baidu*,[87] *Alibaba* and *Tencent*[88] (also known as BAT[89]) dominate the Chinese market. Despite having their core businesses in different sectors, all these corporates since recently have an own financial arm, which successfully complements their respective business model. *Alibaba*'s financial arm, *Ant Financial*, as of September 2016 has been the most

[83]Duflos and Klapper (2015, n.p).

[84]Moon (2016, n.p).

[85]Wai (1992, p. 342 ff), Elliot et al. (2015).

[86]Chan (2016, n.p).

[87]*Baidu* is the Chinese pendant to the search engine *Google*.

[88]*Tencent* is a provider of games and social media.

[89]*BAT* by 2015 has become a popular acronym for the three internet service providers made up from the initials of *Baidu*, *Alibaba* and *Tencent*.

Table 4.4 The world's most prospective FinTech unicorns in terms of valuation[a]

Rank	Company	Capitalisation in billion USD	Valuation in billion USD
1	Ant financial	4.5	60.0
2	Lufax	1.7	18.5
3	JD finance	1.0	7.0
10	ZhongAn insurance	0.9	2.0

[a]Desjardins (2016)

promising FinTech unicorn in the world (see Table 4.4), with a market capitalisation of USD 4.5 billion and an estimated value of USD 60 billion.[90] *Tencent* is a shareholder of the world's FinTech number three, *JD Finance*, which offers a variety of online financial services. Moreover, *Alibaba* has another affiliate FinTech unicorn among the global top ten, *ZhongAn Insurance*, which holds a promising future. Even though, there are also some less established companies amongst Chinese FinTech champions, often these are backed or have been partly acquired by one (or several) of China's internet giants. I will further refer to this aspect in Sect. 4.4.2.

Like their Western peers, China's FinTech companies primarily address SMEs and households, and people who are less well-off. KPMG China (2016) in its recent FinTech report on China's leading 50 companies discovered that new financial technologies are mainly used in the fields of *consumer finance, lending to small and micro businesses, lending to SMEs, personal finance and wealth management, personal insurance products* and *comprehensive personal financial services*.[91] Of the six categories of FinTech identified by Arner et al. (2015),[92] China's FinTech unicorns are said to focus on *online payments* and *lending*,[93] which make up to 80% of their value.[94] More often than not, Chinese FinTech companies "focus[...] their attention on underbanked communities including students, blue-collar workers and rural residents."[95] Once these groups of people have better access to finance, they can contribute to China's economic development. Presumably, this is a strong argument for the Chinese government to support recent FinTech developments.

KPMG further analysed the underlying idiosyncrasies of Chinese FinTech companies. Thereby, it identified *big data* and *big data analysis* as the most

[90]The second rank is held by *Lufax* or *Lu.com* respectively, China's second largest P2P platform, which is an associate of the *Ping An Insurance Group*.

[91]KPMG China (2016, pp. 10–12).

[92]See Sect. 2.5,"(1) finance and investment, (2) operations and risk management, (3) payments and infrastructure, (4) data security and monetization, [...] (5) customer interface, [...] [and (6)] the use of technology in regulation itself" (Arner et al. 2015, p. 18).

[93]Chan (2016). Thus, according to the categorisation by Arner et al. (2015), Chinese FinTech companies focus on category (3) and (1).

[94]"[I]nsurance, enterprise/software-as-a-service, financial services and consumer financing account for the remaining 20%." Linnane (2016, n.p.).

[95]KPMG China (2016, p. 10).

prevailing business models of the analysed companies (see Fig. A.1). In terms of their core technologies, again *big data* and *data analysis* dominated by far before *quantitative models*, *mobile computing* and other technologies such as *cloud services*, *blockchain* and *internet of things*.[96] Big data supports FinTech companies to estimate their clients' creditworthiness and reliability. Apparently, big data analysis enables FinTech companies to serve the allegedly difficult clientele.

Crowdfunding mirrors the recent developments in FinTech, and originally crowdfunding belongs to the category of finance and investment (see Arner et al. 2015). However, the Chinese versions of crowdfunding, besides finance and investment, are also closely related to other fields of FinTech, above all, to e-commerce, payments and customer interface. All of the latter are driven by mobile internet applications.[97] Thus, I argue that in particular these interdependencies characterise the development of crowdfunding in China. The following chapter will therefore first sketch China's internet industry and the ecosystem of China's internet corporates, and thereupon elaborate China's mobile internet sector, its e-commerce industry, and also its payments market. Based on these findings, the role of crowdfunding in China becomes more obvious.

4.4 China's Internet Industry

Yueguo changcheng, zou xiang shijie. (Across the Great Wall, we reach the world.)[98]

This was the heading of China's first email in 1987, which was sent from scientists of a Beijing research project to their cooperation partners at Karlsruhe University in Germany.[99] Eight years later, the internet was opened to Chinese citizens and within only 5 years, by 2000, China had 22.5 million internet users, compared to 95.1 million American netizens at that time.[100] Since then, the "[i]nternet has become a key sector that affects the development of [China's] society and economy and changes people's lifestyle".[101] By the end of 2014, the China Internet Network Information Center (CNNIC) registered 649 million internet users, which then accounted for a 47.9% penetration rate of the entire country,[102] and more than one fifth of the entire number of global internet users. As a comparison,

[96] KPMG China (2016, p. 8).
[97] Arner et al. (2015, p. 19).
[98] 越过长城，走向世界. Wang [王珊] (2014a).
[99] China Education and Research Network[中国教育和科研计算机网] (2001).
[100] Pingdom.com (2010).
[101] China Internet Network Information Center (2015, preface).
[102] China Internet Network Information Center (2015, p. 1).

India, for instance, had about 243 million netizens in 2014,[103] and the world's average internet penetration was at 46.4% in November 2015.[104] The importance of the internet for China and vice versa becomes obvious not least from the fact that "Chinese is the second most widely used language on the internet".[105]

Besides density and the high absolute numbers, the dynamics and growth rates of China's internet are of equal importance. Within only 4 years, between 2010 and 2014, China's internet user base grew by 42%,[106] primarily connecting the urban population to the World Wide Web.[107] Even though growth rates of new internet users have slightly declined as the market is maturing, the ubiquity of the internet in daily life cannot be denied: cities like Beijing and Shanghai already demonstrate a rate above 70%. Although provinces further towards the West and South like Yunnan or Sichuan have internet penetration levels below national average,[108] even their rates are higher than the average national penetration rates in many other developing countries.[109]

Chinese netizens are young, well-educated and well-endowed. According to the CNNIC, in 2014, the typical Chinese internet user was between 20 and 29 years old (31.5%), holding a secondary level education (88.9%), and was either a student (23.8%), self-employed (22.3%), or a manager/staff member of an enterprise (17.0%). Chinese netizens were amongst those with the highest monthly income levels ranging from RMB 2001–3000 (18.8% of all netizens), RMB 3001–5000 (20.2%), and above (14.4%).[110] On average, a Chinese netizen in 2014 spent 26.1 h online on a weekly basis,[111] compared to 13 h of an average German adolescent[112] and 22.4 h of the average German youth.[113] The profile of the typical Chinese netizen is likely to alter over time, not least due to demographic changes. In any case,

---

[103]Internet Live Stats (n.d.).

[104]Internet World Stats (n.d.).

[105]So and Westland (2010, p. viii).

[106]Own calculation based on China Internet Network Information Center (2011) and China Internet Network Information Center (2015).

[107]By 2014, China's internet users comprised to 72.5% of urban netizens. Although the government puts a lot of effort in establishing internet infrastructure in rural regions, the rural-urban gap in terms of internet penetration is widening (China Internet Network Information Center 2015, p. 31).

[108]China Internet Network Information Center (2015, p. 29).

[109]See Internet World Stats (n.d.).

[110]China Internet Network Information Center (2015, p. 32 ff).

[111]China Internet Network Information Center (2015, p. 37).

[112]Statista Inc. (2016c).

[113]Statista Inc. (2016f). Unfortunately, there are no numbers on German netizens between the age of 20 and 29, whose internet usage is probably higher than the one of the average German adolescent or teenager.

there is an emergent and aspiring group of *digital natives* and *digital immigrants*,[114] which will shape China's new society.

Although the internet is an American invention, which from there was imported to China, "the character of the Chinese internet, and the experience for China's internet users, is likely to remain substantially different from the experiences of those in the West."[115] First, this stems from the fact that most "Chinese internet users [are] young people looking for fun".[116] Whereas in America, 70% of all netizens are elder than 30 years, the Chinese internet community looks just the opposite. Secondly, Americans rather search the internet for information, e.g. on topics like mortgage, insurances or diseases. Chinese youngsters, on the other hand, search for entertainment and a contrast to their real life, which partly explains the success of companies focussing on gaming, community and communication tools being amongst China's top internet companies.[117] Thirdly, China's internet and its netizens not least differ from the West in that China's internet corporates differ substantially from their Western counterparts.

China's internet corporates are very profitable, they contribute progressively more to China's economic growth and thus are very attractive for investors. By 2025, the internet industry is estimated to create 46 million new jobs in China.[118] Although in 2013, the internet sector's share of China's GDP was only 4.4% and thereby fifth in the world,[119] it is expected that the share will rise to a percentage between 7.0% and 22% by 2025. In that case, the internet sector would contribute between 0.3% to 1.0% to China's overall economic growth rate.[120] "In 2014, the Top 100 [Chinese internet] companies generated RMB 573.5 billion[121] in revenue, [which] [...] increased by 47%"[122] from the previous year. Rising gains simultaneously increase expected returns. In the first half of 2015, VCs and PE companies invested USD 6.6 billion into Chinese internet companies, which operate in the fields of "E-commerce, Online Education, Internet Services, Online Entertainment, Social

---

[114]"Digital native is a term coined by Mark Prensky in 2001 used to describe the generation of people who grew up in the digital age. Digital natives are comfortable with technology and computers at an early age and consider technology to be an integral and necessary part of their lives. Teenagers and children today are generally considered to be digital natives as they mainly communicate and learn via computers, SMS, and texting. The opposite of digital natives is digital immigrants—people who have had to adapt to the new language of technology" (Investopedia n.d.).

[115]So and Westland (2010, p. ix).

[116]So and Westland (2010, p. 121).

[117]Ibid.

[118]McKinsey Global Institute (2014, p. 6).

[119]UK's internet, in 2013, economy generated 6.7% of its GDP, followed by South Korea (5.9%), Japan (5.6%), Sweden (5.0%) and China (4.4%) (Kwan n.d.).

[120]McKinsey Global Institute (2014, p. 13).

[121]This equals to USD 87.2 billion and EUR 79.9 billion as of 2016-01-28.

[122]Niko Partners (2015, n.p).

Table 4.5 Top ten global internet companies in terms of market capitalisation as of 2014

Rank	Company	Market capitalisation in bn USD	Headquarters
1	Google	390.5	US
2	Facebook	193.9	US
3	Alibaba	165.0	China
4	Amazon.com	149.6	US
5	Tencent	147.6	China
6	Baidu	73.9	China
7	ebay	63.3	US
8	The Priceline Group	60.5	US
9	Yahoo!	42.3	US
10	JD.com	39.5	China

Media, Internet Marketing and Internet Finance".[123] The lion's share of these investments (33%) went to e-commerce,[124] which reflects the sector's relevance and its promising future. China's largest internet companies are well-endowed in terms of market capitalisation. On a global base, there were four Chinese players amongst the Top 10 internet companies as of 2014 (see Table 4.5 (China Daily 2014b)).

The growth of China's internet market happened not by chance but was boosted by several players. First, Chinese network operators accelerate the facility of 4G systems and lately provide much more flexible and user-friendly service packages like combinations of "Fixed-line Broadband + Mobile Communication",[125] which eventually attract more netizens. Secondly, China's internet was mainly steered by the government. The latter from early on has put the development of the internet on its political agenda and authorities are actively promoting the internet industry. Thirdly, internet giants like *BAT* determine public discourse and eventually convince non-netizens to familiarise themselves with the internet.[126] The second and the third aspect are further elaborated in Sects. 4.4.1 and 4.4.2.

4.4.1 The Role of the Government

China's government was and is the major driving force behind the development of China's internet sector. In contrast to e.g. the US, where the internet developed from the private sector, China has followed a stringent and centrally planned strategy. "This state-precipitated development of the Internet [...] ensured the state

[123]PricewaterhouseCoopers Zhong Tian LLP (2015, p. 27).

[124]Own calculation based on PricewaterhouseCoopers Zhong Tian LLP (2015).

[125]China Internet Network Information Center (2015, p. 25 ff).

[126]Ibid.

ownership and control of main Internet infrastructure and the use of Internet."[127] Since the government is aware of the economic gains that the internet can yield, it has actively promoted the internet sector with respective planning and regulation. Against the background of the government's intention to develop a new growth model driven by domestic consumption, the internet plays an essential role. The more Chinese have access to internet services like internet finance and e-commerce, the more domestic consumption will increase. Yet, internet promotion in China has always come along with tight control as the internet should develop "without destabilizing the country".[128]

China's internet development followed the government's plans. In its 9th Five-Year Plan (1996 to 2000), the government "set the goal of facilitating national economic informationization through rigorous development of the Internet."[129] The subsequent Five-Year Plan (2001 to 2005) defined "electronic government, electronic commerce, and the software industry as the development priorities".[130] Thereafter, the 11th Five-Year Plan (2006 to 2010) stipulated "the integration of the networks of telecommunications, radio, television and the Internet."[131] In the 12th Five-Year Plan (2011 to 2015), the building of a new generation IT industry, including a new generation of the internet, was stressed.[132] Moreover, in March 2015, China's premier, Li Keqiang, announced the *Internet Plus Action Plan* to "integrate mobile Internet, cloud computing, big data and the Internet of Things with modern manufacturing, to encourage the healthy development of e-commerce, industrial networks, and Internet banking, and to help Internet companies to increase their international presence."[133] The recent Five-Year Plan (2016 to 2020) stresses the establishment of a *cyber economy* with a focus on big data and information security.[134] In the end, the strengths of China's internet today can be traced back to the foci the Chinese government set in the past.

China's internet sector is highly regulated and marked by censorship. Liang and Lu (2010) mention three features which characterise China's internet regulation, namely the great firewall, self-censorship and multidimensional regulations.[135] The great firewall is an installation that enables supervision at the infrastructure level. Agencies that establish internet interconnecting networks need to be approved by the government, all private internet service providers need to hold a licence from such an approved agency, and all internet users need to register with internet service providers before accessing the internet. Thereby, control is affected on several

[127]Liang and Lu (2010, p. 105).

[128]Tan et al. (1999, p. 44).

[129]Shao (2012, p. 46).

[130]Ibid.

[131]Ibid.

[132]Gov.cn (2011).

[133]English.Gov.cn (2015, n.p).

[134]The People's Republic of China (2016, pp. 99–109).

[135]Liang and Lu (2010, p. 105).

levels. The government has proclaimed nine categories of potential violations by internet users, for instance, the distribution of information that harms the interests or reputation of the state. Besides, there are some sensitive topics like the *Falun Gong* or *Taiwan* which are filtered or simply blocked by the firewall.[136] In addition, an internet police force supports the government with surveillance. However, as most Chinese netizens are aware of domestic internet regulation and potential consequences of a violation, they often comply with the regulation by self-censorship. "Given the broad and vague nature of government regulations, many [Chinese] decide[...] to play safe and end up with even more sweeping censor mechanisms".[137] Another aspect is the multidimensionality of China's internet regulation. There are several actors involved in internet regulation, e.g. the Ministry of Information Industry, the State Council, the Ministry of Public Security, the State Secrets Bureau, etc., and often their responsibilities overlap. Moreover, some laws and regulations are redundant, others are ambiguous and others lead to confusion. Whilst this regulatory structure may enable comprehensive internet control, it also creates some inefficiencies and destruction.[138]

Irrespective of efficiency and effectiveness, authorities justify regulation and censorship with internet security. The 13th Five-Year Plan stresses the protection of data resources and the establishment of cyberspace governance to, for instance, "clear out illegal and bad information".[139] However, the definition of bad and illegal issues falls to agencies appointed by the government. Therefore, it is questionable whether instalments like the *social credibility system*[140] serve national security or rather the interests of the Chinese government (Denyer 2016).

Internet regulation and restrictions do not only affect Chinese netizens, but also online providers, in particular foreign ones, whose websites are not accessible via a Chinese server. Prominent examples are the American social network *Facebook* or *Alphabet Inc.'s* internet service provider *Google*, which both can only be accessed within China via a Virtual private network (VPN).[141] One consequence of this censorship is the emergence of Chinese equivalents, i.e. Chinese companies, which

---

[136]For more information on internet censorship in China see e.g. Becker (2011) or Shi-Kupfer (2015).

[137]Liang and Lu (2010, p. 107).

[138]Liang and Lu (2010, pp. 105–109).

[139]The People's Republic of China (2016, p. 107).

[140]In the 13th Five-Year Plan, the idea of a *social credibility system* is elaborated. It aims at the citizens' increased integrity and is based on data "relating to key areas such as government administrative integrity, commercial and business integrity, social integrity, and judicial credibility" (The People's Republic of China 2016, p. 289). The idea is that authorities "will establish a mechanism for encouraging and rewarding those who act in good faith. [...] and establish in every industry a blacklist of enterprises which lack credibility and a mechanism for having them exit the market" (The People's Republic of China 2016, p. 290). This credit system is said to serve an easier and faster evaluation of the creditworthiness of Chinese individuals and companies, however, critics fear that the individual scores could be misused in terms of totalitarian control.

[141]In January 2017, the Chinese government announced that all unauthorised VPNs henceforth are declared illegal (Ye 2017).

provide similar services to their prohibited international counterparts. *WeChat*, a sophisticated hybrid of *Facebook*, *Instagram* and *Twitter*, is such an example. Yet, there are authors who claim that Chinese internet applications like *WeChat* are not mere copies of Western counterparts.[142] They rather argue that "American Internet companies such as Twitter or Facebook-owned WhatsApp take[...] inspiration from the best ideas of Chinese companies such as Sina Weibo or Tencent's WeChat."[143] I will discuss this issue more in detail below. All in all, despite the government's harsh controls, the Chinese internet sector has developed affluently, but in a kind of parallel universe.[144]

The Chinese government appreciates its internet giants, and despite rare controversy on certain issues—e.g. *Alibaba*'s dispute with Chinese regulators on counterfeit products on *Taobao*[145]—China's big internet corporates enjoy relatively great freedom. However, all Chinese private companies of respectable size need the support of the authorities in order to prosper. Therefore, successful entrepreneurs try to keep a harmonious relationship with the local and central governments. For example, "Tencent's [CEO] Pony Ma and Xiaomi's[146] [CEO] Lei Jun are members of the country's parliament, the National People's Congress, and Baidu's [CEO] Robin Li is a member of the Chinese People's Political Consultative Conference".[147] Such engagement can ensure some governmental patronage and at the same time demonstrates the entrepreneurs' interest in political issues. At the same time, "the government expects loyalty, particularly in politically sensitive areas".[148] Still, China's big internet corporates indeed have influence on the political setting.[149] In sum, the companies' freedom of action and political influence ultimately derives from their size and impact on the Chinese market, in particular, on China's consumerism and therefore, on their impact on China's GDP.

4.4.2 The Ecosystem of China's Internet Giants

> [In the West,] the Internet hasn't fundamentally changed which kind of companies remain on top. Banks and financial companies still dominate finance, automotive companies remain carmakers, energy companies are still energy companies. In China, however, [...] we not only see online businesses jumping into finance, logistics, and the media, but

[142]See e.g. So and Westland (2010, p. v), Tse (2015).

[143]Tse (2015, p. 191).

[144]Fischer (2014, p. 492).

[145]Congressional-Executive Commission on China (2015).

[146]*Xiaomi [小米]* is a leading Chinese mobile phone producer.

[147]Tse (2015, p. 81).

[148]Tse (2015, p. 80).

[149]Interview with Sean (founder of the Chinese CFP *I fund u*), 2015-04-27.

> delivery companies jumping into retailing and e-commerce; battery companies jumping into carmaking; appliance makers reinventing themselves as Internet businesses; and computing, telecom-equipment, and start-up firms all leaping into smartphones, to name just a few.[150]

Whilst there are only few examples like *Alphabet* and *Apple* which pursue a horizontal business expansion approach, China's internet champions apparently follow such an approach by default. Moreover, although the latter operate in different sectors, their businesses often overlap. *Baidu* started out as search engine, whilst *Alibaba* and *JD.com*[151] have their core business in e-commerce. *Tencent*, on the other hand, originally provided games, social media and instant messaging services. By 2016, all of the latter directly or indirectly provided e-commerce, social media, a search engine and, above all, financial services.

China's internet companies are often considered to be copycats of Western counterparts which are prohibited in the PRC[152]—e.g. *Baidu* is said to be the Chinese *Google*, *Alibaba* resembles *Amazon*, and *Tencent* supposedly is a mixture of *Facebook*, *Twitter* and *WhatsApp*. However, Chinese internet corporates differ essentially from their Western peers for several reasons. First and foremost, Chinese corporates are much younger than their Western competitors. Secondly, the role of the government and the interrelation of business and politics is much more distinct in China than in the West. Thirdly, the motivations for the companies' horizontal business expansion are likewise different.[153] A prosperous core business enables Chinese internet corporates to explore new sectors, and acquire and merge with companies of other industries by cross-financing and utilising existing assets. Moreover, a substantially large customer base from the core business ensures broad and fast recognition of their other ventures. Not least, these companies follow the typical Chinese *trial-and-error approach*[154] and thereby foster their omnipresence and overall impact on the internet industry and far beyond.

In fact, *BAT*, and to a certain extent also *JD.com*, have managed to establish robust *business ecosystems*.[155] Taking the examples of *Alibaba* and *JD.com*, one can see that these companies are not just successful e-commerce platforms, but indeed multifaceted corporates which continuously reinvent themselves and eventually have also expanded into the financial service sector. Both companies started out with financial services in the early 2010s and since then have spurred the expansion of their financial arm. Thereby, they can rely on an abundance of customer data which they gather from their respective e-commerce business. Besides a range of

[150]Tse (2015, p. 186).

[151]*JD.com* is China's number four, see Table 4.5.

[152]Rabkin (2011).

[153]Backaler (2014, pp. 9–28). The author mentions four reasons why Chinese corporates emerge into horizontally new businesses: uninformed opportunism, competition-driven diversification, the guanxi effect (i.e. the acquisition of a horizontal business is recommended to them), and market driven diversification.

[154]Harford (2011).

[155]Hendrichs (2015).

other services, *Alibaba* and *JD.com*, both also provide crowdfunding. On the one hand, this broadens the companies' ecosystem; on the other hand, it puts crowdfunding in another context. *Alibaba* and *JD.com* have integrated crowdfunding into e-commerce, thus I denominate this type of crowdfunding (CF) as *e-commerce CF*. *Tencent* also supports crowdfunding, though not deliberately and only indirectly via its social medium *WeChat*. Chinese utilise their *WeChat* accounts in order to set up rather private crowdfunding campaigns. I label this type of crowdfunding as *WeChat CF*. In Sects. 5.3 and 5.4 I will discuss both *WeChat CF* and *e-commerce CF* and some further forms of Chinese crowdfunding. In order to illustrate the nature of Chinese corporates and demonstrate how crowdfunding is embedded in their business structures, the following paragraphs depict the ecosystems of *Alibaba* and *Tencent*.

4.4.2.1 Alibaba

> [Alibaba] is a marketplace, a search engine and a bank, all in one.[156]

Alibaba is mainly known for its online retailing platforms, however, the company's success derives from its competitive edge in the three fields of e-commerce, logistics and finance. This triad is also described as *Alibaba*'s *iron triangle*, which fosters the company's uniqueness.[157] Originally, *Alibaba*'s financial and logistics arms supported its e-commerce business. Yet, nowadays the employment of either of *Alibaba*'s services reinforces the usage of the other two: For instance, customers that utilise *Alibaba*'s mobile wallet, *AliPay*, are likely to purchase via one of *Alibaba*'s e-commerce platforms for a matter of convenience. Thereafter, the purchased good is likely to be delivered by one of *Alibaba*'s distribution partners. Thereby, the company has created three individual business branches that automatically boost each other.

Founded in 1999 in Hangzhou (Zhejiang province), by Jack Ma, a former English teacher, *Alibaba Group* envisions "to build the future infrastructure of commerce".[158] At first, Jack Ma intended to create a virtual market place, an online communication platform for small businessmen leaned on a so-called *souq*[159] from ancient Arabic times. This is where the company's name stems from: *Alibaba* is associated with a poor boy who unlatches a hidden treasure with a simple magic formula.[160] Ma's formula for e-commerce was likewise simple: He created a platform where businessmen can directly deal with each other; middlemen subsequently are superfluous and entrepreneurs can make a good living from their

[156] Lajoie and Shearman (n.d., n.p).

[157] Clark (2016, p. 5).

[158] Alibaba Group (n.d.(a).

[159] I.e. market.

[160] So and Westland (2010, p. 79 ff).

trading. Information can be posted individually, instantly and at any time without being centrally controlled. Within the first 3 years, *Alibaba.com* did not charge any fees for its service, but only relied on advertisement. Later on, it introduced several premium membership services, which guaranteed paying traders e.g. a better ranking or the display of product pictures, and which eventually generated some income for *Alibaba*. Luckily, Ma also could convince several investors who believed early in the success story of *Alibaba*.[161]

This venture capital was predominantly used for the establishment of *Alibaba*'s second endeavour, *Taobao*,[162] which was launched in May 2003.[163] Whilst *Alibaba.com* started out as a pure Business-to-business (B2B) platform, *Taobao* originally was a Consumer-to-consumer (C2C) auction site initiated to counterbalance the American platform *ebay* which in the early 2000s had entered China.[164] Eventually, China's C2C market turned out to be even larger than its B2B segment; still, Ma did not charge any fees for *Taobao* services, which amongst others is one reason why *Taobao* finally succeeded over *ebay* in China.[165] "Taobao [...] was quickly adding new features and making its design more and more appealing to Chinese users. It added an online chat function that allowed buyers and sellers to communicate before trading. [...] It made its page design more feminine to appeal to a growing number of female users."[166]

Alibaba's competitive edge in logistics is based on its cooperation with numerous low-cost delivery companies. Notably, *Alibaba* does not employ any own couriers (like e.g. *JD.com*), but instead has jointly established a logistics data platform called *Cainiao Logistics* with its partners. "Cainiao is building a propriety information platform that knits together logistics providers, warehouses and distribution centers across the country [and] Alibaba owns 48% of Cainiao".[167] Furthermore, *Alibaba* does not carry any inventory like e.g. *Amazon*. Instead, the goods are delivered straight from the vendors to the customers,[168] which reduces *Alibaba*'s fixed costs. By means of the data platform Cainiao, delivery services are optimised and transaction costs are reduced, which eventually leads to increased customer satisfaction.

---

[161] So and Westland (2010, pp. 79–92).

[162] *Taobao* [淘宝] literally means *bargaining for treasure*. "Just as Google is synonymous with searching online, in China to "tao" something is shorthand for searching for a product online" (Clark 2016, p. 4).

[163] Alibaba Group (n.d.(b).

[164] In fact, Ma feared that *ebay* could eventually also approach the B2B market (So and Westland 2010).

[165] According to So and Westland (2010, p. 98), "what really caused eBay to lose its dominance in China was its decision to move its technology platform from China to America."

[166] So and Westland (2010, p. 100).

[167] Clark (2016, p. 15).

[168] Clark (2016, p. 5).

In 2004, *Alibaba* set the cornerstone for its financial edge. It integrated an online payment solution, called *AliPay*,[169] which henceforth could be utilised by all *Taobao* customers. When *Taobao* started out, only about 1% of the Chinese population held a credit card, which made e-commerce close to impossible. As China lacked an adequate payment solution, *Alibaba* invented its own. Therefore, on behalf of *Taobao*, Ma started to open bank accounts in major branches in major cities and deposited money in them, which further built the foundation of *Alibaba*'s escrow service. The latter has contributed a lot to enhance customer trust. Once a customer pays via *AliPay*, with the escrow service her money is held in trust by *Alibaba* until the seller has sent the purchased good. Once the buyer has received this good and signalled her confidence to *Alibaba*, the latter transfers the buyer's money to the seller. Other service providers imitated Alibaba's escrow service; however, even today *AliPay* is the most successful payment provider in China (see also Sect. 4.4.5).[170]

Yet, *Alibaba*'s financial edge comprises of much more than just *AliPay* and its eschrow service. The company's financial arm is called *Ant Financial Service Group* or *Ant Financial*,[171] which by 2016 listed eight sub-business units. As before, when Jack Ma had recognised a lack of credit cards and therefore introduced *AliPay*, he identified the lack of financial services as a barrier to SME business on *Alibaba.com*. Therefore, in 2008, he started to provide loans to SMEs built on an own credit rating system. This system was based on "the total value of business [that an entrepreneur] conducted through *Alibaba.com* and the ratings [he] received from [his] customers."[172] By 2014, *Alibaba* had provided USD 2 billion in small commercial loans, with an average amount of less than USD 10,000 and a default rate below 2%.[173]

In line with its e-commerce branch which started out with B2B and subsequently included C2C and Business-to-consumer (B2C) services, *Alibaba* since 2013 has also started to provide consumer finance. *Yu'e Bao* [余额宝] is an online investment fund, which enables consumers to deposit and withdraw money instantaneously via their *AliPay* account. This fund is attractive to consumers because besides this flexibility, *Yu'e Bao* offers far higher interest rates on deposits than established banks.[174] Within the first 10 months, the fund absorbed USD 90 billion of Chinese deposits.[175] Whilst *Yu'e Bao* focusses on savings, since 2015, *Alibaba* also has been

---

[169]In Chinese *AliPay* it is called *Zhifubao [支付宝]*, which literally means "paying for a treasure".

[170]Tse (2015, p. 35 ff).

[171]Its Chinese name is *mayi jin fu [蚂蚁金服]*, which can be translated as "ant money service" (Alibaba Group (n.d.(b)).

[172]Tse (2015, p. 39).

[173]Ibid.

[174]Presumably, *Yu'e Bao* can offer far higher interest rates as it is first of all an online based fund without costs incurred by physical branches. Secondly, investments are likely to be steered by a computer and algorithms, instead of by human beings, which further saves costs.

[175]Cheng (2014, n.p).

Fig. 4.3 Alibaba's core business before its Initial public offering

offering loans via *MyBank*. As one of five privately owned banks which recently have gained a banking licence, *MyBank* is an exclusive direct bank. It provides an interesting alternative to Chinese offline banks as it offers small loans to people who previously had no access to formal finance.

All of *Alibaba*'s financial services are based upon big data analysis and a corresponding credit system. In particular, in 2015, *Ant Financial* launched its subsidiary *Sesame Credit Management Co.*, which then was one of eight institutions that obtained a licence by the PBOC to run proprietary credit rating systems.[176] As Chinese increasingly shop online (see Sect. 4.4.4), in particular via one of *Alibaba*'s platforms, and extensively use online payment systems (see Sect. 4.4.5), in particular *AliPay*, *Alibaba* has plenty of data which can be used to optimise credit rating. In summary, *Alibaba* has created and internalised a comprehensive financial service system including the provision of debt, assets and credit rating.

Until the early 2000s, *Alibaba*'s business resembled an integration of the analogue services of *Amazon*, *ebay* and *PayPal* (see Fig. 4.3 (Spiegel Online 2014)). Since the run-up to its IPO on the New York stock exchange in 2014,[177] the company has started to pursue a horizontal strategy. According to its corporate website, as of 2015 *Alibaba Group* comprises of ten major businesses, which either are affiliates or related companies. Besides its five e-commerce platforms, *Taobao.com* (a C2C platform), *Tmall.com* (B2C), *Alibaba.com* (a global B2B platform), *1688.com* (domestic B2B), and *AliExpress* (B2C wholesale for customers from abroad), and the *Cainiao Logistics* platform, it also includes an online marketing technology platform called *Alimama.com*, an own cloud platform for data management of sellers and third-party customers (*AliCloud* or *aliyun.com* respectively), China's

---

[176]Li (2015b, n.p).

[177]*Alibaba*'s listing on the Wall Street in 2014 surpassed all expectations and was the highest IPO in history then. In total, *Alibaba* collected USD 25 billion with a share price of USD 68. Yet, within the first day of trading, *Alibaba*'s shares exceeded the price of USD 92 (Spiegel Online 2014).

most popular online group buying marketplace called *Juhuasuan.com*,[178] which is comparable to the Western *Groupon*,[179] and its financial arm, *Ant Finance*.

Besides the above mentioned affiliates, *Alibaba* further maintains several strategic partnerships and has acquired stakes in other companies, both in China and overseas, which complement and diversify *Alibaba*'s portfolio. Exemplifying industries are digital mapping,[180] entertainment,[181] mobile browsers,[182] and high-end department stores.[183] *Alibaba* further has a 30% stake in *Sina Weibo*[184] and holds 17% of *Youku Tudou*.[185] *Alibaba*'s operations are not limited to China. With *Tango*, *Alibaba* has invested in a US-based start-up that provides a mobile communication app. Moreover, *Alibaba* has accessed the US gaming industry with an investment in the company *Kabam*.[186] Although the e-commerce giant still focusses on mainland China as this market has not yet matured, *Alibaba* has the assets and also the capabilities to become a true global player.

The complexity of *Alibaba*'s ecosystem becomes clear from Fig. 4.4 (Lajoie and Shearman n.d.). This further reveals that *Baidu*, *Alibaba*, *Tencent* and *Jingdong*, despite the fact that they are all competitors in the Chinese internet industry, are all directly or indirectly cooperating with each other.

Alibaba is a powerful actor within China's economy and lately also within the financial sector. In 1999, Jack Ma started out with 17 peers and within 15 years, he has created a total of 14 million jobs with *Alibaba*.[187] Not least due to this fact, the Chinese government tolerates *Alibaba*'s expansion tour and promotes its path by e.g. issuing the above mentioned licences. Besides promoting the country's economy by pushing consumerism through e-commerce and providing jobs, *Alibaba*, and in particular *Ant Finance*, is transforming China's financial system towards more market orientation. For instance, as *Yu'e Bao* continuously withdraws consumer deposits from state-owned banks, the latter are likely to ultimately increase their interest rates for deposits.[188] In fact, *Alibaba* could evoke some banking reform

---

[178] *Ju huasuan [聚划算]*, which can be translated as "collective calculating".

[179] According to *Groupon*'s website, the platform is "a global leader of local commerce" offering discounts for offline products and services (Groupon 2016).

[180] *Alibaba* holds assets in the company *AutoNavi* (Alibaba Group n.p).

[181] *Alibaba Group* has acquired about 60% in the movie and television producer *ChinaVision* (Alibaba Group n.p).

[182] *Alibaba Group* has fully acquired the company *UCWeb* (Alibaba Group n.p).

[183] *Alibaba* has established a joint venture with Intime Retail Group in order to expand its online-to-offline (O2O) business in China (Alibaba Group n.p).

[184] *Sina Weibo* or *Xinlang weibo [新浪微博]* is China's most popular microblog website, owned by *Sina Corporation*.

[185] "Youku Tudou [优酷土豆] is a leading online video site [comparable to *YouTube*], formed by the March 2012 merger of formally rancorous rivals Youku and Tudou Holdings." Lajoie and Shearman (n.d.).

[186] Lajoie and Shearman (n.d.).

[187] Helft (2014, n.p).

[188] Tse (2015, p. 40).

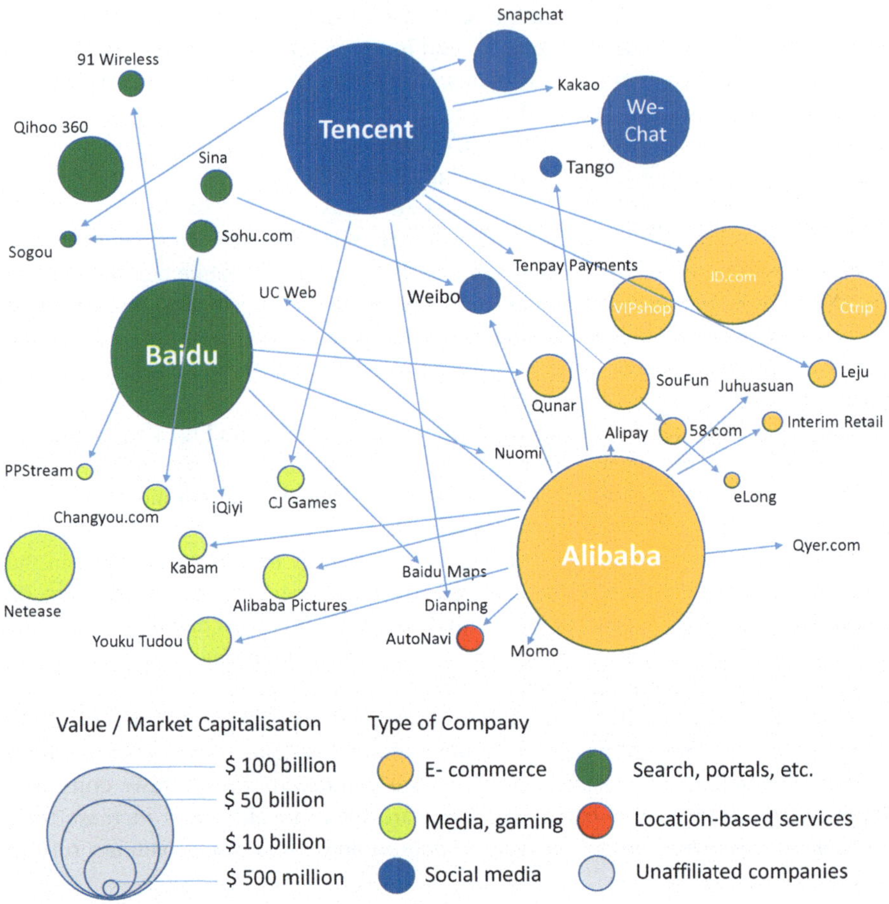

Fig. 4.4 The ecosystem of China's internet giants

from outside the banking sector. In line with this, Jack Ma once referred to his enterprise and stated: "If banks don't change, we will change banks."[189]

4.4.2.2 Tencent

China's number two in terms of market capitalisation, *Tencent*, like *Alibaba* has established a conglomerate of diverse businesses within less than 20 years. Founded in 1998 by Ma Huateng (Pony Ma), the company describes itself as "China's largest

[189]Tse (2015, p. 39).

and most used internet service portal".[190] Indeed, whilst *Tencent* is mainly known for its instant messengers, *WeChat* and *QQ*, its service portfolio further includes entertainment, online payment services, search engines, information security and also e-commerce. The strategic idea behind this diversity is to "provid[e] users with 'one-stop online lifestyle services'".[191]

Pony Ma initially launched the PC-based *QQ* as a copy of the American chat service *ICQ*. When China's state-owned cellphone operators opened their platforms for third parties, in 2000, *mobile QQ* was launched and became a success. Chinese mobile phone users henceforth could communicate with others for a small monthly fee and could exchange data via their phones. In addition, *Tencent* started to offer ring tones, pictures, news and other features for tiny fees and people were willing to pay for these as well. "This became a fundamental strategy for Tencent's future development. It kept adding new services—dating, email, alumni club, portals, auction, search, online games, blogs, etc. Some were for keeping users happy, others were for making money, and some were for both. [...] Some of the trials were not very successful, [...b]ut others became extreme successful."[192] "Almost by chance, Tencent had stumbled over its business model: selling value-adding extras to users of a product giv[en] away for nothing."[193] In sum, Tencent understands quite well to monetise China's unique internet community as its services in particular target on young netizens who are longing for entertainment (see also Sect. 4.4).

In this regard, *Tencent*'s business model is quite unique. In contrast to its local and international competitors like *Baidu*,[194] *Facebook*[195] or *Google*,[196] *Tencent* derives only about 10% of its revenues from advertising; 80% of its revenues are based on value-added services and virtual goods.[197] All of the above mentioned companies have in common that they provide their main services for free, and thereby have established a broad customer base. Yet, instead of relying on advertisement, which creates certain dependencies, *Tencent* has accomplished to offer additional services "such as avatars (icons representing users' identities), virtual pets, and online games"[198] and converts these into cash. Therefore, *Tencent* leads the world's online game market with its affiliate *Tencent Games*.[199] By using *Tencent*'s social media for free, customers become loyal and eventually pay for *Tencent*'s

[190] Tencent (n.d., n.p).

[191] Tencent (n.d., n.p).

[192] So and Westland (2010, p. 116 ff).

[193] Tse (2015, p. 86).

[194] *Baidu*'s revenues as of 2012 comprised of 100% from advertising (The Economist 2013).

[195] *Facebook*'s revenues as of 2012 comprised of about 85% from advertising and of about 15% from e-commerce (The Economist 2013).

[196] *Google*'s revenues as of 2012 comprised of about 88% from advertising and of about 12% from e-commerce (The Economist 2013).

[197] The Economist (2013, n.p).

[198] So and Westland (2010, p. 112).

[199] Business Wire (2014, n.p).

value-added services. In this regard, *Tencent*'s business model is both, quite unique and very successful.[200]

Still, *Tencent* is best known for its instant messengers, *QQ* and *WeChat*, which are not only excessively used by teenagers but also by businessmen. "Many people print their QQ numbers [and/or *WeChat* nicknames] on their business cards as a way of contacting them."[201] Whilst *QQ* used to be China's number one communication app, *WeChat* inexorably is on the rise. The range of Chinese instant messenger providers is broad and competition is fierce; yet, the market is controlled by a few strong players. With about 700 million Monthly active users (MAUs) as of March 2016, the app *WeChat*[202] currently dominates the Chinese market.[203] With a user base of 576 million, *QQ* is ranked second in China. *Alibaba*, has also launched two instant messaging apps: *Momo*, originally a dating app, and *Wangxin*, an app which supports *Taobao*'s e-commerce business by providing a communication tool for its users. However, in terms of MAUs, these two apps are far behind *Tencent*'s success story of *WeChat*. Besides, there are further instant messenger apps, which dominate niche markets as long as they provide some additional value services.[204] Still, from observations of the recent market development, it is likely that *WeChat* will continue to dominate the Chinese market.

The underlying reason behind *Tencent*'s success is *WeChat*'s broad functionality, which is unique not just in China but in the entire internet world. Chan (2016) has described this functionality in the following way:

> Along with its basic communication features, WeChat users in China can access services to hail a taxi, order food delivery, buy movie tickets, play casual games, check in for a flight, send money to friends, access fitness tracker data, book a doctor appointment, get banking statements, pay the water bill, find geo-targeted coupons, recognize music, search for a book at the local library, meet strangers around you, follow celebrity news, read magazine articles, and even donate to charity ··· all in a single, integrated app.[205]

Since 2013, *WeChat* has an integrated payment system called *TenPay* (see also Sect. 4.4.5). *WeChat* users can link their account to their cash card or credit card and make direct and instant transfers to their *WeChat* contacts. *Tencent* has also experimented with offline payments via so-called *QR codes*[206] (see also Sect. 4.4.5). The advantage of *WeChat*-integrated *TenPay* derives from the fact that users do not have to utilise several apps, but instead, they can search, book and pay via one and the same application. Chinese users probably trust *TenPay* as *Tencent* requires an

[200]The Economist (2013, n.p).

[201]So and Westland (2010, p. 118).

[202]In Chinese, *WeChat* is called *Weixin [微信]*, which can be translated as *micro letters*.

[203]Business Insider (2016).

[204]Wan (2015a).

[205]Chan (2016, n.p).

[206]*QR codes* are two-dimensional bar codes which, in contrast to ordinary bar codes, contain horizontal as well as vertical information (Hartz 2013).

authentication for all payments. Last but not least, *TenPay* was highly promoted by *Tencent* with several campaigns (see Sects. 4.4.4 and 4.4.5).

Next to *TenPay*, *WeChat* provides millions of other "apps within an app",[207] which Chan (2016) denominates as *lightweight apps*. On *WeChat* these are called "'official accounts'. Approved by WeChat after a brief application process, there are well over 10 million of these official accounts on the platform—ranging from celebrities, banks, media outlets, and fashion brands to hospitals, drug stores, car manufacturers, internet startups, personal blogs, and more."[208] *WeChat* users can easily connect to such official accounts, which is like "following" an official account on *Facebook* and which replaces the downloading of additional apps. For example, by connecting to the lightweight site of a library, the user is able to directly manage his book orders via *WeChat*, instead of accessing the library via its official website or its app. With *WeChat*, such services are convenient and easy to handle; above all, the app is extremely time-saving.[209]

Whilst the numbers of *WeChat* and *TenPay* users are still growing, *Tencent* tries to keep its cutting edge with research and investments. On the one hand, the company intends to innovate from within, on the other hand, it acquires external assets and capabilities. With more than 50% of the entire staff working in research and development and with research institutes located at several campuses of China's top universities, *Tencent* extensively invests in innovation.[210] Likewise, the company spends large amounts to obtain stakes in firms, which complement its core business. Currently, *Tencent* holds a 37% stake in *Sogou*, a search engine, which is owned by *Sohu.com*, and one of *Baidu*'s major rivals. With a 20% stake investment in *Dianping*, *Tencent* also got access to (the customers of) a popular restaurant reviewing app. It further differentiated its portfolio with investments in several e-commerce companies; presumably not least in order to challenge *Alibaba*'s supremacy. Amongst these investments, *Tencent*'s alliance with *JD.com* or *Jingdong* respectively[211] is the most promising one. Thereby, *Tencent* obtained a 15% stake in *JD.com* for USD 215 million cash. In exchange, *JD.com* received total ownership of two of *Tencent*'s pre-existing e-commerce sites and stakes in a third one.[212] In addition, between 2011 and 2014, "Tencent has spent more than $2 billion on overseas acquisitions".[213] For instance, it invested USD 500 million in a

[207]Chan (2016, n.p).

[208]Ibid.

[209]Own experience.

[210]Tencent (n.d., n.p).

[211]In September 2011, the Wall Street Journal described *JD.com* as "The Biggest IPO You Haven't Heard of" (Chao and Burkitt 2011, n.p). Indeed, few people outside China have heard about *Jingdong*, China's second largest online retailer, though within China, the company is a respectable player.

[212]As *Alibaba*'s major competitor, *Jingdong* is likely to also profit from *Tencent*'s social media prominence.

[213]Tse (2015, p. 135).

28% stake in South Korean based *CJ Games* in 2014.[214] Moreover, *WeChat* already has a growing international user community and according to Tse (2015) it is rather a question of time when it "becomes a global powerhouse".[215] In fact, *Tencent* has managed to establish a diversified ecosystem of various businesses (see Fig. 4.4; the arrows demonstrate investment directions); and aspires to become a global player.

In order to understand the role of crowdfunding, its embedding and integration into other features, this chapter illustrated the complex structures of Chinese internet corporates. The latter are complex ecosystems with commonly one core business and a plurality of other businesses, which not necessarily need to be related to the core business. Initially, "Alibaba, Tencent [and] Baidu [...] all used American-developed business models as inspiration for their own businesses, but then transformed them by adding features appropriate for Chinese users."[216] Several of them have already entered the financial sector, either via a payment solution, the provision of own financial services or through cooperation with existing financial service providers. Some of them also provide crowdfunding, however, crowdfunding often is only a small component within the corporates' broad portfolio of financial services.

4.4.3 China's Mobile Internet Market

> Until recently, each of the BATs occupied its own demarcated space, Baidu in search, Alibaba in e-commerce, and Tencent in online games and messaging. The arrival of the mobile Internet has upset this balance. With more people now accessing the Internet from their phones than from desktop computers, both Alibaba's dominance of e-commerce and Baidu's of search look vulnerable to Tencent, thanks to its near-universal presence of its WeChat messaging app on people's phones and the possibilities this offers the company to link directly to its own e-commerce and other services.[217]

Chinese predominantly access the internet via their mobile phones. In total, the number of mobile internet users grew from 303 million in 2010 to 557 million in 2014, then accounting for 23% of all worldwide mobile internet users[218] and for a share of 85.8% of all Chinese netizens.[219] Putting this number in a global perspective, where mobile phone internet penetration was at 48.8% by 2014,[220] and further considering that those Chinese who for their first time access the internet,

---

[214]Lajoie and Shearman (n.d., n.p).

[215]Tse (2015, p. 139).

[216]Tse (2015, p. 191).

[217]Tse (2015, p. 83 ff).

[218]Own calculation based on GSM Association (2015, p. 3).

[219]China Internet Network Information Center (2011, 2015).

[220]Statista Inc. (n.d.).

Table 4.6 Mobile phone and mobile internet usage in China and the world as of 2014

	China	World
Mobile phone penetration	94.5%	< 40.0%
Share of mobile internet users of all internet users	85.8%	48.8%

predominantly do this via their phones,[221] one can say that China is a true nation of mobile internet users. One driver for this development is China's overall high rate of mobile phone penetration, which was at 94.5% by the end of 2014[222] compared to less than 40% on a global scale.[223] Table 4.6 (Statista Inc. n.d.; China Internet Network Information Center 2015; GSM Association 2015) illustrates these discrepancies. Another driver for the high level of mobile internet acceptance is that mobile internet just better suits the Chinese lifestyle. In particular, urban citizens, who often have to bridge long distances from home to work and correspondingly commute long hours, prefer mobile internet instead of using a desktop computer once they have reached their homes. Thirdly, from my own observations I claim that the popularity of personal internet apps like instant messaging and microblogs has also led to the dominance of mobile internet, whereas both presumably have enforced each other's growth.

Instant messengers are by far the most dominating internet apps in China, in terms of both stationary and mobile internet. In 2014, Chinese netizens used their PC predominantly for online communication tools (90.6%), followed by search engines (80.5%) and online news (80.0%). This situation is reflected in mobile internet apps as 97.2% of Chinese netizens use mobile instant messengers, 77.1% utilise mobile search engines, and 74.6% of all netizens regularly consume mobile Netnews.[224] One could presume that the Chinese are a highly interactive people. Having a closer look, however, reveals that Chinese mobile messengers like *WeChat* are more than just communication apps (see also Sect. 4.4.2.2). "Mobile instant messaging [...] has evolved from a mere communication tool into a user interface for payment, game-playing, O2O,[225] etc."[226] As a consequence, "mobile instant messaging will be of great commercial value for other value-added services".[227]

[221] According to China Internet Network Information Center (2015, p. 26), 64.1% of Chinese new netizens exclusively access the internet via their mobile phones.

[222] China Internet Network Information Center (2015, p. 28).

[223] GSM Association (2015, p. 2).

[224] China Internet Network Information Center (2015, p. 43 ff).

[225] O2O i.e. online-to-offline commerce, which will be further elaborated in Sect. 4.4.4.

[226] China Internet Network Information Center (2015, p. 42).

[227] Ibid.

4.4.4 China's E-Commerce Market

In the U.S., e-commerce is just online shopping. In China, e-commerce is a lifestyle.[228]

According to the 2015 Global Retail E-Commerce Index,[229] China in 2015 was the second most attractive e-commerce market in the world, right after the US.[230] Yet, in terms of market volume, China's e-commerce market in 2015 already surpassed the United States, generating EUR 269 billion in sales.[231] This figure becomes more intriguing against the background that in 2008, China's e-commerce market generated only EUR 16 billion.[232] The growth of China's e-commerce sector has been driven by several factors and actors, which will be elaborated in the following paragraphs.

Predominantly, the evolution of China's e-commerce sector has been pushed and steered by the government. China's 12th Five-Year Plan stressed the importance of raising domestic consumption.[233] Online retailing was a key sector to reach this goal and was meant to contribute a 9% share to overall retail sales by 2015.[234] Shortly after the release of this Five-Year-Plan, guidelines on the online retail market were published in October 2011 and January 2012. Large retail companies were encouraged to install online stores, and third-party transaction platforms were supposed to serve the needs of small and medium merchants.[235] The Chinese government made several efforts to increase domestic consumption. For instance, as a countermeasure to the global financial crisis, it subsidised the purchase of home appliances by rural households. Moreover, in 2012 it invented a so-called *Consumption Promotion Month*, which henceforth was to run from April to May on a yearly basis.[236] In 2014, China's e-commerce penetration rate stood at 55.7%. Within only 1 year, from end 2013 on, China had gained 60 million online shoppers.[237] Although, only about 16% of all retail purchases were conducted online in 2015—compared to e.g. about 50% in Germany, the largest European e-commerce market[238]—these figures were far ahead of the government's prognosis.

---

[228] Jack Ma, the founder of *Alibaba*, made this statement during a keynote speech at the 16th Credit Suisse Asian Investment Conference (PTL Group 2013).

[229] This index is based on the size of the online market, the consumer behaviour, the market's growth potential and the market's infrastructure.

[230] Kearney (2015).

[231] Statista Inc (2016a). By contrast, the US e-commerce market generated EUR 265 billion in 2015 (Statista Inc. 2016b).

[232] Own calculation based on Kearney (2011, p. 2).

[233] Gov.cn (2011).

[234] Li & Fung Research Center (2016, p. 46 ff).

[235] Ibid.

[236] Tse (2015, p. 73).

[237] China Internet Watch (2015f).

[238] Ecommerce News (2015b).

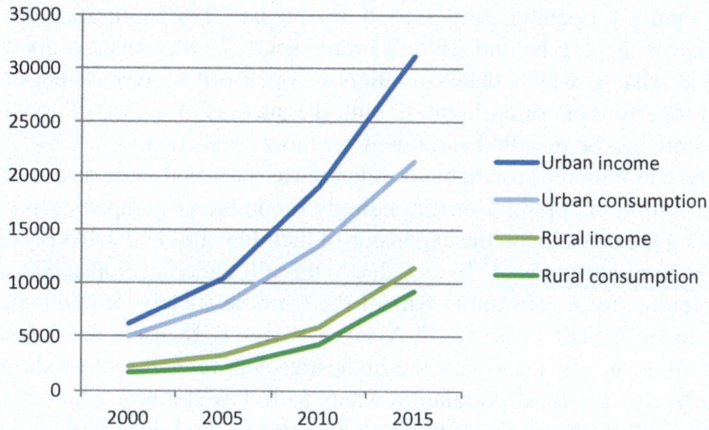

Fig. 4.5 Development of disposable income and consumption of Chinese rural and urban citizens

Table 4.7 China's rural and urban income and consumption from 2000 to 2015

	2000 (in RMB)	2015 (in RMB)	Growth rate
Urban income	6280.0	31,194.8	397%
Urban consumption	4998.0	21,392.4	328%
Rural income	2253.4	11,421.7	407%
Rural consumption	1607.1	9222.6	452%

Secondly, China's overall consumption, and in particular its e-commerce growth, is driven by the increasing income of Chinese consumers (see Fig. 4.5 (National Bureau of Statistics of China 2006, 2016)).[239] As Table 4.7 (National Bureau of Statistics of China 2006, 2016) demonstrates, an urban Chinese citizen in 2015 on average had a yearly disposable income of RMB 31,194.8[240]; and a rural Chinese had an average income of RMB 11,421.7.[241] From 2000, these were cumulative growth rates of 397% (urban) and 407% (rural income).[242] During the same period, urban consumption increased by 328%, which was even surpassed by rural consumption, which increased by 452% from 2000 to 2015.

A third reason for China's growing e-commerce sector is the lack of established offline retail networks.[243] China's overall retail market is quite young considering

[239]Kuo (2016).

[240]This figure equals to USD 4564.5 or EUR 4270.9 as of 18th January 2017.

[241]This figure equals to USD 1671.2 or EUR 1563.7 as of 18th January 2017.

[242]Own calculation based on National Bureau of Statistics of China (2006), and National Bureau of Statistics of China (2016).

[243]Clark (2016, p. 8 ff).

that the country's opening only started in the late 1970s. In fact, the offline retail market is lagging behind China's online spurt.[244] Moreover, property prices in China are rising, which deters retailers to open offline representations.[245] In addition, property rents often increase with the success of a shop.[246] By contrast, an online store can be installed and run at very low fixed costs.

Fourthly, e-commerce growth has accelerated as more and more rural netizens are attracted by online shopping. Correspondingly, e-commerce companies like *Alibaba* and *Jingdong* are investing in the expansion of their logistics and delivery services in order to reach remote areas.[247] In fact, due to the still underdeveloped infrastructure in some regions, for a substantial part of the Chinese society "e-commerce is the only way to fulfil their desires".[248] A survey by A.T. Kearney has revealed that lower tier cities are the ones with the highest growth rates in online shopping.[249] As probably also the rural population wants to follow the new Chinese lifestyle, e-commerce will further increase in line with a rise of rural disposable income.

Furthermore, KPMG has identified four technological drivers of e-commerce growth in China: "e-commerce platforms, social media platforms, digital payments platforms and mobile devices."[250] Not least, e-commerce in China is also driven by low logistic costs,[251] inventions like the *Single's Day*,[252] and by the utilisation of Online-to-offline (O2O) marketing.[253] The following paragraphs will focus on these issues. As payments are central, not just for e-commerce, but also for crowdfunding, a separate Sect. 4.4.5 is dedicated to this topic.

4.4.4.1 Mobile E-Commerce

Mobile e-commerce is the main driver of China's entire online shopping market. In line with the general internet user behaviour, Chinese online shoppers predominantly purchase via their mobile phones. In contrast to Germany and the US, where in 2014 only 10% of all online shoppers utilised their smartphones,[254] in China 34% of all online retail sales derived from mobile (m-) purchases. By 2015, this

---

[244] Lee (2014).

[245] Wei (2013).

[246] Clark (2016, p. 9).

[247] China Internet Watch (2015g).

[248] PTL Group (2013, n.p).

[249] Kearney (2016, p. 3).

[250] KPMG (2014, p. 2).

[251] GO-Globe (2013).

[252] Internet World (2016).

[253] Innovation is Everywhere (n.d.).

[254] Ecommerce News (2015a).

Table 4.8 Distribution of China's online sales via PC vs. mobile devices

GMV (in tn RMB)	2011	2012	2013	2014	2015	2016e	2017e	2018e
PC-based shopping	0.8	1.1	1.6	1.9	1.7	1.6	1.7	2
Mobile shopping	0	0.1	0.3	0.9	2.1	3.4	4.5	5.5

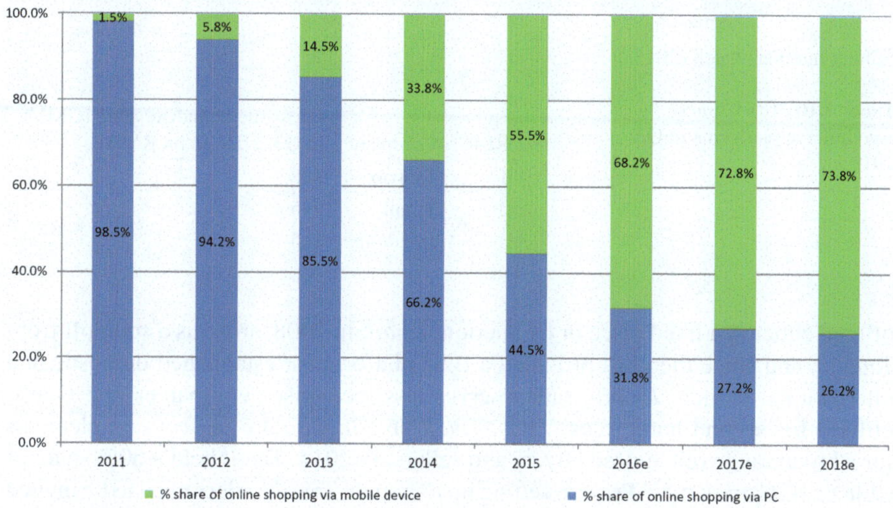

Fig. 4.6 Share of mobile vs. PC-based online sales in China

number had increased to 55.5% totalling to a RMB 2.1 trillion sales volume (see Table 4.8 (iResearch 2016d,e)). iResearch has estimated that by 2018, mobile sales could account for up to 74% of all online sales (see Fig. 4.6 (iResearch 2016e)).[255] With 84.2% market share, *Alibaba* in 2015 dominated China's m-commerce market, followed by *Jingdong*[256] (see Table 4.9).

4.4.4.2 E-Commerce Platforms

China's entire e-commerce market is dominated by *Alibaba*'s two affiliates *Taobao*, and *Tmall* (Table 4.10 (China Internet Watch 2015e (ranks of the companies); Statista Inc. 2016d (GMV of Taobao); Statista Inc. 2016e (GMV of Tmall); China Internet Watch 2015j (GMV of Jingdong))).[257] As stated in Sect. 4.4.2.1, *Taobao* is regarded as the Chinese pendant to *ebay* as it is a platform on which goods are

[255] iResearch (2016e).

[256] Ibid.

[257] In Chinese *tianmao* 天猫, which literally means "sky cat".

Table 4.9 Revenue distribution of China's m-commerce market in 2014[a]

Rank	Company	Mobile Revenue (in bn RMB)
1	Alibaba (Taobao & Tmall)	801.4
2	Jingdong	39.0
3	Slipshod	19.5
8	Amazon	2.8

[a]China Internet Watch (2015a)

Table 4.10 Top Chinese e-commerce platforms in Q3 2015

Rank	Company	Gross merchandise value (GMV) in Q3 2015 (in bn RMB)
1	Taobao	438
2	Tmall	275
3	Jingdong	115

offered either at a fixed price or by auction. *Tmall*, in 2008, arose as a spun off from *Taobao*, and since then has provided a B2C platform for established domestic and international brands. *Taobao* rather serves less recognised companies and is also utilised for second-hand sales. Thus, *Tmall* and *Taobao* are perfect complements for a broad range of Chinese buyers and sellers. In 2014, *Tmall* held a 60% share of China's B2C market.[258] Prior to setting up a shop on *Tmall*, sellers need to be invited to the platform; they pay a deposit in order to be listed and an extra commission for each transaction. *Taobao*, on the other hand, with more than 500 million registered users in 2014 held 80% of the Chinese C2C market, which probably derives from the fact that it does not charge any transaction or commission fees, but instead—as mentioned in Sect. 4.4.2.1—the platform is financed by advertisement.[259]

Alibaba's most challenging competitor, and ranking third in 2015, right after *Taobao* and *Tmall*,[260] is the e-commerce giant *Jingdong* (JD.com). Formerly known as *Jingdong Mall* and *360buy*, *JD.com* is an exclusive B2C online direct sales platform focussing on electronic devices or 3C[261] e-commerce. In 2014, *Jingdong* held an overall market share of about 15%,[262] yet only about 5% of China's mobile shopping market.[263] As mentioned in Sect. 4.4.2.2, *JD.com* in March 2014 has

[258]Wan (2015b).

[259]Wan (2015b), KPMG (2014, p. 3).

[260]China Internet Watch (2015e).

[261]3C stands for computer, communications, and consumer electronics.

[262]KPMG (2014, p. 3), referring to Steven Millward. The primary source unfortunately was not available any longer.

[263]China Internet Watch (2014).

acquired a mobile app from *Tencent*, called *Paipai*; in exchange, *Tencent* gained a 10% stake in *JD.com*, and since then, the two have been cooperating strategically. Just like at *Taobao*, merchants can install small mobile stores within *Paipai*; however, they can only get access by using a *QQ* identification number. As mentioned above, *QQ* belongs to *Tencent*. Therefore, through the interlinkage of *Paipai* with *QQ*, *Tencent* indirectly competes with *Alibaba*'s platforms. Additionally, merchants and sellers can share their latest offers and purchases at their *WeChat* and *mobile QQ* account; moreover, purchases and also payments can easily be cleared via *WeChat*'s payment function, *TenPay*. In fact, *Paipai* targets at the C2C shopping segment, it thus complements *Jingdong*'s B2C business, and thereby *JD.com* directly competes with *Alibaba*'s *Taobao*.[264] With the help of strategic alliances, *JD.com* (and *Tencent*) managed to catch up in the race for Chinese online consumers. Recently, *JD.com* announced that it would terminate the C2C business of *Paipai.com* by December 2015,[265] yet, it will continue the mobile shop provision via *WeChat* and *mobile QQ*.

Besides strategic partnerships, *Jingdong* has increased its market share with slick marketing efforts. One prominent example is the disbursement of so-called *hong baos*.[266] According to China Internet Watch, *JD.com* in 2014 gave out RMB one billion (USD 156 million) in red envelopes to *mobile QQ* users for free.[267] *QQ* users could give these small amounts of money as a virtual gift to their friends, and the latter could e.g. use the money for future purchases at *JD.com*. Thereby, *JD.com* increased customer loyalty in twofold respect as both, the donor and also the final donee of the hong bao, were given *face*.[268] Another effective means to increase its market share that *Jingdong* applies, is *group buying*.[269] Similar to services provided by the American platform *Groupon* and *Alibaba*'s *Juhuasuan*, *Jingdong* provides a discount for certain products and services as long as a sufficiently high number of people is willing to take the offer.[270]

Whereas *Jingdong* ranks behind *Alibaba* in most categories, *Jingdong* excels with its independent logistics system with 196 warehouses in 46 cities, a total of

---

[264]China Internet Watch (2015b).

[265]China Retail News (2015).

[266]*Hong baos (红包)* literally mean *red envelopes*, which Chinese exchange during Chinese New Year or as a gift on other occasions. The envelope commonly contains some money, and the exchange of hong bao between family members and friends has a long tradition in China. China's internet companies have transformed this common ritual and invented the virtual hong bao. Although, *Sina Weibo* and *AliPay* have offered digital hong baos much earlier than *Tencent* or *Jingdong*, virtual hong baos only have become very popular since their integration in *WeChat* (Dong 2014).

[267]China Internet Watch (2014).

[268]According to Ho (1976, p. 883), *face* is "the respectability and/or deference that a person can claim for him/herself from others, by virtue of the relative position he occupies in the social network and the degree to which he is judged to have functioned adequately in the position as well as acceptably in his social conduct."

[269]Group buying is *Tuan gou [团购]* in Chinese.

[270]China Internet Watch (2014).

4760 delivery and pickup stations, and its same-day/next-day delivery programme in 135 counties.[271] *Jingdong*'s relevant impact and reach become clearer once those figures are viewed from an international perspective. *Amazon*, for instance, by 2015 maintained only a total of 121 warehouses.[272] Both, *Jingdong* and *Amazon* run their logistics independently, whilst other players like *Alibaba* voluntarily or compulsorily rely on external logistics providers. Yet, time will show whether *Jingdong* (and *Amazon*) can use this independence to their advantage.

Not least due to the discrimination of international players by the Chinese government (see also Sect. 4.4.2), Chinese e-commerce platforms are often compared to their US counterparts. "*Taobao* versus *ebay*, *JD.com* versus *Amazon*, *Suning*[273] versus *Walmart*".[274] Yet, in fact, Chinese e-commerce companies just like other Chinese internet companies demonstrate distinctive features which make such a comparison rather obsolete. First of all, in contrast to their US peers, Chinese internet companies were only founded around the year 2000, and are therefore still relatively young. Compared to more established companies, young companies tend to be more flexible and thus can adapt much quicker and easier to changing market settings. Secondly, China's e-retailers pursue different business models. Instead of merely building on listing or transaction fees like *Amazon*, China's e-commerce companies mainly rely on advertising models,[275] which is not just accepted by Chinese merchants, but by Chinese customers as well. Thirdly, Chinese online retailers are highly service-oriented[276] and customer-focussed. For instance, they guarantee discounts and free delivery, and offer refunds and free replacement for unsatisfying orders.[277] In 2014, China had already overtaken the US as the biggest online retail market[278] despite the fact that overall (online + offline) retail sales then were still much higher in the US than in China.[279]

Alibaba, *Jingdong* and their peers have managed to evoke trust amongst Chinese consumers which not least is due to their specific terms of payment and delivery. First of all, most e-commerce platforms provide a Cash on delivery (COD) service in addition to online banking, third-party and credit card payment, and in 2011, COD has been the most common payment method in China.[280] Thereby, all risks

---

[271] Wang (2015a).

[272] Of these 121 warehouses 96 ones were located in the US, four in India, nine in Germany and twelve in China (Ahmed 2015).

[273] *Suning [苏宁]* is a Chinese retailer for electrical appliances.

[274] Wei (2013, n.p).

[275] Whereas *Tencent* hardly builds on advertising (see Sect. 4.4.2.2), China's other e-commerce companies predominantly derive their revenues from advertisement.

[276] Wei (2013, n.p).

[277] Clark (2016, p. 6).

[278] China Internet Watch (2015g), Centre for Retail Research (n.d.).

[279] In 2014, overall retail sales were at USD 4.23 trillion in China and at USD 4.79 trillion in the US (own calculation based on China Internet Watch (2015k) and eMarketer Inc (2015)).

[280] Li & Fung Research Center (2016, p. 13).

are outsourced to the seller, and customer satisfaction can be raised. Likewise, the already mentioned *escrow service* (see Sect. 4.4.2.1), which is very popular in China, enhances trust. Thirdly, the integration of e-commerce into instant messengers like *WeChat* enables a direct and immediate interaction between merchants and customers, which reinforces trust. Customers can easily oversee a merchant's offers, his track of records, his existing contacts including customers, and communicate instantaneously with him via the messenger. The merchant, on the other hand, can provide more transparency and evoke trustworthiness through prompt replies and an overall confidential online appearance. Once a merchant lags behind customer expectations, he can easily be degraded, e.g. by a post from a unsatisfied customer. Thereby, he runs in danger to lose his online reputation, not just within the e-commerce platform but also within the interlinked social medium. Such mechanisms are employed to deter fraudulent merchants from dubious offers, and eventually strengthen overall trust in e-commerce.

4.4.4.3 Social Commerce

China's online retail market is not least promoted by social media. "Consumers in China use these platforms for immediate 'buy/don't buy' advice from friends, to post product reviews, and to seek product knowledge/advice from key opinion leaders".[281] Denominated as *social commerce*, merchants provide product information and purchase opportunities in social media like *WeChat* and *Sina Weibo*. Whilst Western social media have experimented with *social commerce* since 2013 and achieved modest to poor results,[282] *social commerce* is very popular and well accepted in China. By contrast, German netizens, for example, perceive advertisement within social media as rather annoying; therefore, ad blockers are quite common there.[283] Moreover, the overall importance of social media for shopping decisions is much less prevalent in Western countries compared to China. A study by Capgemini (2014) has revealed that for Chinese consumers the relevance of social media almost converges with the standing of the traditional store experience.[284] German consumers, in contrast, consider social media as far less central for their shopping decisions, and rather emphasise the offline store experience.[285] Furthermore, China's shoppers do care about their peers' opinion and

---

[281] KPMG (2014, p. 4).

[282] For instance, *Twitter* in summer 2015 introduced a so-called *buy button*; users could offer their products via *Twitter* and interested people could easily buy these within the social medium. However, 1 year later, *Twitter* declared the project as failed (Ptoch 2016).

[283] Henkel (2015, n.p).

[284] In China, social media reached a score of 3.65, whilst the traditional shopping experience scored 4.04, based on a scale from 1=not at all important to 5=extremely important (Capgemini 2014, p. 18).

[285] In Germany, social media scored 2.19, whilst the traditional store experience stood at 4.08 (Capgemini 2014, p. 18).

also like to share their shopping experience. 40% of Chinese consumers regularly read and post reviews on online purchases.[286] Thus, social media contribute a lot to the exponential growth of China's e-commerce market.

4.4.4.4 Cost Advantage and Innovative Capacity

E-commerce in China is affordable due to low shipping costs, which further increases the popularity of e-retailing. One kilogram in China on average costs one USD, whereas American merchants or shoppers have to face about six USD for a parcel of the same weight.[287] Therefore, online shopping in China is a cost-effective and convenient alternative for customers in remote areas with difficult access to specialty shops or well-assorted supermarkets. However, also urban consumers who live close-by shopping centres progressively utilise e-commerce with included delivery service, not just for specialised products but also for daily necessities like food[288] in order to save time and avoid queues.[289] A keyword for this trend is the expansion of *O2O commerce*, which will be discussed below. Ultimately, many Chinese, rural as well as urban citizens, appreciate the advantages of online shopping and prefer it to traditional offline stores, not least due to its high convenience-to-price ratio.

In addition, China's online retail market is a source of innovation and market evolvement. According to a report by China Internet Watch, 22% of all capital spent via online shopping satisfies newly created demand, which so far has not been served by traditional retailers.[290] Moreover, e-commerce giants understand to exploit China-special rituals in order to reinforce shopping behavior. Besides the above mentioned *hong bao*, another prominent example is the so-called *Singles Day*, the 11th of November,[291] a day which originally had been invented by Chinese students in the 1990s to celebrate their singledom. *Alibaba* since 2009 has transformed this day into China's most valuable online sales event providing consumers with rocketing discounts and granting merchants above-average sales volumes, so-called *Double 11 deals*.[292] In 2016, *Alibaba* achieved sales worth of USD 17.8 billion through its e-commerce platforms within that single day.[293] Over the last few years, *Alibaba*'s competitors have joined the *Singles Day*; thus overall sales in China on that day are even higher.

---

[286] GO-Globe (2013, n.p).

[287] Ibid.

[288] China Internet Watch (2015i).

[289] Innovation is Everywhere (n.d.).

[290] China Internet Watch (2015h).

[291] The date of 11th November comprises of four 1s, standing for singles.

[292] dpa (2015), Berke (2015).

[293] Internet World (2016).

4.4.4.5 O2O Commerce: A Trillion Dollar Business

Another example for the innovativeness of China's e-commerce sector is the excessive utilisation of *O2O commerce* by both, Chinese retailers and consumers. Per definition, O2O "is the link between 'online discovery' and actual commerce in the physical world".[294] Yet, the payment transaction commonly occurs already online; therefore, customer data can be tracked easily.[295] Whilst *O2O commerce* is not a Chinese invention but also available in the West, e.g. with *Groupon* or *Uber*,[296] the setting for *O2O* in China is much more favourable. The link between offline and online commerce or services is often established by a *Quick response (QR) code*, which can be scanned by a mobile device. Thereby, a customer e.g. can easily be led from a product image to an online shop within just 1 s or scan respectively.

In contrast to the West, where *QR code* usage is pretty low[297] and seems to be already in decline,[298] Asians excessively use *QR codes* for a variety of purposes.[299] This discrepancy can be attributed to several causes. First of all, Chinese predominantly access the internet via their mobile phones instead of PCs, and for them scanning a *QR code* is much faster and more convenient than typing a long web address with Western characters.[300] Secondly, whereas Western customers need to install an additional app on their smart phone in order to be able to read *QR codes*, Chinese who use the instant messenger *WeChat* automatically hold an integrated *QR code* reader. Thirdly, Chinese use *QR codes* on a daily basis. For instance, every *WeChat* user has her own personal *QR code*, which is like an ID. Instead of typing someone's name and contact number, one can just scan the person's *QR code* and thereby easily get connected. Henceforth, the connected parties have access to each other's *WeChat* profiles, can start chatting, transfer cash, and much more. In sum, for Chinese customers *QR codes* are a convenient and fast tool for a variety of purposes.

To my best knowledge, there are no statistics on the current usage volume of *QR codes*. One census by the mobile coupon company *Imageco* in 2013 counted 113.6 million scanned *QR codes* in China within just 1 month.[301] Another survey assessed a number of 486 billion scanned *QR codes* for the entire year of 2013.[302] As the application of *QR codes* is not exclusive for online retailers and customers, the

---

[294] Innovation is Everywhere (n.d., n.p).

[295] Rampell (2010, n.p).

[296] *Uber* is an online mediation company for private car transportation. It connects private people with cars willing to drive other private people who seek transportation. The latter order and pay online, whilst the actual service is offline. (Own explanation.)

[297] QRC (n.d.).

[298] Morris (2015).

[299] Roselli (2015).

[300] Advertising Age (2014).

[301] Ibid.

[302] 199IT.com (2014).

actual number of uses could theoretically grow infinitely. Western corporates, which operate in China, like *BMW* or *Nike*, have also started to exploit the prominence of *QR codes* for their marketing purposes.[303] Ultimately, *QR codes* link people as well as offline with online actions, and thereby can promote commerce.

O2O commerce is further reinforced by instant messaging and voice-based apps.[304] As mentioned above, merchants and customers can communicate directly, immediate and at no costs via *WeChat* and similar tools, which reinforces overall trust. Different from emails or other text-based software, *WeChat* enables the user to record short voice messages and transfer these directly to his contacts. It is thus not just a fast and easy tool, but also independent from written language. Notably, *WhatsApp*, the Western pendant to *WeChat* also started to provide this voice-feature in 2013,[305] a move which appears to have been a copycat of the Chinese original. All in all, instant voice-based messaging promotes direct communication between buyers and sellers, which contributes to *O2O commerce*.

Last but not least, *O2O commerce* is accelerated by the integration of mobile payment systems in instant messaging and e-commerce. Once people have interlinked their *WeChat* profiles, e.g. via a *QR code*, money can easily be transferred via *TenPay* to other *WeChat* accounts. For example, traditionally, restaurant bills in China are paid by one person (usually the host). More recently, however, Chinese follow the Western style of separate payments. Yet, instead of paying individually, commonly there is still only one person settling the bill; the others thereafter simply transfer their share of the bill to the payer's *WeChat* account via *TenPay*. Nowadays, *WeChat* payment is much more accepted in China than e.g. paying with debit or credit card. In particular, *WeChat* payment is more convenient for vendors as they only need a smart phone compared to some expensive electronic payment devices. Moreover, they can save fees which usually arise with debt or credit card settlements. Therefore, fruit sellers on the street or retailers on China's night markets naturally accept *WeChat* payments, but probably have never accepted any other e-payments before. Taking the example of buying fruits, people can order their daily fruit ration via *WeChat* instant messaging from their trusted street hawker, pay in advance via *TenPay*, and later on either pick it up from the stall or have it delivered straight home. Therefore, the integration of mobile payments in instant messaging in the end promotes *O2O commerce*.

In fact, *O2O* back in 2010 was already considered to be "a trillion dollar opportunity",[306] though experts at that time did not refer to China but to the entire world. However, 6 years later, *O2O* seems to be a niche market in the West, whereas it is omnipresent in China. One explanation for this development probably is the general focus on add-on services by Chinese retailers. For example, newly established supermarkets like *Dmall* in Beijing turn their shopping mall into

---

[303]Ibid.

[304]Innovation is Everywhere (n.d., n.p).

[305]Merz (2013).

[306]Rampell (2010, n.p).

inventory warehouses, which can be accessed online. Customers living close-by place their orders via their smart phone and pay online, and all goods will be delivered within 1 h.[307] Western providers are more likely to charge their customers for such additional services, whilst Chinese expect delivery to be included in the purchase price. In the end, *O2O* and integrated services contribute a lot to the acceleration of Chinese consumption, which is in line with China's 12th Five Year Plan.

Whilst the Chinese government appreciates the increase in domestic consumption, and the e-commerce sector is flourishing, platform providers earn little from the rising online sales. As e-commerce margins continuously decline due to fierce competition, payment systems become more important. This is not a Chinese but a global phenomenon, which can be seen from the example of *PayPal*. Until July 2015, *PayPal* belonged to the e-commerce platform *ebay*. Whilst in 2002, *PayPal* contributed only 16% to *ebay*'s revenues, by 2014, this share had increased to 44%.[308] Likewise, *AliPay* has become of crucial importance for the *Alibaba Group*, and *TenPay* is simultaneously essential for *Tencent*. However, China's payment systems are more than just Chinese equivalents of *PayPal*; they have an even greater impact, not just on e-commerce providers but also on the entire society.[309] The following chapter will discuss this issue further.

4.4.5 China's Payments Market

> [P]ayment is not about replacing cash, and potentially it is not even about payment itself. Instead, it can unlock the key to much bigger revenue generating opportunities such as targeting behaviour for product sales resulting in refined loyalty programmes and better customer insights.[310]

Commerce in China until recently has been dominated by cash payments. Even though China's highest banknote is only RMB 100, which equals to about EUR 14 or USD 15,[311] Chinese rather carried bundles of cash to pay large bills, instead of using a credit card or other electronic (e-) money. Whilst in the West, only a few scholars talk about the abolition of cash,[312] China seems to leapfrog credit cards with third-party payment systems. This development is mainly driven by "young, digital-savvy consumers [...]. Living in a fast-moving economy, Chinese consumers have proven themselves to be early adopters of

[307] Innovation is Everywhere (n.d.).

[308] WalktheChat (n.d., n.p).

[309] Hendrichs (2015).

[310] PricewaterhouseCoopers (2013, p. 1).

[311] This is based on the exchange rate as of 13th December 2015.

[312] E.g. Peter Bofinger (Reiermann 2015).

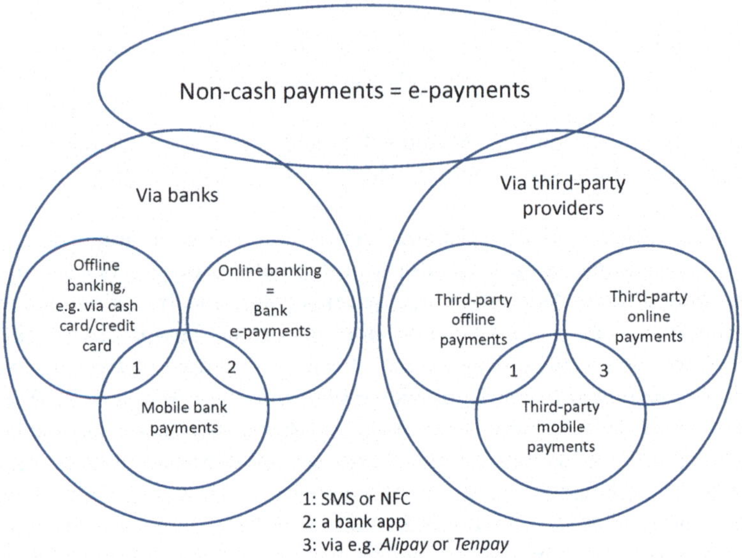

Fig. 4.7 Categories of non-cash transactions

disruptive new technologies."[313] Although Western consumers also have access to similar technologies, they are much more reluctant to change established habits,[314] presumably due to safety concerns and the involved transaction costs.

According to a recent study by Capgemini and the Royal Bank of Scotland (2015), China experienced a growth rate of 37.7% in non-cash financial transactions from 2012 to 2013,[315] and thereby globally ranked fourth, just behind the US, the Eurozone, and Brazil.[316] However, whilst the latter countries are dominated by debit and credit card usage and e-banking, China's recent gain in e-transactions is foremost due to the increased use of third-party payment systems,[317] in particular online and mobile third-party payment systems.[318] Figure 4.7 illustrates the different categories of e-payments, and Table 4.11 (China Internet Watch 2015c; iResearch 2016f,g) provides a snapshot of the Chinese payments market in Q2 2015 with regard to the number of transactions (TA) and the respective volumes of e-payments by banks and third-party payments providers. At this time, the volume of online payments via third-party payment providers was comparably low (USD 0.41 tn versus USD 72.66 tn of online payments

[313]Griffiths (2015, n.p).

[314]Ibid.

[315]Capgemini Consulting and Royal Bank of Scotland (2015, p. 6).

[316]Capgemini Consulting and Royal Bank of Scotland (2015, p. 3).

[317]Capgemini Consulting and Royal Bank of Scotland (2015, p. 9).

[318]iResearch (2015).

Table 4.11 Distribution of non-cash transactions in China in Q2 2015[a]

	Non-cash payments	
	via banks	via third-party providers
Total	24.976 bn TA USD 92.99 tn	20.66 bn USD 1.73 tn
Offline	14.578 bn TA USD 20.33 tn	N/A USD 1.32
Online	10.398 bn TA USD 72.66 tn	N/A USD 0.41 tn
Mobile	N/A USD 0.48 tn	N/A USD 0.36 tn

[a]All figures have been transferred into USD, based on an own calculation and the exchange rate of 2017-01-19

via banks),[319] yet, the volume of mobile transactions via third-party payment providers was only slightly lower than the one of banks (USD 0.36 tn versus USD 0.48 tn). Moreover, third-party payments experience huge growth rates. In 2015, online payments via third-party providers accumulated to RMB 11.9 tn, and by 2018, this volume is expected to double.[320] Mobile payments via third-payment providers reached RMB 10.2 tn in 2015, and by 2018 this number is expected to almost triple.[321] Thus, in the long run, China's third-party payment providers will challenge China's banks with regard to e-payments, in particular in terms of mobile e-payments.

China's payments market is highly competitive and the current situation is associated with a "payments war".[322] As of Q1 2015, the majority of the payment market was distributed between three players: *AliPay*, the mobile wallet launched by Alibaba, *ChinaPay*, a payment system provided by *China Union Pay*,[323] and *TenPay*, the mobile wallet by Tencent, holding 36.4%, 35.5% and 12.6%

[319]In terms of the sum of transactions, third-party payment providers in 2015 already challenged banks and their payment services. China Internet Watch refers to data released by the PBOC, which for Q2 2015 assessed a sum of 20.66 bn transactions by non-bank agencies. These transactions accumulated a total volume of USD 1.73 tn (China Internet Watch 2015c). These figures suggest that transactions by third-party payment providers, in contrast to transactions settled via banks, are comparably of low volume. On the other hand, the high frequency of transactions tells that Chinese are integrating third-party payments in their daily lives. Once they have experienced the convenience and safety of such services, they are likely to apply non-bank payments also for transactions of higher amounts.

[320]iResearch (2016b).

[321]iResearch (2016c).

[322]Griffiths (2015).

[323]*China Union Pay* is a bank card association founded in 2002, which until recently was the only entity in China to issue credit cards and settle bank card transactions (China Internet Watch 2013).

Table 4.12 China's mobile payment champions in Q2 2015[a]

Rank	Company	Revenue in Q2 2015 (bn USD)	Market share in Q1 2015	Number of users (in million)
1	AliPay (AliPay wallet)	1.53	36.4%	300 (Jan 2015) 190 (Dec 2014)
2	ChinaPay	1.49	35.5%	260 (Aug 2015)
3	TenPay	0.53	12.6%	650 (Jan 2015)

[a]Revenues as of Q2 2015 are own calculations based on China Internet Watch (2015c). Market shares as of Q1 2015 are drawn from China Internet Watch (2015d). Numbers of users are based on Gokey (2014) (AliPay); Alibaba (2014) (AliPay Wallet); China Internet Watch (2015d) (Unionpay); and PYMNTS (2015) (TenPay)

respectively of the Chinese mobile third-party payment market.[324] Each of the three mentioned Chinese payment providers has specific capabilities. Until 2014, *China UnionPay* had a monopoly on the clearing of all e-payments, and consequently, all electronic transactions providers had to process their payments via *China UnionPay*. Yet, in 2014, this monopoly was dissolved.[325] In the same year, *Alibaba* and *Tencent* both received a banking licence[326] and thus since then have been able to clear payments on their own. Contrasting *ChinaPay*, *TenPay* and *AliPay*, not only their individual strengths and competitiveness become obvious, but also their superiority over their Western counterparts.[327] *ChinaPay* due to its mother company has links to more than 280 banks across the world,[328] and thereby can issue, acquire and clear payments for a broad range of bank depositors. *TenPay* and *AliPay*, on the other hand, have access to millions of Chinese customers, who either utilise *Tencent*'s applications like *WeChat* or *QQ*, or purchase via one of *Alibaba*'s e-commerce platforms. In the end, *TenPay* and *AliPay* have access to plenty of data, which Chinese consumers are willing to provide in order to enjoy other value-adding services.[329]

Most articles and statistics on payments in China focus on the competition of *AliPay* versus *TenPay* or *Alibaba* versus *Tencent*, despite *ChinaPay*'s respectable market share and the existence of further market players. One explanation for this could be that *ChinaPay* due to its mother company is considered a bank institution, and most assessment on payments in China focus on third-party (i.e. non-bank) payment providers. Moreover, *AliPay* and *TenPay* have much more users than *ChinaPay* (see Table 4.12). Another explanation could be the multiple features that

[324]China Internet Watch (2015d).

[325]Transact24 (n.d.).

[326]See e.g. Wildau (2014), Wong (2015); *Alibaba*'s bank is called *MyBank*; *Tencent*'s bank is called *WeBank*. The latter reminds of *Tencent*'s currently most valuable asset, *WeChat*.

[327]Examples of Western payment providers are *Visa*, which since 2015 has provided a *V.me Wallet* (Zachariae 2015). Another example is *Apple*, which in 2014 launched *Apple Pay* (Swider 2016). A further example is *PayPal*.

[328]China Internet Watch (2015d).

[329]China Internet Watch (2013).

AliPay and *Tenpay* offer. "In addition to simply buying goods online, AliPay and WeChat [i.e. TenPay] allow users to pay at restaurants and convenient stores, shop online, and even pay parking fines and utility bills".[330] Moreover, *WeChat* is said to be "an effective customer relationship management tool"[331] (see also Sect. 4.4.4). In contrast to email, which is generally a less accepted communication tool in China,[332] companies can utilise social media like *WeChat* not only for marketing and customer services, but also for customer data collection. As mentioned in Sect. 4.4.2.2, *WeChat* users can follow the corporate channel (i.e. official account) of a brand or company; thereby, demographics, personal preferences and other respective customer data can be tracked from the user's personal *WeChat* account. *AliPay*'s main asset, on the other hand, is its integration in the largest and most prominent e-commerce platform, *Alibaba*. In the end, it has become obvious that both, *AliPay* and *TenPay* or *WeChat* payment respectively, are more than pure payment apps; they have rather converted into true "lifestyle app[s]".[333]

Ultimately, the acceptance of a payment system depends on the surplus of customer value that the financial service can generate, and additionally, on the level of trust a provider can create. Both, *AliPay* and *WeChat* are offering discounts if people choose their mobile wallets instead of paying in cash or via card. In early 2015, more than 40,000 supermarkets and convenient stores like *Walmart*, *Carrefour*, and *7-Eleven* all over China have started to accept *AliPay* and *TenPay* payments; groceries and snack stands are following. Whereas *AliPay* and *TenPay* are seen as competitors, they also cooperate occasionally in order to build a bulwark against third players. This can be seen, for instance, in the case of *Didi Kuaidi*,[334] China's largest taxi service provider which is backed by both, *Alibaba* and *Tencent*, and correspondingly also accepts both, *AliPay* and *WeChat* payments.[335]

Western payment providers lag far behind the Chinese success story. Their point of departure and their different projections of online, and in particular mobile payments give an explanation for this development. Taking the example of *Apple Pay*, this system has principally been designed to reinforce the sales of *Apple*'s electronic devices,[336] and it started out as a new and rather independent app. Chinese payment providers, on the other hand, "have found a way to embed payments in services that consumers are already using",[337] for example, in instant messaging or

---

[330] Griffiths (2015, n.p).

[331] Ibid.

[332] Interview with Sean, 2015-04-27.

[333] Griffiths (2015, n.p).

[334] *Didi Kuaidi [滴滴快的]* was founded in 2015, resulting from a merger of *Didi Dache [滴滴打车]* (partly owned by *Tencent*) and *Kuaidi Dache [快的打车]* (financed by *Alibaba*). This cooperation proved to be a success as in August 2016, *Didi Kuaidi* acquired *Uber*'s China business (Kharpal 2016).

[335] Huang (n.d.).

[336] PYMNTS (2015, n.p).

[337] Ibid.

e-commerce. Therefore, Chinese payment system providers typically already had an existing customer base before they started providing their payment services. Although *Alphabet* with its *Google Wallet* also attempts to integrate mobile payment into e-commerce, the company faces the challenge to change established consumer behaviour, from debit and credit card usage towards online and mobile payments. By contrast, *AliPay* and *WeChat* only had to convince Chinese customers to replace cash payments. Notably, *Apple* recently has launched a cooperation with *ChinaPay* in order to get access to the Chinese market. Moreover, *Baidu*, the third big internet player next to *Alibaba* and *Tencent* (see *BAT*, Sect. 4.4 and Table 4.5.), has acquired *99Bill*, another electronic payment provider,[338] presumably in order to not stand behind its competitors. Still, I expect that neither *Apple* nor *Baidu* will be able to challenge the success of *AliPay* and *TenPay*.

In the end, China's payments war seems to rule over more than just the future of Chinese payments. As mentioned in Sect. 4.4.4, payments are getting more important as margins on e-commerce and similar services are decreasing. By 2015, neither *AliPay* nor *TenPay* charged end-users for utilising their payment systems. Yet, *Tencent* since 2016 claims a transaction fee of 0.1% from all users who "transfer[…] funds above 1000 yuan from their wallets to their bank cards".[339] However, this fee probably just covers *Tencent*'s costs that it is charged by the settlement bank; therefore, *Tencent* in fact subsidises the transfers of its customers. On the other hand, both, *AliPay* and *TenPay* seem to profit from B2C transactions, in particular, if foreign traders are involved. "Foreign companies [utilising *AliPay*] must pay a $1000 setup fee and are charged a 2.5–3% transaction fee depending on their annual volume. The set-up [sic!] fee is waived for Chinese companies; transaction fees [for Chinese] range from 0.7 to 1.2% of annual sales with a $5000 minimum."[340] With *TenPay*, domestic companies allegedly face transaction fees of 1% without any setup fee, while the conditions for foreign companies are said to be about the same as provided by *AliPay*.[341] Although these fees appear to be quite low, on a cumulative basis they create large revenue streams. Furthermore, I argue that the customer data which are automatically gathered through the provision of payment systems are of much higher value than the direct revenues generated through fees. These data can be used to create future customer value. I will further discuss this issue in Sect. 6.4. In any case, it is safe to assume that the Chinese war on supremacy over payments is not just about the distribution of revenues from transaction fees.

Presumably, this war could even become international some time in the future. The strength and global recognition of *AliPay* and *TenPay* can be inferred from

---

[338] Young (2016, n.p).

[339] CCTV (2016, n.p.) "The problem is that when money is moved from [a] WeChat wallet to [a] bank card, the bank charges WeChat for the transfer. Tencent used to bear that cost, but the expenses are adding up."

[340] Lets Talk Payments (2013, n.p).

[341] Ibid.

the fact that foreign retailers have started to accept *AliPay* and *WeChat* payments on their e-commerce websites.[342] Besides, Chinese tourists at Frankfurt airport since September 2015 can pay via *AliPay* at a merchant called *Tripidi*. Within the first month of operation, *Tripidi* announced that more than half of all Chinese purchases had been paid via *AliPay*. Correspondingly, *AliPay* intends to expand its service in Europe in the near future.[343] Even though, such installations still predominantly target at Chinese customers shopping abroad, the mere presence of Chinese payment providers increases the competition amongst established payment systems. Ultimately, Chinese (and potentially also people of other nations) will have a true alternative to cash and "*UnionPay*'s payment cards, which are not accepted universally".[344]

[342]Griffiths (2015, n.p).

[343]Ecommerce News (2015c).

[344]Griffiths (2015, n.p).

Chapter 5
Crowdfunding in China

Once idealistic, crowdfunding is now an unholy hybrid of retail, investment, and risk.[1]

5.1 The Evolution of Crowdfunding in China

Eight years after its invention in the US, crowdfunding was introduced in China, in July 2011,[2] by He Feng [何峰], a Chinese graduate from Stanford University. Having learned about crowdfunding during his studies abroad, He launched China's first crowdfunding platform with the name *Demohour*[3] in Beijing.[4] Shortly thereafter, another platform, called *Dreamore*,[5] was established by the then 22-year-old Du Mengjie [杜梦杰], who was inspired by the idea of the *share economy*, which he had learned about from a journey abroad.[6] For about 1 year, these two pioneer platforms jointly dominated the small crowdfunding market in China. Four years later, in 2015, they had innumerable competitors, all aspiring to gain a share of the growing Chinese crowdfunding market. Due to the dynamics of the still immature market and an overall lack of data, there are no exact numbers on China's CFPs.[7]

---

[1]Banjo (2015).

[2]Deng (2014, p. 94).

[3]In Chinese, the platform is called *Dianming shijian [点名时间]*, which can be translated as "appeal time".

[4]Email conversation with He Feng, 2013-05-31.

[5]In Chinese, the platform is called *Zhuimeng wang [追梦网]*, which can be translated as "network to follow [your] dreams".

[6]Interview with Du Mengjie, 2013-08-10.

[7]According to the Asia-Pacific Alternative Finance Benchmarking Report (Zhang et al. 2016), there are more than 1600 CFPs on mainland China; however, the majority of these platforms

A. S. Funk, *Crowdfunding in China*, Contributions to Management Science,
https://doi.org/10.1007/978-3-319-97253-4_5

From my analysis I conclude that, compared to the US and Europe, China has adopted crowdfunding much faster, despite its regulatory tentativeness.

Moreover, China's crowdfunding landscape is highly dynamic and in the process of change. *Demohour* and *Dreamore*, both companies still existed in 2015. However, *Dreamore* in March 2015 transformed its CFP into a mobile app.[8] By contrast, *Demohour* has become a sales platform for high-tech devices. After shifting their business model several times, the former pioneers and founders of China's first CFP finally exited the crowdfunding market due to diminishing margins and loss of market share towards bigger players.[9] These two examples mirror the volatile situation for CFPs in China. In particular, since the release of draft regulations for equity crowdfunding, new players have been entering the market and others have been forced to resign. As a result, especially smaller players with few assets and low capitalisation face difficulties to compete with well-endowed platforms.[10]

China's crowdfunding market differs a lot from the one in the West. Whilst some aspects of the original model have been adopted by Chinese actors—e.g. the idea of donation-based crowdfunding—other features have been amended or invented according to China specific needs—e.g. *e-commerce crowdfunding*. Moreover, whilst America and Europe provide many examples of typical *start-up CFPs*, which grew self-sufficiently and by means of commission, China's crowdfunding market is dominated by established players and *start-up CFPs* with substantial capitalisation. For instance, *Dreamore* has already received three rounds of VC investments and thereby collected about USD 260 million.[11] Other *start-up CFPs* without external investment sooner or later had to resign.[12] In the end, the institution of crowdfunding is shaped by different market settings and the respective circumstances of the actors which apply that institution. With regard to Chinese crowdfunding, I argue that it is foremost affected by the country's long history of informal finance and its advanced internet sector; therein, in particular, by China's mobile internet sector, its e-commerce industry and also its payments sector. Moreover, the influence of cultural dimensions and specific Chinese habits, beliefs and values should not be underestimated. Ultimately, crowdfunding in China has become a hybrid of Western crowdfunding, China's culture and Chinese capitalism.

provides P2P; the survey counted 128 reward-, donation- and equity-based CFPs. Other institutions like iResearch or Zero2IPO came to different conclusions, see further below.

[8]Interview with Water (Head of Crowdfunding at *Dreamore*), 2015-04-16.

[9]Interview with Jason (former employee at *Demohour*), 2015-05-19.

[10]Interview with Sean, 2015-04-27.

[11]Interview with Water, 2015-04-16.

[12]Interview with Sean, 2015-04-27.

5.2 Crowdfunding Education and Regulation

Currently, crowdfunding in China is facing two major challenges, namely education and regulation. By 2015, to the majority of Chinese citizens the term *crowdfunding* or its Chinese equivalent *zhongchou [众筹]* was still indefinite. In addition, a substantial number of those Chinese who have actually heard about crowdfunding interpret its concept rather differently from the original Western understanding. For example, several of my interview partners still considered *Demohour* a CFP in 2015. Others take the term *crowd-funding* literally, and count all ventures, which have been realised through the joint investment of a certain group of people as crowdfunding. Others do not distinguish between group buying,[13] crowdfunding and sales discounts,[14] or mix it up with pre-sales or lottery.[15] Yet, *zhongchou* has become a trend word in China, as can be seen from the soaring presence of the term in China's everyday life. Considering the confusion about the meanings of crowdfunding, one challenge of crowdfunding in China is education, as people should understand how it works.

In line with this comes China's second challenge, which is crowdfunding regulation. Whereas donation- and reward-based crowdfunding are unregulated, Chinese authorities in December 2014 quietly published draft regulations for equity crowdfunding, which are similar to Chinese regulations on PE. Previous to that, Chinese equity CFPs were operating in a grey or informal, if not illegal area of finance. On the one hand, the release of draft regulations demonstrates the government's generally positive attitude towards crowdfunding. On the other hand, not all crowdfunding actors are satisfied with these draft regulations as they particularly support big CFPs and force smaller CFP to resign.[16]

Regardless the deficiencies in regulation, the government pins its hopes on the positive impacts which crowdfunding could have on the entire economy. According to the Chinese research institution *Zero2IPO*, equity crowdfunding in China could have the following five effects:

> first, alleviating the financing difficulties of micro and small enterprises and encouraging innovation and entrepreneurship; second, diversifying investment & financing channels and stimulating financial innovation; third, guiding informal finance onto the well-regulated development track, expanding and improving the multi-layered capital markets; fourth, decentralizing financial risk, enhancing flexibility and stability of the financial system; and fifth, creating jobs and facilitating technological innovation and economic growth.[17]

These five goals are challenging and regulation needs to strike a balance between liberal development and fierce restriction.

[13]Group buying in Chinese is *tuan gou [团购]*, see also Sect. 4.4.4.

[14]Discounts are *tou jian [头减]* in Chinese.

[15]Interview with Sean, 2015-04-27, and own observations from field studies in 2013 and 2015.

[16]Interview with Sean, 2015-04-27.

[17]Cao (2015, n.p).

In this regard, the association responsible for equity crowdfunding in China, the CSRC, has defined that the number of shareholders for one crowdfunding project may not exceed 200. Moreover, crowdfunding projects may only be offered by means of a crowdfunding platform where potential crowdfunders have to register.[18] The draft regulations further define the criteria of a Chinese equity crowdfunding platform, which include the following:

> An EC[19] platform provides an online finance solution service between entrepreneurs and investors. The service includes publication of information, business matching, and assistance in financial transactions. An EC platform needs to register at the Securities Association of China (SAC) and apply to be a member. An EC platform has to be a legal Chinese company or a partnership enterprise. This company has to have net assets of RMB 5 million or greater. The platform must have a specialist in EC and at least two senior management staff with work experience in finance or IT of over three years. The platform must have legal support and the appropriate technological facilities. The platform must have appropriate project management standards. The platform must have real-name authentication and perform due diligence on both the entrepreneur and investors. The platform has the responsibility to keep a record of all investments and transactions for at least 10 years.[20]

Whilst these regulations ensure a certain stability of the Chinese crowdfunding market and presumably aim at default prevention of CFPs, they also ban weakly capitalised and less experienced players from the market. As a consequence, a substantial number of Chinese equity-based CFPs, in particular *start-up CFPs* (see Sect. 5.4) resigned after the draft regulations had been released.[21] By contrast, *corporate CFPs*[22] profit from the implementation of these draft regulations, which quasi automatically reduced the number of potential competitors. This platform oligopoly seems to be the result of the government's trade-off between security and diversity of market players. Whilst such an oligopoly is likely to harm market development, other aspects of the draft regulations for Chinese equity CFPs are more plausible, in particular against the backdrop of recent fraud cases in P2P lending.

> The platform CANNOT offer its own company or related companies as an investment opportunity on the platform. The platform CANNOT provide [a] guarantee or be a shareholding nominee for projects on the platform. The platform CANNOT offer shares for resale. The platform CANNOT publish investment information to unaccredited users. The platform CANNOT offer underwriting securities services, investment advice, asset management, unless the company has a relevant license. The platform CANNOT offer online P2P lending services at the same time.[23]

---

[18] Cao (2015).

[19] I.e. equity crowdfunding.

[20] Translation of draft regulation by BOP Consulting (2015, n.p).

[21] Interview with Sean, 2015-04-27.

[22] *Corporate CFPs* and *start-up CFPs* will be introduced in Sect. 5.4.

[23] Translation of draft regulation by BOP Consulting (2015, n.p). The capitalisation of "cannot" originates from BOP Consulting.

The draft regulations further contain instructions for crowdfunders. Investors become eligible for equity crowdfunding by either "invest[ing] at least RMB 1 million[24] in a single project [...], [by] hav[ing] net assets of RMB 10 million or [by] hav[ing] net assets of RMB 3 million and an average annual income of RMB 500,000 for the past 3 years".[25] Whereas in the past, potential crowdfunders just had to register with their personal ID, most Chinese equity CFPs nowadays additionally conduct a financial check on each applicant, which is in line with the draft regulations.[26] In the end, the CSRC has defined the nature of a Chinese (equity) crowdfunder, and notably, Chinese (equity) crowdfunding does not fit my definition of crowdfunding (see Sect. 3.1) as the regulations explicitly exclude some people from becoming a crowdfunder.

Chinese authorities also published some guidelines for PIs. The draft regulations state that "[e]ntrepreneurs CANNOT issue securities. [...] Entrepreneurs CANNOT promise zero loss or guarantee a minimum return. Entrepreneurs CAN only promote a project for investment on an EC platform but not through any other public venues or platforms, and CAN only showcase one project on one EC platform at a time."[27] Whilst most of these rules sound plausible, the explicit mentioning of such guidelines evokes the impression that there have been entrepreneurs in the past who neglected those points.

Although, the CSRC explicitly distinguishes crowdfunding from venture capital and PE and has stated that crowdfunding should "be more grass-root-based",[28] the concept of equity crowdfunding in China in fact is very close to classical PE.[29] One aspect that can be found in both, Chinese PE and crowdfunding, is the instalment of so-called *lead-investors*. Some Chinese CFPs[30] try to reduce the risks of their projects by appointing some expert investors. In this regard, Chinese scholars differentiate crowdfunders into *lead-investors* (*ling tou [领投]*) and *follower-investors* (*gen tou [跟投]*). The former are rather professional, they can rely on certain investment experience and therefore are likely to execute a project's due diligence. *Lead-investors* typically also have expertise in the project's respective industry. Thus their investment decisions can give good advice to *follower-investors*, who have less pre-knowledge.[31] Yet, Chinese CFPs are not obliged to provide *lead-investors*.

---

[24] This equals to USD 150,049 and EUR 134,823 as of 4th July 2016.

[25] BOP Consulting (2015, n.p).

[26] Interview with Grace (Head of Agricultural Crowdfunding projects at the Chinese CFP *Zhong-chou wang*), 2015-09-18.

[27] Translation of draft regulation by BOP Consulting (2015, n.p). The capitalisation of "cannot" originates from BOP Consulting.

[28] Cao (2015, n.p).

[29] Interview with Grace, 2015-09-18.

[30] E.g. *Zhongchou wang [众筹网]*.

[31] Sheng et al. (2014, p. 37).

According to Chinese authorities, equity crowdfunding is said to contain higher risks than product- and debt-based crowdfunding.[32] Whilst this may be true in the case of product-based CF, it hardly applies to P2P (i.e. debt-based crowdfunding) in China, at least in its current form of execution. Although Chinese do not consider P2P a form of crowdfunding, but rather a separate category of finance (see also Sect. 3.3.2 and Fig. 3.2), I will briefly discuss P2P in China in Sect. 5.3.1 in order to put the role of crowdfunding into perspective. In terms of equity crowdfunding, I argue that it is only risky if crowdfunders lack education and do not understand their investment as risk capital. Therefore, the main risk lies not with equity crowdfunding per se, but with the investors' understanding. Not only regulation but also the understanding of crowdfunding in China differs from the West. The following chapter is predominantly based on my own observations.

5.3 The Chinese Understanding of Crowdfunding

As mentioned in Sect. 3.3.2, Chinese have several ways to categorise crowdfunding. Besides the four-folded classification of the West (donation-, rewards-, debt-, and equity-based crowdfunding), the most common distinction in China is a bipolar one into equity crowdfunding (*guquan zhongchou [股权众筹]*) and product crowdfunding (*chanpin zhongchou [产品众筹]*), which includes donation- and rewards-based crowdfunding. Moreover, some reports only distinguish between rewards- and equity-based crowdfunding,[33] probably because the number of donation-based campaigns in China is rather low. Debt-based crowdfunding is typically referred to as *P2P (crowdfunding)*, and although P2P by 2016 was the largest crowdfunding sector in China, Chinese authorities, scholars and practitioners characteristically contemplate this market separately (see Fig. 3.2). Moreover, Chinese reports on the topic of crowdfunding, usually only comprise of data on product/reward and equity crowdfunding. Before I discuss several further specifications of crowdfunding in China, of which some seem to be unique in the world, I briefly scheme Chinese P2P and refer to rewards- and equity-based crowdfunding.

5.3.1 P2P Finance

P2P is more for consumption; crowdfunding is more for value creation.[34]

In order to illustrate the advantages of concepts like *e-commerce crowdfunding*,[35] I need to briefly outline the current status of P2P finance in China. P2P

[32]Cao (2015, n.p).

[33]See e.g. Zero2IPO (2015) or iResearch (2016a).

[34]Interview with Conor Roche, 2015-05-06.

[35]I will elaborate e-commerce crowdfunding in Sect. 5.4.4.

is omnipresent in China, though it currently is one of the most opaque and controversial industries in China. A keyword search with *"P2P金融"* (i.e. *P2P finance*) on Baidu.com produced 8,450,000 results. A further search with the keyword "互联网金融" *[hulian wang jinrong]* (i.e. internet finance) on Baidu.com produced 7,720,000 records. Moreover, there were 2259 Chinese academic articles incorporating *"P2P金融"* in their headlines.[36] These figures reflect the overall prominence of P2P finance in China compared to the West[37] and also compared to crowdfunding in China (see Sect. 3.3.2). Most Chinese scholars working on P2P finance either focus on the algorithms and search technologies behind P2P,[38] or contemplate the risks associated with this form of direct finance.[39] Recent studies also focus on the criminal dimensions of P2P finance.[40] As such, the theoretical works mirror the reality of the current P2P market in China.

The idea behind Peer-to-peer lending is the direct provision of loans from individuals to individuals, predominantly to those who do not meet the requirements of getting a proper loan. Even though, theoretically, there is no financial mediator, often an online platform without a banking licence mediates between borrowers and lenders. Credit rating is often based on data analysis; however, in China, there is neither a standard nor much regulation of this sector. Similar to informal finance, Chinese borrowers can more easily and much faster obtain a loan via P2P than from a formal bank; creditors, on the other hand, are attracted by potential yields of over 10%.[41] Compared to regular deposit rates, which were at 1.75%[42] in China in January 2016, P2P platforms indeed seem to be attractive alternatives for Chinese savers. Although P2P is a form of risk capital, and typically, there are no guarantees from the platform operators for returns, the Chinese P2P market has grown to a multi-billion dollar market. P2P platforms have mushroomed since 2013, the first year of Chinese P2P platforms.[43] Estimations of the market volume in 2015 varied from USD 33.2 billion[44] to USD 64.7 billion.[45] *Xinhua* counted 3612 P2P platforms in November 2015, however, according to the CBRC, a share of about 1000 platforms was non-performing.[46]

---

[36] All of the latter searches were conducted on 2nd February 2016.

[37] A search via *Google* and *Google scholar* with the keyword *"P2P finance"* produced 75,600 and 45 results respectively (2nd February 2016). A search with the keyword *"P2P"* produced far more results in both, Chinese and Western databases; however, therein also other P2P operations like *"P2P streaming"* are included, which adulterates the results.

[38] See e.g. Wang et al. (2013).

[39] See e.g. Liao (2015) or Guo (2014).

[40] See e.g. Wang and Xu (2015) or Yu (2015b).

[41] Xinhua (2015).

[42] Deposits.org (2016).

[43] Wang and Xu (2015, p. 29).

[44] Gough (2016a) referring to Morgan Stanley.

[45] Xinhua (2015).

[46] Ibid.

Indeed, recent developments impair the image of P2P in China. In February 2016, China's largest P2P platform, *Ezubao*,[47] was accused to have bilked investors of USD 7.6 billion by setting up fictional investments and promising returns of up to 15%. *Ezubao* is said to have attracted about one million Chinese savers who believed in those promising returns.[48] However, 95% of all projects on *Ezubao*'s platform were made up and the entire funding model of the company relied on a ponzi scheme, i.e. new deposits permanently financed the interests and paybacks of previous ones. Thus, P2P got the sobriquet *"P"onzi-2-"P"onzi*, and as about one third of all Chinese P2P platforms are in troubles, further disclosures of failing or fraudulent platforms are expected to happen in the near future.[49]

The case of *Ezubao* is sweeping not least due to the fact that the company in the past obviously enjoyed the government's credibility. Only started in 2014, *Ezubao* gained exponential recognition foremost through advertisement on CCTV, a Chinese state television channel,[50] and through a number of articles on central governmental websites.[51] In addition, *Ezubao* had sponsored several official events like the China Open tennis tournament and its logo was omnipresent in high-speed rail cars.[52] Moreover, *Ezubao*'s annual meeting in 2015 was held in Beijing's Great Hall of the People, which is usually reserved for official events, and several celebrities from politics and other parts of society joined the event.[53] Based on these facts, investors believed in the trustworthiness of *Ezubao* and many of them have lost a several years' salary by its bankruptcy.[54]

As P2P is debt-based, the CBRC has regulation authority of the market. Not least due to the high number of unprofitable P2P platforms, and in the wake of first hints on *Ezubao*'s failing, the CBRC in December 2015 released several new draft regulations on P2P. According to these, P2P platforms may not articulate any guarantees towards depositors, nor pool any deposits in order to fund own projects. In addition, all deposits should be handled in trust by a banking institution. P2P platforms further should install borrowing limits for each debtor and also restrict the number of outstanding loans per person. Still, the CBRC stressed the dangers of P2P, in particular, the involved credit and liquidity risks, and the existence of false advertising and potential fraud. The institution claimed that such incidents "could affect the [entire] financial market order and social stability".[55] Indeed, *Ezubao*'s case has evoked social unrest and still ongoing protests.

---

[47] *Ezubao [e租宝]* in Chinese.

[48] Gough (2016a).

[49] Durden (2016).

[50] Mitchell (2016).

[51] Gough (2016b).

[52] Mitchell (2016).

[53] Gough (2016b).

[54] Mitchell (2016).

[55] Xinhua (2015) referring to CBRC.

Against this background, the draft regulations on equity crowdfunding (see Sect. 5.2), which had been released even earlier than the draft regulations on P2P, sound quite reasonable. CFPs should explicitly perform as mere mediators and not issue projects themselves. They further are not allowed to guarantee a certain return on investment, and ultimately, they may not offer any P2P services at the same time. These regulations prevent cases like *Ezubao* to expand to the equity crowdfunding market.

To conclude, P2P in China is a very risky financial tool, regulation still lags behind the dynamics of the market and so far cannot prevent fraud. Most P2P platforms do not hold sufficient assets in order to avoid liquidity risks; in particular, weakly capitalised platforms cannot ensure permanent liquidity. In contrast, China's equity crowdfunding market is restricted to platforms with substantial capitalisation. Moreover, whilst P2P capital is said to be mainly used for consumption,[56] equity crowdfunding contributes to the establishment of new businesses, which eventually can create new jobs and increase economic growth. In the end, I suppose that the Chinese P2P model, just like crowdfunding, will experience some change in the near future. By means of systematic big data analysis and the integration of P2P into other sectors, e.g. e-commerce, it could become much safer and more efficient, and eventually become a true alternative to classical bank loans.

5.3.2 *Rewards- Versus Equity-Based Crowdfunding*

Data on the Chinese crowdfunding market is still scarce. According to iResearch, by the end of 2014, there have been 110 CFPs in China, including 75 reward-based platforms[57] and correspondingly 35 equity-based ones. An even higher number was reported in November 2015 by South China Morning Post (SCMP) referring to 01caijing,[58] which counted a total of 128 online crowdfunding platforms, yet including only 32 equity-based platforms.[59] The majority of Chinese CFPs are based in first-tier cities like Beijing and Shanghai and the coastal provinces of Guangdong and Zhejiang. They provide projects in the fields of science, technology, film, photography, publications, humanities, music, agriculture, and public welfare.[60] Besides, real estate crowdfunding has become very popular in China, though this "is mostly about presales and debts, instead of equity investment".[61] In 2014, the volume of China's rewards-based crowdfunding market accumulated

[56] Interview with Conor Roche, 2015-05-06.

[57] iResearch (2016a, p. 4).

[58] *01caijing* is a Chinese internet-based medium regularly publishing financial news.

[59] Chiang (2015).

[60] iResearch (2016a, p. 4).

[61] Chiang (2015, n.p).

to at least RMB 440 million,[62] of which 61% or RMB 270 million respectively were collected via the five most successful CFPs, namely *Jingdong*,[63] *Zhongchou wang*,[64] *Alibaba*,[65] *Demohour*,[66] and *Dreamore*.[67] Unfortunately, there are no comprehensive data on Chinese equity-based CFP, probably because until 2014 equity based CFPs still operated in a rather grey area. With the publication of draft regulations in December 2014, the number of new market entrants first soared. However, smaller platforms could not meet the requirements of the draft regulations. They consequently lost market share to bigger players and many of them resigned.[68] These market dynamics contribute to the problems of determining the exact number of Chinese CFPs.

Some quantitative analysis of crowdfunding in China is provided by industry reports, although these reports usually illustrate only parts of the market. For example, Zero2IPO in their *2014 Crowdfunding Report* analysed six rewards-based[69] and three equity based CFPs.[70] In total, the research agency identified 1423 Chinese crowdfunding projects in the first half of 2014, which collectively raised funds of RMB 188 million.[71] In its *2015 China Crowdfunding Market Research Report*, based on data of the entire year 2014, the analysis was extended to 13 CFPs,[72] of which four platforms were equity-based.[73] In total, these 13 CFPs counted 9088 crowdfunding projects, which intended to raise RMB 3.78 billion; in the end, the total funding sum amounted to RMB 1.38 billion.[74] Tables 5.1 (Zero2IPO 2014, pp. 17; 22; Zero2IPO 2015, p. 15) and 5.2 (Zero2IPO 2014, pp. 17; 22; Zero2IPO 2015, p. 15) summarise the findings for reward- and equity-based

[62]iResearch (2016a, p. 4). i.e. USD 66.91 million or EUR 59.96 million respectively (as of 7th February 2016).

[63]*Jingdong zhongchou [京东众筹]*.

[64]*Zhongchou wang [众筹网]*.

[65]*Taobao zhongchou [淘宝众筹]*.

[66]*Dianming shijian [点名时间]*.

[67]*Zhuimeng wang [追梦网]*.

[68]Interview with Sean, 2015-04-27.

[69]*Zhongchou wang [众筹网], Dianming shijian [点名时间], Zhuimeng wang [追梦网], Tao meng wang [淘梦网], Zhongguo meng wang [中国梦网], Letong yinyue [乐童音乐]* (Zero2IPO 2014, p. 17).

[70]*Yuanshi hui [原始会], Tianshi hui [天使汇], Dajia tou [大家投]* (Zero2IPO 2014, p. 17).

[71]I.e. USD 29 million or EUR 25 million respectively (as of 10th February 2016).

[72]*Tianshi hui [天使汇], Yuanshi hui [原始会], Dajia tou [大家投], Tianshi ke sijia guquan zhongchou pingtai [天使客私家股权众筹平台], Zhongchou wang [众筹网], Dianming shijian [点名时间], Zhuimeng wang [追梦网], Taobao zhongchou [淘宝众筹], Letong yinyue [乐童音乐], Jue [觉], Jingdong zhongchou [京东众筹], Zhongguo meng wang [中国梦网], Tao meng wang jiu jia jiangli zhongchou pingtai [淘梦网九家奖励众筹平台]*.

[73]*Tianshi hui [天使汇], Yuanshi hui [原始会], Dajia tou [大家投], Tianshi ke (sijia guquan zhongchou pingtai) [天使客(私家股权众筹平台)]*.

[74]I.e. USD 210 million or EUR 187 million respectively (as of 10th February 2016); Zero2IPO (2015, p. 15).

Table 5.1 Collected data of reward-based crowdfunding in China of 2014 by Zero2IPO

Reward-based CF	2014 Report based on data from Q2 2014	2015 Report based on data from entire 2014
Number of analysed CFPs	6	9
Number of identified CF projects	993	5997
Total expected target sum	RMB 26.59 million	RMB 280.90 million
Total sum of actual funding	RMB 32.28 million	RMB 349.46 million
Ratio of actual to expected funds	121.40%	124.41%

Table 5.2 Collected data of equity-based crowdfunding in China of 2014 by Zero2IPO

Equity-based CF	2014 Report based on data from Q2 2014	2015 Report based on data from entire 2014
Number of analysed CFPs	3	4
Number of identified CF projects	430	3091
Total expected target sum	RMB 2.04 billion	RMB 3.50 billion
Total sum of actual funding	RMB 0.16 billion	RMB 1.03 billion
Ratio of actual to expected funds	7.84%	29.43%

crowdfunding. Unfortunately, the authors of both Zero2IPO reports do not state any criteria for the selection of the CFPs. Presumably at the respective times of evaluation, these were the most renowned and successful CFPs then. Even though the data only represent a certain share of the entire market, they still mirror the perceived development of China's crowdfunding market.

Despite its short history in China, equity-based crowdfunding already dominates the Chinese CF market. According to Zero2IPO (2015), equity CF in 2014 already accounted for 74.7% of the total Chinese crowdfunding volume.[75] However, in contrast to rewards-based crowdfunding, equity campaigns in China fell quite short of expectations. As Table 5.2 demonstrates, only 29.4% (or RMB 1.03 bn) of the intended total target sum (i.e. RMB 3.50 bn) were reached in 2014. Reward-based campaigns, on the other hand, in sum outreached the intended target volume by 124% (see Table 5.1). Zero2IPO explains the discrepancy in success between rewards- and equity based crowdfunding campaigns with the fact that share-based venture financing is more challenging than raising funds for a rewards-based project. The authors claim that investors can more easily be convinced to contribute to a rewards-based project with a definite goal than to buy shares (i.e. invest in equity crowdfunding), presumably due to the relative short investment duration of the former. Moreover, crowdfunders of reward-based projects do not need to care about the situation of the company, which is providing the project they invest in. Furthermore, the risks of reward-based crowdfunding can be overseen more easily as the return of investment mostly is a physical good. In the worst

[75]Own calculation based on Zero2IPO (2015, p. 15).

case, the expected reward is of low quality. In addition, the entry threshold for investors in reward-based crowdfunding is rather low.[76] Still, like in the West, the total volume of funds collected by rewards-based projects, according to Zero2IPO (2015), accounted for only about one-third of those by equity-based projects.[77] Moreover, on average a reward-based project gained only about a sixth of the sum of an equity-based campaign (RMB 58,273 vs. RMB 333,590).[78] Therefore, equity-based CF increasingly dominates China's crowdfunding market.

Chinese CFPs differ a lot in terms of the number of projects, their funding volumes, the number of crowdfunders and also their funding ratios. With 2607 campaigns, *Tianshi hui [天使汇]* in 2014 was the most attractive (equity-based) CFP for Chinese PIs, which probably has been reinforced by its relatively high funding rate of 76.9%. In total, 2000 registered investors contributed RMB 769 million,[79] making *Tianshi hui* the most valuable Chinese CFP in 2014, followed by *Yuanshi hui [原始会]* (RMB 194 million) and *Jingdong zhongchou [京东众筹]*[80] (RMB 147 million). Notably, *Jingdong zhongchou* by Q2 2014 only provided reward-based crowdfunding, but still ranked third in terms of funding volume. This indicates that equity-based CFPs not necessarily incorporate higher funding volumes compared to pure rewards-based platforms. Among those nine reward-based CFPs that Zero2IPO analysed in the 2014 Report in terms of the number of projects, *Zhongchou wang [众筹网]* led with 1964 campaigns followed by *Dianming shijian [点名时间]* (1091) and *Zhuimeng wang [追梦网]* (871). However, regarding the success rate, all of the above stood far behind *Jingdong zhongchou [京东众筹]* and *Taobao zhongchou [淘宝众筹]*,[81] who surpassed their funding goals at 1240.9% and 267.8%. Regarding the number of crowdfunders, *Jingdong zhongchou* and *Taobao zhongchou* were again far outstanding from the other CFPs, with 591,742 and 585,933 registered investors respectively. These numbers derive from the huge customer base of the platforms' parent companies, i.e. *JD.com* and *Alibaba* respectively, which have their core business in e-commerce. Yet, individual contributions at *Taobao zhongchou* and *Jingdong zhongchou* were comparably low. A crowdfunder at *Taobao* on average invested RMB 108 in 2014, one at *Jingdong* about RMB 249, which both appear very low compared to the average RMB 384,500 that a crowdfunder had invested at the equity-based CFP *Tianshi hui*. Just like in the West, equity-based investments are commonly much higher than contributions for reward-based projects. The results of the comparison of all 13 CFPs can be found in the appendix (Fig. A.4) contrasting their number of registered projects, the total target volume and the actual total funding sum. Unfortunately, the data do neither reveal the exact number of successfully funded

[76]Zero2IPO (2015, p. 16).

[77]RMB 349 million for rewards-based projects vs. RMB 1.03 billion for equity-based projects.

[78]Own calculation based on Zero2IPO (2015, p. 15).

[79]I.e. USD 117 million or EUR 104 million respectively (as of 2nd November 2016).

[80]*Jingdong zhongchou* is the CFP of the e-commerce corporate *Jingdong.com*.

[81]*Taobao zhongchou* is the CFP of the ebay-like platform *Taobao* (belonging to *Alibaba Group*).

projects at each platform, nor give any idea about the distribution of the funds. Still, the data imply that different CFPs address different kinds of PIs and also different types of crowdfunders (e.g. in terms of their capitalisation). Last but not least, the rankings based on data from 2015[82] show a very different picture. For instance, in 2014, *Dianming shijian [点名时间]* ranked third in terms of the number of crowdfunding projects. By 2015, *Dianming shijian* has been no CFP any longer, but transferred its business model into presales of high-tech devices. Moreover, *Jingdong zhongchou [京东众筹]* and also *Zhongchou wang [众筹网]* since 2015 have been providing equity-based crowdfunding, which presumably pushes the overall rankings of these CFPs. Therefore, as the entire Chinese crowdfunding market is changing rapidly, crowdfunding data should be taken rather as a snapshot of the market than as a basis for extrapolation.

Besides their absolute numbers, funding volumes and the numbers of offered projects, the nature of Chinese CFPs is also changing. iResearch identified that Chinese CFPs increasingly focus their business on specific industries which leads towards more specialised platforms.[83] This statement was underlined by the fact that the *2014 Report* Zero2IPO distinguishes between *specialised*[84] and *comprehensive*[85] rewards-based CFPs.[86] However, for unknown reasons this differentiation has no longer been applied in the *2015 Report*. As a second trend, Chinese CFPs constantly increase their level of service integration, which ultimately leads towards a new development stage,[87] and which is incomparable to Western CFPs. Particularly, as Chinese PIs are reluctant to pay commission for a successful crowdfunding campaign, CFPs are forced to change their business model accordingly. Thus, they often offer their intermediation function for free and additionally provide value-added services like offline road shows for certain crowdfunding projects (see also Sect. 5.4).[88]

5.3.3 "Crowdfunding kafei" and "Playing with Crowdfunding"

During the analysis of literature on crowdfunding in China, I often came across the terms *zhongchou kafei [众筹咖啡]* and *wan zhongchou [玩众筹]*, which seem to be unique Chinese connotations of crowdfunding. The former literally means "*crowdfunding coffee*", but rather stands for "*crowdfunding café*"; the latter can be

---

[82] I.e. in a potential *2016 Zero2IPO Report*, which by the time of writing this thesis was yet to be released.

[83] iResearch (2016a, p. 4).

[84] *chuizhi lei [垂直类]*, i.e. "vertical type".

[85] *zonghe lei [综合类]*, i.e. "integrated type".

[86] Zero2IPO (2014, p. 17).

[87] iResearch (2016a, p. 4).

[88] Interview with Grace, 2015-04-15.

translated as "*play (with) crowdfunding*" and hints at the main utility function of the internet for Chinese netizens. The backgrounds of these two specifications tell a lot about the underlying nature of crowdfunding in China. As mentioned in Sect. 5.1, Chinese tend to adapt and amend Western concepts according to their special needs and cultural habits. *Crowdfunding kafei* and *wan zhongchou* are two examples of such specification with regard to crowdfunding.

With *crowdfunding* and *coffee* in fact two recent Chinese trends are combined to a neologism for financial innovation. China originally has been a tea drinker nation. However, in line with the country's opening up and its progressive westernisation, increasingly more Chinese indulge in drinking coffee. Indeed, drinking coffee is considered to be classy, not least due to the relatively high prices for a standard cup of coffee. Coffee shops are mushrooming in urban China, despite quite high real-estate prices. "Ultimately, many people dream of having their own coffee shop."[89] In addition, coffee shops just like restaurants are considered to be safe investments. In contrast to e.g. software, a café can be physically seen and visited by its investors. Thereby, any investor, regardless of financial education, can easily understand whether his investment is profitable or not by just observing the number of customers. "[Chinese p]eople will never stop eating, and more and more are drinking coffee".[90] Thus, crowdfunding cafés are popular amongst Chinese founders as well as investors.

Yet, crowdfunding cafés are more than just a place to consume coffee. They started out as a social "forum for ideas",[91] where people, in particular students, went to stay and exchange views. In particular, they offered comfort for students who usually live in rather crowded dormitories.[92] In general, private space in China is often limited and reserved for the *inner circle*.[93] Since the popularity of coffee shops has grown, their social function has been extended for business purposes. "[T]hey are becoming important networking tools for entrepreneurs, who utilize the gatherings of students and recent alumni to meet and assess young talent."[94] Against this background, there have been several *crowdfunding cafés* established in Beijing,

[89]Interview with Helen (Co-founder of *Her's café*), 2014-10-10.

[90]Interview with Water, 2015-04-21.

[91]Luo (2015, n.p).

[92]In his book *Remaking Chinese urban form: Modernity, scarcity, and space, 1949–2005*, Duanfang Lu describes the housing situation in China's urban dormitories. "While centralized common restrooms are provided on each floor, there are no kitchens, dining rooms or shower rooms; people are expected to eat in unit canteens and take showers in public bathhouses" (Lu 2006, p. 62). Although Lu mainly refers to work units and the period between 1949 and 2005, from my own observations I know that the situation in Chinese student dormitories has not changed essentially since then.

[93]Chinese commonly distinguish people between belonging either to one's *inner* or one's *outer circle*. The *inner circle* typically comprises of one's family, relatives, and close friends, whereas colleagues, other friends, acquaintances and strangers belong to the *outer circle*. Traditionally, one's home is reserved for the *inner circle*; and people from the *outer circle* are usually not received at home.

[94]Luo (2015, n.p).

Hangzhou, Guangzhou and similar first- and second-tier cities within the last few years.

Chinese describe such places as *crowdfunding cafés* as they are based on quasi offline equity crowdfunding. The first and most famous one is called *1898 café*, which was founded by 200 alumni of Peking University (PKU), led by an entrepreneur called Yang Yong [杨勇]. *1898* refers to the founding year of PKU, and the café is located close-by, in the district *Zhongguancun [中关村]*, also dubbed China's Silicon Valley. It is a members-only café, restricting the place to like-minded PKU alumni. Similar to the US, Chinese cultivate close networks to their alma mater and appreciate this affiliation. Inside *1898 café*, there is not just a coffee-house, but also a number of small seminar rooms for discussions, idea creation, and teambuilding. According to Yang Yong, the coffee shop should "become a leading platform for PKU entrepreneurs, and the home of the leading companies and businesspeople of the future".[95] Arguably, such a café rather resembles an *incubator*,[96] however, the founders of *1898* insist on the term *crowdfunding café*.

Particularly, they claim that their creation of *offline* crowdfunding is much more effective than online crowdfunding, and the only form of crowdfunding suitable for the Chinese market, which ultimately could be the beginning of something much bigger. "Chinese people don't trust crowdfunding Internet sites. China is a nepotistic society; sometimes people trust the binding force of friendship more than a legal contract".[97] Therefore, investors of a crowdfunding café often know each other personally; they have something in common like their graduation from the same university; or they were all chosen by a core group of investors who have some form of relation (or *guanxi*) to each co-investor.

Jinrong café[98] or *JRCoffee* respectively, another prominent crowdfunding café in Beijing, has been financed by 200 selected investors, who all have a distinct background in banking, insurance, or internet finance. Each person has contributed an amount of RMB 300,000 to the offline crowdfunding. Besides a 0.005% share of the café, each investor also received "a coffee consumption card worth the same value with a five-year validity period. That is roughly the equivalent of about 164 yuan per day, which is equal to about seven lattes from Starbucks".[99] Yet, this is a mere driver for the investors of *JRCoffee*. Rather, they see in *JRCoffee* a predecessor of a new stock market for Chinese start-ups. In line with the tradition of *Lloyd's of London*, an insurance market, which was founded at Edward Lloyd's coffee house,

[95] Luo (2015, n.p).

[96] An incubator is an "organization designed to accelerate the growth and success of entrepreneurial companies through an array of business support resources and services that could include physical space, capital, coaching, common services, and networking connections" (Entrepreneur n.d).

[97] Yang according to Lan (2014, n.p).

[98] *Jinrong kafei [金融 咖啡]*, which can be literally translated as "*finance coffee*" or rather "*finance café*", is a crowdfunding café located at Jinrong Street in Beijing.

[99] Lan (2014, n.p).

and the *London Stock Exchange*, which derived from another coffee house, *JRCoffee* is to turn into a venue for investors and new businesses.[100]

Besides *1898 café* and *JRCoffee*, Beijing until recently had at least one more crowdfunding café, which derived from a rather altruistic cause. Female entrepreneurs from all over China had gathered in a *WeChat* group in order to exchange views, discuss gender and business specific topics and support each other. Once the group had grown to a number of 100 participants, those women desired to meet offline as few of them knew the others personally. However, as they could not find an appropriate place for such a meeting, they decided to create such a place by founding *Her's kafei*. They pooled RMB 10,000 from each member of the *WeChat* group, distributed tasks according to the females' professions and within 3 months opened their café in Beijing, in August 2013. *Her's café* was intended to be a place where business women could meet and advise each other; and the founders denominated it a *crowdfunding café*. Yet, due to the high costs and no further business model, the café had to close in October 2014; at least, it had fulfilled its original purpose.[101]

Crowdfunding cafés are a Chinese alteration of the original crowdfunding model. Even though those ventures are a form of equity crowdfunding, the shareholders hardly use the term *guquan zhongchou [股权众筹]*, but *zhongchou kafei [众筹咖啡]*. Moreover, although the collection of the capital is not done online, investors of crowdfunding cafés heavily rely on internet tools, which support their business. "We always thank Tencent and its messaging app WeChat which provided instant communication tools for 200 funders".[102] Coincidentally, a *WeChat* group is also restricted to a number of 200 people; likewise an equity crowdfunding project in China is restricted to 200 shareholders (see also Sect. 5.2). Once trust is established and the investment is accomplished via offline relations, business can be processed online. Thus, *crowdfunding kafei* is not pure offline fundraising, but rather a combination of *offline crowdfunding + online crowdsourcing*.

Whilst the founders of crowdfunding cafés utilise crowdfunding for certain ends, other Chinese see in crowdfunding rather a game or a form of gambling. In Chinese literature and also in colloquial language the term *wan zhongchou [玩众筹]* can often be found,[103] which can be translated as "having fun with crowdfunding". On the one hand, this expression is an analogy of *wan wang [玩网—"have fun with the internet"]* as Chinese rather consider the online space a place for entertainment and joy.[104] On the other hand, the term seems to refer to the nature of donation- and reward-based projects, which are not necessarily business oriented. Some crowdfunders contribute to a project in order to be part of a group

---

[100]Interview with Yi Hui [易辉], the founder of *JRCoffee*, 2015-09-16.

[101]Interview with Helen, 2014-10-10.

[102]Yang according to Lan (2014, n.p).

[103]See e.g. Yi (2015), Wang (2014b, 2015c), Dumas (2014).

[104]So and Westland (2010, p. 121).

or just for their own entertainment.[105] PIs are aware of such crowdfunders and often succeed by framing their offered project accordingly. An example of such a project is the one created by Lin, a young Chinese who intended to travel around Europe, but who lacked the money for his trip. Therefore, he had set up a donation-based crowdfunding campaign at the CFP *Dreamore*. In return, he promised his backers to take videos during his trip so that they could follow him and virtually participate in his journey. Ultimately, Lin had a substantial community of followers who contributed to his crowdfunding campaign.[106]

The fun aspect of crowdfunding was also mirrored by the responses of the questionnaires that I had distributed to PIs and crowdfunders in 2014 (see Chap. 1). This questionnaire also included one question regarding the entertainment function of crowdfunding. Although the sample size was rather small with only 25 participants, and the answers are not representative for the Chinese crowdfunding market,[107] it is still significant that 22 probands agreed or even strongly agreed to the statement that crowdfunding is fun.[108] At the same time, not a single respondent agreed to the statement that he applied crowdfunding because he could not obtain a bank loan. Rather, the majority of the probands saw in crowdfunding a supplement to other finance. The participatory aspect is further stressed by the fact that almost all respondents stated to have a friend who had previously successfully utilised crowdfunding. Still, overall joy and fun with crowdfunding could be diminished by potential frauds and idea theft; only three individuals of all respondents disagreed that others could copy their business idea once they present it on a CFP. As mentioned before, the data collected did not suffice to do a more detailed quantitative analysis as it was limited in scope and partly biased. Still, the results supported the impression I gathered from my observation of different national crowdfunding markets, namely that *wan zhongchou* is a genuine Chinese aspect of crowdfunding.

5.3.4 WeChat Crowdfunding

Chinese PIs do not necessarily rely their crowdfunding campaign on a CFP, but often conduct their campaign independently via their *WeChat* account. I denominate this kind of crowdfunding as *WeChat crowdfunding*. Whilst there are only few examples from the West, for PIs that have set up a crowdfunding appeal on a personal website, referred to their bank account and thereby asked people to contribute to a project, Chinese often decide to start their crowdfunding campaign without the support of a CFP. Moreover, sometimes a *WeChat crowdfunding*

[105]Interview with Water, 2015-04-21.

[106]Interview with Lin, 2013-08-10.

[107]90% of all respondents were either PIs or crowdfunders of the platform *Dreamore*.

[108]In the questionnaire, the statement was "觉得好玩 (I think [crowdfunding] is entertaining)".

campaign is upstream before the actual campaign on a CFP, and therefore functions as a proof of concept.[109] More specifically, Chinese PIs either (like some of their Western peers) simply set up a website for their project and spread the website's link via social media, or they totally do without a website and simply state their crowdfunding request via social media channels. Irrespective of the visual appearance of the crowdfunding campaign, Chinese PIs often utilise *WeChat* for their fundraising appeal. In the end, the comprehensive features of the mobile app *WeChat* including its payment function can replace the services of classical CFPs.

There are several reasons for the existence of *WeChat crowdfunding*. First and foremost, Chinese PIs feel reluctant to pay commission to a CFP in the case of a successful crowdfunding.[110] Secondly, as the first contributors of a campaign often are the PI's friends[111] and as *WeChat* primarily is a social medium to communicate with friends, it is convenient for a PI to spread the word on a crowdfunding campaign via *WeChat*. Thirdly, *WeChat* provides all features of a classical CFP, predominantly the communication and payments functions. With *TenPay*, Chinese PIs can directly accept contributions from their crowd. Furthermore, contents can easily be shared and spread via *WeChat*'s personal websites and its instant messenger. Crowdfunders can follow a project in real time and PIs can instantaneously update the crowd. All in all, *WeChat crowdfunding* is a cost-saving, easy to handle and speedy alternative to common CFPs.

Besides, with *WeChat crowdfunding* the PI keeps the entire control of her crowdfunding campaign. Although *WeChat* still is some kind of platform at which the crowdfunding campaign is presented, there is no longer any intermediary entity between the PI and the crowd. Moreover, all contributions can directly be transferred from the crowdfunders' *WeChat* wallet to the PI's account. In addition, the PI can update her followers both individually and as a group, as long as the followers are connected to each other via *WeChat*. Ultimately, *WeChat crowdfunding* ensures a PI full control over her campaign.

However, *WeChat crowdfunding* limits the potential size of the crowd to one's own friends and relies on the latters' willingness to spread the word about the project. Therefore, the success of *WeChat crowdfunding* is, first, highly dependent on the actual size and quality of a PI's social networks and secondly, on his capability of good PR. Moreover, in line with the Chinese virtue of *guanxi*, people belonging to a PI's social network are likely to feel obliged to contribute to the latter's campaign. Whilst this could be advantageous for the PI, his friends could feel annoyed by the request for money. Therefore, I assume that some crowdfunders prefer to invest via a CFP instead of applying *WeChat crowdfunding*. Moreover, the CFP could function as a guarantor for the investment, e.g. if the *AON* model is applied. On the other hand, due to the reciprocal character of *guanxi*, with *WeChat CF* the PI is likely to be asked to also financially contribute to other crowdfunding

[109]Interview with April and Tina (employees at *Attkon*), 2015-04-28.

[110]Interview with April and Tina, 2015-04-28.

[111]Agrawal et al. (2011).

campaigns in the future. Ultimately, despite the attractiveness and obvious benefits of *WeChat crowdfunding*, it is not the default choice for every Chinese PI aspiring to conduct a crowdfunding campaign.[112] Irrespective of this, *WeChat crowdfunding* is quite popular in China and arguably by 2016 still unique in the world.

5.4 China's Crowdfunding Platforms

Chinese CFPs do not just differ a lot from their Western counterparts, but also amongst each other. Whilst the West is dominated by *start-up CFPs* (see Sect. 5.4.1) which share many similarities, the Chinese market holds a variety of distinguished CFPs, of which some seem to be unique in the world. Literature on crowdfunding in China so far solely applies Western categorisation and differentiates between donation-, rewards-, and equity-based CFPs. Yet, based on my observations and the interviews carried out with Chinese practitioners, Chinese CFPs can be classified into further categories. Below, I present my own classification of Chinese CFPs. In the end, this classification helps to better characterise different CFPs and also to make propositions regarding their advantages and drawbacks.

5.4.1 Start-up Crowdfunding Platforms

Analyses of CFPs in America and Europe show that all renowned actors originally were start-up companies, which have been founded exclusively for the purpose of intermediating between PIs and crowdfunders. Likewise, in China there are CFPs like *Dreamore [Zhuimeng wang 追梦网]*, which started out as genuine CFPs, without any other business operations and without cross-financing from other business units. At least in the beginning, such CFPs relied on their own funding and lived on the commissions collected from successfully funded crowdfunding campaigns. However, just like many of their Western peers, Chinese CFPs could hardly become profitable with this kind of business model. In particular, as Chinese PIs are reluctant to pay any fees for their crowdfunding (see Sects. 5.3.2 and 5.3.4), many CFPs in the beginning of their operation had to keep their commission claims very low or even did without any revenue in order to attract PIs' attention.[113]

[112]Interview with Water, 2015-04-21.

[113]*Dreamore* in its first year claimed a commission of 0% on each successfully funded crowdfunding project; in 2012, the rate was raised to 6%, but again reduced to 3.5% in 2015 (Interview with Du Mengjie, 2015-04-16).

All existing Chinese *start-up CFPs* sooner or later obtained external finance like venture capital in order to sustain their operations.[114] In fact, the low market capitalisation is the main handicap of such companies, which further hinders them to expand their brand recognition, their overall presence and eventually their market share. With the help of angel or venture capital, such *start-up CFPs* can keep their commission fees low and at the same time invest in promotion. "Between 2010 and 2014, any internet start-up could easily at least get an A round of investment".[115] Likewise, Chinese *start-up CFPs* could easily obtain venture finance during that period. "Investors just believed in the market. Even though there are no high revenues just from commission, there might be future services which then generate revenues."[116] I will further discuss some of such additional services in Sect. 5.4.2. To put it in a nutshell, there are indeed Chinese *start-up CFPs*, which have their genuine and sole business in crowdfunding intermediation; however, to my best knowledge, there are no exclusively self-sufficient players like the German CFP *Startnext*, which are run without any external finance. *Start-up CFPs* in China can only sustain on the market with substantial external financial resources.

5.4.2 Specialised Versus Comprehensive Versus Combined CFPs

As mentioned in Sect. 5.3.2, an increasing number of Chinese CFPs, both equity- and reward-based ones, specialises in a certain industry due to a lack of resources. Thereby, expertise can be bundled. For example, the platform *Musikid [letong yinyue 乐童音乐]* exclusively provides music-related projects; over the past years, it has become an uncontested player in this crowdfunding field. Moreover, some CFPs have identified certain industries, which are particularly suitable for the crowdfunding model and set the focus of their business accordingly. The equity-based platform *Tian shi jie [天使街 ("Angel Street")]*, for instance, predominantly offers campaigns which aim at the establishment of a restaurant. As explained in Sect. 5.3.3, Chinese are more easily convinced to invest into physical hardware like a café or a shop than to contribute to e.g. invisible software because they can personally visit the former and assure themselves of the profitability of those businesses. "[Chinese] people don't trust the internet, but if I open a restaurant or a shop, they dare to invest as they believe that I can earn money with that business. Having a restaurant gives me some stable revenue".[117] Thus, more than half of

[114] Interview with Sean, 2015-04-27; interview with Du Mengjie, 2015-04-16; interview with Water, 2015-04-21.

[115] Interview with Water, 2015-04-16.

[116] Interview with Sean, 2015-04-27.

[117] Interview with Water, 2015-04-21.

Angel Street's projects refer to the opening of a new (hot pot) restaurant, which suits the Chinese mentality.

Apart from the specialised CFPs, there is a substantial share of Chinese CFPs which offers a broad spectrum of crowdfunding categories, which I denominate as *comprehensive CFPs*. According to Zero2IPO, in the first half of 2014, the ratio of comprehensive to specialised crowdfunding projects was at 2.5.[118] One example for a *comprehensive CFP* is *Dream China [Zhongguo mengwang* 中国梦网*]*,[119] a reward-based CFP which in 2014 had offered 291 crowdfunding projects[120] in eleven categories, namely *publishing, music, film and TV, design, games, science and technology, social services, events, peripheral regions, animation*, and *others*.[121] Notably, according to Zero2IPO, projects at *comprehensive CFPs* were less likely to be funded than projects at *specialised CFPs*; moreover, the former received comparably less funds than projects on specialised platforms.[122] I assume that crowdfunders approach *specialised CFPs*, if they deliberately intend to invest in a certain industry, e.g. music, whereas potential investors rather browse *comprehensive platforms* for interesting projects and spontaneously decide in which project to invest in.

Besides the distinction in *specialised* versus *comprehensive CFPs*, platforms can also be categorised in terms of the compensation they offer to crowdfunders (see Sect. 3.3.2 and Fig. 3.2). Whilst in the West, most CFPs *either* offer rewards-/product-based CF *or* equity-based CF, in China, there are some CFPs that in fact offer both types of crowdfunding. I coin these platforms as *combined CFPs*. These CFPs often recommend their PIs to apply the two different crowdfunding modes consecutively. In this case, the upstream reward-based crowdfunding campaign serves as proof of concept which demonstrates whether there is a market for the respective product or service. As an employee at *Zhongchou wang* put it "reward investors are actually consumers; equity investors are real investors".[123] Correspondingly, a reward-based campaign helps to assess the actual market value of the PI's business idea, which is helpful to set an adequate price per share for a possibly following equity crowdfunding.[124] Once a reward-based campaign has been successfully funded, the PI can instantaneously approach an equity-based campaign on the same CFP. At that time, the PI needs to incorporate her product or service in order to be able to offer shares. In the end, with a *combined CFP* the crowd

[118]Zero2IPO (2014, p. 19 ff).

[119]The founders of *Dream China* in 2015 have changed the platform's name and domain into *Qingju zhongchou [*青橘众筹*]*, i.e. *"young tangarine"*.

[120]Zero2IPO (2015, p. 17).

[121]Qingju.com (n.d.).

[122]According to Zero2IPO (2014), projects on specialised platforms on average collected RMB 54,247 (though these on average only asked for RMB 22,892, and thus outreached their funding goals), whilst projects on comprehensive CFPs on average collected RMB 23,758, which was below the average target sum of RMB 28,347 (own calculation based on Zero2IPO 2014, p. 17).

[123]Interview with Grace, 2015-04-15.

[124]Interview with Sean, 2015-04-27.

does not merely decide upon the success of a (rewards-based) funding, but also on whether there will be a further (equity-based) crowdfunding. Although Chinese PIs may start an equity-based campaign without a previously accomplished reward-based project, the advantages of the combined *reward-equity-model* are obvious, and thus is recommended by the majority of such platform providers.[125]

5.4.3 Financial Corporate Crowdfunding Platforms

Since 2014, some established Chinese financial corporates have integrated crowd-funding into their business model. Whilst in the West, there are also a few examples of corporate crowdfunding,[126] the overall number and the impact of such platforms is very small. Moreover, those Western financial corporates seem to have little interest in shaping the crowdfunding market, but rather utilise the buzz word crowdfunding to improve their dusty image. By contrast, China's *financial corporate CFPs* have much greater impact on the crowdfunding market. At the same time, as established corporates apply crowdfunding, the concept itself gains in credibility in China. As a result, the application of crowdfunding by financial corporates benefits both, these financial corporates and entrepreneurs that seek funding.

The most prominent example for a financial corporate CFP is *Shenzhen Qianhai Puhui Crowdfunding Exchange Co. Ltd. (Puhui)*, which is a subsidiary of *Ping An Insurance (Group) Co.*, China's second-largest insurer,[127] *Puhui* is an equity-based CFP launched in 2015.[128] Although *Ping An*'s P2P platform, *Lufax*, is far more renowned than its equity affiliate, presumably also because *Ping An* has announced *Lufax*'s IPO for 2016/2017,[129] *Puhui* is likely to follow *Lufax*'s success story due to *Ping An*'s prominence and market capitalisation. Yet, to date there are still very few information on *Puhui*'s business model, its actual market share and current operations.

A second example is the already mentioned CFP *Zhongchou wang [众筹网]*, which is an affiliate of the *Net Credit Finance Group (NCFG)*.[130] In the *2015*

[125]Interview with Grace, 2015-04-15.

[126]One example would be the German cooperative *Volksbanken Raiffeisenbanken*, which since 2013 has provided its members with a crowdfunding tool-kit for the creation of an own CFP (for further information see Harms 2015).

[127]Li (2015c).

[128]Xie (2015).

[129]Maxwell (2016).

[130]"Net Credit Finance Group (NCFG) was co-founded by UCF Group [Unified Compliance Framework Group, an integrated financial service group with headquarters in Beijing (in Chinese 先锋集团),] and various professional investment institutions. Leveraging on UCF Group's 10+ years' experience in investment and financing for SMEs, NCFG strategically covers 7 [sic!] key areas in third-party payment, on-line loans, crowdfunding, wealth management, media,

Crowdfunding Report by Zero2IPO, based on data from 2014, the platform with 1964 projects ranked second in terms of the number of successful campaigns, just behind *Tianshi hui*. A comparison of these data to more recent numbers from the company's website reflects the dynamics of the Chinese crowdfunding market, and at the same time reduces the significance of outdated figures. By February 2016, *Zhongchou wang* had provided a total of 13,307 crowdfunding projects (on a cumulative basis since 2013), which attracted 720,988 investors who conjointly contributed more than RMB 162 million.[131] However, *Zhongchou wang* is unlikely to have kept its second rank on the Chinese crowdfunding market beyond 2014 as other players like *Jingdong zhongchou* and *Taobao zhongchou* since then have gained much ground (see below). *Zhongchou wang* offers both rewards- and equity-based crowdfunding, and recommends its PIs to apply the combined model. Whilst in the past, crowdfunding campaigns at *Zhongchou wang* were free of charge, since 2015, the platform has been charging a 1.5% commission of the target sum of each successful project. In 2015 this has summed up to RMB 2.44 million, considering the volume of successfully funded campaigns.[132] As the platform can hardly live on that commission, it has started to provide additional services, including offline road shows, taste parties (e.g. for agricultural projects intending to do a reward-based crowdfunding), and further online and offline promotion through cooperation with other platforms. In fact, *Zhongchou wang* has a comprehensive list of services, from which a PI can choose, ranging from RMB 1000 to RMB 123,000. In fact, the platform has created a kind of *O2O crowdfunding*. Eventually, these value-added services are *Zhongchou wang*'s main business model. Besides, the platform together with Tsinghua University has launched a *Crowdfunding University*, a virtual institution which provides short courses for students interested in crowdfunding. This instalment also serves crowdfunding education.[133]

Financial corporate CFPs have several advantages compared with *start-up CFPs*. First, due to their corporate structure and likely support from the established parent company, these CFP can be cross-financed and thereby face less pressure to be profitable from the very beginning. Secondly, financial corporate affiliated CFPs automatically have some credibility due to the track record of the holding company. Thirdly, any corporate CFP can more easily attract PIs and investors if they get access to the existing customer base of the parent company. Last but not least, the corporate can serve as a guarantor against risks and potential defaults. *Financial corporate CFPs* in addition can demonstrate industry know-how, which enforces overall trust and credibility. Moreover, they have the capabilities to provide

mobile communication and lifestyle services. With the vision of 'connecting people and finance', NCFG established a new mobile web-based ecology of financial services by connecting finance, commerce, services, lifestyle and investments" (NCFG n.d.).

[131]Zhongchou.com (n.d.).

[132]Own calculation based on the total funding sum of all successful projects (Zhongchou.com n.d.); i.e. USD 374,256 or EUR 336,199 respectively (as of 17th February 2016).

[133]Interview with Grace, 2015-04-15.

a portfolio of different financial products; for example, an investor at *Ping An* could either invest via *Puhui* (equity crowdfunding) or *Lufax* (P2P finance) without changing the provider. All in all, *corporate CFPs*, and particularly those with their core business in financial services, provide advantages for both, PIs and investors, and can more easily provide crowdfunding due to the backing of their holding companies.

5.4.4 E-Commerce Crowdfunding Platforms

Besides financial corporates, the Chinese crowdfunding market provides another rather unique form of CFPs, which I denominate *e-commerce crowdfunding platforms*. Several Chinese e-commerce actors nowadays also offer crowdfunding. Thereby, just like their financial corporate peers, they can draw on assets from their parent company's core business, in particular, on the established customer base: merchants can easily become PIs, and consumers can eventually become crowdfunders. This explains why Chinese often equate (rewards-based) crowdfunding with pre-buying (see Sect. 5.2). As stated in the previous chapter, the corporate group behind the CFP can function as warrantor, it increases the CFP's reputation from the very beginning, promotes the latter's image through broad market coverage and, last but not least, can cross-finance the CFP with revenues from the e-commerce business. The emergence of *e-commerce CFPs* is a genuinely Chinese phenomenon, which is on the rise.

Retailing in general shares many characteristics with (reward-based) crowdfunding, and e-commerce platforms have a special expertise in the intermediation of transactions. An e-commerce platform matches sellers with buyers, cares for financial transaction (via online banking, e-cash or third-party-payment services) and the exchange of goods. Likewise, a CFP matches PIs with crowdfunders, and handles the transfer of investments and rewards. The tasks of a CFP are very similar to the ones of an e-commerce platform. Therefore, e-commerce platforms can easily provide crowdfunding as additional service. A customer who is satisfied with a platform's e-commerce service is likely willing to use its crowdfunding features. Importantly, e-commerce platforms hold a vast amount of customer data which can also be used for crowdfunding purposes. For instance, a PI's consumption and payment history can indicate his creditworthiness. In the end, an established e-commerce platform is likely to more easily evoke trust and credibility for crowdfunding compared to a nameless *start-up CFP*.

A prominent example for an *e-commerce CFP* is *Alibaba*'s *Taobao zhongchou [淘宝众筹]*, a platform which provides rewards-based crowdfunding projects. According to Zero2IPO, *Taobao zhongchou* in 2014 only ranked fifth in China in terms of the number of crowdfunding projects. However, these projects were overfunded with 267.8%, which reflects the platform's success rate. Although, the ratio of fundings per investor at *Taobao zhongchou* was relatively low,[134] this CFP in 2014 could attract a total of more than half a million crowdfunders.[135] Moreover, even though, *Taobao zhongchou* (or *Alibaba* respectively) is unlikely to gain high revenues from its current reward-based CF business model, crowdfunding has the potential to lure further customers to one of *Alibaba*'s websites and eventually pledge revenues from other business operations. Simultaneously, *Alibaba* and its financial arm, *Ant Financial*, are considering to start a proprietary equity-based crowdfunding platform.[136] Ultimately, crowdfunding is an expansion of *Alibaba*'s business model and supports the company's aspiration to become a comprehensive financial service provider.[137]

Besides *Alibaba*, China's second largest e-commerce platform, *Jingdong*, since 2014 also has been providing crowdfunding via an affiliate, the already mentioned *Jingdong zhongchou [京东众筹]*. However, in contrast to *Taobao zhongchou*, *Jingdong zhongchou* already provides both rewards- and equity-based crowdfunding, and recommends its PIs to apply the combined model.[138] At the end of 2014, *Jingdong zhongchou* had by far the highest number of registered crowdfunders, namely 591,742,[139] and despite its fair rank in terms of the number of listed projects,[140] on average its projects were heavily over-funded by 1240.9%.[141] These figures are even more striking against the background that *Jingdong* only started its (rewards-based) CFP in July 2014.[142] Thus, I assume that either the projects at *Jingdong zhongchou* were very attractive or that *Jingdong*'s customers generally are eager to invest via crowdfunding. Furthermore, even though *Jingdong* only in March 2015 launched its equity-based CFP, by 2016, it was the leading Chinese CFP in terms of collected funds and market share.[143] In a nutshell, *Jingdong* has succeeded in applying the resources and capabilities from its core business for the purpose of crowdfunding and thereby has become China's largest *(e-commerce) crowdfunding platform*.

[134] RMB 108 compared to RMB 372 at, for instance, *Zhongchou wang*. (Own calculation according to Zero2IPO 2015, p. 17).

[135] Zero2IPO (2015, p. 17).

[136] Li (2015c).

[137] Sugawara (2014, n.p).

[138] Interview with April and Tina, 2015-04-28.

[139] Zero2IPO (2015, p. 17).

[140] 301 projects compared to e.g. 871 projects by *Zhuimeng wang [追梦网]* (Zero2IPO 2015, p. 17).

[141] Zero2IPO (2015, p. 17).

[142] Interview with Bolly, Senior Manager for equity crowdfunding at *Jingdong*, 2015-05-14.

[143] Ibid.

5.5 Embedding Crowdfunding in China's Financial Spectrum

The previous chapters drew a picture of the range of China's crowdfunding landscape. The major forms of crowdfunding identified for China differ in their degree of institutionalisation. Accordingly, Fig. 5.1 presents an approach to locate the different types of Chinese crowdfunding on the spectrum between informal and formal finance. Whilst other countries almost exclusively rely on crowdfunding provided by *start-up CFPs* and a few financial corporates, China features three unique forms of crowdfunding, namely *crowdfunding kafei*, *WeChat crowdfunding* and *e-commerce crowdfunding*. Of these, *WeChat CF* is a modification of traditional informal finance (TIF); *e-commerce CF* is an integrated form of crowdfunding in established e-commerce institutions. *Crowdfunding kafei*, on the other hand, only refers to crowdfunding by its name.

Crowdfunding kafei or *cafés*, in fact, are places which have been created through collective funding by a group of selected people. Similar to a ROSCA, which can be set up for a shared purpose (see Sect. 2.4.3), participants of a *crowdfunding kafei* have a shared investment aim; they enjoy equal rights in line with equal shares of investment. Commonly, all investors know each other, either directly or indirectly, and share a similar background. At least initially, they meet offline and in person, which enforces overall trust. Therefore, according to my definition of crowdfunding, *crowdfunding kafei* actually does not count as crowdfunding as it lacks the online component. Yet, once the group is established offline, most interactions are lifted to the online level (see also Sect. 5.3.3). At the same time, crowdfunding cafés highlight the similarities between traditional informal finance (TIF) and crowdfunding.

In comparison, *WeChat crowdfunding* more obviously is an online extension of TIF. Interactions are primarily confined to personal *(WeChat)* contacts, however,

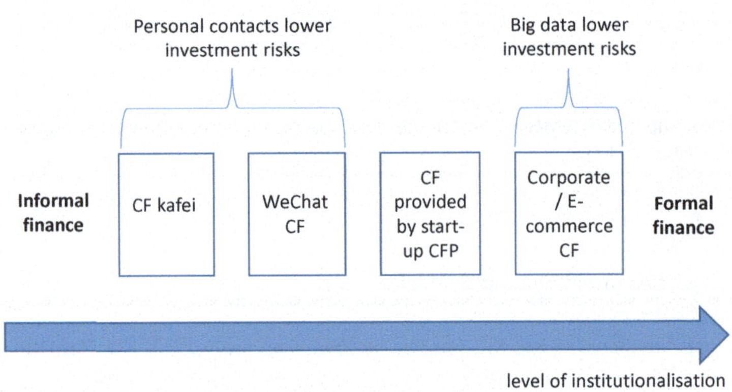

Fig. 5.1 Location of Chinese crowdfunding forms on the financial spectrum

different from TIF, communication and transactions are processed exclusively online. Internet applications are utilised in order to accelerate processes, to ease communication and extend a project's scope. This type of crowdfunding does not include any intermediary; all crowdfunding steps can be implemented by the PI on his own. Typically, financial transactions are cleared via *WeChat*'s integrated payment function, *TenPay*. In the end, *WeChat*'s functionality lowers the costs of informal financial transactions. Like *crowdfunding kafei*, *WeChat crowdfunding* is tolerated by authorities, though not officially recognised as a form of crowdfunding.

E-commerce crowdfunding, on the other hand, is an amplification of customary online retailing. Platforms like *Alibaba* and *Jingdong* are established online players, which can rely on an abundance of assets and long track records. They enjoy government authority, not least due to the importance of e-commerce and consumption for the Chinese economy. Therefore, they are recognised actors and their business is entirely institutionalised. Consequently, *e-commerce crowdfunding* is simultaneously authorised and has enjoyed formalisation from the very beginning. Thus, in comparison to the other mentioned forms of crowdfunding, *e-commerce crowdfunding* is the most established crowdfunding type in China.

Still, all of the above mentioned three types of crowdfunding are able to reduce risks and uncertainties. In terms of *crowdfunding kafei* and *WeChat crowdfunding*, investment risks can be reduced by the fact that PIs and investors commonly know each other personally. Therefore, investors can better estimate the PI's credibility. *E-commerce crowdfunding*,[144] on the other hand, reduces risks through big data analysis. For instance, a PI who has previously purchased a good via *Alibaba* and paid via *AliPay* has concurrently left some marks on his liability, his solvency and ultimately his credit rating.[145] Thus, *e-commerce CFPs* are able to pre-select campaigns according to the trustworthiness of the respective PIs. Likewise, such platforms are able to check the credibility of investors. In the end, the Chinese types of crowdfunding can better reduce risks as they either rely on personal contacts or on big data analysis.

5.6 Case Studies on Crowdfunding in China

The following three case studies shall give further insight into the various forms of crowdfunding in China, in the diverse approaches of respective CFPs, the different means by which PIs spread the word about their campaigns, and the corresponding results they have achieved. Although these cases do not draw a complete picture of crowdfunding in China, the features of these examples give an idea of some typical characteristics. The following campaigns were run on different Chinese

[144]This also refers to financial *corporate crowdfunding*.

[145]Likewise, a client who has previously utilised other financial products from a financial service provider has left some data on his credibility and liability with the financial service provider.

CFPs, namely on *Demohour*, *Dreamore* and *Zhongchou wang*. Whilst *Dalan Youth Hostel* and *Dita* are two real crowdfunding campaigns, which have been carried out by Chinese entrepreneurs in 2011 and 2014 respectively, *DECIDER* describes an experiment conducted by myself in 2015, based on a real German product. Eventually, these cases shall also provide a notion of the dynamics of crowdfunding in China, once a PI understands to employ the power of the crowd.

5.6.1 *Case Study of* Dalan Youth Hostel

The founder of *Dalan Youth Hostel (DYH)*, Jia Yuhao [加于昊], previously had worked as an employee at *AliPay* and *Yahoo* in Beijing. According to him, he started *DYH* out of boredom, in 2011, right after he and his colleagues had quit their jobs at *Yahoo*. Their idea was to open a guest house in Lhasa, Tibet province. As they lacked the money for the hostel's interior and did not want to approach a business angel in order to keep full control of their project, they decided to ask their friends whether the latter had any things they wanted to get rid of.[146] As all of the co-founders had a background in the IT sector, they had well established online networks; Jia himself during that time could already rely on about 2500 personal *Weibo* contacts and even more people followed Jia's *Weibo* account. Correspondingly, his request met great response as "anyone has something to give away".[147] Initially, the founders merely intended to collect second-hand furniture via their online channels.

Due to the broad online coverage of *DYH*, the founders of *Demohour (Dianming shijian [点名时间])*, China's first reward-based CFP, also learned about *DYH*'s success story shortly after *DYH*'s initiation. *Demohour* approached the founders of *DYH* and the platform finally persuaded them to set up a campaign on its website. From then onwards, the founders of *DYH* started to ask for money from the crowd. *DYH* was planned to become *Demohour*'s first successful crowdfunding project; in fact, *Demohour* intended to utilise *DYH*'s fame to make the crowdfunding platform more popular, and this plan worked out pretty well. *DYH* started with a target sum of RMB 1000, which was quickly extended to a multiple of that amount. "A target sum of RMB 40,000 sounded far too high for me, but we agreed with Demohour's suggestion. Only later, we were thinking about how we could spend the money."[148] In the end, there were 2595 investors from whom *DYH* collected a total of RMB 146,400. Comparing this sum to the average amount of collected funds for projects at *Demohour* in 2014, i.e. RMB 40,863,[149] and considering that by 2011, hardly any Chinese was familiar with the concept of crowdfunding, *DYH*'s campaign was a great success. As a reward, the founders of *DYH* promised each crowdfunder free

[146]Interview with Jia Yuhao, 2013-08-28.

[147]Interview with Jia Yuhao, 2013-08-26.

[148]Ibid.

[149]Own calculation according to Zero2IPO (2015, p.17).

accommodation in their guesthouse.[150] Presumably, Jia and his colleagues could easily engage the crowd as Tibet is an attractive destination also for domestic tourists and as the story of the founders—their transformation from IT nerds to adventurous drop-outs—was quite appealing. Ultimately, *DYH* helped *Demohour* to kick-start its CFP. The *DYH* project accelerated from the very beginning as the co-founders, all previous employees of *Sina*, *Baidu*, *Alibaba*, or *Yahoo*, knew exactly how to apply the power of the internet.

DYH already had a substantial crowd when *Demohour* started to push the project with and for the purpose of crowdfunding. Furthermore, the campaign was promoted with the help of a Chinese celebrity called Lao Luo.[151] In 2011, Lao had about seven million online fans. According to *DYH*'s founder, Jia Yuhao, Lao Luo shared the project on his *Weibo* account and thereby kick-started the crowdfunding campaign.[152] The support by Lao Luo increased the project's prominence and added to its credibility way beyond the personal networks of the project initiators. People henceforth trusted *DYH* and *Demohour* without knowing the founders personally; they transferred money via *Demohour*'s platform to strangers, just because Lao Luo, someone they appreciated, had recommended the project to them. Probably, *DYH* would have collected less capital without the support by Lao Luo.

An additional success factor of the *DYH* project was Jia Yuhao's ability to win the crowd for his idea. He frequently informed all of his followers via several social media channels; he posted pictures from the evolving *DYH* so that e.g. early contributors could find and actually see their discarded furniture placed in the guest house. "This is the key to make a project popular: People need to be integrated, you need to make them feel excited and interested about a project. Make the project explicit; explain what you are actually doing with the money, and continuously update investors in order to make them trust. Other founders think that the crowdfunding platform does PR for them, but this does not work."[153] Jia furthermore stressed that crowdfunding in fact is not about money, but about the originality and fun[154] that a project provides. Correspondingly, *Demohour* wanted to engage Jia Yuhao as a consultant to train other PIs on how to utilise tools like *Weibo*, *WeChat* and *Facebook*, yet he rather pursued the opening of another *DYH* in Nepal. The ambitious founder was certain that if he had run his crowdfunding campaign in China some years later, it would have been even more successful, as by then more Chinese knew about the concept of crowdfunding and his strategy of integrating the crowd probably would have worked out even better.[155]

---

[150] Xu (2012).

[151] Luo Yonghao [罗永浩] also known as Lao Luo [老罗], i.e. "Old Luo".

[152] Interview with Jia Yuhao, 2013-08-26.

[153] Ibid.

[154] Jia explicitly said "zhongchou hen hao wanr [众筹很好玩儿]", i.e. "crowdfunding is a lot of fun". Interview with Jia Yuhao, 2013-08-28.

[155] Interview with Jia Yuhao, 2013-08-26.

Jia Yuhao identified the benefits and pitfalls of crowdfunding in China and drafted the crowdfunding campaign for *DYH* accordingly. First of all, with (rewards-based) crowdfunding, PIs rather set the funding target low[156] and raise it later if they have achieved it. This reflects Jia's experience, because *DYH* started out with RMB 1000 and raised the level to RMB 40,000 once the previous target was outreached; thereafter, even the second target was outreached. Secondly, as Chinese netizens and therefore potential crowdfunders are quite young (see Sect. 4.4), they need to be addressed with the right online communication tools. Jia Yuhao and his colleagues were experts in China's social media landscape due to their professional backgrounds and knew exactly how to reach the crowd.

A notable characteristic of this early crowdfunding project was the relatively low age of all crowdfunders and the high number of female investors.[157] Likewise the founders of the platform *Zhuimeng wang [追梦网]* concluded from an internal analysis of projects run on their platform that the male to female ratio of its investors differed from the general male to female ratio on Chinese websites. Whereas the latter is usually 3:2, investors were evenly distributed in terms of gender at *Zhuimeng wang*.[158] Considering the fact that females are generally underrepresented in China's internet industry, crowdfunding seems to attract disproportionally more women. Whether this can be explained by the fact that "females are more easily exited for crowdfunding projects"[159] as Jia Yuhao claims, may still need further research. In any case, PIs in China may be well advised to use this finding and draft their campaigns accordingly.

As discussed before in Sects. 5.3.3 and 5.4.2, the greatest challenge for crowdfunding in China is to gain the trust of the crowd. In this regard, Jia criticised *Demohour*'s initial lack of due diligence: "Dianming's [i.e. Demohour's] previous methods were wrong, there was no prior observation of the founders nor a check of their reliability; there was little advice and guidance from the platform, and no post communication after the project was accomplished."[160] Therefore, Jia and his colleagues tried to evoke trust through regular updates and direct communication with the crowd. Whilst many PIs limit their interaction with the crowd to the running period of the campaign, *DYH* and its founders continued their communication with the crowd after the accomplishment of the project. They also profited from the fact that many crowdfunders later "collected" their reward by visiting the guest house, and by telling their friends about it. These crowdfunders further spread the success story of *DYH* by sharing their experience in social networks.

As early as 2013, Jia Yuhao recognised crowdfunding as a means to prove a concept before companies approach a VC for support. Even today, at a time when marketing strategists find ways to artificially increase the number of fans or

---

[156]See also Sect. 3.3.1.2 and Frydrych et al. (2014).

[157]Interview with Jia Yuhao, 2013-08-28.

[158]Interview with Water, 2015-04-21.

[159]Interview with Jia Yuhao, 2013-08-28.

[160]Interview with Jia Yuhao, 2013-08-28.

followers of a product, person or brand, crowdfunding can still serve as a proof of concept as support of a crowdfunding campaign goes beyond the push of a "Like-button". Whilst it is rather easy to convince people to demonstrate their consent to a certain issue, it takes far more effort to make them invest into a certain project, unless they intend to actively support the project.

All in all, *DYH* and its founders had a rather enthusiastic view on crowdfunding, and managed to succeed with their campaign by telling an exciting story, which was spread extensively with the help of a celebrity and the application of internet communication tools. Although *DYH* has had many imitators, these stayed far behind *DYH*'s success story.[161] One explanation could be *DYH* founders' capabilities, including their professional backgrounds and extensive (online) networks. Another reason could be the impetus which the campaign already had reached before the founders asked for money. Certainly, the offer of free accommodation as reward contributed to the viral spread of the project's story. Finally, Jia Yuhao and *Demohour* were also lucky with the timing of *DYH*'s campaign: Even though crowdfunding was still unknown in China in 2011 and (particularly equity crowdfunding) situated in an absolutely grey area of regulation, Chinese at the time started to become open for the phenomenon of the *share economy*. Thus, *DYH*, besides all other factors mentioned above, in the end also benefited from a first mover advantage.

5.6.2 Case Study of Beverage DECIDER

In order to get a better idea of the Chinese crowdfunding market, in particular, the processes of a Chinese crowdfunding campaign, I initiated my own crowdfunding campaign on the Chinese CFP *Zhongchou wang [众筹网]*. In August 2015, I launched a project which aimed at the introduction of a German alcoholic beverage on the Chinese market, called *DECIDER*. Before setting up a campaign, a PI needs to hold a Chinese mobile number as well as a domestic bank account. *Zhongchou wang* recommends PIs to start with a rather low target sum and rather do several campaigns consecutively. For my project, the target sum was set at RMB 5000 and the running period at 30 days. After some consultation from Grace, the Head of Agricultural Products campaigns at *Zhongchou wang*, I decided on four different reward categories, ranging from RMB 30 (which incorporated one bottle of *DECIDER* plus a promised personal message from the PI) to RMB 1000 (which included six cases or 36 bottles of *DECIDER* plus a cup of coffee with the PI during a personal meeting plus the invitation to join the Decider team and become a priority user for testing new products as reward). In contrast to the majority of Western crowdfunding projects, which commonly include a crowdfunding video, Grace recommended pictures instead as they could be loaded much faster than a video, in particular, if people viewed the project on their mobile devices. The

[161] Interview with Jia Yuhao, 2013-08-26.

project description was bilingually presented, in Chinese (simplified) and English respectively. The campaign was easily set up within 1 day; there was no due diligence by *Zhongchou wang*,[162] presumably as the target sum was very low and as *Zhongchou wang* (or Grace respectively) already knew me personally from a previous interview. Eventually, the crowdfunding campaign collected a total of RMB 2408, and therefore failed.

As this experiment was not controlled for variables like industry, target sum, chosen pictures, etc., it cannot be taken as universally representative for other projects in China; still, its dynamics tell something about crowdfunding in China. Although I had already used Chinese social media previous to the time of the campaign and also maintained some personal contacts to Chinese natives, I deliberately abstained from any (viral) marketing on the *DECIDER* crowdfunding campaign for the first 15 days of the campaign. In line with Jia Yuhao's statement (see Sect. 5.6.1), the CFP did not promote the campaign as I had not paid for additional services like online banner advertisement. There was also no crowdfunder that was coincidentally attracted by the campaign. Of course, this always depends on the nature of the project. After 15 days of inactivity, I started to inform my personal Chinese networks on the *DECIDER* campaign and asked my friends and acquaintances to spread the word about the crowdfunding project. Within 5 days, the project received 41 "Likes" on *Zhongchou wang* and collected 48% of its target sum. Breaking down the collected amount, there were a total of 21 potential investors comprising of seven crowdfunders willing to invest RMB 30, twelve people planning to give RMB 99, zero attracted by the third category (i.e. RMB 189 for a reward including six bottles of *DECIDER* plus a T-shirt plus a personal phone call from the PI), and one person intending to invest RMB 1000. However, all investors belonged either to my direct or first-grade contacts, which demonstrates that the campaign did not become viral by then. Ultimately, as I was not eager to deliver the rewards and hence wanted the campaign not to be accomplished, I stopped promoting the project and instantaneously also the contributions ebbed. Therefore, I conclude that the dynamics of a crowdfunding campaign in China—just like in the West[163]—are highly dependent on a PI's personal networks and her efforts to spread the word about her campaign.

---

[162]Usually, *Zhongchou wang* conducts a two-stage check before a campaign is launched: First, a PI needs to provide general information on his business idea, which is checked by *Zhongchou wang*; secondly, a platform employee calls that PI or meets him in person in order to make a risk assessment; moreover, often PIs need to show respective certificates (Interview with Grace, 2015-04-15).

[163]See e.g. Agrawal et al. (2011).

5.6.3 *Case Study of Air Pollution Meter* Dita

In June 2014, MJ[164] together with three co-founders established a company called *Attkon*, based in Guangzhou. MJ's wife and child both had suffered from allergies caused by air pollution, which is one of the most severe environmental issues that China is facing. From the very beginning, the founders intended to establish not just one single product, but a hardware company with a range of intelligent products, of which *Dita*[165] should become the company's first success. In fact, *Dita* within seconds measures the level of air pollution in- and outdoor and tells the user whether he can stay in his environment without harming his health. Whilst there are comparable smart devices on the market, *Dita* distinguishes with its relatively small size, easy handling and attractive design, and is available in a plastic and wooden version. Whilst the first prototype of *Dita* was soon created after the company's foundation, *Attkon* lacked the capital to marketise its product on a broad scale. Yet, there seemed to be a market for *Dita* from the very beginning as the product addresses the fear of many Chinese consumers.[166]

From 2015 onwards, *Attkon* used a combination of different crowdfunding models in order to finance the acceleration of its business. Initially and during the beta version of *Dita*, the company relied on *WeChat crowdfunding*, though there was no explicit target sum set. *Attkon* thereby pre-sold 200 devices to the founders' friends exclusively via *WeChat*; the customers directly paid online via *TenPay* or *AliPay*, and were asked to provide feedback to *Attkon*, which eventually shaped the final version of *Dita*. As the founders of *Attkon* and a majority of their friends belonged to the IT scene, eventually the e-commerce platform *Jingdong* learned about *Dita* and was attracted by the product. Similar to the case of *Demohour* and *DYH*, *Jingdong* in fact approached *Attkon*; the e-commerce company was convinced by the high quality of *Dita* and wanted to gain the product for its crowdfunding platform. After a successful campaign at *Jingdong zhongchou*,[167] *Jingdong* further promoted *Dita* at its e-commerce platform where people could directly buy the device. During that time, *Attkon* projected its internationalisation and therefore started another crowdfunding campaign at the American CFP *Crowdsupply*.[168] However, *Attkon* stopped this project before the actual crowdfunding period had expired as the campaign lost momentum.[169] In the end, *Dita*, at least within China,

---

[164]My interview partners did not mention MJ's Chinese name. They apparently addressed their boss only with his English nickname.

[165]The name derives from the sound, which occurs once the device is turned on.

[166]Interview with April and Tina, 2015-04-28.

[167]See JD Finance (2015): In total, the campaign collected RMB 317,016.

[168]See Crowdsupply (n.d.).

[169]According to April, an employee at *Attkon*, the company untimely stopped the campaign in order to do another crowdfunding on America's most popular CFP, *Kickstarter*; however, by the end of 2016, there was no such campaign on *Kickstarter*.

became a success due to *WeChat* and *Jingdong*.[170] In this case, *WeChat crowdfunding* served *Attkon* as a proof of concept and kick-started viral marketing, whilst *e-commerce crowdfunding* fostered marketing and eventually secured financing.

Attkon was easily convinced by *Jingdong* to launch a campaign on its CFP for several reasons. First of all, *Jingdong* promised the start-up broad PR after reaching a threshold of RMB 150,000 via crowdfunding. Only 15 min after the campaign's start, the threshold was reached as MJ and his co-founders had pushed *Dita* in the forefront of the launch via *WeChat*. Thereafter, *Jingdong* placed an advertisement banner of *Dita* on the starting site of its homepage, which further increased the interest in *Attkon*'s crowdfunding campaign. Secondly, *Dita* at *Jingdong* was indirectly subsidised by the government. Whilst the project offered seven different categories of rewards, ranging from RMB one (including the chance to win a *Dita* device by lottery) to RMB 1099 (including two wooden *Dita* devices), the second-, third- and fourth-ranked reward categories all included a voucher worth of RMB 100; this money according to *Jingdong* was provided by the government[171] and was put on the crowdfunders' *Jingdong e-card* so that the amount could be used for any purchases at *JD.com*. Thus, any crowdfunder contributing to the *Dita* project and opting for the middle reward categories automatically received a voucher. Ultimately, *Attkon* was convinced by *Jingdong*'s market power, though it took the founders a lot of upstream effort to make their crowdfunding project stick out from the mass of crowdfunding projects at *JD.com*.[172]

It is worth to mention that, although *Dita* at *Jingdong* was framed as a crowdfunding project, the campaign was rather a mixture of lottery and pure sales. First and foremost, each reward category except the lowest one included one or two *Dita* devices plus some minor extras. In addition, *Attkon* did not state explicitly what the company actually needed the funding for. Despite the previously set target sum, the production start of *Dita* was not dependent on whether this goal was reached. Rather, *Attkon* could have fulfilled the pre-orders individually, which diminishes the idea of *the power of the crowd*. Once *Dita* had reached critical sales numbers (i.e. RMB 150,000), *JD.com* was willing to reward *Attkon* with free advertisement on its e-commerce platform, which further increased *Dita*'s sales figures. Thus, *Attkon*

---

[170]Interview with April and Tina, 2015-04-28.

[171]Unfortunately, my interview partners from *Attkon* could not explain the reasons behind this subsidy. I assume that the Chinese government supported projects like *Dita* at *Jingdong* for one or several of the following reasons: First, *Attkon* with *Dita* addresses a social issue and raises awareness for environmental problems. As the PRC in particular struggles with air pollution, the government could have subsidised *Dita* in order to demonstrate its appreciation for the product. Secondly, in 2013, China's premier, Xi Jinping, proclaimed the *Chinese Dream* (see also Sect. 6.2), which should be achieved by means of reform and innovation (Feng 2015, p. 166.) The Chinese government could have subsidised *Dita* as it is an innovative venture. Moreover, as crowdfunding is a means to promote innovative projects, the government could have intended to reward those who invest into crowdfunding. Thirdly, this kind of subsidy could have been meant to increase overall domestic consumption, which is a strategic goal of China's recent policies (see Sect. 4.4.4).

[172]Interview with April and Tina, 2015-07-28.

actually was not dependent on the crowd to start its business, the enterprise rather employed crowdfunding to accelerate the company's growth.

However, this case demonstrates how a typical Chinese crowdfunding expands and how the win-win situation evolves: In the beginning, *Jingdong* scouted for attractive projects in order to promote its crowdfunding platform. For *Dita*, on the other hand, a powerful CFP could yield not just funding but also sustainable PR. After the successful accomplishment of the campaign, *Attkon* could continue selling its product via *JD.com* and the latter could confidently list *Dita* on its e-commerce platform as the alleged crowdfunding had functioned as proof of concept. Thus, in a nutshell, crowdfunding (or rather just the term crowdfunding) was employed as a means to make a new product marketable on an established e-commerce platform.

5.6.4 Conclusion of Cases

Even though the above mentioned case studies were chosen randomly and they do not represent the entire Chinese crowdfunding market, still several conclusions can be drawn. Some of these findings, however, are not China specific but refer to crowdfunding in general.

Crowdfunding (in China and elsewhere) is first and foremost about inspiring and integrating the crowd. Although, crowdfunding per se is a tool based on anonymity, the mobilisation of friends, relatives and acquaintances is essential. Only if a substantial number of supporters can be motivated in the very beginning (like in the case of *DYH* and *Dita*) a crowdfunding can succeed. The founders of *DYH* perfectly translated the integration of the crowd by offering free accommodation as reward to all contributors. Likewise, regular updates of the crowd are important in order to give the crowd a feeling of participation. In the end, the cases demonstrate that crowdfunding is not a method that succeeds without any personal contacts, but in fact is an intensive process that relies heavily on the support of a PI's networks, at least in the very beginning.

Secondly, crowdfunding is about utilising online tools. If PIs know how to exploit the power of the internet, including social media, search engine optimisation, etc., they can leverage their crowdfunding campaign. The founders of both *DYH* and *Dita* had a relevant IT background and could employ their skills from previous jobs. In the end, this IT expertise also supported them to attract a large crowd.

Thirdly, crowdfunding should help solving a problem of the crowd or at least create customer value. In the case of *Dita* and with their campaign on *Jingdong zhongchou*, the founders addressed Chinese crowdfunders with a China specific problem (i.e. air pollution) and eventually succeeded with their campaign as the crowd easily could see value in that product. In contrast, *Attkon* failed with the same product on an American CFP. Whilst the failure of this campaign probably had several reasons, I argue that for American crowdfunders *Dita* provided less value than for Chinese crowdfunders as smog is a less prominent problem in the US compared to China. Therefore, campaigns which direct at a crowd's problem are more likely to be funded.

Fourthly, because Chinese crowdfunders tend to be young and 50% female, Chinese PIs should arrange their campaigns accordingly in order to address a potentially large crowd. The relatively low age of Chinese crowdfunders is no surprise as this is reflected by the average low age of Chinese netizens (see Sect. 4.4). However, it is indeed striking that *Zhuimeng wang* identified a relatively high number of female crowdfunders on their platform as there is commonly a sharp bias towards male investors.[173] This could have further impact on the entire crowdfunding landscape as the number of female crowdfunders eventually contributes to the number of female entrepreneurs.[174] Irrespective of this correlation, Chinese PIs should have the constitution of the Chinese crowd in mind when they set up their crowdfunding campaign.

Fifthly, crowdfunding is about creating trust. The founders of *DYH* managed to generate trust with the help of a celebrity's reputation. People who did not know the founders personally could rely on Lao Luo's recommendation. As the latter shared *DYH*'s campaign via his social media channels he kind of functioned as a warrantor for the reliability of the project. *Dita*, on the other hand, could rely on *Jingdong*'s reputation, once the project was set up at the e-commerce platform's CFP. *DECIDER*, by contrast, could neither rely on any famous supporter nor on an *e-commerce CFP*. There are certainly further means, which PIs can utilise in order to create trust. Yet, the above mentioned—*celebrities and e-commerce CFPs*—were proven to be very effective.

Finally, a successful *WeChat CF* campaign can pave the way for an *e-commerce CF* campaign. As mentioned before, a *WeChat crowdfunding* can function as a proof of concept as an entrepreneur thereby can demonstrate the demand for his product. Once *Dita* succeeded with its *WeChat crowdfunding*, *Jingdong zhongchou* was eager to list the product on its CFP. Moreover, by means of *WeChat crowdfunding*, a PI can establish a fan-base which potentially would also support a subsequent *e-commerce CF* campaign. Ultimately, *WeChat CF + e-commerce CF* provides a combined crowdfunding mode similar to the combined principle of *rewards-based CF + equity-based CF* (see Sect. 5.4.2). I argue that for Chinese PIs *WeChat crowdfunding* is easier to handle, more convenient and much more effective than the original *rewards-based crowdfunding*. Thus, I recommend Chinese PIs to opt for *WeChat crowdfunding* and complement a successful campaign with *e-commerce CF*, which could be either rewards- or equity-based.

The question remains whether crowdfunding in China will eventually evolve towards a fully institutionalised financial tool or whether rather informal forms like *WeChat crowdfunding* will exist simultaneously. This will not least depend on whether *e-commerce CF* and other forms of *corporate crowdfunding* can meet the entire demand and serve all Chinese PIs. Certainly, there will always be projects,

---

[173] Teare and Desmond (2016, n.p).

[174] de Vasconcelos (2015).

which do not fit the business model of certain CFPs. For instance, *Jingdong zhongchou* is unlikely to be interested in a campaign like *DYH* as the project does not incorporate a product which after a successful crowdfunding could be marketised on *Jingdong*'s e-commerce platform. Thus, projects like *DYH* need alternative forms of crowdfunding, e.g. *WeChat crowdfunding*. In the end, China's different types of crowdfunding—just like informal and formal finance—serve a different clientele with different purposes. Therefore, I assume that China's crowdfunding landscape will stay just as multifaceted as its traditional (informal) finance sector is. For the subsequent analysis, I subsume *WeChat CF* and *e-commerce CF* as *Chinese crowdfunding*.[175]

5.7 Embedding Chinese Crowdfunding in the Theoretical Context

5.7.1 Principal-Agent-Relations and Transaction Cost Economics of WeChat Crowdfunding and E-Commerce Crowdfunding

Similar to Sect. 3.4, which analysed the Original crowdfunding (OCF) model in terms of principal-agent-relations and transaction costs, this chapter specifically considers *WeChat CF* and *e-commerce CF* and embeds the latter in the theoretical context of Chap. 2. As introduced previously, an executing agent usually has more information than his principal. These information asymmetries bear the risks of *adverse selection*, *moral hazard* and *hold up*. Moreover, transaction costs influence an actor's decision, for instance, in terms of his choice of finance. I therefore refer to the classification of transaction costs by Dahlmann (1979) and Furubotn and Richter (1991), and distinguish between costs for information search, bargaining + preparing, decision making, and policing + enforcement. By contrasting Chinese crowdfunding with OCF and with each other in terms of principal-agent-relationships and transaction costs, similarities and differences become obvious.

Figure 5.2 (Kortleben and Vollmar 2012) illustrates that in *WeChat crowdfunding* there are only two different actors involved. There is no immanent intermediary, because the PI executes the campaign by himself by means of the features of *WeChat* and the crowd. Thus, there are only two P-A-relations. As the PI primarily addresses his direct *WeChat* contacts and consequently both the crowd and the PI know each other personally, the risk of adverse selection is negligible. For the same reason, situations of moral hazard and hold up in both relationships, though immanent, are reduced to a minimum.

[175] As *crowdfunding kafei* does not fit my (online) definition of crowdfunding, it is not part of my subsequent analysis.

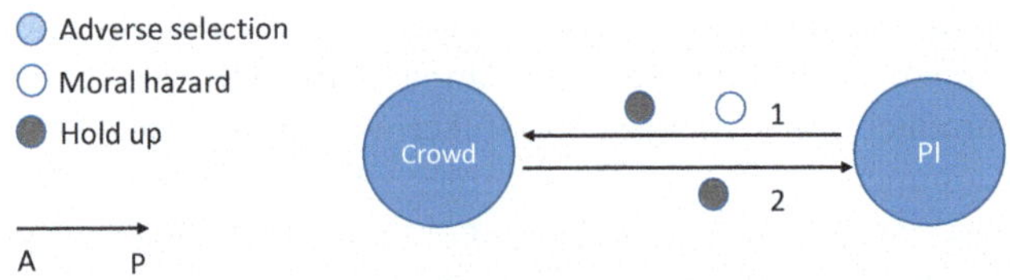

Fig. 5.2 Principal-agent-relations and potential threats of a WeChat crowdfunding campaign

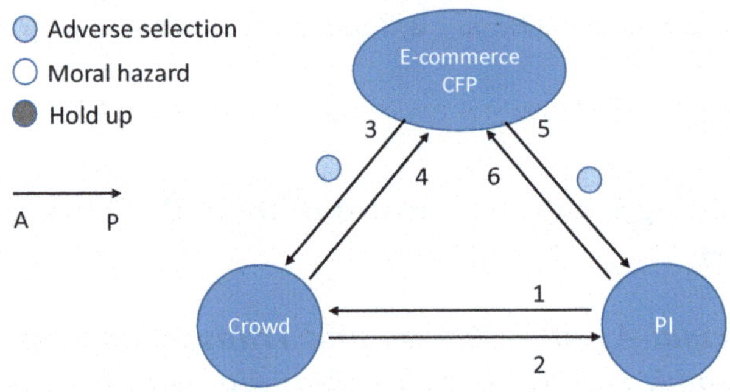

Fig. 5.3 Principal-agent-relations and potential threats of an e-commerce crowdfunding campaign

For instance, after a successful campaign the PI as agent (relationship one) could theoretically use the collected funds for other purposes than previously stated in front of his crowd (i.e. a *moral hazard* problem); likewise, he could run away with the crowd's investments (i.e. *hold up*). However, in both cases he probably would be dismissed by his *WeChat* contacts (i.e. his friends). Moreover, as *WeChat* crowdfunders are often interconnected, one suspicious investor could easily warn his peers of the PI's (potential) misconduct. Therefore, a PI applying *WeChat crowdfunding* is likely to have an interest in avoiding P-A-problems. On the other hand, the crowd as agent (relationship two) theoretically could steal the PI's business idea (i.e. a *hold up* problem) once it has heard about it via a *WeChat crowdfunding* appeal. However, the principal (i.e. the PI) would only share his project with people he trusts. Although a *WeChat crowdfunding campaign* can easily be shared amongst friends' friends, the spread of the word is still restricted to a manageable group of people. In case someone within that circle cheated on the PI, it would be very likely that that person could be identified. Thus, with *WeChat crowdfunding*, situations of *hold up* are manageable for the PI as long as he has wisely pre-selected his crowd.

In terms of *e-commerce crowdfunding*, the same P-A-relationships as in the OCF model (see Sect. 3.4.1, Fig. 3.3) can be identified, which are depicted in Fig. 5.3 (Kortleben and Vollmar 2012). However, *e-commerce CF* compared to OCF bears less risk. First of all, an e-commerce CFP, in contrast to a *start-up CFP*, can rely on big data gathered from its core business. Big data enables the platform to screen and pre-select both creditworthy PIs and solvent investors. Consequently, *adverse selection* problems of the CFP as principal (relationship four and six) are reduced to a minimum. Yet, there is still the danger that the PI chooses the wrong CFP (*adverse selection* problem in relationship five) or the crowd selects an inappropriate platform (*adverse selection* problem in relationship three). Secondly, as most Chinese utilise online retailing and thereby leave more or less virtual marks—for instance by creating a purchaser's account, a customer typically states personal contact details which often need to be verified prior to a purchase—every PI and crowdfunder utilising e-commerce crowdfunding is traceable. As a consequence, theoretically, an *e-commerce CFP* can prevent all situations of *moral hazard* and *hold up* between PIs and the crowd. If, lets say, a PI after a successful campaign on an *e-commerce CFP* falls short of his previously stated project plans or even commits some fraud and runs away with the collected funds (*moral hazard* and *hold up* situations in relationship one), he can relatively easily be tracked unless he changes his identity. Likewise, a crowdfunder who obviously copies a PI's business idea (*hold up* situation in relationship two), can be persecuted if he has previously left his data with the e-commerce platform.[176] Ultimately, the fact that an *e-commerce CFP* and consequently the e-commerce platform itself could lose its good reputation, increases the probability that the platform would go after fraudulent (and maybe also after default) cases.

From the analysis above, it becomes obvious that *WeChat crowdfunding* and *e-commerce crowdfunding* economise on transaction costs. As illustrated in Fig. 3.5 in Sect. 3.4.1, with the OCF concept, PIs usually face relatively high costs of information search, bargaining + preparing and decision making. Crowdfunders, on the other hand, are confronted with transaction costs for information search and monitoring. If a PI opts for *WeChat crowdfunding*, she no longer has to choose between several CFPs. Moreover, her crowd is already largely pre-defined as it is based on her direct and indirect *WeChat contacts*. Still, she has to put efforts on the setup of her campaign and decide on issues like rewards. Yet, regular updates for the crowd can easily be handled and distributed via *WeChat*'s instant messenger or blog function, though the PI has to conceive the contents for these updates. From the perspective of the crowdfunders, information search costs are close to zero within a *WeChat crowdfunding* campaign as all information are likely to be presented by the PI.[177] Furthermore, as the crowdfunders directly or indirectly know the PI and would only transfer money via *TenPay* (i.e. directly to the PI's account) if they trust that person, I assume that their aspirations for monitoring of the PI are rather low. Thus, compared to the OCF model, in which the PI and the crowdfunders commonly do not know each other in advance, *WeChat crowdfunding* incurs less transaction costs for both PIs and also crowdfunders.

---

[176]Of course, the success of such persecution also depends on the legislature and the courts in action.

[177]It is very unlikely that a crowdfunder would deliberately search for a suitable *WeChat crowdfunding* project amongst his *WeChat* contacts.

E-commerce crowdfunding, in contrast to *WeChat crowdfunding*, cannot rely on personal contacts and informal information, which would reduce overall transaction costs. Yet, the integration of crowdfunding with an e-commerce platform, which is an established institution, likewise reduces transaction costs (see also Fig. 2.2). In addition, by means of big data analysis the e-commerce CFP can check the reliability of all involved actors. Framed differently, all PIs and potential crowd-funders more or less voluntarily provide relevant data to the e-commerce platform (and thereby indirectly to the *e-commerce CFP*) when they utilise e-commerce. Therefore, e-commerce crowdfunding includes some form of *signalling*. With big data analysis, *screening* and monitoring theoretically can be outsourced completely to the CFP. From my interviews, I have learned that Chinese *e-commerce CFPs* commonly support PIs with the setup and preparation of their campaigns. Thereby, PIs who launch their crowdfunding campaign on an e-commerce CFP have low bargaining power. Consequently, not only their preparation but (involuntarily) also their decision making power and therefore their decision making costs are rather low. Probably, some PIs are deterred from *e-commerce crowdfunding* because of this low bargaining power. Still, from a transaction cost perspective and compared to OCF and *WeChat crowdfunding*, *e-commerce crowdfunding* incurs the least transaction costs for both, PIs and the crowd.

Finally, *WeChat CF* and *e-commerce CF* differ in terms of their governance structure, which is due to their disparities in the pivotal dimensions *frequency*, *uncertainty* and *ease of verification*. Although any *WeChat crowdfunding* campaign is a unique event, the relation between the respective PI and his crowd (i.e. his direct or indirect *WeChat* contacts) typically is based on frequent or at least occasional interaction. By contrast, actors of an *e-commerce CF* campaign commonly have no relationship beyond the crowdfunding campaign and interaction between the PI and the crowd is at most occasional. Uncertainties increase with the level of information asymmetries. These are relatively high with any form of crowdfunding (see also Sect. 3.4.1), yet the personal characteristic of *WeChat CF* lowers these to a modest level. Likewise, the reliability of the involved actors can relatively easily be verified within *WeChat CF*. On the other hand, in terms of *e-commerce CF* verification is much harder, unless it is based on a well-founded big data analysis. In sum, *WeChat CF* is characterised by frequent interaction amongst involved actors, modest uncertainties and relative ease of verification. According to Williamson (1985) (see also Fig. 2.3) the recommended governance structure for transactions with such criteria is a bilateral or relational contract respectively, which is just the case with *WeChat crowdfunding*. In contrast, e-commerce CF incorporates low frequency, high uncertainties and difficulties in terms of verification, and thus in line with Williamson's assumptions is ruled by a third party (the *e-commerce CFP*) and neoclassical contracts respectively.

5.7.2 Chinese Crowdfunding Versus Classic Financial Intermediaries

Similar to Sect. 3.4.2, which contrasted the OCF concept with a commercial bank, this chapter analyses the differences and similarities of Chinese crowdfunding with a classical financial intermediary. In terms of their transformational functions, *WeChat CF* and *e-commerce CF* do not essentially differ from Western crowdfunding or OCF respectively as neither type of crowdfunding fulfils the dimensions of lot-size transformation, term transformation, and risk transformation. *WeChat CF* does not rely on any immanent financial mediator; rather the PI handles his transactions himself by means of the platform *WeChat*. Consequently, *WeChat crowdfunding* does not incur financial coordination per se.

In *e-commerce crowdfunding*, on the other hand, the *e-commerce CFP* takes over financial coordination between PIs and crowdfunders. As stated in Sect. 2.3.1, the job of a commercial bank commonly includes the acquisition and processing of data, and sometimes also the repackaging and sale of information to other entities. By contrast, *e-commerce CFPs* do not need to acquire external data as they can directly obtain (processed) data from their mother companies.[178] Moreover, in comparison to *start-up CFPs*, *e-commerce CFPs* are typically more renowned and thus often enjoy a better reputation. Therefore, in case they cannot exclusively rely on (internal) data from their mother company, they could relatively easily obtain external information from other entities. Irrespective of where an *e-commerce CFP* derives its data from, by means of big data analysis, it—at least in theory—can easily estimate the PIs' creditworthiness. Furthermore, as *e-commerce CFPs* commonly also rely on assets from their mother company, they are not forced to specialise in order to create economies of scale. In conclusion, *e-commerce CFPs* compared to *start-up CFPs* or *WeChat CF* rather fulfil the role of formal financial intermediaries. However, neither *WeChat CF* nor *start-up CFPs* nor *e-commerce CFPs* have a transformational function like a commercial bank.

5.7.3 E-Commerce Crowdfunding in the Context of Financialisation

As illustrated in Sect. 2.3.2, large corporates increasingly finance themselves, banks thus have to search for a new business model and therefore progressively approach SMEs and households. At the same time, because the state increasingly withdraws

[178] *Demohour*, the first Chinese CFP has changed its business model from rewards-based crowdfunding into a pre-sales of high-tech devices. Legrand (2016, n.p.) argues that *Demohour* has become an *e-commerce CFP*. Yet, I disagree, as *Demohour* first of all is not backed by an established e-commerce platform, and thus the CFP cannot rely on big data, unless the platform collects data itself. Secondly, *Demohour* offers pure pre-sales, rather than projects which are based on sufficient demand from the crowd.

from providing public services (like housing, education, etc.), households need to care for these services themselves, and of late, such services are offered by banks, which thereby not only fill the service gap created by the state, but also increasingly transform their business model. This entire process, which according to Lapavitsas (2013a,b) originated from the abolishment of the *Bretton-Woods-Agreement* in the early 1970s, is called financialisation.[179]

I argue that in China, financialsation 2.0 has already started. Admittedly, China's currency, the Yuan, is far from being freely floated and capital controls continue to be in place.[180] Yet, China's financial sector is currently undergoing crucial change. Established banks are losing ground as new players from outside the financial sector are entering the market. These players predominantly are internet corporates like *BAT*, which since recently are providing financial services besides their core business. For this expansion they rely on an established customer base and a leap of faith resulting from the reputation from their core business. As discussed in Sect. 4.1, formal banks traditionally played a minor role for Chinese POEs and households. Therefore, the latter are used to apply alternative financial sources. As a consequence, those new financial players have a walk-over to fill the financial gap of Chinese POEs and households. In the end, financialisation in China looks like financialisation in the West, except from the fact that it is internet corporates who take over the role of the banks.

Traditionally, Chinese banks served the interests of SOEs, not least due to the fact that the banks themselves were mainly state-owned. Thus, POEs and households had to rely on internal or informal finance (see Fig. 5.4). Since the rise of large private internet corporates, one can observe that these companies not only have been financing themselves, but increasingly also have started to provide capital and other services to POEs and to households (see Fig. 5.5). Tse (2015) also sees these typical developments of financialisation in China, though he does not subsume these under financialisation. "Take finance, health care, and the media. All three sectors have traditionally been state-run, and the government continues to regard each as a strategic area that it is responsible for and wants to control. Yet in each of these industries, despite continuing restrictions, entrepreneurs are finding opportunities and reworking regulatory boundaries in ways that advance the government's broader goals for developing China."[181] In fact, Chinese entrepreneurs are invading industries which traditionally have been reserved for SOEs. The government, on the other hand, tolerates these developments as it sees the benefits of more people having access to such services.

E-commerce crowdfunding per se does not provide finance to households. Rather, P2P finance, consumer finance, the provision of payments, and other services would fit the scheme of Fig. 5.5. At most, *e-commerce crowdfunding* provides finance for PIs and is an alternative investment opportunity for households. Still,

[179] Lapavitsas (2013a, p. 3).

[180] Bloomberg (2016).

[181] Tse (2015, p. 149).

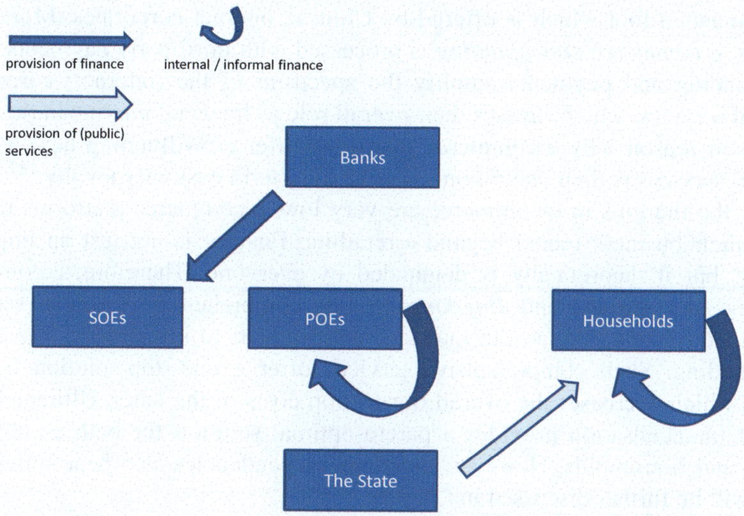

Fig. 5.4 Provision of finance and public services in China before the era of financialisation 2.0

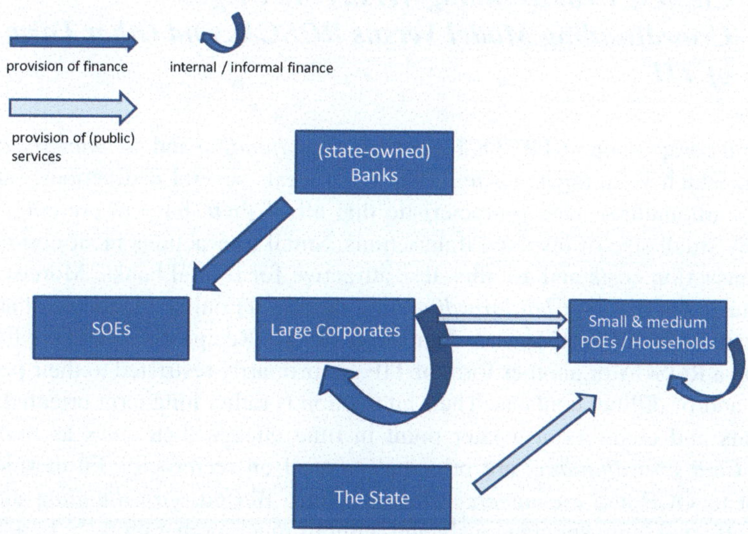

Fig. 5.5 Provision of finance and public services in China since the era of financialisation 2.0

it is a financial tool which is offered by Chinese internet corporates. More often than not, *e-commerce crowdfunding* is processed with third-party payments. Both, crowdfunding and payments amplify the spectrum of the (internet) corporates' financial services, which stresses their overall role as financial intermediaries.

A main reason why e-commerce platforms offer crowdfunding next to other financial services is their aspiration to evoke long-term customer loyalty.[182] Moreover, as the margins in e-commerce are very low, e-commerce platforms need to extend their business model beyond e-retailing. Finance is not just an important industry, but it theoretically is demanded by everyone. Therefore, e-commerce platforms like *Alibaba* and *Jingdong* provide comprehensive financial services, ranging from loans over wealth management products to investments like equity-crowdfunding. Such comprehensive services offer a one-stop-solution for customers, which decreases the overall transaction costs of the latter. Ultimately, this form of financialsation provides a pareto-optimal solution for both e-commerce players and households. However, these interdependencies also bear some risks, which will be further discussed in Chap. 6.

5.7.4 Chinese Crowdfunding Versus the Original Crowdfunding Model Versus ROSCAs and Other Forms of TIF

A general comparison of TIF, OCF, *WeChat crowdfunding* and *e-commerce crowdfunding*, which is summarised in Table 5.3, reveals several distinctions, but also some commonalities. One characteristic that all of them have in common is the relatively small size of involved transactions. Small transactions incur comparably high transaction costs and are thus less attractive for formal banks. Moreover, the table illustrates that *WeChat crowdfunding*, despite its online character, shares several features with ROSCAs and other forms of TIF. Recipients[183] and creditors[184] applying a ROSCA or another form of TIF are primarily restricted to their personal (online and/or offline) contacts. Their interaction is rather long term oriented; often recipients and creditors at a later point in time change their roles as both, TIF and *WeChat crowdfunding*, are principally based on reciprocity. Furthermore, in contrast to OCF and *e-commerce crowdfunding*, *WeChat crowdfunding* and TIF can be effected quite spontaneously and without much preparation.[185] In addition, both types of finance are based on closed circles of people, transactions are neither

[182]Interview with Bolly, 2015-05-14.

[183]Under the term "recipients" I subsume entrepreneurs, start-ups, SMEs, POEs, etc., all kinds of individuals and entities searching for and receiving capital.

[184]Under the term "creditors" I subsume depositors, investors, crowdfunders, etc., all kinds of individuals and entities providing funds.

[185]Presumed that the actor has an established offline or online network respectively.

Table 5.3 Contrasting features of TIF, ROSCAs, OCF, WeChat crowdfunding and e-commerce crowdfunding[a]

	Type of financial tool				
Feature	**TIF**	**ROSCA**	**OCF**	**WeChat CF**	**E-commerce CF**
Size of transactions	Small	Small funds pooled to large sums	Small funds pooled to large sums	Small sums pooled to large sums	Small funds pooled to large sums
Feasibility	Rather spontaneous	Requires planning	Requires planning	Rather spontaneous	Requires planning
Addressees	All kinds	All kinds	All kinds	All kinds	PIs with product-based projects
Networks	Personal	Personal	Relatively anonymous	Personal	Anonymous
Fundament of trust	**Offline contacts/** guanxi; experience; informal information	**Offline contacts/** guanxi; experience informal information	PI's online presence; CFP's due diligence; AON principle	Online/WeChat contacts; personal relationships	Reputation of CFP; big data analysis
Durability	Long term	Long term	Non-recurring	Relatively long	Non-recurring
Incl. reciprocity	Yes	Yes	No	Presumably expected	No
Communication	Face to face	Face to face	Virtual	Virtual	Virtual
Transparency	Low	Low	High	Low	High
Primary location	Developing countries; rural areas	Developing countries; rural areas	Originally in developed countries; rather urban, but everywhere	Chinese phenomenon rural and urban	Chinese phenomenon rural and urban
Interest rates	High	None	Low (just commission)	None	Low (just commission)
Savings capacity	High	High	Only in case of debt- and equity-based crowdfunding	None (as most campaigns are donation- or reward-based	Only in case of debt- and equity-based crowdfunding

[a]Same colours demonstrate similar characteristics

mediated nor supervised by external entities and thus, from an outer perspective, they are rather opaque.

All three types of crowdfunding are based on online tools, which is reflected in the integrated online communication. Furthermore, crowdfunding like ROSCAs per se does not include any interest; only some Chinese CFPs stipulate a fee in form of commission for successfully funded projects. In the West, this commission varies between five and 20%, whilst in China it is usually not higher than 10% and thus lower than the above mentioned average interest rate of TIF. In this regard, *WeChat crowdfunding* is an exception: As PIs can use the app *WeChat* and its payment function *TenPay* for free and there is no additional mediator between recipient and creditors, *WeChat crowdfunding* can be applied without any fees or commission.

From Table 5.3 one can see that TIF and ROSCAs feature some special characteristics. First, they are based on face-to-face interactions, which traditionally enhances trust. Moreover, they are primarily a phenomenon of developing countries and concentrated in rural areas. Thirdly, and as mentioned above, informal finance is known for its savings function and its relatively high deposit rates. Savings imply guaranteed interest rates at preferably low risks. Funds incorporated in TIF commonly have a warrantor who is responsible for the payback of debts and the distribution of potential earnings. In the case of ROSCAs, the role of the warrantor is commonly taken over by the organiser of the association. In sum, social ties evoke compliance and at the same time would enforce punishment in case of default.

So far, there are no studies on the savings function of crowdfunding; most authors primarily see it as a financial tool for start-ups and entrepreneurs. Examining the four different types of crowdfunding (donation-, reward-, debt-, and equity-based crowdfunding), neither donation- nor reward-based crowdfunding yield interest or financial profit for involved creditors. By contrast, debt-based crowdfunding can include some interest payment, and equity-based crowdfunding incorporates shares whose value may increase over time. Yet, any capital collected via any type of crowdfunding must be denoted as risk capital as there is no entity that guarantees the crowdfunders' investment, neither the PI nor the CFP. Previous studies on crowdfunding mainly concentrate on the perspective of the PIs and rather neglect the view of the crowd. The risky character of OCF probably is one explanation for this one-sided focus. *E-commerce crowdfunding* could bring some change, not just in terms of risks but potentially also regarding future research on the savings function of crowdfunding. This point will further be elaborated below.

The peculiarities of TIF, ROSCAs, OCF, *WeChat crowdfunding* and *e-commerce crowdfunding* identify the advantages of each financial institution in terms of transaction costs. On the one hand, the overall transaction costs of each institution can be compared, on the other hand, the respective transaction costs for each actor can be contrasted. The following paragraphs and Table 5.4 illustrate the comparison of overall transaction costs, whilst Chap. 6 deals with the individual costs and implications for the respective players. Both approaches take the transaction costs of TIF as a benchmark.

TIF and ROSCAs incur relatively low information search costs for recipients and creditors as both financial tools are based on personal contacts and close (offline)

Table 5.4 Transaction costs of TIF vs. ROSCA vs. OCF vs. WeChat CF vs. e-commerce CF

	Type of financial tool				
Type of transaction costs	TIF	ROSCA	OCF	WeChat CF	E-commerce CF
Information search	Low	Low	High	Low	Low
Bargaining and preparing	Low to modest	Low	Modest	Low to modest	Low
Decision making	Low to modest	Low	High	Modest	Modest
Policing and enforcement	Low	Low	High or not relevant	Modest or not relevant	Low

relationships. All involved actors commonly know each other due to a shared background, location, occupation, or interest, and correspondingly can estimate each other's reliability and creditworthiness. Of course, maintaining social contacts affords a lot of transaction costs. However, as informal financial actors do not maintain these contacts exclusively for the purpose of finance, costs for the maintenance of networks are neglected at this point. Depending on the type of TIF, bargaining and preparing costs are either low with pre-defined conditions by the creditor, or may vary according to the bargaining power of the recipient.[186] Simultaneously, decision making costs vary with the share of pre-defined conditions. Ultimately, social ties also fulfil a policing role. Consequently, monitoring and enforcement costs of creditors are kept at a very low level.

By contrast, OCF demands much more efforts (see also Figs. 3.4 and 3.5 in Sect. 3.4.1). Although there are standardised procedures and all stages of the campaign are commonly explained by the CFP, the utilisation of OCF incurs at least modest transaction costs for the PI in terms of preparing and bargaining. Likewise, information search and decision making costs are high, not only for the PI but also the crowdfunders. Moreover, in case the CFP or the crowdfunders decide to do a due diligence of the project or monitor the PI's actions during and after the campaign, policing and enforcement costs are very high. In particular the PI and the CFP have to bear relatively high transaction costs with OCF. Yet, in case of a successful campaign—and different from TIF—the CFP gets compensated with a commission, and the PI can enjoy the additional marketing insights gained from crowdfunding.

[186] If a recipient has no bargaining power at all and all conditions of the transaction are pre-defined by the creditor, then bargaining costs are automatically low. If, on the other hand, the recipient has much bargaining power (e.g. due to a high supply in creditors), then his (and the creditors') bargaining costs are correspondingly high. In fact, the recipient needs to make a trade-off between bargaining power and bargaining costs. Likewise, if there is a standard procedure of the respective type of finance, then both recipients and creditors can follow the processes according to the book and preparation costs are relatively low. For example, within a ROSCA, conditions are often pre-defined by the organiser of the association, whilst borrowing and lending amongst friends is often subject to individual bargaining and demands more preparation.

However, as both commission and marketing only come into effect with a successful campaign and as neither the PI nor the CFP know about the campaign results in advance, these benefits may not be deducted from the involved transaction costs. Instead, transaction costs need to be considered individually from the respective perspectives of the different actors. Therefore, I conclude that overall transaction costs of OCF are much higher than transaction cost of TIF.

Chinese crowdfunding incurs less transaction cost than OCF, though the underlying reasons differ for each type. In terms of *WeChat crowdfunding*, a PI no longer needs to inform himself about different CFPs, once he has decided to utilise *WeChat* as platform. Moreover, he addresses his direct contacts which he is likely to know, and therefore can easily set up his campaign without high information search and preparing costs. Moreover, the PI does not have to bargain with a counterpart, unless he asks his crowdfunders which kind of compensation they would prefer; therefore bargaining and decision making costs are kept quite low. Like with OCF, policing and enforcement costs in *WeChat crowdfunding* are dependent on the crowdfunders' willingness to monitor the PI. However, *WeChat crowdfunding* has the advantage that it (like TIF and ROSCAs) relies on social ties, which function as warrantor against fraud. *WeChat* crowdfunders are likely to trust the PI due to their personal connection; the latter can further enhance this trust by frequently updating his crowd via *WeChat*. In sum, monitoring costs are relatively low.

On the other hand, if a PI decides to apply *e-commerce crowdfunding* and his business idea gets accepted, he receives assistance from the *e-commerce CFP*, which reduces his information search and preparation costs. Moreover, with *e-commerce crowdfunding*, the PI's bargaining power is relatively low vis à vis the established e-commerce platform, and overall bargaining costs are accordingly low. *E-commerce crowdfunding* is based on anonymous contacts, therefore PIs and crowdfunders commonly do not know each other in advance. Still, *e-commerce crowdfunding* can provide trust, not just through the reputation of the established e-commerce platforms, but foremost through the utilisation of big data analysis. Finally, the utilisation of big data keeps policing and enforcement costs low as unreliable PIs (and potentially also unreliable investors) would be rejected by *e-commerce CFPs* in advance.

In the end, from Table 5.4 it becomes obvious that ROSCAs incur the least transaction costs, due to their personal and tight organisation, which stresses its reputation as benchmark for (formal and informal) finance (see Sect. 2.4.3). By contrast, OCF demands high efforts in almost all of the mentioned categories. *E-commerce crowdfunding* can economise on transaction costs through big data analysis and the capabilities from the e-commerce platform, whilst *WeChat crowdfunding* just like TIF keeps costs low through social ties and informal information. From a transaction cost perspective, Chinese PIs and investors with established social contacts are likely to opt for *WeChat crowdfunding*, a ROSCA or another form of TIF. Of course, this choice would further depend on the internet and social media affinity of the involved actors. On the other hand, PIs and investors without established social contacts are likely to be more successful with OCF or *e-commerce crowdfunding*. For a Chinese PI, *e-commerce CF* is the better option as long as

Table 5.5 Likely choices of finance by different types of entrepreneurs

	Type of financial tool				
Type of entrepreneur	TIF	ROSCA	OCF (excl. equity CF)	WeChat CF	E-commerce CF
Craftsman	x	x	(x)	x	
Opportunist	x	x	x		x
Inventor	x	x	x	x	x
Life-style	x	x	(x)	x	
Serial	x	x	x		x

he provides a product which the e-commerce platform could be interested in. By contrast, PIs with service-oriented projects or products, which are less suitable for e-retailing should rather opt for OCF. Moreover, as TIF, ROSCAs and *WeChat CF* preclude equity finance, PIs who intend to offer an equity project and investors who are interested to obtain shares of a company would rather opt for (equity-based) *e-commerce crowdfunding* or OCF. Therefore, the choice for a certain financial tool not only depends on the relative level of transaction costs, but also on the purpose which the tool is intended for.

Ultimately, the PIs' choice of finance also depends on the nature of their entrepreneurial character. As craftsmen and life-style entrepreneurs appreciate entrepreneurial independence, I assume that they would neither opt for an equity-based OCF project nor for any form of *e-commerce CF*,[187] but rather choose TIF, the membership in a ROSCA or *WeChat CF*. However, *WeChat crowdfunding*, in comparison to other forms of finance, typically collects smaller sums. Thus, opportunists and serial entrepreneurs would choose any of the other financial tools in order to have a higher leverage effect. Finally, inventor entrepreneurs do not care about 100% ownership, but would choose a financial tool which promotes the progress of their invention best. In sum, as depicted in Table 5.5, it becomes obvious that both TIF and ROSCAs fit the criteria of all types of entrepreneurs. With regard to OCF, only product-based (donation- and reward-based) crowdfunding is suitable for all kinds of entrepreneurs. Equity-based crowdfunding, on the other hand, and *e-commerce CF* only fit the characteristics of opportunists, inventors and serial entrepreneurs. On the other hand, *WeChat CF* can be the best solution for craftsmen, inventors and life-style entrepreneurs.

A PI's choice of finance also depends on his strategic business approach. TIF, *WeChat CF* and rewards-based OCF rather suit for a just-do-it strategy. With these financial tools, a PI can relatively quickly reach a certain milestone of his venture. In comparison, collecting money within a ROSCA takes more time,[188] and both

[187] An e-commerce CFP has considerable bargaining power and thus can exert influence on the entrepreneur.

[188] The more members a ROSCA has, the longer it can take until each individual member has obtained the collected money, unless the PI in question receives one of the first hands.

equity-based projects as well as campaigns on an *e-commerce CFP* tend to demand more preparation and planning.[189] Thus, in the end, the choice of finance also depends on the business strategy of the PI.

The above mentioned analysis is based on theoretical deliberation. In order to verify the results, all considerations would need to be contrasted to empirical findings on entrepreneurs' choice of finance. Moreover, such a comparison would need to have control variables in order to avoid biases resulting from e.g. differences in culture. For instance, it would be very interesting to see whether Western craftsmen, inventors and life-style entrepreneurs would also opt for *WeChat CF* as it is expected for Chinese PIs.

[189]In case of an equity-based project, the venture needs to be incorporated prior to the start of the campaign. A (rewards- or equity-based) campaign on an *e-commerce CFP* commonly demands more preparation (i.e. time and other resources) compared to a *WeChat crowdfunding* campaign (interview with April and Tina, 2015-04-28).

Chapter 6
Traditional Informal Finance Versus Crowdfunding in China

Informal finance has been omnipresent in China for a long time and for certain reasons. Crowdfunding, in particular, the Chinese versions of crowdfunding provide true alternatives to informal finance and eventually could bring some change to China's financial sector. However, the advantages and disadvantages of TIF and crowdfunding respectively differ according to the actor in perspective. Therefore, this chapter deals with the stakeholders of TIF and crowdfunding. It considers the implications for each stakeholder, the benefits of TIF vs. CF for the respective actors, and tries to evaluate under which circumstances crowdfunding for them could become a game changer of informal finance.

6.1 Implications for Chinese Project Initiators

Project initiators, start-ups and individual entrepreneurs demand capital in order to make their venture run. As illustrated in Sect. 2.2, a PI's choice of finance depends on several strands, not least on the stage of the venture, a PI's personal preferences, and also the availability of resources. Any choice brings certain transaction costs but also potential benefits along. A Chinese PI having the choice between TIF and crowdfunding should first ask himself the following questions, and thereupon consider his respective transaction costs.

- Which financial sources do I have?
- How much capital do I intend to rise and how important is independence for me?
- What do I aim to achieve with the financial tool?—The pure financing of my venture or something beyond financing (like marketing)?
- How distinct is my risk aversion? Do I pursue a "just-do-it" or rather a "wait-and-see" strategy?
- How large and how effective are my online and offline networks?
- In how far does the legal status of the respective financial tool affect me?

A. S. Funk, *Crowdfunding in China*, Contributions to Management Science,
https://doi.org/10.1007/978-3-319-97253-4_6

- How can I protect my Intellectual property?
- Which financial tool fits the nature of my venture best?
- Can I rely on any partners or reciprocal support?
- Which means do I have to create trust amongst my creditors?

A PI's choice of finance foremost depends on the availability of financial sources. The majority of Chinese entrepreneurs has no access to established formal financial tools and therefore has to opt for informal alternatives. However, as mentioned in Sect. 5.3.3, amongst the participants in my survey, there was not a single PI who applied crowdfunding because he could not obtain a bank loan, which weakens the idea that crowdfunding is a substitute for formal finance. Still, the question remains, whether crowdfunding, and in particular the Chinese types of crowdfunding, are rather complements or substitutes for TIF. During my research, I came across PIs who initially did not demand any capital or have a project idea at all, but who learned about crowdfunding and wanted to apply it, and only thereupon designed a special project. In fact, a person could possibly apply crowdfunding not out of a financial demand, but rather out of a certain interest. This explains the Chinese connotation of crowdfunding with "fun" and "entertainment". However, for those entrepreneurs who indeed demand capital, their decision between TIF and crowdfunding depends on a number of other issues.

For a recipient of capital, there is often a trade-off between the principal amount that he can obtain and the degree of dependency he is willing to bear. Obtaining larger amounts of capital usually comes along with more obligations and a higher degree of dependency. ROSCAs, equity-based crowdfunding and all kinds of *e-commerce crowdfunding*[1] can be utilised to raise large funds, however, all of the latter are rather long-term oriented financial tools, which incorporate certain duties. Williamson (1985) in this respect spoke of *bonding costs* (see also Sect. 2.1.1). Members of a ROSCA need to have a steady cash-flow and continuously have to contribute a certain amount of capital to the collective. They are obliged to stay within the association, at least until the completion of one cycle. In the end, they will have saved the entire amount of obtained capital themselves, though they are likely to receive the amount to a much earlier point in time. In contrast, with equity-based crowdfunding, a PI gives out shares of his venture to each contributor of the campaign. These stakeholders can be either silent shareholders or actively take part in the venture's decision-making. In any way, with equity crowdfunding the PI needs to render some of his ownership. In terms of (rewards- or equity-based) *e-commerce crowdfunding*, a PI starts a long-term relationship with a powerful entity, *the e-commerce (crowdfunding) platform*, which can provide many resources but at the same time is not merely dependent on one single PI as it has many other interested PIs in the pipeline.[2] Therefore, if a PI opts for *e-commerce crowdfunding*, he will have to follow the platform's instructions in order to enjoy the benefits of

[1]This includes rewards- and equity-based crowdfunding.

[2]Interview with Jason, 2015-05-19.

this form of crowdfunding. ROSCAs, equity-based CF and *e-commerce CF* all come along with relatively high bonding costs, albeit are suitable for raising larger funds, *WeChat CF* and donation-/rewards-based crowdfunding on a *start-up CFP* enable a PI to keep his independence. However, the latter on average raise smaller sums of capital, though exception proves the rule (see e.g. Sect. 5.6.1). TIF also tends to include small scale finance, yet theoretically it is not capped. In TIF, a recipient's degree of dependency is negotiable, though it is probably dependent on the ratio of supply to demand. All in all, a Chinese PI should consider his financial demand and his desired level of dependency before deciding on TIF versus ROSCA versus any type of crowdfunding.

As stated in Sect. 3.2, crowdfunding is more than just a financial tool. With crowdfunding, a PI has the chance to raise money and simultaneously marketise, pre-test and pre-sell his product or service. These features are particularly included in *e-commerce crowdfunding*, though all kinds of crowdfunding evoke certain customer feedback and (positive or negative) PR. However, these benefits do not come for free. Crowdfunding also demands more preparation than TIF. These efforts only pay, if a PI can use the additional benefits for his purpose.[3] Therefore, if an entrepreneur exclusively demands capital and wants to obtain money with little efforts, then he should rather opt for TIF, a ROSCA or (if possible) some form of formal finance. On the other hand, if an entrepreneur pursues added value beyond capital from a financial tool, then he should opt for crowdfunding despite the higher efforts.

Moreover, the trade-off between CF and TIF also depends on the PI's level of risk aversion. Besides his own default risk and the potential consequences of the latter, a PI further faces the risk that he cannot obtain funds at all. Comparing the above mentioned categories of finance, on first sight, donation- and reward-based crowdfunding, particularly with the Keep-It-All crowdfunding (KIA) model, seem to be the least risky financial options for a Chinese PI. Likewise, equity-based and *e-commerce crowdfunding* include low risks for the PI as he typically is not obliged to pay back the crowdfunding investments in case of his default. Yet, this advantage is diminished by the relative modest chance to succeed with crowdfunding, particularly with the All-or-nothing crowdfunding (AON) model, and obtain capital at all. Therefore, if an entrepreneur definitely needs to obtain capital, then he should rather opt for a ROSCA, some other form of TIF or formal finance. However, as illustrated in Sect. 2.4.2, with TIF a PI commonly runs in danger to be socially stigmatised if he defaults. To date, there are no investigations whether a default with crowdfunding (after a successful funding) also evokes (online) stigmatisation. In line with my classification of Chinese crowdfunding in terms of institutionalisation (see Fig. 5.1), *WeChat CF* is likely to incorporate higher

[3] In this regard, *WeChat crowdfunding* is an exception: It affords relatively little time and efforts to set up a *WeChat CF* campaign, still the marketing effect is included. However, on the other hand, the range of the campaign is limited to one's direct (and indirect) *WeChat* contacts.

risks of social punishment in contrast to OCF, *e-commerce CF* and other forms of *corporate crowdfunding* as the former relies more extensively on personal contacts.

In addition, the benefits of CF vs. TIF also depend on whether a PI aims at a "wait-and-see" or rather a "just-do-it" strategy.[4] As for the latter, *WeChat CF* and TIF are appropriate tools; all other forms of finance demand not just more time for preparation and execution, but also take relatively long until the capital is disbursed. Finally, a PI should know whether he is able and willing to pay back the funds (with or without interest), or whether he would rather provide some rewards or shares as investment compensation, or whether he wants to obtain capital for free. In the latter case, he would have to opt for donation-based crowdfunding, though keeping in mind that this financial tool is rather suitable for smaller target sums. If the PI is neither willing to provide rewards nor enjoys giving out shares, then he has to opt for debt-based funds in the form of TIF or a ROSCA.[5] In conclusion, both Chinese CF and TIF have advantages, yet, a PI needs to consider his preferences in terms of guarantee of funds, the degree of obligation to pay back the crowdfund-investments, the consequences in case of a default, and the speed of receiving the funds.

Another crucial argument for or against TIF vs. CF is the number and also the quality of a PI's online and offline contacts. For TIF, and particularly a ROSCA, sound offline networks are the prerequisite for any transaction. Crowdfunding, on the other hand, per definition can be applied by any individual or entity, who or which understands to employ the power of the crowd (see Sect. 3.1). However, a successful campaign demands a fascinated crowd. Moreover, as illustrated in Sect. 5.6, key contacts can initiate the automation of a self-fulfilling crowdfunding campaign. Thus, a PI either has to establish a substantial crowd before the actual start of his campaign, or he optimally can revert to already existing networks. As crowdfunding typically is an online tool, predominantly online contacts are valuable. Amongst others, the number of an entrepreneur's *WeChat* contacts has an impact on his choice for or against crowdfunding, in particular for or against *WeChat CF*.[6] My questionnaire has revealed that this number can differ a lot amongst Chinese founders, from 50 to 4000 *WeChat* contacts respectively. Yet, offline relationships are likewise important to spread the word about an online campaign. Ultimately, all forms of alternative finance, at least initially, rely on support from sustainable contacts in order to establish the ground for financial transactions.

Furthermore, a Chinese entrepreneur is likely to choose his financial sources on the basis of their legality. By 2015, (equity-based) crowdfunding in China still relied on draft regulations. The legal status of informal finance in China, on the other hand, often depends on the eye of the beholder (see Sect. 2.4.1). Depending on the amount of his capital demand, a PI is more or less willing to approach grey or illegal creditors. Furthermore, his personal status, the location of his business, and potential

[4]See also Sect. 2.2.2.

[5]Or P2P finance.

[6]Interview with April and Tina, 2015-04-28.

patronage could also affect his choice in terms of the legality of financial tools. For instance, a renowned businessman located in Shanghai without any patronage from city authorities probably is more reluctant to utilise dubious funds compared to a lower ranked entrepreneur on the countryside, who enjoys immunity from persecution by local authorities. Besides the above mentioned factors, a PI's trade-off between CF vs. TIF ultimately and again depends on his risk aversion and thus his ability to cope with the externalities of illegal or informal finance.

In addition, IP considerations are likely to influence a PI's choice of finance. With TIF, ROSCAs and *WeChat CF* a PI's business idea can only be seen by a pre-defined circle of people. On the other hand, campaigns in line with OCF and those on an *e-commerce CFP* are specially designed for the public. Therefore, PIs with projects of a high degree of IP should either find a way to not disclose sensitive information or fairly refrain from the latter forms of crowdfunding. Yet, considering the current state of equity-based crowdfunding in China, which is rather a re-framed version of PE, the circle of investors and thereby potential spies is limited to 200 people. Finally, as both TIF, ROSCAs, and any type of crowdfunding essentially rely on the exchange of information, a PI with highly sensitive IP should try to opt for formal finance.

Besides, the general nature of a venture is essential for the appropriateness of TIF or CF respectively, and ultimately also determines the success of a venture. Whilst TIF (and consequently also ROSCAs) can be applied for all kinds of endeavours as usually the creditor does not care about the borrower's purpose of the funding,[7] certain types of crowdfunding only fit certain types of projects. Social and non-profit projects rather suit for donation- and rewards-based CF, whilst for-profit start-ups, and particularly those with a marketable product, can more easily pursue a (rewards- or equity-based) *e-commerce CF* campaign. By contrast, for incorporated and service-oriented ventures equity-based CF would be a better option. A project, which is highly associated with its founder, on the other hand, is rather suitable for *WeChat crowdfunding*. These examples demonstrate that a PI's choice of crowdfunding, not only depends on his personal characteristics (see Sects. 3.4.4 and 5.7.4 and Tables 3.3 and 5.5), but should also be based on the nature of his venture.

Moreover, the priority of TIF or CF respectively depends on whether a PI can rely on any partners or rather runs his project on his own. Although, for instance, a *WeChat CF* campaign is easily set up within a short period, the word is spread faster and more extensively if several partners refer to the same campaign in their respective networks at the same time (see e.g. the examples in Sects. 5.6.1 and 5.6.3). Moreover, existing partners could share the workload of preparing a crowdfunding campaign. A single founder of a venture is likely to opt for TIF or another form of finance, which demands less preparation; this not exclusively refers to Chinese PIs, but equally applies to PIs from other nations.

[7] An exception to this is a special type of ROSCA that has been set up by its members for a shared purpose.

In addition, the anticipated success of a Chinese crowdfunding campaign, and thus the general choice for crowdfunding and against TIF is also dependent on the number of projects a Chinese PI has previously invested in. Specifically, as reciprocity is a deep-seated value in Chinese culture,[8] potential crowdfunders probably feel obliged to support the PI, if the latter has patronised them or others before. In my survey, all founders except one had previously invested in other crowdfunding projects. Although my study is far from representative and should have a control sample from the West, it demonstrates that reciprocity in China is not restricted to TIF but is also reflected in crowdfunding.

Finally, trust or any other form of security is the currency necessary for all kinds of financial sources. Therefore, a Chinese PI needs to consider the assets that he can offer to the respective financial institutions. Whilst formal institutions typically demand collateral or a track of records, and informal finance usually requires social ties in order to create trust and estimate a borrower's creditworthiness, with crowdfunding, a PI needs to find other and often individual means to evoke credibility. With OCF, a PI typically creates trust by the provision of sufficient information on him and the project via the CFP, by continuous updates and direct communication with the crowd. However, in my opinion, with OCF a PI's capabilities to create trust are limited. With Chinese crowdfunding, on the other hand, a PI's scope for trust creation is broader. In particular, with *WeChat crowdfunding* a PI targets at his direct and indirect contacts. Like with TIF, *WeChat CF* includes social ties as a form of currency, and thus compared to OCF enables the PI to more easily evoke trust. Once a PI has been chosen by an *e-commerce CFP*, he probably had been checked on his reliability and creditworthiness by means of big data analysis. The *e-commerce CFP* can refer to the PI's track of records from his e-shopping (and e-payments) history and thereupon conduct a due diligence. Thus, with *e-commerce CF*, a PI is patronised by an established *e-commerce (crowdfunding) platform*, which automatically enhances the PI's credibility. In sum, whilst with OCF a Chinese PI has only limited means to demonstrate his creditworthiness, with *WeChat crowdfunding* a PI can evoke trust via personal contacts like with TIF; with *e-commerce crowdfunding*, a PI profits from the CFP's high degree of institutionalisation and its capabilities conduct a sound due diligence.

Section 4.4 has demonstrated that Chinese consumers have exceptionally integrated the internet into their daily lives. Mobile internet, e-commerce and (mobile) online payments in China have become very natural, more than accessing the internet via a desktop computer, going shopping offline or paying with credit card. From the perspective of a Chinese PI, I argue that crowdfunding could indeed become a game changer of informal finance in China, once it is fully integrated into social media, e-commerce and mobile payment systems. As Chinese excessively employ the internet for all kinds of services, the impact of TIF, which traditionally is offline, will automatically decrease with the rise of online services.

---

[8] Song et al. (2012).

However, in terms of transaction costs, crowdfunding, and in particular OCF, affords high efforts from a PI (see also Fig. 5.4). These costs only outweighed, if a PI can appreciate the potential benefits of crowdfunding beyond finance; otherwise, TIF is the better, i.e. more cost-effective, choice. The most striking advantage of crowdfunding over TIF is its marketing function, including pre-testing and pre-selling. Yet, if a PI has neither a demand nor an interest to publicly marketise her venture, crowdfunding is no valuable alternative for her.

Even though crowdfunding per definition can be applied by any individual or entity regardless of his/her/its status, background, etc., the PI needs to be able to employ the power of the crowd. This means that a PI either can rely on established networks or that she has to create respective networks of potential crowdfunders prior to the start of her campaign. I claim that Chinese crowdfunding, in particular, *WeChat CF*, is able to tackle the network issue pretty well and thereby can leverage a PI's campaign. As the majority of Chinese extensively utilises *WeChat* on a daily basis and for all kinds of other services, it is relatively easy for a Chinese to exploit the app for crowdfunding. Similar to *WeChat CF*, *e-commerce CF* can boost a venture's reach. Once a PI has managed to list her project on an *e-commerce CFP*, she not only gets support for the preparation of her campaign, but is also likely to have a distribution channel for her product subsequent to a successful campaign. Thus, if a Chinese PI first is willing to share her business idea—either just with her direct and indirect contacts via *WeChat* or publicly via a CFP, if her venture secondly suits one of the available crowdfunding modes and if thirdly her chosen CFP is willing to list her project on the platform, then for her crowdfunding is a true alternative to traditional informal finance.

6.2 Implications for the Chinese Government

Crowdfunding's standing in China has been elevated, which not least is a result of its promotion by the Chinese government. Still, the underlying motivation of the central government to support crowdfunding is yet to be fully announced. I argue that crowdfunding in fact could facilitate a solution for at least three issues. Currently, China is facing several challenges. Foremost, the world's second largest economy is suffering from declining growth rates. Secondly, China is struggling to reform its formal financial sector, and thirdly, China's authorities have to deal with the opacity of informal finance and a pervasive shadow banking sector. The combination of these three circumstances could provide an answer to the sudden official promotion of crowdfunding in China.

When I started my research on crowdfunding in China, in early 2013, there was hardly any Chinese literature on that topic. It was not clear whether the OCF model in China belonged to the formal or rather the informal finance sector; in fact, crowdfunding then was neither explicitly sanctioned nor illegal as only few people and consequently few authorities had ever heard about it. Private fundraising, on the other hand, was and is explicitly prohibited by Chinese law.[9] However, even though conviction can lead to draconic punishment,[10] illegal fundraising was and still is omnipresent in China. Official data specified the growth rates of such illegal cases to 79% from 2011 to 2012; and those cases which were discovered from 2005 to 2013 have summed up to a yearly amount of USD 3.26 billion.[11] As informal finance, and shadow banking can lead to financial instability, the Chinese government wants to curtail these sectors. Yet, the authorities' impact is limited as non-formal financial institutions often operate underground and sanctions hardly deter. At the same time, the government is aware that currently formal finance cannot meet overall financial demand. Once there are neither formal nor informal sources of finance, Chinese entrepreneurs and consequently China's economic growth are in danger to end up in a blind alley. Crowdfunding and other forms of internet finance could be a solution for this dilemma: By providing legal alternatives, the government can close the financial gap of PIs and indirectly influence the scale and scope of informal finance.

Back in 2013, it was incalculable which stand the Chinese government would eventually take in terms of crowdfunding, which in fact is a sort of private fundraising via a platform.[12] In 2014, Chinese officials and scholars started to put crowdfunding on their agenda and mentioned it in the same breath with "internet finance" and "innovation". By the end of that year, draft regulations on equity-based crowdfunding had been published by the CSRC demonstrating that Chinese authorities officially supported crowdfunding. As a consequence, the number of Chinese CFPs sky-rocketed, crowdfunding became a buzzword and increasingly more Chinese knew about it.

The statement by Zero2IPO on the potential effects that equity crowdfunding in China could have (see Sect. 5.2), in particular, "guiding informal finance onto the well-regulated development track", lets me suppose that the Chinese government is making a trade-off between TIF and crowdfunding. However, in fact, this statement and not least the publication of draft regulations on equity-based crowdfunding give the impression that the trade-off has already been made in favour of crowdfunding.

Referring to China's current challenges, and specifically to the issue of reform, there is a struggle within the government between one fraction aiming at a more liberalised formal financial sector and another one postulating enhanced state control.[13] From my observations and literature research, I argue that crowdfunding like other forms of internet finance could subliminally bring some reform to the entire financial sector from the outside. With internet finance a third strand is

---

[9]Zui gao renmin fayuan [最高人民法院] (n.d.).

[10]See for instance the case of Wu Ying, who was sentenced to death for her illegal fundraising (Xinhua [新华网] 2012).

[11]Robertson (2014).

[12]Simultaneously, it was difficult to foresee the dimensions that P2P would reach by 2015, as in early 2013 P2P was non-existent in China.

[13]The internal struggle within the Chinese government between reformists and traditionalists on economic policies is further discussed by Fischer (2015, 2016).

emerging next to formal and informal finance, and it is challenging both, the formal and the informal financial sector. Instead of reforming the formal finance sector and/or integrating the informal sector, some scholars see in internet finance the solution to lagging reforms and prevalent opacity.[14] In fact, online tools have the potential to replace established institutions as they decrease overall transaction costs for all involved players. Moreover, digital technologies and online financial service providers could evoke some change without official pressure from the reformers. For example, since third-party providers have been offering convenient mobile transfers, increasingly more Chinese banks have introduced mobile banking services to be able to compete with FinTech companies.[15] Indeed, internet finance could not just provide an alternative to informal finance, but also transform China's formal financial sector through increased competition. In sum, by institutionalising financial tools like crowdfunding, governmental debates on reforms become rather obsolete.

In terms of China's greatest challenge, the economy, some analysts claim that there is a trade-off between growth and reform.[16] However, I argue that crowdfunding could not just quiet the reform debate on China's financial sector, but eventually also help to tackle China's major challenge, to enhance its economic growth. In the past, China's GDP was excessively driven by exports and investment, and the latter were predominantly financed by households savings.[17] In order to reach a more sustainable GDP, China's leadership aspires a growth model which is based on domestic consumption and innovations. Although consumption rates have increased over the last few years, the Chinese people still has a relatively high savings rate. Therefore, Chinese authorities are highly dependent on e-commerce giants like *Alibaba*, which can boost overall domestic spending. At the same time, China's government backs innovative ideas in order to foster the entrepreneurial environment. Thereunder, online financial tools like equity crowdfunding are explicitly mentioned as drivers for entrepreneurship.[18] Ultimately, crowdfunding is seen as an innovative tool which could evoke not just reform but also growth.

These aspects fit Xi Jinping's political slogan of the *Chinese Dream*. In 2013, China's president first articulated this term,[19] which resembles his vision of the PRC and which stands for the integration of the "twin goals of reclaiming national pride and achieving personal well-being."[20] In order to accomplish the *Chinese Dream*, both reform and innovation are essential.[21] In this context, Chinese authorities

[14] Xie et al. (2016).

[15] Xie et al. (2016, p. 30).

[16] Lopez (2015, n.p.).

[17] Lardy (1998, p. 9).

[18] Beijing backs equity crowdfunding to develop entrepreneurial economy: State Council encourages more entrepreneurial activity and vows to cut red tape for new firms (2015).

[19] Feng (2015).

[20] Chi Daily (2014a, n.p.).

[21] Feng (2015, p. 166).

often talk of "mass innovation" *(dazhong chuangye [大众创业])* and "a million innovations" *(wanzhong chuangxin [万众创新])*,[22] which eventually should realise the dream. Thereby, the term crowdfunding *(zhongchou [众筹])* perfectly fits this wording. At the same time, China's government has set up numerous innovation centers all over the country to enhance the entrepreneurial spirit top down.[23] Furthermore, China's officials have been visiting start-up hubs,[24] which demonstrates their overall support. Besides the hope for more economic growth, start-ups hold the chance to create additional jobs. Having in mind that China in 2015 had 7.49 million graduates,[25] unemployment is a great challenge to China's economic and social stability. Admittedly, the rhetoric of China's authorities is changing and since 2016, the *Chinese Dream* has lost in relevance. Still, the Chinese government sets on "[m]ass entrepreneurship and innovation as new growth engine".[26]

Against the above mentioned circumstances, it seems plausible that recent regulation on (equity) crowdfunding predominantly benefits Chinese *corporate CFPs*. In order to be an eligible equity CFP, Chinese providers need to hold net assets of at least RMB 5 million.[27] Thereby, many *start-up CFPs* are forced out of the market as they cannot meet the asset requirements.[28] In consequence, only few but established players are remaining and dominating the Chinese crowdfunding market. From the perspective of the Chinese government, this constellation provides several advantages: First, the monitoring task is outsourced to few reliable institutions which already have a broad market coverage. These institutions can easily fulfil this task as they can build on an abundance of customer data from their core business, for instance, e-commerce or corporate finance. Secondly, such *corporate CFPs*, in contrast to *start-up CFPs*, are unlikely to fail as they are cross-financed from the players' other businesses. Thirdly, these platforms due to their reputation are unlikely to default or commit fraud. Finally, it seems as if the central government voluntarily has assigned the task of financial monitoring to private enterprises for the sake of more control.[29]

In fact, the Chinese government is highly dependent on China's internet corporates, in particular on e-commerce platforms, which is another explanation for the recent developments in crowdfunding regulation. E-commerce is the main driver for domestic consumption and economic growth, therefore, e-commerce platforms

[22]Zhang (2015).

[23]By contrast, innovation centers and start-up hubs in Western countries tend to be private initiatives and rather bottom-up.

[24]China's premier joins the start-up crowd at entrepreneurs' café in innovation push (2015).

[25]Could start-ups revitalise the Chinese economy? The government thinks so (2015).

[26]English.Gov.cn (2016, n.p.).

[27]BOP Consulting (2015).

[28]Interview with Sean, 2015-04-27.

[29]Tse (2015) claims that "there is clearly a degree of irony in one of the world's most authoritarian and control-minded regimes seeing the rapid emergence of some of the world's most open [and powerful] organizations" (Tse 2015, p. 164 ff.).

and consequently *e-commerce CFPs* have a great stake in the central government. Moreover, *e-commerce crowdfunding* could further transfer investments from the informal to the formal financial sector. The example of *Alibaba*'s online fund, *Yu'e bao*, which has attracted millions of deposits since its introduction in 2014 (see also Sect. 4.4), demonstrates that Chinese are willing and eager to utilise alternative investment tools. Although *e-commerce crowdfunding*, particularly the equity-based type, per se is a form of risk capital and not the optimal tool for every investor, the Chinese government could have an interest to see more savings invested in *e-commerce crowdfunding* than in informal finance for two reasons. First, *e-commerce CF* compared to TIF is more transparent, and therefore more easily traceable for authorities. Secondly, *e-commerce CF* eventually serves innovation, entrepreneurship and again domestic consumption (see Sect. 6.4), which are all priorities on the agenda of China's government. Thus, it sounds plausible that the Chinese government favours *e-commerce CF*.

In terms of *WeChat crowdfunding*, Chinese authorities generally so far have neither sanctioned not banned this form of finance per se. As thereby, financial transactions are carried out via (though not by means) of an online platform, the question remains whether *WeChat crowdfunding* is a form of private fundraising, and thus illegal by Chinese definition. Presumably as *WeChat crowdfunding* commonly incurs low amounts of capital, authorities by 2016 have refrained from regulation or even annotation. Yet, in September 2016, the new Chinese *Charity Law* came into effect,[30] and henceforth bans collecting donations for charity issues via *WeChat* and *Weibo*. Based on the new law "public donation campaigns initiated by unauthorized parties will be prohibited."[31] This seems to be a setback for *WeChat crowdfunding* as it used to be an important tool for charities and non-profit organisations. However, apparently, this new regulation in particular addresses charities and less *WeChat crowdfunding* per se. Ultimately, China's government will not be able to prevent its citizens from donating to their friends or the latter's business ideas.

Finally, the question remains whether, from the perspective of the Chinese government, crowdfunding could become a game changer for informal finance. The Chinese state has an interest to first, provide enterprises and households with finance; secondly, enhance innovation and entrepreneurship in order to boost economic growth, and thirdly, control the financial markets to uphold social stability. Comparing TIF with crowdfunding from the perspective of the Chinese government, I argue that crowdfunding, in particular *e-commerce CF*, is more favoured. Crowdfunding like TIF provides PIs with finance and both financial tools can be utilised to create innovative businesses. Yet, crowdfunding due to its online character becomes much more seizable for authorities than TIF, which is rather opaque and commonly happens without any documentation. Once crowdfunding is processed via an established corporate, it is overseen by a reputable institution, which can function as a gatekeeper. Therefore, the government's monitoring costs,

---

[30] Ohlrich (2016).

[31] AllChinaTech (2015, n.p.).

which make the majority of its overall transaction costs, can be outsourced to these corporates to a large extent. Not least due to this aspect, from the perspective of the Chinese government, I see in *corporate crowdfunding* (like in other financial tools provided by established internet corporates) a true alternative to informal finance in China.

6.3 Implications for Chinese Crowdfunders

Crowdfunding extends the scope of investment opportunities for Chinese creditors. Yet, only equity crowdfunding[32] can yield financial returns, whilst donation-based CF serves philanthropic ends and rewards-based CF yields a material compensation. Still, this analysis includes equity- as well as product-based crowdfunding as crowdfunders are not exclusively driven by financial motivations.

With the publication of draft regulations on equity-crowdfunding, Chinese savers[33] have been offered a further legal investment tool. Low interest rates have pushed savers away from formal bank deposits. Since the latest turmoil on China's stock exchanges, investors have been even more extensively searching for alternative opportunities. Some Chinese try to invest overseas and thereby get their capital out of the country. Yet, not least on behalf of the Chinese government, but also for the sake of China's innovativeness and thus their own sake, Chinese depositors should rather invest within China and in Chinese ventures. However, equity-based crowdfunding is a long-term investment tool and thus not suitable for savers that pursue short-term financial returns. Yet, for other depositors, Chinese equity-based crowdfunding indeed is an interesting and legal alternative to informal finance and foreign investment opportunities.

Inarguably, the online character of crowdfunding provides several benefits for Chinese investors. By means of the internet, physical borders can be overcome, and thus, savers theoretically have access to innumerable investment opportunities. Furthermore, as illustrated in Sect. 4.4, Chinese are extremely internet-savvy and are used to employing online solutions for all kinds of services. They increasingly replace cash payments with online (and in particular mobile) payments. Therefore, I assume that it is only a matter of time until online investments become as common as payments via *TenPay* or *AliPay* as CF fits the Chinese lifestyle.

Still, in comparison to ROSCAs or other forms of TIF, original crowdfunding is very risky as it lacks social ties and other (informal) institutions that reduce information asymmetries. Therefore, I doubt that OCF becomes a game changer

[32] Besides, equity crowdfunding, also P2P finance can yield financial returns.

[33] This chapter does not differentiate between savers/depositors and investors. Even though, a saver depositing money differs a lot from a professional investor pursuing financial profits, crowdfunders are not further distinguished into contributors (to donation- and reward-based projects) and investors (of equity-based crowdfunding projects) for the purpose of simplification.

for informal finance in China. By contrast, the Chinese versions of crowdfunding better manage to reduce investor risk and thus, from the perspective of the crowd, are true alternatives to informal finance.

WeChat CF like TIF relies on social ties; the addressed crowdfunders commonly know the PI from which they receive the crowdfunding appeal, either directly or indirectly via their *WeChat* connection. The personal character of *WeChat CF* automatically reduces information asymmetries and provides the crowd with trust. Moreover, the relationship with the PI beyond the crowdfunding campaign (via a social medium or otherwise) further reduces the crowdfunders' transaction costs for bargaining and monitoring. Yet, *WeChat CF* commonly does not yield any financial return as it is typically based on donations or rewards. Therefore, whilst it reduces investment risks and could provide additional value like reciprocity, participation in an interesting project, early access to an innovative product, entertainment, etc., *WeChat CF* in its current stage is unlikely to revolutionise the informal finance landscape.

On the other hand, *e-commerce CF* includes equity crowdfunding, and at the same time is a relatively secure and transaction cost saving investment tool. Thereby, crowdfunders can rely on a CFP that has the expertise and capabilities to thoroughly pre-select promising campaigns, which further reduces the crowd's searching costs. Moreover, *e-commerce CFPs* have the skills and capacities to prepare, advise and also monitor the selected PIs as they can rely on assets from their mother companies. In fact, the crowd can outsource the due diligence to the platform. In case a chosen PI commits any fraud, the crowdfunders can expect the *e-commerce CFP* to jump in in order to save the corporate reputation. Although to my best knowledge, there has been no such case by 2016, *Alibaba, JD.com* and other *corporate CFP*, in contrast to *start-up CFPs*, would not have to shut down their operations due to such failure. I assume that they would persecute the deceiver and possibly compensate affected crowdfunders.

In sum, *e-commerce CF* is an attractive investment tool for Chinese crowdfunders as it is integrated in e-commerce and thus institutionalised. The reputation of *e-commerce CFPs*, their capabilities to process crowdfunding, and the inclusion of big data analysis make *e-commerce crowdfunding* an attractive alternative to informal finance for Chinese investors. If Chinese *corporate CFPs* manage to replace social ties (i.e. the currency of trust) with big data analysis (i.e. the currency of credits), crowdfunding could become a game changer of informal finance from the perspective of Chinese crowdfunders.

6.4 Implications for Chinese Crowdfunding Platforms

Considering the implications for Chinese CFPs, I need to distinguish between *start-up CFPs* and *corporate CFPs*, and amongst these between *financial corporate CFPs* and *e-commerce CFPs* as the indications differ for each type of platform. All of the latter have in common that they provide online-based crowdfunding as an alternative to offline TIF. As depicted in Chap. 4, Chinese excessively utilise online services, particularly mobile services, e-commerce and online (mobile) payment services, driven by an internet savvy Chinese youth. Thus, all online based platforms per se hit the zeitgeist of China's society. However, some CFPs are less predestined to offer crowdfunding, whereas others have sufficient capabilities. Furthermore, only few platforms can actually create value for themselves out of crowdfunding, whereas the majority of Chinese CFPs is still in search for a suitable business model.

Start-up CFPs often lack a track of records and thus need to put much effort in the creation of trust and credibility for PIs and crowdfunders. Moreover, they lack the data and capabilities to conduct a reliable due diligence. Unless a *start-up CFP* can provide additional customer value—for instance, by providing a mobile crowdfunding app like *Zhuimeng wang* does—it can hardly attract a sufficiently large customer base. In contrast to *corporate CFPs*, their overall transaction costs and financial costs are just too high. Therefore, unless Chinese *start-up CFPs* can rely on external investors, they sooner or later have to resign.

By contrast, *corporate CFPs* typically can build on the reputation of their mother company, and thus have an easier stand from the very beginning. More specifically, *financial corporate CFPs* have an expertise in financial services, thus crowdfunding seems to be just an extension of their traditional business model. The latter can rely on data collected from their core business to evaluate a person's creditworthiness, i.e. its eligibility to become a PI or a crowdfunder respectively. However, as crowdfunding usually is applied by people without access to formal finance, it is unlikely that *financial corporate CFPs* have much advantage over *start-up CFPs*, except from their reputation and their corporate assets. Therefore, unless the PIs and the crowdfunders are clients of the financial corporate, the *financial corporate CFP* (just like a *start-up CFP*) needs to make a big effort to conduct a due diligence. Against this background, it seems irrational that some Chinese financial corporates (like NCFG with its affiliated CFP *Zhongchou wang*) provide crowdfunding, despite low margins and a lack of customer data.

Yet, I see several motivations behind this apparently unprofitable business. First, I assume that financial corporates provide crowdfunding as they do not want to leave the crowdfunding field, which in fact is a category of financial services, to other players. Secondly, due to crowdfunding's posh image, with the integration of this innovative tool a corporate can enhance its dusty appearance. Thirdly, according to Du Mengjie,[34] a main idea behind the provision of (corporate) crowdfunding is the extension of the customer base and the creation of customer loyalty. "First create traffic or a customer base respectively, and thereafter think about how to make money out of it."[35] In sum, China's *financial corporate CFPs* currently are not making much profit with crowdfunding, and they are not necessarily experts to provide this kind of financial tool due to a lack of customer data; yet, they do offer

[34]Founder and CEO of the CFP *Zhuimeng wang*.

[35]Interview with Du Mengjie 2015-04-16.

crowdfunding in order to compete with other financial service providers and as they aspire to create future revenues from value-added services.

By further contrast, for *e-commerce CFPs* crowdfunding in fact is just an extension of the e-commerce platforms' core business as both, crowdfunding and e-commerce are very similar in terms of their processes. In both cases, the platform connects a supplier (the seller or the PI respectively) with a bidder (the purchaser or the crowdfunder respectively), it mediates the purchase crowdfunding agreement, settles payments and the exchange of goods or rewards/debt certificates/shares respectively. The greatest advantage that *e-commerce CFPs* have over other types of CFPs is that they can rely on an abundance of customer data from their core business. Chinese extensively utilise and enjoy e-commerce services, regardless of their location and status. The number of Chinese who do not shop online is decreasing, and thus, most Chinese sooner or latter have left their marks or data respectively on one of China's leading e-commerce platforms. This amplitude of data increases further, if the e-commerce platform next to e-retailing also offers an integrated payment system like *Alibaba* does with *AliPay*. For example, a potential PI who has been in default for any online payments in the past can easily be identified and automatically be excluded from the crowdfunding platform. Thus, I assume that the Chinese government has consciously outsourced crowdfunding governance to those actors which can easily supervise crowdfunding transactions. In sum, *e-commerce CFPs* first of all have a very broad customer base from the core business of their mother companies, and secondly, have the capabilities to conduct a sound due diligence with the data collected from the platform's e-commerce (and potentially payments) services.

Yet, crowdfunding like e-commerce only creates low margins. One explanation, why e-commerce platforms still provide crowdfunding, is the fact that crowdfunding and e-commerce can be used for each other's ends. As mentioned in Sect. 3.1, crowdfunding is a means for pre-testing a certain product or service. Once a campaign has been funded successfully, one can imply that there is a market for the respective business idea. In terms of an end-user product, which is launched on an *e-commerce CFP*, this can be instantaneously promoted and sold via the e-commerce platform after the successful crowdfunding campaign. Thus, I assume that e-commerce platforms mainly utilise crowdfunding in order to attract additional customers to their platform. The consumers first make a statement on their demands via investing or not investing into certain crowdfunding projects; secondly, the products of those campaigns, which have been successfully funded, are then automatically adopted for the e-commerce platform; and thirdly, those crowdfunders could potentially become the first customers of that product by purchasing it via the e-commerce platform. Therefore, I subsume that *Alibaba* and *Jingdong* in fact approach the same strategy like *BMW*, *Procter & Gamble* and other corporates (see Sect. 3.2), which utilise crowdfunding primarily for testing and marketing purposes. Indeed, these e-commerce platforms outsource the testing of new products to its CFP.

A second explanation, why *Alibaba* and its corporate peers provide crowdfunding is the pure nature of crowdfunding as a financial tool. As illustrated in Sect. 4.4.2,

Chinese internet corporates are invading in all spheres of Chinese daily lives. Finance has been identified as a core sector, all big internet corporates since recently have established a financial arm, and even if crowdfunding per se creates low revenues (or even losses for the platform providers), it accomplishes the portfolio of financial services providers. Finally, e-commerce players who already provide other financial services probably have integrated crowdfunding in their range of services in order to not lose customers to other CFPs. This is in line with a statement by Bolly, the Senior Manager of equity crowdfunding at *Jingdong zhongchou*, who claimed that *Jingdong* offers crowdfunding in order to stress its financial service arm.[36]

I expect that China's *e-commerce CFPs* will continue to dominate the Chinese crowdfunding market for several reasons. First, as China's e-retail platforms already control the Chinese e-commerce and m-commerce market, they are likely to also dominate China's crowdfunding market. Chinese customers trust e-commerce platforms and likewise they will easily trust CFPs provided by e-commerce players. Secondly, *e-commerce CFPs* can easily integrate all services from their e-commerce business into crowdfunding, for instance, their payments function or an escrow service. Thirdly, *e-commerce CFPs*, in contrast to other CFPs, have the capacity to make a new venture big. Therefore, any PI, who intends to reach a broad market scale with his product will try to list his project on an *e-commerce CFP*. Consequently, an increased preference for *e-commerce CFPs* will automatically lower the impact of other CFPs. Last but not least, current draft regulations favour large CFPs with respective assets and expertise, which *e-commerce CFPs* can easily produce.

[36]Interview with Bolly 2015-05-14.

Chapter 7
Learnings from Crowdfunding in China

Crowdfunding is a recent but promising phenomenon as it provides an alternative financial tool with an integrated marketing function for people and organisations that lack access to traditional forms of finance. The global crowdfunding market is driven by China, though the country has a comparably short history of crowdfunding. In fact, the Chinese market provides unique prerequisites for a prosperous development of crowdfunding. First and foremost, it has an established informal finance sector as formal finance cannot meet overall financial demand. Therefore, Chinese are used to applying alternative financial tools. Secondly, China has an agile internet sector, driven by e-commerce giants and social media providers, which next to their core business also provide financial services like crowdfunding. As a consequence, banks and other traditional financial institutions have to face competition. Thirdly, the Chinese government welcomes and promotes this development as internet finance could become a motor for financial reform. This triad of an underdeveloped formal financial sector, an established informal finance sector, and a dynamic internet finance sector provides a unique setting for crowdfunding in China.

This thesis investigated whether crowdfunding could become a game changer for traditional informal finance in China, from the perspective of the respective stakeholders, i.e. China's project initiators (entrepreneurs, start-ups, etc.), its crowdfunders (savers, investors, etc.), the government, and China's crowdfunding platforms. It applied a New Institutional Economics approach to analyse the principal-agent-relations and transaction costs involved in a typical crowdfunding campaign. Furthermore, it analysed a PI's choice of finance, the role of financial intermediaries before and since the era of financialisation, and the features of traditional informal finance. Thereby, Rotating Savings and Credit Associations served as a benchmark for formal and informal finance. Based on this theoretical framework, this dissertation analysed the principal-agent-relations and transaction cost of both, Original crowdfunding (OCF) and the Chinese versions of crowdfunding.

A. S. Funk, *Crowdfunding in China*, Contributions to Management Science,
https://doi.org/10.1007/978-3-319-97253-4_7

In the West, crowdfunding as a subcategory of internet finance started out in the aftermath of the global financial crisis, which was the catalyser for the FinTech 3.0 development. The recent FinTech era in America and Europe is determined by tech-savvy start-ups, which provide financial services as non-financial companies. Whilst the global FinTech market is increasingly dominated by Chinese players, FinTech there has a different point in departure. In fact, FinTech in China is a product of entrepreneurial and regulatory forces. By further contrast, the Chinese FinTech market is controlled by huge internet corporates which can rely on an extensive ecosystem made of a variety of different businesses. Recently, the Chinese government has started to push internet finance, presumably as it hopes that this third strand of finance could fill the gap of formal finance and replace some forms of informal finance. As FinTech in China (like in other emerging economies) differs substantial from FinTech in the West and people living there adopt these technologies much faster than in the developed world, scholars concluded that China has already reached the era of FinTech 3.5.

In order to understand the function and features of crowdfunding in China, this thesis has analysed China's path from informal to internet finance. It first highlighted the shortcomings of China's formal finance sector, secondly illustrated the characteristics of informal finance in China, and thirdly concentrated on the country's dynamic internet sector. Thereby, the role of the central government as main driver for China's internet industry was depicted. Moreover, China's internet service providers, exemplified by the ecosystems of *Alibaba* and *Tencent*, were analysed. As China's internet market is predominantly shaped by mobile internet, e-commerce and (third-party) online payments, and as all of the latter have a direct or indirect impact on China's crowdfunding market, individual chapters analysed these industries in detail. Thereby, some unique and China specific aspects have been identified, amongst others, the dimensions of mobile e-commerce, the dominance of Chinese e-commerce platforms, and the acceptance of social commerce by Chinese consumers. Ultimately, these characteristics of China's internet sector explain the specificities of China's crowdfunding market.

Crowdfunding was introduced in China in 2011, and since then has experienced exponential growth rates. However, crowdfunding in China faces several challenges, above all education and regulation. Moreover, the understanding of crowdfunding in China differs a lot from the Original crowdfunding model. This first of all can be seen by the typical classification of crowdfunding by Chinese scholars, who deliberately exclude *P2P finance* from crowdfunding and mainly distinguish between product- and equity-based crowdfunding. Secondly, Chinese literature has picked up the terms *crowdfunding kafei* and *playing with crowdfunding*, which are China specific connotations of crowdfunding. Whilst *crowdfunding kafei* is a kind of offline group-fundraising for the purpose of creating special investment hubs, the latter refers to *playing with the internet*, a term that describes a typical Chinese association with the World Wide Web. Thirdly, Chinese netizens have invented *WeChat crowdfunding*, which is crowdfunding processed via China's most popular social media application, *WeChat*. As another specificity, crowdfunding in China is integrated into e-commerce, which I coined *e-commerce crowdfunding*.

The differences of crowdfunding in China become further obvious from its prevailing crowdfunding platforms. This thesis distinguished between *start-up CFPs*, *specialised* vs. *comprehensive* vs. *combined CFPs*, *financial corporate CFPs* and *e-commerce CFPs*. Last but not least, the dynamics and processes of China's crowdfunding market were illustrated by means of three short case studies.

The embedding of Chinese crowdfunding in the theoretical context revealed that both *WeChat crowdfunding* and *e-commerce crowdfunding*, in contrast to OCF, manage to reduce dangers of *adverse selection*, *moral hazard* and *hold up* quite effectively. With regard to transaction costs, the direct comparison of the different types of crowdfunding with Traditional informal finance (TIF) demonstrated that again, Chinese crowdfunding performs better than the OCF model. Whilst *WeChat CF* resembles several features of TIF like personal contacts as the basement for trust, *e-commerce CF* economises transaction costs through the utilisation of big data analysis and the reputation and capabilities of the e-commerce platform. Therefore, from a NIE's perspective, it seems plausible that Chinese employ Chinese crowdfunding just as ROSCAs and other forms of informal finance.

Yet, whether crowdfunding eventually could become a game changer for informal finance in China depends not least on the stakeholder in perspective. Therefore, the penultimate chapter has considered crowdfunding from the point of view of Chinese project initiators, crowdfunders, the government and China's crowdfunding platforms. Although, a PI's and an investor's choices of finance both depend on individual and external factors, crowdfunding like other online services are becoming increasingly interesting for Chinese citizens as they are in line with the Chinese (online) lifestyle. Therefore, offline alternatives are automatically losing in attractiveness. Yet, the OCF model is only of limited suitability and can hardly compete with TIF as it demonstrates no distinctive features to create trust, test the reliability of the involved actors, or provide any guarantee in cases of default or fraud. *WeChat CF*, on the other hand, sticks out for its convenience and its easy handling for both, PIs and crowdfunders. Trust is created through direct or indirect online relationships, which reduces bargaining and monitoring to a minimum. However, *WeChat CF* so far is only employed for donation- and rewards-based crowdfunding. Whilst a PI still has the chance to raise a formidable funding sum, for a saver or investor, *WeChat crowdfunding* is not a true alternative to informal finance. Even if crowdfunders appreciate *WeChat CF* for its additional features like the participation in a venture, *WeChat CF* per se cannot be seen as a game changer of informal finance for Chinese investors. On the contrary, equity-based crowdfunding indeed is an alternative investment tool for risk-friendly investors, in particular, equity-based crowdfunding provided by *e-commerce CFPs*. The latter can utilise big data analysis and thereby conduct a due diligence on both, PIs and investors. Moreover, theoretically, an *e-commerce CFP* has the capabilities and assets to jump in in cases of severe fraud. Thus, *e-commerce crowdfunding* for both, Chinese PIs and investors likewise provides an attractive financial tool. From my analysis I conclude that Chinese crowdfunding indeed could become a game changer of informal finance for those Chinese PIs that appreciate the benefits of crowdfunding beyond finance. For those PIs crowdfunding's marketing potential will outweigh all necessary efforts, i.e. transaction costs to process a CF campaign. On the other hand, for savers and investors, Chinese crowdfunding only contingently will become a game changer of informal finance as donation- and reward-based CF do not yield any financial returns. Equity crowdfunding, on the other hand, is a long-term financial tool and thus not the first choice by every Chinese investor. Yet, the general integration of alternative finance into established institutions like e-commerce platforms is likely to pull investors away from the informal (and shadow) finance sector, if corporates sufficiently manage to replace social ties (i.e. the currency of trust) with big data analysis (i.e. the currency of credits).

From the perspective of the Chinese government, *corporate crowdfunding* is an attractive alternative to traditional informal finance. Generally, the central government regards TIF with suspicion as it could harm financial stability. Thus, any alternatives which provide more transparency and traceability to authorities are likely to be favoured. Recent draft regulations on crowdfunding in particular strengthen *corporate crowdfunding* and force *start-up CFPs* out of the market. *Corporate CFPs* have the advantage that they hold sufficient assets and capabilities to function as gatekeepers. Not least due to their reputation, corporates possibly would jump in in cases of fraud. Therefore, the Chinese government for the sake of control has outsourced crowdfunding monitoring to China's corporates. Amongst these, China's e-commerce players seem to enjoy a special status. This first of all derives from the fact that the Chinese government is highly dependent on the latter as they push domestic consumption and therefore China's GDP. Secondly, e-commerce corporates like *Alibaba* and *Jingdong* own a vast amount of data from their core businesses, which they can easily employ for crowdfunding due diligence. Against this background and from the perspective of the Chinese central government, crowdfunding, and in particular *e-commerce CF*, could become a true game changer of informal finance. By contrast, *WeChat crowdfunding*, which is like an online extension of TIF, is only tolerated for non-charity actors. Campaigns are processed via private accounts of the social media app *WeChat*, thus *WeChat crowdfunding* is less traceable for authorities and therefore less favoured than *e-commerce crowdfunding*.

Even though, Chinese CFPs are a recent phenomenon and presumably not a single platform previously has offered informal finance, we can still ask whether from their point of view crowdfunding could become a game changer of informal finance. More specifically, the question is why Chinese platforms provide crowdfunding despite low margins. The answers and corresponding implications for China's crowdfunding platforms differ according to the different nature of the platform. First, any Chinese CFP aspires to gain profits from value-added services that could be offered next to crowdfunding, once a substantial customer base has been established. Secondly, *financial corporate CFPs* additionally utilise the buzzword crowdfunding to de-dust their old-fashioned image. Thirdly, *e-commerce CFPs* can easily offer crowdfunding as it is an extension to their core business model. However, as mentioned above, recent regulation impedes the success of certain CFPs. Whilst equity-based *start-up CFPs* can hardly sustain with the new draft regulations in place, donation- and reward-based *start-up CFPs* need to find their niche market to be able to compete with their corporate peers. All remaining players need to build on value-added services in order to make their crowdfunding business profitable.

China's liberalising financial market is highly competitive, and Chinese consumers will eventually opt for those providers that offer the most attractive financial services. Therefore, all Chinese financial service providers—those which originally have their core business in finance, and also those which have their core business in any other industry—have an interest to perfect their financial service portfolio to not lose any customers to competitors. Once a provider manages to offer a broad range of convenient and secure services, it will automatically pull customers away from the informal finance sector. In sum, for those CFPs, which next to crowdfunding also offer further financial services, crowdfunding indirectly could become a game changer of informal finance.

This thesis tried to draw a comprehensive picture of China's crowdfunding market, yet the research included certain limitations. Because literature on Chinese crowdfunding, in particular quantitative data, is still limited, this work followed a qualitative approach to grasp the scope of the topic. By today, China's crowdfunding market is still young, however, it is highly dynamic. As it is hard to hit a moving target, this dissertation focussed on the developments of Chinese crowdfunding from 2011 until 2015. In order to verify the theoretical deliberations of this thesis, further empirical studies are necessary. Moreover, to exclude any biases deriving from e.g. cultural influences, a cross-cultural analysis with crowdfunding actors from different markets would be helpful.

Future research should further consider P2P finance and its potential to become a game changer for informal finance in China. In addition, Chinese crowdfunding should be tested in terms of its transferability to other markets. I could imagine a *WhatsApp crowdfunding* just like further forms of *corporate crowdfunding*. Any large corporate platform holding a vast amount of customer data—e.g. *Facebook* or *Google*—could de facto provide some form of crowdfunding. Notably, *Facebook* since November 2016 has been holding a licence for financial payments[1] and therefore theoretically could provide a one-stop crowdfunding solution like *Alibaba*. Such a copycat of Chinese crowdfunding based on big data analysis could equip the OCF mode with more security. In the end, Chinese crowdfunding could not just become a game changer for informal finance in China, but also for formal finance in the West.

[1] The Irish Times (2016).

Appendix A

See Tables A.1, A.2, A.3, and A.4 (Zero2IPO 2015, p. 17) and Fig. A.1 (KPMG China 2016, p. 7).

Table A.1 Interviews conducted during field research between 2013 and 2016

Date	Place/medium	Name of interviewee	Position of interviewee
2013-08-10	Beijing	Du Mengjie	Founder and CEO of the CFP Zhuimeng wang
2013-08-10	Beijing	Lin	PI at the CFP Zhuiming wang
2013-08-26	Lhasa	Jia Yuhao	Co-founder of *Dalan Youth Hostel*
2013-08-28	Lhasa	Jia Yuhao	ibid.
2014-10-10	Beijing	Helen	Co-founder of *Her's café*
2015-04-15	Beijing	Grace	Head of Agricultural Crowdfunding at the CFP Zhongchou wang
2015-04-16	Beijing	Du Mengjie	Founder and CEO of the CFP Zhuimeng wang
2015-04-16	Beijing	Water	Head of Crowdfunding at Zhuimeng wang
2015-04-21	Beijing	Water	ibid.
2015-04-27	Foshan	Sean	Founder of ifundu
2015-04-28	Guangzhou	April and Tina	Employees at *Attkon*
2015-05-14	Beijing	Bolly	Senior Manager for equity crowdfunding at *Jingdong*
2015-05-19	Shenzhen	Jason	Former employee at the CFP Dianming shijian
2015-05-06	Shanghai	Conor Roche	Consultant at BOP Consulting
2015-09-16	Beijing	Yi Hui	Founder of *JRCoffee*
2015-09-18	Beijing	Grace	Head of Agricultural Crowdfunding at the CFP Zhongchou wang
2016-01-21	via Skype	Luke Deer	Co-editor of *The Asia-Pacific Alternative Finance Benchmarking Report*

A. S. Funk, *Crowdfunding in China*, Contributions to Management Science,
https://doi.org/10.1007/978-3-319-97253-4

Table A.2 Literature on PIs' motivation for applying crowdfunding

Author(s)	Drivers of crowdfunding for PIs
Agrawal et al. (2013)	Lower cost on capital; better match of PIs and crowdfunders on a global basis; mutual exchange of information
Belleflamme et al. (2013)	Feedback from the crowd; public attention
Dorfleitner et al. (2014)	Reduced search costs; presentation in front of broad audience of potential investors
Gerber et al. (2012)	Long term relationships; mutual interaction with the crowd; online validation; feeling of success replication of others
Hui et al. (2012)	Protection of project ownership; quick transfer of collected capital; low entry barriers; low risk
Mollick (2014)	Access to potential customers; access to outside funding (like VCs and BAs)
Kim and Hann (2016)	Democratising access to capital

Table A.3 Literature on methods and features of a successful crowdfunding campaign

Author(s)	Methods for and features of a successful crowdfunding
Agrawal et al. (2011, 2013)	Social networks
Ahlers et al. (2012)	Signalling of a companiy's/project's value; signalling of financial roadmap; signalling of internal governance; signalling of risk factors
Belleflamme et al. (2010, 2013)/Lambert and Schwienbacher (2010)	Non-profit project
Burtch et al. (2014)	Cultural and geographical proximity to funders
Colombo et al. (2015)	Internal social capital
Frydrych et al. (2014)	A project's legitimacy; lower target sums; shorter duration period; a convincing project narrative
Giudici et al. (2013)	Individual (exclusive) social capital
Kuppuswamy and Bayus (2016)	Lower target sums; shorter duration period; project video; provision of social information of PI
Lehner (2012)	Social capital, which can be transferred into economic captial
Mollick (2014)	A PI's personal networks; large number of friends on online networks; high quality projects
Mollick and Kuppuswamy (2015)	Listed on *Kickstarter*; many *Facebook* friends of PI; appropriate background of the PI; outside endorsements
Saxton and Wang (2014)	Size of social network; non-profit projects, particularly health-related projects
Zheng et al. (2014)	Structural, relational and cognitive social capital

Table A.4 Analysis of 13 Chinese crowdfunding platforms by Zero2IPO in 2014

Name of CFP	Number of projects	Actual funding volume in mn RMB	Number of active crowdfunders	Expected funding volume in mn RMB	Success rate
Tianshihui	2607	769.0	2000	1000.0	76.9 %
Zhongchou wang	1964	61.5	165,137	75.2	81.7%
Dianming shijian	1091	44.6	183,512	N/A	N/A
Zhuimeng wang	871	16.2	54,803	35.7	45.5%
Taobao zhongchou	544	63.5	585,933	23.7	267.8%
Letong yinyue	400	4.2	35,961	6.0	69.8%
Jue.so	329	1.3	3434	2.0	65.9%
Jingdong zhongchou	301	147.2	591,742	11.9	1240.9%
Zhongguo mengwang	291	8.2	42,217	30.3	27.2%
Yuanshihui	281	194.0	1526	2391.5	8.1%
Taomeng wang	206	2.7	2207	96.1	2.8%
Dajiatou	185	39.3	932	85.5	46.0%
Tianshike	18	28.8	556	26.3	109.3%

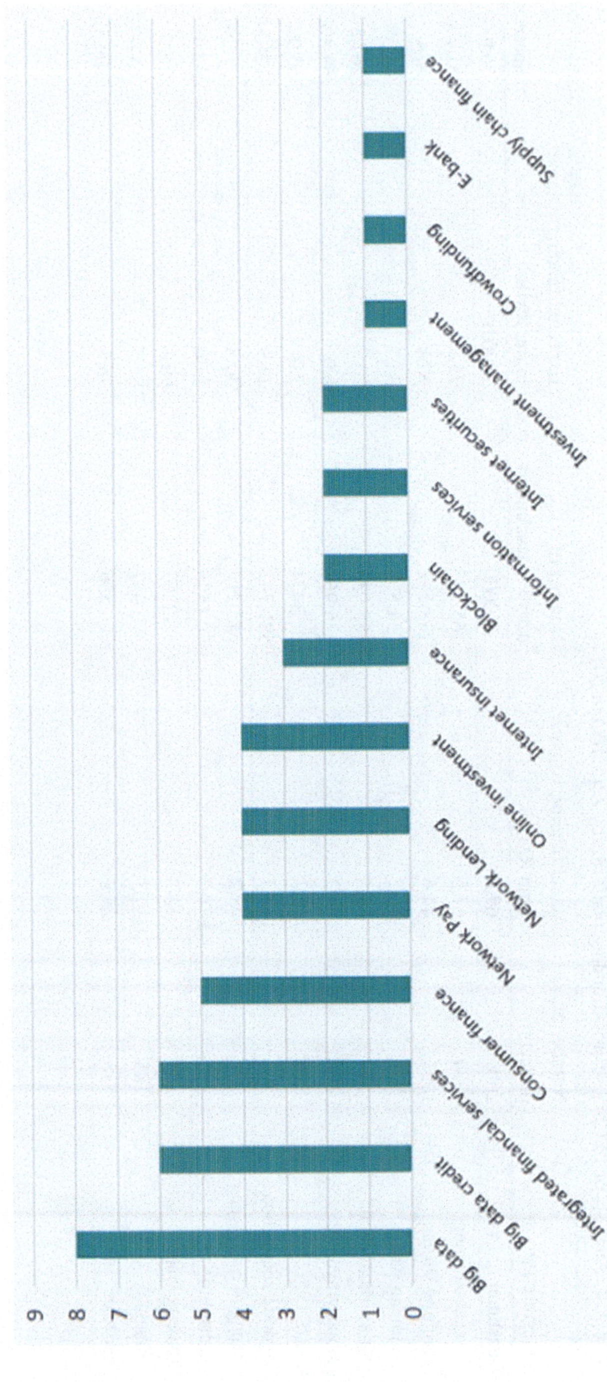

Fig. A.1 Business models of China's FinTech 50 companies

众筹在中国

欢迎参与调查“众筹在中国”！亲爱的参与者，非常感谢您能抽出 5 分钟的时间参与此次“众筹在中国”的问卷调查。您的所有回答都将是匿名的。我想就中国众筹写一本书。因此，我需要您的故事和经历。非常感谢您能跟我分享它们！诚挚问候，Andrea Funk (德国维尔茨堡大学博士在读学生)

1、您第一次听说众筹是什么时候？ (填空题 *必答)

____

2、您从何种途径得知众筹? (单选题 *必答)

- ○ 朋友
- ○ 媒体
- ○ 海外
- ○ 其他 ________

3、您是项目启动者还是投资人？ --请选择您与众筹的关系。 (单选题 *必答)

- ○ 项目启动者
- ○ 投资人
- ○ 既是项目启动者也是投资

4、迄今为止您使用过哪些众筹途径？您使用哪个平台？ (单选题 *必答)

- ○ 奖励众筹 ；所使用的平台： ________
- ○ 股权众筹； 所使用的平台： ________
- ○ 捐款众筹； 所使用的平台： ________
- ○ P2P 众筹； 所使用的平台： ________
- ○ 还没用众筹

5、众筹拥有许多优点。您欣赏众筹的那些优势? (排序题 请填 1-5 数字排序 *必答)

_____众筹是一种很好的口碑营销

_____众筹是一种资金来源

_____能在市场中预测试我的产品或服务

_____众筹为我的产品或服务带来 PR(公共关系 / 人脉)

_____能够预售我的产品或服务

1064. **KPMG.20162**

6、　　　您为何使用众筹方式？请注明赞同或不赞同。(5 = 完全赞同　4 = 赞同　3 = 无所谓　2 = 不赞同　1 = 完全不赞同 ）(打分题 请填 1-5 数字打分 *必答)

觉得好玩 _____
是其他融资方式的一种补充 _____
无法获得银行货款 _____
其他融资方式手续繁琐 _____
众筹不需支付利息 _____
在众筹之中展示项目，我担心其他人会剽窃我的创业理念 _____
我的一个朋友也成功运用了众筹 _____
从前我成功地投资了一个众筹项目 _____
其他融资方式比众筹更耗时 _____
比起其他融资方式我更喜欢众筹，因为这样可以保持独立性 _____
其他 _____

7、以下两个因素哪个在先，您对众筹的兴趣还是您的创业 / 项目方案？ (单选题 *必答)

○ 对众筹的兴趣
○ 创业 / 项目方案

8、为了您的项目 / 生意，您还使用过哪些其他融资手段？ (多选题 *必答)

☐ 个人资金
☐ 家人提供资金
☐ 朋友提供资金
☐ 天使投资
☐ 风险资本（VC）
☐ 银行贷款
☐ 政府补贴
☐ 只使用众筹
☐ 其他 __________

9、您是如何操作您的众筹的？ (多选题 *必答)

☐ 使用众筹平台
☐ 使用微信
☐ 用自己的网站
☐ 通过线下众筹
☐ 其他 __________

10、从您开始拥有创业 / 项目的想法到开始落实和实施您的创业 / 项目理念时间间隔多久？ (填空题 *必答)

____

11、您的项目属于哪个领域？（单选题 *必答）

- ○ 艺术
- ○ 时尚
- ○ 电影音像
- ○ 视频
- ○ 游戏
- ○ 新闻
- ○ 设计
- ○ 音乐
- ○ 科技
- ○ 其他 ________

12、您打算通过众筹募集多少资金？（填空题 *必答）

____

13、您投资过多少其他项目？（填空题 *必答）

____

14、您有几个合作伙伴？（填空题 *必答）

____

15、您的众筹面临的主要挑战有哪些？（填空题 *必答）

____

16、请设想，我送给您￥450 作为礼物。现在您可以选择拿走这 450 元或者赌博——赢 1000 元或是全输光。您会怎么做呢？（单选题 *必答）

- ○ 拿走这 450 元
- ○ 赌一把，并希望能赢 1000 元

17、您的性别是？（单选题 *必答）

- ○ 女性
- ○ 男性

18、您的年龄？（填空题 *必答）

____

19、您的教育背景是什么？（单选题 *必答）

○ 初中
○ 高中
○ 中专
○ 大专
○ 本科
○ 硕士
○ 硕士以上

20、您拥有多少年的商界经历？（填空题 *必答）

____

21、您的户口在哪儿？（填空题 *必答）

____

22、您有多少微信联系人？（填空题 *必答）

____

23、您会怎样用一句话定义众筹?（填空题 *必答）

____

Welcome to the survey "Crowdfunding in China"!

Dear Participant,

Thank you very much for spending 10 minutes of your time to join this survey on "Crowdfunding in China."

All of your answers will be anonymized. If you wish to receive the results of this survey after evaluation, or if you find time for a personal interview, you may provide your email-address towards the end of the survey. Still, this is optional/voluntarily.

I would like to write a book on "Crowdfunding in China". Therefore, I need your story and experience. Thank you very much for sharing both with me!

Best regards,

Andrea Funk (PhD student of University of Wuerzburg, Germany)

Q1: When did you first hear about crowdfunding?

Q2: Where do you know crowdfunding from?

- Friends
- Media
- From abroad
- Other source:

Q3: Are you a project initiator or a crowdfunder/investor, or both? - Choose your relation to crowdfunding.

- Project initiator
- Crowdfunder
- Both, a project initiator and a crowdfunder

Q4: Which kinds of crowdfunding have you used so far? Which platforms have you applied?

- Reward-based crowdfunding; utilised CFP:
- Equity-based crowdfunding; utilised CFP:
- Donation-based crowdfunding; utilised CFP:
- P2P crowdfunding; utilised CFP:
- I have not yet used crowdfunding

Q5: Crowdfunding has many advantages. What do you appreciate crowdfunding for? – Please rank all aspects which are important for you, from most important to least important.

- Crowdfunding is a source of finance
- I can pre-test my product or service on the market
- Crowdfunding is a good word-of-mouth marketing
- Crowdfunding brings PR for my product or service
- I can pre-sell my product or service.

Q6: Why do you use crowdfunding? – Please state whether you agree or disagree. (5 = I absolutely agree; 4 = I agree; 3 = I am indifferent; 2 = I do not agree; 1 = I do not agree at all)

- I think it is fun.
- It is a supplement to other finance.
- I cannot obtain a bank loan.
- Other finance is more bureaucratic.
- Crowdfunding includes no interest rate.
- By disclosing my project via crowdfunding, I fear that others copy my idea.
- A friend of mine has also successfully used crowdfunding.
- I have invested in a crowdfunding project before.
- Other finance is more time consuming than crowdfunding.
- I prefer crowdfunding instead of other forms of finance in order to stay independent.
- Other reasons:

Q7: What was first – your interest in crowdfunding or the idea of your project?

- My interest in crowdfunding.
- My idea to start a project/business.

Q8: Which other kinds of sources have you also used for your project/business?

- Personal/own finance
- Finance from family
- Finance from friends
- Angel investors
- Venture capital
- Bank loan
- Government subsidies
- Only crowdfunding
- Others

Q9: How do you conduct your crowdfunding?

- I use a crowdfunding platform
- I use WeChat
- I have my own website
- I have used offline crowdfunding
- Other tools:

Q10: How much time passed since the invention of your project/business idea and the actual implementation?

Q11: Which category does your project belong to?

- Art
- Fashion
- Film & Video
- Internet video
- Games
- Journalism
- Event
- Music
- Technology
- Other

Q12: How much capital do you intend to collect via crowdfunding?

Q13: In how many other projects have you invested in?

Q14: How many business partners do you have?

Q15: What are currently the major challenges of crowdfunding?

Q16: Imagine, I have just given you 450 RMB as a gift. Now you have the choice of either take these 450 RMB or gamble, and either win 1000 RMB or loose it all. What would you do?

- Take the 450 RMB
- Gamble and hope to win 1000 RMB

Q17: What is your gender?

- Male
- Female

Q18: What is your age?

Q19: What is your educational background?

Q20: How many years of business experience do you have?

Q21: What is your Hukou?

Q22: How many WeChat contacts do you have?

Q23: Can you define crowdfunding in one sentences?

References

199IT.com (ed) (2014) 灵动快拍 [Smart snap]: 2013 年二维码使用统计数据调查 [Statistics on a survey on QR code usage in 2013]. http://www.199it.com/archives/201000.html. Accessed 18 Jan 2017

Acharya V, Khandwala H, Öncü TS (2013) The growth of a shadow banking system in emerging markets: evidence from India. J Int Money Financ 39:207–230

Adams D (1992) Taking a fresh look at informal finance. In: Adams D, Fitchett D (eds) Informal finance in lowincome countries. Westview Press, Boulder, pp 5–24

Adams D, Canavesi, M (1992) Rotating savings and credit associations in bolivia. In: Adams D, Fitchett D (eds) Informal finance in low-income countries. Westview Press, Boulder, pp 313–323

Adams D, Fitchett D (eds) (1992a) Informal finance in low-income countries. Westview Press, Boulder

Adams D, Fitchett D (eds) (1992b) Introduction. In Adams D, Fitchett D (eds) Informal finance in low-income countries. Westview Press, Boulder, pp 1–4

Advertising Age (ed) (2014) QR codes are alive and well and living in China. http://adage.com/article/global-news/qr-codes-alive-living-china/291026/. Accessed 11 Dec 2015

Agrawal A, Catalini, C, Goldfarb, A (2011) Friends, family, and the flat world: the geography of crowdfunding: working paper. National Bureau of Economic Research. http://nber.org/papers/w16820.pdf

Agrawal A, Catalini, C, Goldfarb, A (2013) Some simple economics of crowdfunding: working paper 19133, Cambridge, MA. https://doi.org/10.3386/w19133

Agrawal A, Catalini, C, Goldfarb, A (2015) Crowdfunding: geography, social networks, and the timing of investment decisions. J Econ Manag Strateg 24(2):253–274

Ahlers G, Cumming D, Guenther C, Schweizer D (2012) Signaling in equity crowdfunding. SSRN Electron J. http://ssrn.com/abstract=2161587. Accessed 12 Feb 2014.

Ahmed S (2015) How many warehouses does Amazon have and where are they located? Edited by Quora. https://www.quora.com/How-manywarehouses-does-Amazon-have-and-where-are-they-located. Accessed 8 June 2016

Akerlof G (1970) The market for lemons: quality uncertainty and the market mechanism. Q J Econ 84(3):488–500

Alibaba Group (ed) (2014) Alipay 2014 spending report sheds light on Chinese online spending behavior: press release. http://www.alibabagroup.com/en/news/press_pdf/p141208.pdf. Accessed 13 Dec 2015

Alibaba Group (ed) (n.d.(a)) Company overview. http://www.alibabagroup.com/en/about/overview. Accessed 13 Dec2015

A. S. Funk, *Crowdfunding in China*, Contributions to Management Science,
https://doi.org/10.1007/978-3-319-97253-4

Alibaba Group (n.d.(b)) Our business. Edited by Alibaba Group. http://www.alibabagroup.com/en/about/businesses.

Alibaba Group (ed) (n.p.) History and milestones. http://www.alibabagroup.com/en/about/history?year=2014. Accessed 13 Dec 2015

Alijani S, Assadi D, Ashta A (2016) Can social dynamics be channeled from offline to online communities? Commitment, compliance, and cooperation from microfinance to crowdfunding. In: Assadi D (ed) Strategic approaches to successful crowdfunding. Advances in business strategy and competitive advantage. Business Science Reference, Hershey, pp 210–227

AllChinaTech (ed) (2015) China's newly proposed Charity law will ban donations collected through WeChat and Weibo. http://www.allchinatech.com/chinas-newly-proposed-charity-law-will-ban-donationscollected-through-wechat-and-weibo/. Accessed 8 Dec 2016

Aoki M (2007) Endogenizing institutions and institutional changes. J Inst Econ 3(1):1–31

Arner D, Barberis J, Buckley, R (2015) The evolution of fintech: a new post-crisis paradigm? University of Hong Kong Faculty of law research paper no. 2015/047. https://papers.ssrn.com/sol3/papers.cfm?abstract_id=2676553. Accessed 27 Oct 2016

Arrow K (1969) The organization of economic activity: issues pertinent to the choice of market versus non-market allocation. In: Joint Economic Committee, 91st congress 1st session

Artmorpheus (ed) (2012) How to run a successful crowdfunding campaign. https://artmorpheus.wordpress.com/2012/02/27/postshow-to-run-a-successful-crowdfunding-campaign/. Accessed 30 Nov 2016

Bachmann A, Becker A, Buerckner D, Hilker M, Kock F, Lehmann M, Tiburtius, P, Funk, B (2011) Online peer-to-peer lending – a literature review. J Internet Bank Commer 16(2):1–18

Backaler J (2014) China goes West: everything you need to know about Chinese companies going global. Palgrave Macmillan, Basingstoke

Banjo S (2015) Once idealistic, crowdfunding is now an unholy hybrid of retail, investment, and risk. Edited by Quartz. http://qz.com/389001/once-idealistic-crowdfunding-is-now-an-unholy-hybrid-of-retail-investment-and-risk/. Accessed 31 July 2015

Baydas MM, Bahloul Z, Adams DW (1995) Informal finance in Egypt: banks within banks. World Dev 23(4):651–661

BBC News Magazine (2013) The statue of liberty and America's crowdfunding pioneer. http://www.bbc.com/news/magazine-21932675. Accessed 15 Jan 2016

Becker K-B (2011) Internetzensur in China: Aufbau und Grenzen des chinesischen Kontrollsystems. 1. Aufl. VS research, VS Verl. für Sozialwiss, Wiesbaden. http://bvbr.bib-bvb.de:8991/F?func=service&doc_library=BVB01&local_base=BVB01&doc_number=024143323&line_number=0001&func_code=DB_RECORDS&service_type=MEDIA

Begashaw G (1978) The economic role of traditional savings and credit institutions in Ethiopia. Sav Dev 2(4):249–262.

Beijing backs equity crowdfunding to develop entrepreneurial economy: state council encourages more entrepreneurial activity and vows to cut red tape for new firms (2015). http://www.scmp.com/business/chinabusiness/article/1861840/beijing-backs-equity-crowdfunding-developentrepreneurial. Accessed 28 June 2016

Bell C (1990) Interactions between institutional and informal credit agencies in rural India: a symposium issue on imperfect information and rural credit markets. World Bank Econ. Rev. 4(3):297–327.

Bell S, Feng H (2013) The rise of the people's bank of China: the politics of institutional change. Harvard University Press, Cambridge

Belleflamme P, Lambert T, Schwienbacher A (2010) Crowdfunding: an industrial organization perspective. In: Workshop on digital business models: understanding strategies, Paris

Belleflamme P, Lambert T, Schwienbacher A (2013). Individual crowdfunding practices. Ventur Cap 15(4):313–333. https://doi.org/10.1080/13691066.2013.785151

Belleflamme P, Lambert T, Schwienbacher A (2014) Crowdfunding: tapping the right crowd. J Bus Ventur 29:585–609

Benda C (2013) Community rotating savings and credit associations as an agent of well-being: a case study from northern Rwanda. Community Dev J 48(2):232–247

Benston G, Smith, C (1976) A transaction cost approach to the theory of financial intermediation. J Financ 31(2):215–231

Berke J (2015) How Alibaba turned an obscure, made-up Chinese holiday into a 14.3 billion shopping extravaganza that's bigger than Black Friday. Edited by Business Insider Deutschland. http://www.businessinsider.de/how-alibaba-made-143-billion-on-singles-day-2015-11?r=US&IR=T. Accessed 12 Oct 2015

Besley T, Levenson A (1996). The role of informal finance in household capital accumulation: evidence from Taiwan. Econ J 106(434):39–59

Blohm I, Gebert M, Wenzlaff K, Leimeister JM (eds) (2013) Crowdfunding-Studie 2013/2013: Analyse, Perspektiven und Erfolgsfaktoren innovativer Unternehmens- und Projektfinanzierungen. epubli GmbH, Berlin

Bloomberg (ed) (2015) China development bank is reportedly planning two Hong Kong IPOs. http://www.bloomberg.com/research/stocks/private/snapshot.asp?privcapId=3590896. Accessed 20 Jan 2016

Bloomberg (ed) (2016) Yuan free float seen a decade away as China keeps strict control. http://www.bloomberg.com/news/articles/2016-08-11/yuan-free-float-seen-a-decade-away-as-china-keeps-strictcontrol. Accessed 11 June 2016

Bofinger P, Scheuermeyer P (2015) Das "Kapital" im 21. Jahrhundert. In: Bofinger P, Horn G, Schmid K van Treeck T (eds) Thomas Piketty und die Verteilungsfrage. SE Publishing, Leipzig, pp 98–129

BOP Consulting (ed) (2015) Progress towards equity crowdfunding in China: draft regulations suggest a new era for crowdfunding in China. http://bop.co.uk/articles/progress-towards-equity-crowdfunding-in-china. Accessed 4 July 2016

Boston University (ed) (2014) Profiting without producing: how finance exploits us all — a lecture by Costas Lapavitsas. https://www.youtube.com/watch?v=6GoQWkyVZq4. Accessed 26 Oct 2016

Bouman FJA, Moll HAJ (1992) Informal finance in Indonisia. In: D Adams, D Fitchett (eds) Informal finance in low-income countries. Westview Press, Boulder, pp 209–223

Bradley T (2008) Final fundraising figure: Obama's 750M. Edited by abc News. http://abcnews.go.com/Politics/Vote2008/story?id=6397572&page=1. Accessed 16 Jan 2016

Burtch G, Ghose A, Wattal S (2014) Cultural differences and geography as determinants of online prosocial lending. MIS Q 38(3):773–794

Business Insider (ed) (2016) WeChat breaks 700 million monthly active users. http://www.businessinsider.com/wechat-breaks-700-million-monthly-active-users-2016-4?IR=T. Accessed 31 Oct 2016

Business Wire (ed) (2014) Robot entertainment partners with Tencent games for Orcs must die! unchained to extend global reach: signature Orcs must die! franchise to be published in 2015 by Tencent Games for PC in China, joining North America and Europe as confirmed Territories. http://www.businesswire.com/news/home/20141126005071/en/Robot-Entertainment-Partners-Tencent-Games-Orcs-Die!. Accessed 20 June 2016

Cai H [蔡海宁], Wang L [王雷] (2014) 互联网金融之众筹的法律思考 [Legal considerations on crowdfunding as an art of internet finance]. 仲裁研究 [Zhongcai yanjiu] 37:116–120

Callier P (1990) Informal finance: the rotating saving and credit association — an interpretation. KYKLOS 43(2): 273–276

Cao O (2015) China crowdfunding market research report 2015 is released; encouragement from the State Council presents huge opportunities for crowdfunding. Edited by Zero2IPO. http://en.pedaily.cn/Item.aspx?id=220256. Accessed 29 Jan 2016

Capgemini (2014) Digital shopper relevancy research report 2014: understanding and anticipating the changing perspectives of digital customers.

Capgemini Consulting, Royal Bank of Scotland (eds) (2015) World payments report 2015

Carni US (2014) Protecting the crowd through escrow: three ways that the SEC can portect crowdfunding investors. Fordham J Corp Financ Law 19:681–706

Castree N, Kitchin R, Rogers A (2013). A dictionary of human geography: guanxi. Oxford quick reference collection, 1st edn. Oxford University Press, Oxford

CBRC (ed) (2009) China banking regulatory commission 2009 annual report

CBRC (ed) (2011) China banking regulatory commission 2011 annual report

CBRC (ed) (2014) China banking regulatory commission 2014 annual report: part I

CCTV (ed) (2016) Tenpay starts charging withdrawal fees whild [sic!] the banks cancel them. http://english.cntv.cn/2016/03/02/VIDEWmwCtPcMC2rEULQrXXId160302.shtml. Accessed 2 Dec 2016

Centre for Retail Research (ed) (n.d.) Online retailing: Britain, Europe, US and Canada 2015. http://www.retailresearch.org/onlineretailing.php. Accessed 9 Dec 2015

Chai K [柴珂楠] (2014) '欧盟众筹金融监管法律框架及评 [A review of the legal framework of crowdfunding in the European union]'. 南方金融 July(455):40–47.

Chan J (2016) China leads the way as Asia-Pac fintech investments hit $13 bil. Edited by The Edge Markets. http://www.theedgemarkets.com/my/article/china-leads-way-asia-pac-fintech-investments-hits13-bil. Accessed 31 Oct 2016

Chandler, D, Munday R (2011) Institutions. In: A Dictionary of media and communication. Oxford University Press, Oxford. http://www.oxfordreference.com/view/10.1093/acref/9780199568758.001.0001/acref-9780199568758-e-1360. Accessed 21 Feb 2016

Chao L, Burkitt L (2011) The biggest IPO you haven't heard of: Chinese online retailer hopes to raise up to $5 billion in U.S. Edited by The Wall Street Journal. http://www.wsj.com/articles/SB10001424053111904491704576570612044417314. Accessed 7 June 2016

Chapman J, Marshall U (eds) (2012) China's banking system, currency policy and economic conditions. In: Asian economic and political issues. Nova Science, New York

Cheng A (2014) Yu'e Bao Wow! how Alibaba is reshaping Chinese finance: Jack Ma's money market fund has raised 90 billion in just ten months, posing a threat to the country's banks and challenging its regulators. Edited by Institutional investor. http://www.institutionalinvestor.com/article/3346365/investors-sovereign-wealth-funds/yue-bao-wow-how-alibaba-isreshaping-chinese-finance.html#.V2g4hqKkyJ0. Accessed 20 June 2016

Chiang L (2015) Real estate crowdfunding booms in Asia despite regulatory uncertainties. http://www.scmp.com/property/hong-kong-china/article/1881739/real-estate-crowdfunding-booms-asiadespite-regulatory. Accessed 10 Feb 2016

China Daily (ed) (2014a) Potential of the Chinese dream.http://usa.chinadaily.com.cn/epaper/2014-03/26/content_17380146.htm. Accessed 29 June 2016

China Daily (ed) (2014b) Top 10 internet companies by market value. http://www.chinadaily.com.cn/bizchina/2014-11/18/content_18931467.htm. Accessed 28 Jan 2016

China Education and Research Network [中国教育和科研计算机网] (eds) (2001) Evolution of internet in China. http://www.edu.cn/introduction_1378/20060323/t20060323_4285.shtml. Accessed 21 Aug 2016

China Internet Network Information Center (ed) (2011) Statistical report on internet development in China: January, 2011

China Internet Network Information Center (ed) (2015) Statistical report on internet development in China

China Internet Watch (ed) (2013) UnionPay new policy targeting third-party online payment. http://chinainternetwatch.com/3799/unionpaytargeted-at-third-party-payment/. Accessed 30 Nov 2015

China Internet Watch (ed) (2014) Jingdong launched shopping channel on mobile QQ. http://www.chinainternetwatch.com/8179/mobile-qq-jdshopping/. Accessed 7 Dec 2015

China Internet Watch (ed) (2015a) Alibaba has over 86% share of China mobile shopping market in 2014. http://www.chinainternetwatch.com/12323/mobile-shopping-market-2014/. Accessed 9 Dec 2015

China Internet Watch (ed) (2015b) JD.com marketplace reached 60,000 merchants in 2014. http://www.chinainternetwatch.com/12599/jingdong-q4-2014/. Accessed 6 Dec 2015

China Internet Watch (ed) (2015c) China mobile payment reached $4.19 trillion, up by 445% in Q2 2015. http://www.chinainternetwatch.com/14808/mobile-payment-q2-2015/. Accessed 9 Dec 2015

China Internet Watch (ed) (2015d) China union pay totaled 260 million usesrs [sic!] in Aug 2015. http://www.chinainternetwatch.com/14924/china-unionpay-260-million-usesrs-aug-2015/. Accessed 30 Nov 2015
China Internet Watch (ed) (2015e). China top 100 e-commerce companies in Q3 2015. http://www.chinainternetwatch.com/14911/top-100-ebusiness-companies-q3-2015/. Accessed 6 Dec 2015
China Internet Watch (ed) (2015f) China online shopping insights in 2014. http://www.chinainternetwatch.com/14875/china-online-shoppinginsights-2014/. Accessed 7 Dec 2015
China Internet Watch (ed) (2015g) China to become largest e-commerce market in 2015. http://www.chinainternetwatch.com/15235/retail-e-commerce-2015/. Accessed 6 Dec 2015
China Internet Watch (ed) (2015h) 22% Online shopping spend are newly created demand. http://www.chinainternetwatch.com/15094/online-shoppers-insights-2015/. Accessed 10 Dec 2015
China Internet Watch (ed) (2015i) Most China food delivery users pay online in 2015. http://www.chinainternetwatch.com/15508/chinese-food-delivery-pay-online-2015/. Accessed 12 Dec 2015
China Internet Watch (ed) (2015j) JD GMV exceeded $17.5B, 76% increase YoY in Q3 2015. http://www.chinainternetwatch.com/15699/jd-q3-2015/. Accessed 9 Dec 2015
China Internet Watch (ed) (2015k) China retail V.S. online shopping 2015. http://www.chinainternetwatch.com/15610/china-retail-v-s-onlineshopping-2015/. Accessed 9 Dec 2015
China Retail News (ed) (2015) JD.com to close Paipai.com by end of December. http://www.chinaretailnews.com/2015/11/19/8001-jd-comto-close-paipai-com-by-end-of-december/. Accessed 17 Aug 2016
China's premier joins the start-up crowd at entrepreneurs' café in innovation push (2015). http://www.scmp.com/tech/innovation/article/1788229/chinas-premier-joins-start-crowd-entrepreneurs-cafe-innovation-push. Accessed 29 June 2016
Clark D (2016) Alibaba: the house that Jack Ma built, 1st edn. HarperCollins, New York
Coase, RH (1937) The nature of the firm. Economica 4(16):386–405
Coase, RH (1960) The problem of social cost. J Law Econ 3:1–44.
Colombo M, Franzoni C, Lamastra CR (2015) Internal social capital and the attraction of early contributions in crowdfunding. Enterp Theory Pract 39(1):75–100
Congressional-Executive Commission on China (ed) (2015) Alibaba's dispute with officials highlights lack of transparency and weak role of law. http://www.cecc.gov/publications/commission-analysis/alibaba%E2%80%99s-dispute-with-officials-highlights-lack-of-transparency. Accessed 27 Jan 2016
Could start-ups revitalise the Chinese economy? The government thinks so (2015). http://www.scmp.com/business/companies/article/1730847/could-start-ups-revitalise-chinese-economy-government-thinksso. Accessed 29 June 2016
Cousin V (2011) Banking in China. Palgrave Macmillan studies in banking and financial institutions, 2nd edn. Palgrave Macmillan, Basingstoke
Crowdsupply (ed) (n.d.) Attkon tech. https://www.crowdsupply.com/attkon-tech. Accessed 21 Feb 2016
Cryptocoinsnews.com (ed) (n.d.) Top 10 countries in which bitcoin is banned. https://www.cryptocoinsnews.com/top-10-countriesbitcoin-banned/. Accessed 10 Feb 2017
Cumming D, Leboeuf G, Schwienbacher A (2016) Crowdfunding models: keep-it-all vs. all-or-nothing. http://papers.ssrn.com/sol3/papers.cfm?abstract_id=2447567. Accessed 15 Jan
Dahlmann C (1979) The problem of externality. J Law Econ 22(1):141–162.
Dapp T (2013) Crowdfunding: an alternative source of funding with potential. Edited by Deutsche Bank
Davies R (2014) Three provocations for civic crowdfunding. Inf Commun Soc 18(3):342–355. https://doi.org/10.1080/1369118X.2014.989878
de Buysere K, Gajda O, Kleverlaan R, Marom D (2012) A framework for European crowdfunding. www.europecrowdfunding.org/Resources/Documents/FRAMEWORK_EU_CROWDFUNDING.pdf. Accessed 23 Feb 2014

de Vasconcelos G (2015) Surge of female entrepreneurs thanks to crowdfunding. Edited by Forbes. http://www.forbes.com/sites/goncalodevasconcelos/2015/07/13/surge-of-female-entrepreneursthanks-to-crowdfunding/#5da9bd547a09. Accessed 9 Nov 2016

Deng C [邓晨菲] (2014) 众筹网站 [Crowdfunding platform]: 一种新型营销模式 [A new kind of marketing]. News World, no. November:94–95

Denyer S (2016) China wants to give all of its citizens a score – and their rating could affect every area of their lives: the communist party wants to encourage good behaviour by marking all its people using online data. Those who fall short will be denied basic freedoms like loans or travel. Edited by Independent. http://www.independent.co.uk/news/world/asia/chinasurveillance-big-data-score-censorship-a7375221.html. Accessed 15 Feb 2017

Deposits.org (ed) (2016) China deposits. http://china.deposits.org/deposits/. Accessed 18 Jan 2016

Desjardins J (2016) 27 fintech unicorns, and where they were born. Edited by Visual Capitalist. http://www.visualcapitalist.com/27-fintech-unicorns-where-born/. Accessed 31 Oct 2016

Ding L [丁玲] (2015) 众筹的作用机制与企业融资选择 [The function of crowdfunding and choice of business finance]. 中国物价 [Zhongguo wujia] 10:51–54

Donaldson G (1965) Corporate debt capacity: a study of corporate debt policy and the determination of corporate debt capacity, 4th print. Harvard University, Boston

Dong X (2014) Why virtual hongbao should have WeChat pleased as punch. Edited by Caixin online. http://english.caixin.com/2014-02-12/100637931.html. Accessed 20 Jan 2016

Donoso SB, Altunbas Y, Kara A (2011) The rational behind informal finance: evidence from ROSCAS in bolivia. J Dev Areas 45:191–208

Dorfleitner G, Kapitz J, Wimmer M (2014) Crowdinvesting als Finanzierungsalternative für kleine und mittlere Unternehmen. http://epub.uni-regensburg.de/30104/1/preprint.pdf. Accessed 13 Jan 2016

dpa (2015) Singles Day bricht in China erneut Rekorde. Edited by Handelsblatt. http://www.handelsblatt.com/unternehmen/handel-konsumgueter/alibaba-knackt-bestwert-singles-day-bricht-in-china-erneut-rekorde/12572708.html. Accessed 10 Dec 2015

Draper D, Hoag J (1978) Financial intermediation and the theory of agency. J Financ Quant Anal 13(4):595–611

Duflos E, Klapper L (2015) New accounts in China drive global financial inclusion figure. Edited by World Bank. http://blogs.worldbank.org/eastasiapacific/new-accounts-china-drive-global-financial-inclusion-figures. Accessed 31 Oct 2016

Dumas D (2014) Crowdtilt 随时随地玩众筹 [Crowdtilt (–) Having fun with crowdfunding at any time at any place]. 创业邦 April:53

Dunkley E (2016) China challenges London's fintech lead: UK drops in annual ranking as Brexit concerns hit sector funding. Edited by Financial Times. https://www.ft.com/content/a3c5d652-9914-11e6-8f9b-70e3cabccfae. Accessed 30 Oct 2016

Durden T (2016) More Ponzi-2-Ponzi blowups just a matter of time in China, experts warn. Edited by Zero Hedge. http://www.zerohedge.com/news/2016-02-04/more-ponzi-2-ponzi-blowups-just-mattertime-china-experts-warn. Accessed 7 Feb 2016

Ecommerce News (ed) (2015a) Mobile shopping in Europe and North America: key figures and trends 2014-15. http://ecommercenews.eu/key-figuresmobile-commerce-europe-revealed/. Accessed 6 Dec 2015

Ecommerce News (ed) (2015b) Ecommerce in Germany. http://ecommercenews.eu/ecommerce-per-country/ecommerce-germany/. Accessed 6 Dec 2015

Ecommerce News (ed) (2015c) Alibaba introduces Alipay in Europe. http://ecommercenews.eu/alibaba-introduces-alipay-in-europe/. Accessed 13 Dec 2015

Elliot D, Kroeber A, Qiao Y (2015) Shadow banking in China: a primer. The Brooking Institution, Washington, DC

eMarketer Inc (ed) (2015) US retail sales to near $5 trillion in 2016. http://www.emarketer.com/Article/US-Retail-Sales-Near-5-Trillion-2016/1013368. Accessed 8 June 2016.

Emmerson L (2015) Crowdfunding industry overtakes venture capital and angel investing. Edited by Symbid blog. http://blog.symbid.com/2015/trends/crowdfunding-industry-overtakes-venture-capitaland-angel-investing/. Accessed 6 Jan 2016

English.Gov.cn (ed) (2015) China unveils internet plus action plan to fuel growth. http://english.gov.cn/policies/latest_releases/2015/07/04/content_281475140165588.htm. Accessed 16 Jan 2017

English.Gov.cn (ed) (2016) Mass entrepreneurship and innovation as new growth engine. http://english.gov.cn/premier/news/2016/03/03/content_281475300571752.htm. Accessed 8 Dec 2016

Entrepreneur (ed) (n.d.) Business incubator: definition. http://www.entrepreneur.com/encyclopedia/business-incubator. Accessed 15 Dec 2015

Fan J [范家琛] (2013) 众筹商业模式研究 [Research on the nature of the crowdfunding industry]. Enterp Econ August(396):72–75

Fan Y [樊云慧] (2015) 股权众筹平台监管的国际比较 [An international comparison of the supervision of equity crowdfunding platforms]. 法学 [Faxue] 4:84–91

Feller J, Gleasure R, Treacy S (2013) From the wisdom to the wealth of crowds: a metatriangulation of crowdfunding research: (TOTO working paper 2013.01 v2)

Feng M (2015) The 'Chinese Dream' deconstructed: values and institutions. J Chin Polit Sci **20**(2):163–183. https://doi.org/10.1007/s11366-015-9344-4

Fink A (2015) Protecting the crowd and raising capital through the JOBS Act: SSRN working paper No. 2046051. http://papers.ssrn.com/sol3/papers.cfm?abstract_id=2046051. Accessed 7 Nov

Fischer D (2006) Privatwirtschaft in China: Vom Randphänomen zum Hoffnung- sträger. Osteuropa-Wirtschaft 51(3–4):303–332.

Fischer D (2014) Medien: Alte Reflexe und neue Herausforderungen. In: Fischer D (ed) Länderbericht China. Schriftenreihe / Bundeszentrale für Politische Bildung, vol 1501. bpb Bundeszentrale für politische Bildung, Bonn, pp 463–497

Fischer D (2015) China in 2015 – between a rock and a hard place (2015 年的中国一进退两难). Econet Monit 12:30–33

Fischer D (2016). "Green Growth" or "System Transition"? Competing discourses of China's past economic success and future perspectives. Comparativ 26(2):42–55

Frearson A (2015) Crowdfunded Luchtsingel pedestrian bridge opens in Rotterdam. Edited by dezeen magazine. http://www.dezeen.com/2015/07/16/luchtsingel-elevated-pathways-bridges-rotterdam-cityscapezus-architects/. Accessed 13 July 2016

Freedman D, Nutting M (2015) A brief history of crowdfunding: including rewards, donation, debt, and equity platforms in the USA. http://www.freedman-chicago.com/ec4i/History-of-Crowdfunding.pdf. Accessed 12 Jan 2016

Frydrych D, Bock A, Kinder T, Koeck B (2014) Exploring entrepreneurial legitimacy in reward-based crowdfunding . Ventur Cap 16(3), 247–269.

Fueglistaller U (2012) Entrepreneurship: Modelle, Umsetzung, Perspektiven; mit Fall- beispielen aus Deutschland, Österreich und der Schweiz. 3rd edn. Springer Gabler, Wiesbaden

Funk AS (2016) Institutions influencing the evolution of crowdfunding in China: a review of the world bank report on crowdfunding in the developing world. In: Brüntje D, Gajda O (eds) Crowdfunding in Europe. FGF studies in small business and entrepreneurship. Springer, Cham, pp 125–131

Furubotn E, Richter R (1991) The new institutional economics: an assessment. In: Furubotn E, Richter R The New Institutional Economics. J.C.B. Mohr, Tübingen, pp 1–32

Gabison G (2015) Equity crowdfunding: all regulated but not equal. DePaul Bus Commer Law J 13(3):359–409.

Gerber E, Hui J, Kuo P-Y (2012) Crowdfunding: why people are motivated to post and fund projects on crowdfunding platforms: technical report 12-02. Northwest University, Segal Design Institute, Illinois

Giudici G, Guerini M, Lamastra CR (2013) Why crowdfunding projects can succeed: the role of proponents' individual and territorial social capital. SSRN Electron J. 2255944:1–20. http://ssrn.com/abstract=2255944. Accessed 27 Oct 2015

GO-Globe (ed) (2013) E-commerce in China — atatistics and trends [infographic]. http://www.go-globe.com/blog/ecommerce-in-china/. Accessed 11 Dec 2015

Goebel E (2002) Neue Institutionenökonomik: Konzeption und betriebswirtschaftliche Anwendungen. Betriebswirtschaftslehre, vol 2235. Lucius & Lucius, Stuttgart

Gokey M (2014) Apple pay is just one fingerprint away in China, as Alipay adopts iPhone's touch ID sensor. Edited by Digital Trends. http://www.digitaltrends.com/mobile/alipay-wallet-app-touch-idpayments/. Accessed 27 Jan 2016

Gough N (2016a) Online Lender Ezubao took $7.6 billion in Ponzi scheme, China says. Edited by New York Times. http://www.nytimes.com/2016/02/02/business/dealbook/ezubao-china-fraud.html?_r=0. Accessed 2 Feb 2016

Gough N (2016b) Ponzi scheme in China gained credibility from state media. Edited by New York Times. http://www.nytimes.com/2016/02/06/business/dealbook/alleged-china-ponzi-scheme-ezubao.html?_r=0. Accessed 7 Feb 2016

Gov.cn (ed.) (2011) 国民经济和社会发展第十二个五年规划 [12th five-year-plan for the economic and social development]. http://www.gov.cn/2011lh/content_1825838_2.htm. Accessed 25 Jan 2016

Graham D, Cuevas C (1990) Rural financial markets in Niger: markets, institutions, and experiments: report submitted to USAID/AFR/SWA/SRO. The Ohio State University, Washington, DC

Granville B, Leonard C (2010) Do informal institutions matter for technological change in Russia? The impact of communist norms and conventions, 1998–2004. World Dev 38(2):155–169. https://doi.org/10.1016/j.worlddev.2009.10.010

Griffiths T (2015) China's mobile payments war is going global: what brands need to know to keep up with the fast-changing payment habits of Chinese consumers. Edited by Advertising Age. http://adage.com/article/opinion/china-s-mobile-payments-war-global/301488/. Accessed 13 Dec 2015

GSM Association (ed) (2015) The mobile economy 2015. http://www.gsma.com/mobileeconomy/global/2015/. Accessed 25 Jan 2016

Gugerty MK (2007) You can't save alone: commitment in rotating savings and credit associations in Kenya. Econ Dev Cult Chang 55(2):251–282.

Guha, S, Gupta G (2005) Microcredit for income generation: the role of rosca. Econ Polit Wkly 40(14), 1470–1473

Guo S [郭帅] (2014) P2P 网络融资风险的系统性影响与应对 [The Systemic Risk of P2P online finance and counter-measures]. 金融理论与实践 [jinrong lilun yu shijian] 11(424):63–67

Haas P, Blohm I, Leimeister JM (2014) An empirical taxonomy of crowdfunding intermediaries. Paper presented at the international conference on information systems (ICIS), Auckland

Hainzer M, Stötzer S, Ellmer M (2014) Crowdfunding-basierte Bür- gerkreditmodelle in Kommunen. Zeitschrift für öffentliche und gemeinwirtschaftliche Unternehmen 37(1–2):54–72

Hall P, Soskice D (2001) Varieties of capitalism: the institutional foundations of comparative advantage. Oxford University Press, Oxford

Harford T (2011) How China boomed by trial and error. Edited by Financial Times. https://www.ft.com/content/ad97c282-7b6d-11e0-ae56-00144feabdc0. Accessed 17 Jan 2017

Harms M (2015) Crowdfunding und Banken: Eine Bestandsaufnahme. Edited by crowdfunding.de. http://www.crowdfunding.de/crowdfunding-und-banken-eine-bestandsaufnahme/. Accessed 17 Feb 2016

Harrison R (2013) Crowdfunding and the revitalisation of the early stage risk capital market: catalyst or chimera? Ventur Cap 15(4):283–287. https://doi.org/10.1080/13691066.2013.852331

Hartmann-Wendels T, Pfingsten A, Weber M (2007) Bankbetriebslehre. 4, überarb. Aufl. Springer, Berlin

Hartz W (2013) Basiswissen QR-code. http://qrcode.wilkohartz.de/. Accessed 11 Dec 2015

Heep S (2014) China in global finance: domestic financial repression and international financial power: description based on publisher supplied metadata and other sources, 1st edn. Springer International Publishing, Cham

Helft M (2014) Alibaba's Jack Ma wants to link Alipay with apple pay. Edited by Fortune.com. http://fortune.com/2014/10/28/alibabas-jack-ma-wants-to-link-alipay-with-apple-pay/. Accessed 15 Aug 2016

Hendrichs M (2015) Why Alipay is more than just the Chinese equivalent of PayPal. Edited by Tech in Asia. https://www.techinasia.com/talk/online-payment-provider-alipay-chinese-equivalentpaypal/. Accessed 12 Dec 2015

Henkel M (2015) Social commerce: Verkaufen auf Facebook und Twitter. Edited by Techtag. http://www.techtag.de/it-undhightech/e-commerce/social-commerce-lohnt-sich-der-digitale-handelvia-facebook-und-twitter/. Accessed 11 Dec 2015

Ho DY-F (1976) On the concept of face. Am J Sociol 81(4):867–884. https://doi.org/10.1086/226145

Hodgson G (2006) What are institutions? J Econ Issues 40(1):1–25

Hooghiemstra S, de Buysere K (2016) The perfect regulation of crowdfunding: what should the European regulator do? In: Brüntje D, Gajda O (eds) Crowdfunding in Europe. FGF studies in small business and entrepreneurship. Springer, Cham, pp 135–165

Horwitz J (2016) Your brilliant Kickstarter idea could be on sale in China before you've even finished funding it. Edited by Quartz. http://qz.com/771727/chinas-factories-in-shenzhen-can-copy-productsat-breakneck-speed-and-its-time-for-the-rest-of-the-world-to-getover-it/. Accessed 19 Nov 2016

Howe J (2006) The rise of crowdsourcing. Wired Mag 14(6):1–4. http://www.wired.com/2006/06/crowds/

Hsu S (2009) Introduction. In: Li J, Hsu S (eds) Informal finance in China. Oxford University Press, Oxford, pp. 1–11

Hu X [胡晓军] (2014) 中国金融新生态 [China's new finance ecology?]: 全面解析互联网金融 [A comprehensive analysis of internet finance] SS new management bookshelf. Renmin youdian chubanshe, Beijing

Hu M [胡梦婷] (2015) 众筹的主要法律风险及其防范 [Main legal risks and preventions in crowdfunding]. 连云港职业技术学院学报 [J Lianyungang Tech Coll] 28(2):33–36

Huang J [黄健青], Chen H [陈欢], Li D [李大夜] (2015) 基于顾客价值视角的众筹项目成功影响因素研究 [Investigating successful influencing factors of crowdfunding projects from the perspective of customer value]. Zhongguo ruanke xue 6:116–127.

Huang M (n.d.) How mobile payment works in China. Edited by The Wall Street Journal Blog. http://blogs.wsj.com/digits/2015/11/24/how-mobile-payment-works-in-china/. Accessed 13 Dec 2015

Huang Z [黄震], Deng J [邓建鹏] (2014) 互联网金融 [Internet finance]: 法律于风险控制 [Law and risk control]. Jixie gongye chubanshe, Beijing

Hui J, Gerber E, Greenberg, M (2012) Easy money? The demands of crowdfunding work: technical report no. 4. Northwestern University, Segal Design Institute

Hui J, Greenberg M, Gerber E (2015) Understanding crowdfunding work: implications for support tools. In: CHI'13 extended abstracts on human factors in computing systems, pp 889–894. http://www.juliehui.org/wp-content/uploads/2013/03/. Accessed 7 Nov

Inflation.eu (n.d.) Inflation China 2015. http://www.inflation.eu/inflation-rates/china/historic-inflation/cpi-inflation-china-2015.aspx. Accessed 18 Jan 2016

infoDev (2013) Crowdfunding's potential for the developing world. Edited by The World Bank. Washington, DC

Innovation is Everywhere (ed) (n.d.) O2O: why China leads the online to offline revolution. http://www.innovationiseverywhere.com/o2o-why-china-leads-the-online-to-offline-revolution/. Accessed 11 Dec 2015

Internet Live Stats (ed) (n.d.) Internet users by country (2014). http://www.internetlivestats.com/internet-users-by-country/. Accessed 28 Nov 2015

Internet World (ed.) (2016). Singles Day: Alibaba bricht eigenen Rekord. http://www.internetworld.de/e-commerce/alibaba/singles-day-alibaba-bricht-eigenen-rekord-1148299.html. Accessed 2 Dec 2016

Internet World Stats (ed) (n.d.) World internet users and 2015 population stats. http://www.internetworldstats.com/stats.htm. Accessed 28 Nov 2015

Investopedia (ed) (n.d.) Definition of 'digital native'. http://www.investopedia.com/terms/d/digital-native.asp. Accessed 25 Jan 2016

iResearch (ed) (2015) 2015 China e-payment user report (brief edition)
iResearch (ed) (2016a) 中国权益众筹市场研究报告 [China reward-based crowdfunding market research report]: 2015年 [2015]. http://img1.zczhijia.com/file/20150812/635749694424447890740 7180.pdf. Accessed 29 Jan
iResearch (ed) (2016b) China's third-party online payment market confronts increasing fierce competition. Accessed 19 Jan 2017
iResearch (ed) (2016c) China's third-party mobile payment market shot up 69.7% in 2015. Accessed 19 Jan 2017
iResearch (ed) (2016d) China's online shopping GMV kept rising in 2015. http://www.iresearchchina.com/content/details7_22434.html. Accessed 18 Jan 2017
iResearch (ed) (2016e) China's mobile shopping GMV increased significantly in 2015. http://www.iresearchchina.com/content/details7_22647.html. Accessed 18 Jan 2017
iResearch (ed) (2016f) China's third-party mobile payment GMV broke 6 Tn Yuan in Q1 2016. http://www.iresearchchina.com/content/details7_24301.html. Accessed 18 Jan 2017
iResearch (ed) (2016g) China's third-party online payment GMV hit 4.6 trillion Yuan in Q2 2016. Accessed 19 Jan 2017
JD.com (ed) (n.d.) Corporate website. http://www.jd.com/. Accessed 13th Feb 2017
JD Finance (ed) (2015) Dita 智能便携空气检测仪 [Dita smart convenient and handy device for testing the air]. http://z.jd.com/project/details/7783.html. Accessed 21 Feb 2016
Jensen M, Meckling W (1976) Theory of the firm: managerial behavior, agency costs and ownership structure. J Financ Econ 3:305–360.
Jiang X (1996) The research of informal finance in China. Shandong People's Publishing House, Shandong
Jiang S (2000) China underground finance. Fujian People's Press, Fuzhou
Jiang S (2009a) The evolution of informal finance in China and its prospects. In: Li J, Hsu S (eds) Informal finance in China. Oxford University Press, Oxford, pp 12–38
Jiang X (2009b). A comparative analysis of regional informal financial organizations in China. In: Li J, Hsu S (eds) Informal finance in China. Oxford University Press, Oxford, pp 60–79
Jiang Y [蒋英燕] (2015) 众筹模式与青年创业的契合度初探 [Initial investigation of the compatibility of crowdfunding kinds and start-ups]. Zhejiang Jinrong July:8–12
Jiang X, Ding C (2004) Theoretical analysis of informal finance: conception, comparison and institutional change. J Financ Res 8:100–111.
Jumpstart Our Business Startups: H.R.3606 (2012) 112th congress of the United States of America
Junge R, Eidinger P (2013) Crowdfunding – ein Finanzierungsmodell für Kulturprojekte? Grin Verlag, München
Kearney AT (ed) (2011) China's e-commerce market: the logistics challenges.
Kearney AT (ed) (2015) The 2015 global retail e-commerce index: global retail e-commerce keeps on clicking
Kearney AT (ed) (2016) China's e-commerce market in 2014: the logistics challenges. Accessed 26 Jan
Kharpal A (2016) Taxi app rival Didi Chuxing to buy Uber's China business in $35 billion deal. Edited by CNBC. http://www.cnbc.com/2016/08/01/chinas-didi-chuxing-to-acquire-ubers-chineseoperations-wsj.html. Accessed 21 Aug 2016
Kim K, Hann I-H (2016) Does crowdfunding democratize access to finance? A geographical analysis of technology projects. SSRN Electron J. https://papers.ssrn.com/sol3/papers.cfm?abstract_id=2334590. Accessed 27 Nov
Kleemann F, Voß G (2008). Un(der)paid innovators: the commercial utilization of consumer work through crowdsourcing. Sci Technol Innov Stud 4(1):5–26.
Klein, K (2014) How to raise money for a prototype. Edited by Bloomberg. https://www.bloomberg.com/news/articles/2014-10-30/small-business-how-to-raise-money-for-a-prototype. Accessed 21 Dec 2016
Koch Ramos P (2014). Crowdfunding als Finanzierungsmodell: Am Beispiel von Independent Video Games. 1. Aufl. Saarbrücken: AV Akademikerverlag

Kortleben H, Vollmar B (2012) Crowdinvesting, an innovative option for start-up financing? Conference Paper. In: 7th European conference on innovation and entrepreneurship

KPMG (ed) (2014) E-commerce in China: driving a new consumer culture

KPMG China (ed) (2016) 2016 China leading Fintech 50

Kühl E (2013) Hollywood lässt den Klingelbeutel kreisen. Edited by Zeit Online. http://www.zeit.de/kultur/film/2013-05/hollywood-kickstarter-zach-braff-veronica-mars. Accessed 16 Jan 2016

Kuo Y (2016) 3 great forces changing China's consumer market. Edited by World Economic Forum. https://www.weforum.org/agenda/2016/01/3-great-forces-changing-chinas-consumer-market/. Accessed 18 Jan 2017

Kuppuswamy V, Bayus B (2016) Crowdfunding creative ideas: the dynamics of project backers in Kickstarter: UNC Kenan-Flagler research paper no. 2013-15. SSRN Electron J. http://ssrn.com/abstract=2234765. Accessed 21 Aug

Kwan CH (n.d.) The internet industry has become the growth engine of China. Edited by RIETI. http://www.rieti.go.jp/en/china/15040801.html. Accessed 15 Jan 2017

Lajoie M, Shearman N (n.d.) What is Alibaba? It is a marketplace, a search engine and a bank, all in one. Edited by The Wall Street Journal. http://projects.wsj.com/alibaba/. Accessed 21 Aug 2016

Lambert T, Schwienbacher A (2010) An empirical analysis of crowdfunding: working paper. http://ssrn.com/abstract=1578175. Accessed 1 Feb 2014

Lamberte M (1992) Informal finance in the Philippines' footwear industry. In: Adams D, Fitchett D (eds) Informal finance in low-income countries. Westview Press, Boulder, pp 133–147

Lan L (2014) Beijing coffee shops brews a unique business model. Edited by China Daily. http://www.chinadaily.com.cn/beijing/2014-08/14/content_18307043.htm. Accessed 14 Dec 2015

Lapavitsas C (2013a) Financialization in crisis. Historical materialism book series, vol 32. Haymarket Books, Chicago

Lapavitsas C (2013b) Profiting without producing: how finance exploits us all. Verso, London

Lardy NR (1998) China's unfinished economic revolution. Brookings Institution Press, Washington, DC

Lardy N (2008) Financial repression in China: policy brief, PB08-8. Peterson Institute for International Economics, Washington DC

Larson D, Urquidi R (1987) Competitiveness of informal financial markets in Bolivia: : Economics and sociology occasional paper N. 1426. Edited by Ohio State University. Department of Agricultural Economics and Rural Sociology, Columbus, Ohio

Lawton K, Marom D (2013) The crowdfunding revolution: how to raise venture capital using social media. McGraw-Hill, New York

Leadbeater C, Miller P (2004) The pro-am revolution: how enthusiasts are changing our economy and society. Demos, London

Lee A (2014) How did alibaba capture 80% of Chinese e-commerce? Edited by Forbes and Quora. http://www.forbes.com/sites/quora/2014/05/08/how-did-alibaba-capture-80-of-chinese-e-commerce/#1efcc6676bab;%20https://www.quora.com/How-did-Alibaba-capture-80-of-Chinese-e-commerce. Accessed 9 Dec 2015

Legrand J (2016) E-commerce and crowdfunding: why are they the same in China? Edited by ParisTech Review. http://www.paristechreview.com/2016/04/18/e-commerce-crowdfunding-china/. Accessed 30 Oct 2016

Lehner O (2012) A literature review and research agenda for crowdfunding of social ventures. In: Research colloquium on social entrepreneurship. University of Oxford, Skoll Center of SAID Business School, Oxford

Lets Talk Payments (ed) (2013) Alipay Vs Tenpay – the China payments rivalry. https://letstalkpayments.com/alipay-vs-tenpay-the-china-payments-rivalry-2/. Accessed 2 Dec 2016

Levenson A, Besley, T (1996) The anatomy of an informal financial market: Rosca participation in Taiwan. J Dev Econ 51:45–68

Li J (2009) Informal finance, underground finance, illegal finance, and economic movement: a national analysis. In: Li J, Hsu S (eds) Informal finance in China. Oxford University Press, Oxford, pp 39–59

Li Y [李耀东] (2014) 众筹发展的左和右 [The pros and cons of crowdfunding development]. 金融博览 [Jinrong bolan] November:50–51

Li D [李丹] (2015a) 房地产众筹现状之法律问题探讨 [A discussion of the legal questions of the situation of real estate crowdfunding]. 法制博览 [Leg Vis] 7(中):17–19

Li X (2015b) Ant financial subsidiary starts offering individual credit scores: sesame credit's ratings to appear in Alipay mobile app and take into account range of factors, including whether friends are financially responsible. Edited by Caixin online. http://english.caixin.com/2015-03-02/100787148.html. Accessed 20 June 2016

Li X (2015c) Ping an launches subsidiary to handle new form of net investing: insurer joins JD.com in forming company to get internet users to back startup companies via equity crowdfunding. Edited by Caixin online. http://english.caixin.com/2015-04-10/100799326.html Accessed 16 Feb 2016

Li & Fung Research Center (2016) Online retailing in China. Fung Group. http://www.funggroup.com/eng/knowledge/research/china_dis_issue98.pdf. Accessed 25 Jan

Liang B, Lu H (2010). Internet development, censorship, and cyber crimes in China. J Contemp Crim Just 26(1):103–120. https://doi.org/10.1177/1043986209350437

Liao Y [廖愉平] (2015) 我国互联网金融发展及其风险监管研究 – 以 P2P 平台、余额宝、第三方支付为例 [The supervision research on China's internet financial development and risk – based on P2P platform, Yu'e Bao and the third-party payment as an example]. Econ Manag 29(2):51–57

Liao J, Welsch H, Pistrui D (2003) Patterns of venture funancing: the case of Chinese entrepreneurs. J Entrep Financ Bus Ventur 8(2):55–69

Lin S [林思含] (2015) 互联网时代音乐电台的众筹模式研究——以日本音乐电台众筹模式为例 [Research on the crowdfunding mode of the music radio station in the internet era – an example of japanese crowdfunding of the music radio station]. 中国广播 [Zhongguo guangbo] January:16–19

Linnane C (2016) China's dominance in fintech extends to its 'unicorns': China is the world's biggest peer-to-peer lender, thanks to Tencent. Edited by MarketWatch. http://www.marketwatch.com/story/chinas-dominance-in-fintech-extends-to-its-unicorns-2016-09-09. Accessed 30 Oct 2016

Liu Y (2003). Development of private entrepreneurship in China: process, problems and counter-measures. Research report. The Mansfield Center for Pacific Affairs. Entrepreneurship in Asia. 4th U.S.-Japan Dialogue, Tokyo. 16 April. http://citeseerx.ist.psu.edu/viewdoc/download?doi=10.1.1.465.5186&rep=rep1&type=pdf. Accessed 21 Jan 2016

Liu W [刘文献] (ed) (2015a) 解放众筹 [Crowdfunding revolution]: Crowdfunding revolution. Zhongguo caizheng jingji chuban she, Beijing

Liu Y [刘瑜恒] (2015b) 美国股权众筹立法发展及其借鉴意义 [The development of America's equity crowdfunding legislation and implications from its model]. 证券法苑 [Zhengquan fayuan] 14:361–385

Lopez L (2015) China has a new priority no. 1. Edited by Business Insider. http://www.businessinsider.com/china-has-a-newpriority-1-2015-5?IR=T. Accessed 28 June 2016

Lu D (2006) Remaking Chinese urban form: modernity, scarcity, and space, 1949-2005. Planning, history, and environment series, vol 1. Routledge, London

Luo W (2015) Students full of beans over rise of coffee shops. Edited by China Daily. http://usa.chinadaily.com.cn/china/2015-02/13/content_19578540.htm. Accessed 14 Dec 2015

Luo H [罗弘韬], Cheng N [程楠] (2015) 房地产众筹的非法集资风险分析 [Risk analysis of illegal fundraising of real estate crowdfunding]. 大众理财顾问 [Dazhong licai guwen] 10:86–87

Luo M [罗明雄], Tang Y [唐颖] and Yong L [刘勇] (2012) 互联网金融 [Internet finance] Zhongguo caizheng jingji chuban she, Beijing

Macneil IR (1978) Contracts: adjustment of long-term economic relations under classical, neoclassical, and relational contract law. Northwest Univ Law Rev 72:854

Madestam A (2014) Informal finance: a theory of moneylenders. J Dev Econ 107:157–174.

Maloney C, Ahmed S (1988) Rural savings and credit in Bangladesh. University Press, Dhaka

Martin M (2012) China's banking system: issues for congress. In: Chapman J, Marshall U (eds) China's banking system, currency policy and economic conditions. Asian economic and political issues. Nova Science, New York, pp 1–62

Mas-Colell A (2016) General equilibrium and game theory: ten papers. Harvard University Press, Cambridge

Massolution (ed) (2015) 2015CF crowdfunding industry report: the crowdfunding industry report

Maxwell K (2016) Ping an-backed Lufax sees H2 2016 IPO at earliest, possibly 2017 — chairman. Edited by Reuters. http://www.reuters.com/article/lufax-ipo-idUSL3N1531O7?feedType=RSS&feedName=financialsSector. Accessed 16 Feb 2016

McCulley P (2007) Teton reflections. Edited by PIMCO Global Central Bank Focus. https://www.pimco.com/insights/economic-and-market-commentary/global-central-bank-focus/teton-reflections. Accessed 20 Sept 2016

McDonald S (2015) Islamic state using social media as crowdfunding platform for terrorist activities, expert warns. Edited by ABC Online Services. http://www.abc.net.au/news/2015-11-17/is-using-social-media-to-crowdfund-terrorist-activities/6948374. Accessed 16 Jan 2016

McKinsey Global Institute (ed) (2014) China's digital transformation: the internet's impact on productivity and growth

Meng T [孟韬], Zhang L [张黎明], Dong D [董大海] (2014) 众筹的发展及其商业模式研究 [Research on the development of crowdfunding and its business model]. Innov Entrep 2:50–53

Merz T (2013) Whatsapp now offers voice messages: Whatsapp has added the option of recording and sending voice messages to its smartphone application. Edited by The Telegraph. http://www.telegraph.co.uk/technology/news/10229276/Whatsapp-now-offers-voice-messages.html. Accessed 2 Dec 2016

Miner J, Smith N, Bracker J (1992) Defining the inventor-entrepreneur in the context of established typologies. J Bus Ventur 7:103–113

Mitchell T (2016) Chinese Ponzi scheme sparks calls for protests. Edited by Financial Times. http://www.ft.com/intl/cms/s/0/ade11b08-c9a1-11e5-a8ef-ea66e967dd44.html#axzz3zVOC3vaz. Accessed 7 Feb 2016

Mohieldin M, Wright P (2000) Formal and informal credit markets in Egypt. Econ Dev Cult Chang 48(3):657–670

Mollick E (2014) The dynamics of crowdfunding: an exploratory study. J Bus Ventur 29(1):1–16. https://doi.org/10.1016/j.jbusvent.2013.06.005

Mollick E, Kuppuswamy V (2015). After the campaign: outcomes of crowdfunding: UNC Kenan-Flagler research paper no. 2376997. SSRN Electron J. http://ssrn.com/abstact=2376997. Accessed 7 Nov

Moon H (2016) China unlocks fintech potential. Edited by China Daily. http://www.chinadailyasia.com/asiaweekly/2016-08/12/content_15478469.html. Accessed 30 Oct 2016

Moritz A, Block J (2016) Crowdfunding: a literature review and research directions. In: Brüntje D, Gajda O (eds) Crowdfunding in Europe. FGF studies in small business and entrepreneurship. Springer, Cham, pp 25–53

Morris B (2015) Are QR codes thriving or dying? Edited by Business 2 Community. http://www.business2community.com/marketing/qr-codes-thriving-dying-01228016. Accessed 11 Dec 2015

n.a. (2014) 众筹: 最好的时代, 最坏的时代 [Crowdfunding: the best and the worst time]. China Comput Commun May:43–44

Nahapiet J, Ghoshal S (1998) Social capital, intellectual capital, and the organizational advantage. Acad Manag Rev 23(2):242–266

National Bureau of Statistics of China (ed) (2006) Zhongguo tong ji nian jian 2006: China statistical yearbook 2006, 25th edn. Zhongguo tong ji chu ban she = China Statistics Press, Beijing

National Bureau of Statistics of China (ed) (2007) Zhongguo tongji nianjian – 2007: China statistical yearbook 2007, 26th edn. China Statistics Press, Beijing

National Bureau of Statistics of China (ed) (2016) Zhongguo tongji nianjian – 2016: China statistical yearbook 2016. China Statistics Press, Beijing

NCFG (ed) (n.d.) NCFG profile. http://www.ncfgroup.com/en/aboutncfg.html. Accessed 17 Feb 2016

Niko P (ed) (2015) China's top 100 internet companies. http://nikopartners.com/chinas-top-100-internet-companies/. Accessed 28 Jan 2016

North D (1990) Institutions, institutional change, and economic performance. The Political economy of institutions and decisions. Cambridge University Press, Cambridge

Ohlrich N (2016) What does "charity day" mean in China? Edited by Nonprofit Quarterly. https://nonprofitquarterly.org/2016/09/20/charity-day-mean-china/. Accessed 8 Dec 2016

People's Bank of China (2014) China financial stability report 2014

Picot A, Dietl H, Franck E (2002) Organisation: Eine ökonomische Perspektive. 3. überarb. und erw. Aufl. Stuttgart: Schäffer-Poeschel

Piketty T (2014) Capital in the twenty-first century. The Belknap Press of Harvard University Press, Cambridge

Pingdom.com (ed) (2010) The incredible growth of the internet since 2000. http://royal.pingdom.com/2010/10/22/incredible-growthof-the-internet-since-2000/. Accessed 25 Jan 2016

Pozsar Z, Adrian T, Ashcraft A, Boesky H (2012) Shadow banking. Edited by Federal Reserve Bank of New York

Press G (2015) 15 Most-funded crowdfunding projects on Kickstarter and Indiegogo. Edited by Forbes. http://www.forbes.com/sites/gilpress/2015/02/16/15-most-funded-crowdfunding-projects-on-kickstarterand-indiegogo/#2715e4857a0b6c7357677ba9. Accessed 16 Jan 2016

PricewaterhouseCoopers (ed) (2013) Extending well beyond payments: mobile payment in China's digital age

PricewaterhouseCoopers Zhong Tian LLP (ed) (2015) MoneyTree China TMT report: Q1/Q2 2015. http://www.pwccn.com/webmedia/doc/635786002517607185_moneytree_q1q2_2015.pdf. Accessed 28 Jan 2016

PTL Group (ed) (2013) E-commerce in China: gain entrance into a completely different world: every minute 48,000 e-commerce transactions are made online in China. http://www.ptl-group.com/blogs/en/e-commercein-china-gain-entrance-into-a-completely-different-world. Accessed 6th Dec 2015

Ptoch J (2016) Bye bye social commerce: Twitter legt seinen buy-button auf Eis. Edited by Onlinehändler-News.de. https://www.onlinehaendler-news.de/handel/internationales/25977-social-commercetwitter-legt-buy-button-auf-eis.html. Accessed 9 June 2016

PYMNTS (ed) (2015) What's so different about China's mobile payments' ecosystem? http://www.pymnts.com/in-depth/2015/whats-driving-chinas-mobile-pay-ecosystem/. Accessed 12 Dec 2015

Qingju.com (ed) (n.d.) 浏览梦想 [Discover dreams]. http://www.qingju.com/discover. Accessed 16 Feb 2016

QR Codes (ed) (n.d.) 1 in 5 Americans say they've used a QR code. http://qr-codes.com/1-in-5-americans-say-theyve-used-a-qr-code/. Accessed 11 Dec 2015

Rabkin A (2011) The Facebooks of China. Edited by Fast Company. http://www.fastcompany.com/1715041/facebooks-china. Accessed 28 Jan 2016

Rampell A (2010) Why Online2Offline commerce is a trillion dollar opportunity. Edited by Techcrunch. http://techcrunch.com/2010/08/07/why-online2offline-commerce-is-a-trillion-dollar-opportunity/. Accessed 11 Dec 2015

Reiermann C (2015) Bargeld is ein Anachronismus. Der Spiegel 21. http://www.spiegel.de/spiegel/print/d-134995250.html. Accessed 27 Jan 2016

Ren D (2015) China's internet finance sector challenges state-owned banks. http://www.scmp.com/business/banking-finance/article/1681799/chinas-internet-finance-sector-challenges-stateowned-banks. Accessed 26th Dec 2015

Research and Markets (ed) (2015) China internet crowdfunding and wealth management industry report, 2015. http://www.researchandmarkets.com/reports/3387667/china-internet-crowdfunding-and-wealth-management. Accessed 1 June 2016

Robertson B (2014) Gold mine scams point to trouble ahead, analysts say. http://www.scmp.com/business/banking-finance/article/1424890/gold-mine-scams-point-trouble-ahead-analysts-say. Accessed 29 June 2016

Roselli A (2015) QR codes work, just not in the U.S. http://adrianroselli.com/2015/07/qr-codes-work-just-not-in-theu-s.html. Accessed 11 Dec 2015

Rutherford M (1989) What is wrong with the new institutional economics (and what is still wrong with the old)? Rev Polit Econ 1(3):299–318

Salzsieder L, Cornell D (2013) A critical look at the jumpstart our business startups act: considering the debate surrounding its provisions and implications. CPA J 83(6):18–27

Sands S (2016) George Soros: Is China becoming the US of 2008? Why George Soros sees warning signs in China. Edited by Market Realist. http://marketrealist.com/2016/05/george-soros-says-chinas-surging-credit-growth-warning-sign/. Accessed 11 July 2016

Saxton G, Wang L (2014) The social network effect: the determinants of giving through social media. Nonprofit Volunt Sect Q 43(5):850–868. https://doi.org/10.1177/0899764013485159

Schramm DM, Carstens J (2014) Startup-crowdfunding und crowdin-vesting: Ein guide für gründer: Mit kapital aus der crowd junge unternehmen online finanzieren. Springer Gabler, Wiesbaden

Schwienbacher A (2007) A theoretical analysis of optimal financing strategies for different types of capital-constrained entrepreneurs. J Bus Ventur 22(6):753–781. https://doi.org/10.1016/j.jbusvent.2006.07.003

Schwienbacher A, Larralde B (2012) Crowdfunding of small entrepreneurial ventures. In: Cumming D (ed) The Oxford handbook of entrepreneurial finance. Oxford handbooks. Oxford University Press, New York, pp 369–392

Sciencestarter (ed) (n.d.) Leitfaden für Projektstarter. https://www.sciencestarter.de/Infos/leitfaden.html. Accessed 28 April 2016

Scott S (2015) The moral economy of crowdfunding and the transformative capacity of fan-ancing. New Media Soc 17(2):167–182

Seedmatch (ed) (n.d.) Für Investoren. https://www.seedmatch.de/fuer-investoren. Accessed 29 May 2016

Shao G (2012) Internet law in China. Chandos Publishing, Oxford. http://www.sciencedirect.com/science/book/9781843346487.

Sheng J [盛佳], Ke B [柯斌], Yang Q [杨倩] (eds) (2014) 众筹 [Crowdfunding]. Jixie gongye chubanshe, Beijing

Shi-Kupfer K (2015) Internt in China: Herrschaftssystem Internet? Edited by Der Tagesspiegel. http://www.tagesspiegel.de/themen/china-2014/internet-in-china-herrschaftssystem-internet/11503208.html. Accessed 16 Jan 2017

Shipton P (1992) The rope and the box: froup savings and the gambia. In: Adams D, Fitchett D (eds) Informal finance in low-income countries. Westview Press, Boulder, pp 25–42

So S, Westland JC (2010) Red wired: China's internet revolution. Marshall Cavendish Business, London

Song F, Bram Cadsby C, Bi Y (2012) Trust, reciprocity, and guanxi in China: an experimental investigation. Manag Organ Rev 8(2):397–422

Spiegel Online (2014) Debuet an der Wall Street: Alibaba schafft Rekord-Boersengang. Edited by Spiegel Online. http://www.spiegel.de/wirtschaft/unternehmen/alibaba-boersengang-an-wall-street-wird-groessteripo-aller-zeiten-a-992668.html. Accessed 15 Aug 2016

Spirer G (2014) Crowdfunding: the next big thing: money-raising secrets of the digital age. CreateSpace, North Charleston

Startnext (ed) (2014) Mobility experience challenge. https://bmw.startnext.com/#!home. Accessed 16 Jan 2016

Statista Inc (ed) (2016a) E-commerce: China. https://de.statista.com/outlook/243/117/e-commerce/china#. Accessed 18 Jan 2017

Statista Inc (ed) (2016b) E-commerce: USA. https://de.statista.com/outlook/243/109/e-commerce/usa#market-revenue. Accessed 18 Jan 2017

Statista Inc (ed) (2016c) Entwicklung der durchschnittlichen täglichen Nutzungsdauer des Internets in Deutschland in den Jahren 2000 bis 2015 (in Minuten). http://de.statista.com/statistik/daten/studie/1388/umfrage/taegliche-nutzung-des-internets-in-minuten/. Accessed 7 June 2016

Statista Inc (ed) (2016d) Gross Merchandise Volume von Taobao vom 2. Quartal 2011 bis zum 3. Quartal 2015. http://de.statista.com/statistik/daten/studie/323840/umfrage/gmv-von-taobao-nach-quartal/. Accessed 27 Jan 2016

Statista Inc (ed) (2016e) Gross Merchandise Volume von Tmall vom 2. Quartal 2011 bis zum 3. Quartal 2015 (in Milliarden RMB). http://de.statista.com/statistik/daten/studie/323842/umfrage/gmv-von-tmall-nachquartal/. Accessed 27 Jan 2016

Statista Inc (ed) (2016f) Tägliche Dauer der Internetnutzung durch Jugendliche in Deutschland in den Jahren 2006 bis 2015 (in Minuten). http://de.statista.com/statistik/daten/studie/168069/umfrage/taegliche-internetnutzung-durch-jugendliche/. Accessed 7 June 2016

Statista Inc (ed) (n.d.) Mobile phone internet user penetration worldwide from 2014 to 2019. http://www.statista.com/statistics/284202/mobile-phone-internet-user-penetration-worldwide/. Accessed 28 Nov 2015

Stemler AR (2013) The JOBS act and crowdfunding: harnessing the power—and money—of the masses. Bus Horiz 56(3):271–275. https://doi.org/10.1016/j.bushor.2013.01.007

Stiver A, Barroca L, Minocha S, Richards M, Roberts D (2015) Civic crowdfunding research: challenges, opportunities, and future agenda. New Media Soc 17(2):249–271. https://doi.org/10.1177/1461444814558914

Sugawara T (2014) Alibaba sets out to build financial services empire. Edited by Nikkei Asian Review. http://asia.nikkei.com/Business/Companies/Alibaba-sets-out-to-build-financial-services-empire. Accessed 14 June 2016

Sun X [孙学立] (2015) 我国众筹融资模式及监管问题研究 [China's crowdfunding models and potential research questions]. J Reg Financ Res 6 (511):32–37

Swider M (2016) iOS 9 features – updated for iOS 9.3: Apple's iOS 9 update for iPhone and iPad explained. Edited by TechRadar. http://www.techradar.com/news/software/operating-systems/ios-9-what-wewant-to-see-1253732/3. Accessed 9 June 2016

Tan Y [覃怡敏] (2015) 2015，众筹该怎么玩？ [How to have fun with crowdfunding in 2015?] Zhongguo jingji xinxi July (535):74–75

Tan Z, Foster W, Goodman S (1999) China's state-coordinated internet infrastructure. Commun ACM 42(6):44–52

Teare G, Desmond N (2016) The first comprehensive study on women in venture capital and their impact on female founders. Edited by Techcrunch. https://techcrunch.com/2016/04/19/the-first-comprehensive-study-on-women-in-venture-capital/. Accessed 9 Nov 2016

Techopedia (ed) (n.d.) Web 1.0. https://www.techopedia.com/definition/27960/web-10. Accessed 26 Sept 2016

Tencent (ed) (n.d.) About Tencent. http://tencent.com/enus/at/abouttencent.shtml. Accessed 20 June 2016

The Economist (ed) (2013) Tencent's worth: a Chinese internet firm finds a better way to make money. http://www.economist.com/news/business/21586557-chinese-internet-firm-finds-better-way-make-moneytencents-worth. Accessed 20 June 2016

The Irish Times (ed) (2016) Seen and heard: Facebook secures payments services licence. http://www.irishtimes.com/business/seen-and-heard-facebook-secures-payments-services-licence-1.2875738. Accessed 20 Feb 2017

The People's Republic of China (ed) (2016) The 13th five-year plan for economic and social development of the People's Republic of China: (2016–2020). CCTP

The World Bank (2016) Bank nonperforming loans to total gross loans (%). http://data.worldbank.org/indicator/FB.AST.NPER.ZS?locations=CN. Accessed 14 Jan 2017

Toffler A (1980) The third wave. Bantam Books, New York

Trading Economics (ed) (n.d.) Deposit interest rate in China. http://www.tradingeconomics.com/china/deposit-interest-rate. Accessed 15 Feb 2017

Transact24 (ed) (n.d.) UnionPay clearing monopoly set to end this june. https://www.transact24.com/blog/unionpay-clearing-monopolyset-end-june/. Accessed 17 Aug 2016

Tsai KS (2002) Back-alley banking: private entrepreneurs in China. Cornell University Press, Ithaca

Tsai KS (2009) Beyond banks: the local logic of informal finance and private sector development in China. In: Li J, Hsu S (eds) Informal finance in China. Oxford University Press, Oxford, pp 80–103

Tse E (2015) China's disruptors: how Alibaba, Xiaomi, Tencent, and other companies are changing the rules of business. Portfolio/Penguin, New York

Tu T [涂涛] (2014) 一本书读懂互联网金融 [A guidebook to internet finance]. Di qi e guan li shi wu cong shu hu lian wang jing ji. Renmin youdian chubanshe, Beijing

Volksbanken Raiffeisenbanken (n.d.) Viele schaffen mehr: Gemeinnütziges Crowdfunding mit den Volksbanken Raiffeisenbanken. Edited by Volksbanken Raiffeisenbanken. https://www.viele-schaffen-mehr.de/. Accessed 27 May 2016

von Pischke JD (1992) ROSCAs: state-of-the-art financial intermediation. In: Adams D, Fitchett D (eds) Informal finance in low-income countries. Westview Press, Boulder, pp 325–335

Wai UT (1957) Interest rates outside the organized money markets of underdeveloped countries. Int Monetary Fund Staff Pap 6(1):80–142

Wai UT (1992) What have we learned about informal finance in three decades? In: Adams D, Fitchett D (eds) Informal finance in low-income countries. Westview Press, Boulder, pp 337–348

WalktheChat (n.d.) WeChat payment: 5 reasons Tencent might kill Alipay. Edited by WalktheChat. https://walkthechat.com/wechatpayment-5-reasons-tencent-might-kill-alipay/. Accessed 12 Dec 2015

Wallhäuser M (2014) Crowdfunding for Food: Finanzierungsalternative für landwirtschaftliche Betriebe. Crowdfunding-Studienreihe. epubli, Berlin

Wallis J, North D (1986) Measuring the transaction sector in the American economy, 1870–1970. In: Engerman S, Gallman R (eds) Long-term factors in American economic growth. Studies in income and wealth, vol 51. University of Chicago Press, Chicago, pp 95–161

Walter C, Howie F (2012) Red capitalism: the fragile financial foundation of China's extraordinary rise. Revised and updated edn. Wiley, Hoboken, NJ

Wan A (2015a) Top 5 mobile and instant messaging apps in China. South China Morning Post. http://www.scmp.com/tech/appsgaming/article/1767695/top-5-mobile-and-instant-messaging-apps-china. Accessed 28 Nov 2015

Wan A (2015b) Top 5 business-to-consumer e-commerce platforms in China. http://www.scmp.com/lists/article/1780220/top-5-business-consumer-e-commerce-platforms-china. Accessed 6 Dec 2015

Wang Q (ed) [王钦敏] (20130 中国民营经济发展报告 [Annual report on non-state-owned economy in China]: No. 10 (2012-2013), 1st edn. 民营经济蓝皮书 [Blue book of non-state-owned economy]. Shehui kexue wenxian chubanshe, Beijing

Wang S [王珊] (2014a) 中国互联网: 从第一封邮件走向世界 [China's internet: from the first email across the world]. Edited by ScienceNet.cn. http://news.sciencenet.cn/htmlnews/2014/8/301669.shtm. Accessed 25 Jan 2016

Wang H [王宏宇] (2014b) 一起来玩众筹 [Having fun together with crowdfunding]. 环球市场信息导报 05:62–65

Wang A (2015a) JD GMV exceeded 17.5B, 76% increase YoY in Q3 2015. Edited by China Internet Watch. http://www.chinainternetwatch.com/15699/jd-q3-2015/. Accessed 7 Dec 2015

Wang S [王思惟] (2015b) 中国民营企业的金融支持分析 – 从民营企业融资困境的视角 [An analysis of the financial support of Chinese private enterprises – from the perspective of the misery of private enterprise finances]. 科技视界, no. 36:304

Wang X [王欣芳] (2015c) 谁在济南玩众筹 [Who is having fun with crowdfunding in Jinan]. 齐鲁周刊 [Qilu zhoukan]:30–31

Wang L [王莉娜], Xu Z [徐朱之] (2015) 浅议P2P网络借贷平台经济犯罪特征及防范对策 [Humbly discuss characteristics of economic crime countermeasures involved in loaning platforms of P2P web]. J Shanghai Police Coll 25(2):29–34

Wang J [王婕], Wang Y [王亚美], Liao J [廖婧], Zhao J [赵婧文] (2013). P2P 网络搜索技术 [Search technology of P2P network research]. 计算机系统应用 [Jisuanji xitong yinyong] 1:13–15, 47

Wei D (2013). E-commerce bigger in China than United States. Edited by CNN International Edition. http://edition.cnn.com/2013/09/19/business/on-china-alibaba-e-commerce/index.html. Accessed 9 Dec 2015

Wei J, Burns A (2016) The future of shadow banking in China. Edited by Jerome A. Chazen Institute of International Business. http://www8.gsb.columbia.edu/chazen/globalinsights/sites/globalinsights/files/Shadow%20Banking%20in%20China_Chazen%20Institute.pdf. Accessed 29 Feb

Wen B [闻博] (2015) 国内外众筹融资模式发展现状及我国发展建议 [The current domestic and international development of crowdfunding as well as a proposal for China]. 对外经贸 [Duiwai jingmao] 8(254):75–76, 137.

Westhead P, Wright M (1998) Novice, portfolio, and serial founders: are they different? J Bus Ventur 13:173–204

Wheat R, Wang Y, Bymes J, Ranganathan J (2013) Raising money for scientific research through crowdfunding. Trends Ecol Evol 28(2):71–72. https://doi.org/10.2139/ssrn.2088298

Wildau G (2014) Alibaba affiliate wins approval for bank licence. Edited by Financial Times. http://www.ft.com/intl/cms/s/0/605c26bc-47d3-11e4-ac9f-00144feab7de.html#axzz3sztNFdZ5. Accessed 1 Dec 2015

Williamson O (1975) Markets and hierarchies, analysis and antitrust implications: a study in the economics of internal organization. Free Press, New York

Williamson O (1985) The economic institutions of capitalism: firms, markets, relational contracting. Free Press/Collier Macmillan, New York/London

Williamson O (1986) Economic organization: firms, markets and policy control. Wheatsheaf, Brighton

Williamson O (1990) A comparison of alternative approaches to economic organization. J Inst Theor Econ 146:61–71

Winborg J (2009) Use of financial bootstrapping in new businesses: a question of last resort? Ventur Cap 11(1):71–83

Wong G (2015) Tencent launches China's first private bank. Edited by The Wall Street Journal Blog. http://blogs.wsj.com/digits/2015/01/05/tencent-launches-chinas-first-private-bank/. Accessed 1 Dec 2015

Wong A, Bhatia M, Freeman Z (2009) Angel finance: the other venture capital. Strateg Chang 18(18):221–230. https://doi.org/10.1002/jsc.849

Woo C, Cooper A, Dunkelberg W (1991) The development and interpretation of entrepreneurial typologies. J Bus Ventur 6:93–114

World Bank (ed) (n.d.) Commercial bank branches (per 100,000 adults). http://data.worldbank.org/indicator/FB.CBK.BRCH.P5. Accessed 31 Oct 2016

Xia E [夏恩君], Li S [李森], Zhao X [赵轩维] (2015) 国外众筹研究综述与展望 [Crowdfunding abroad: literature review and prospect]. Technol Econ 34(10):10–16

Xie Y (2015) Chinese insurer Ping An plans listing for P2P loan platform Lufax.com. http://www.scmp.com/business/companies/article/1851554/chinese-insurer-ping-plans-listing-p2p-loanplatform-lufaxcom. Accessed 16 Feb 2016

Xie P, Zou C, Liu H (2016) Internet finance in China: introduction and practical approaches, 1st edn. Routledge, New York

Xinhua W [新华网] (ed) (2012) 吴英集资诈骗案重审改判死缓 [The case of Wu Ying's fradulent fundraising has been resumed, she was sentenced to death on detention]. http://news.xinhuanet.com/legal/2012-05/21/c_112004584.htm. Accessed 22 Nov 2012

Xinhua (ed) (2015) China tightens regulation over P2P lending. http://news.xinhuanet.com/english/2015-12/28/c_134958998.htm. Accessed 2 Feb 2016

Xu J (2012) Pennies from heaven. Edited by China Daily. http://usa.chinadaily.com.cn/china/2012-11/13/content_15924864.htm. Accessed 18 Feb 2016

Yang D [杨东], Huang C [黄超达], Liu S [刘思宇] (2015) 赢在众筹 [How to succeed with crowdfunding]. Zhongguo jinji chubanshe, Beijing.

Yang F (2016) China internet finance — what's in a name? Edited by Kapronasia. https://www.kapronasia.com/china-banking-research/are-you-fintech-or-internet-finance.html.

Yao W [姚文平] (2014) 互联网金融 [Internet finance]: 即将到来的新金融时代 [The coming era of new finance]. Zhongxin chubanshe, Beijing

Ye J (2017) China tightens Great Firewall by declaring unauthorised VPN services illegal: move means all cable and VPN services need prior govenrment approval and comes as Beijing steps up censorship before power-reshuffle party congress. South China morning post. http://www.scmp.com/news/china/policies-politics/article/2064587/chinas-move-clean-vpns-andstrengthen-great-firewall. Accessed 15 Feb 2017

Ye S [叶姝阳], Wu W [吴伟容] (2015) 众筹网络融资模式的监管问题研究——通过对比众筹与非法集资 [An Investigation of the supervision questions on Crowdfunding – by means of contrasting crowdfunding with illegal fundraising]. 财会研究 10:61–63

Yi C [逸尘] (2015) 智能跑鞋玩众筹 [The intellectual power (of) track shoes (and) having fun with crowdfunding]. 中国质量万里行 [Zhongguo zhiliang wanlihang] November:83

Yin M [殷明波] (2015) 众筹模式在中国的发展研究 [Research on the development of the kinds of crowdfunding in China?]. Times Financ 1(577):58–59

You J (1998) China's enterprise reform: changing statesociety relations after Mao. 1. publ. Routledge studies in China in transition, vol. 3. Routledge, London

Young T (2013) The everything guide to crowdfunding: learn how to use social media for small-business funding: understand crowd psychology : gain an online presence : create a successful crowdfunding campaign: promote your campaign to reach hidden funding sources. Adams Media, Avon

Young D (2016) Apple ties up With UnionPay, Baidu Eyes 99Bill. Edited by Seeking Alpha. http://seekingalpha.com/article/2691535-apple-ties-up-with-unionpay-baidu-eyes-99bill. Accessed 30 Nov 2015

Yu T [余涛] (2015a) 众筹规制探究 – 一个规范分析的路径 [A normative study of legal perplexities related to crowd funding] Zhengquan shichang daobao March:12–19

Yu X [俞小海] (2015b) P2P网络借贷平台的刑事责任问题研究 [On the criminal responsibility of P2P network lending platform]. J Shantou Univ (Humanit Soc Sci Ed) 31(5):61–67

Yu Z [余政] (2015c) 众筹与非法集资之分野探究 [Research on the division of crowdfunding and illegal fundraising]. 江西警察学院学报 [J Jiangxi Police Inst] 2.

Yu L [余来文], Wen Z [温著彬], Bian J [边俊杰], Shi L [石磊] (2015) 互联网金融 [Internet finance]: 跨界，众筹于大数据的融合 [The integration of crossover, crowdfunding and big data]. Jingji guanli chubanshe, Beijing

Zachariae S (2015) V.me by Visa: mit Bank- und Kreditkarte sicher und bequem auch über mobile Endgeräte einkaufen. Edited by Visa Europe. https://www.visa.de/uber-visa/presse-und-news/listing?tag$=$v.me%20by%20visa. Accessed 9 July 2016

Zero2IPO (ed) (2014) 中国众模式运行分析告 [Report on the statistical analysis of the dynamics of crowdfunding in China]: 2014 年上半年 [First half of 2014]

Zero2IPO (ed) (2015) 中国众筹市场发展报告 [China crowdfunding market research report 2015]

Zhang Y [张雅] (2014) '股权众筹法律制度国际比较与中国路径 [A comparison of the legal system of equity crowdfunding abroad with china's path]. 西南金融 [Xinan jinrong] November:47–50

Zhang Q [张前荣] (2015) 加快推进 大众创业、万众创新 [Accelerate mass innovation, a million innovations]. Macroecon Manag 6:17–19

Zhang T, Yip C, Wang G, Zhang Q (2014) China crowdfunding report: how to leverage crowdfunding to support China's social and environmental SGBs. Edited by China Impact Fund. http://www.ied.cn/sites/default/files/CIF%20China%20Crowdfunding%20Report_Final.pdf. Accessed 29 Jan 2016

Zhang B, Deer L, Wardrop R, Grant A, Garvey K, Thorp S, Ziegler T et al. (2016) Harnessing potential – the Asia-Pacific alternative finance benchmarking report. Edited by Cambridge Centre for Alternative Finance, University of Tsinghua and The University of Sydney

Zheng H, Li D, Wu J, Xu Y (2014) The role of multidimensional social capital in crowdfunding: a comparative study in China and US. Inf Manag 51(4):488–496. https://doi.org/10.1016/j.im.2014.03.003

Zheng H [郑海超], Qi Z [齐子毫] , Wu J [伍晶] , Wang T [王涛], Wan N [万能] (2015) 产品众筹项目融资绩效的影响因素研究: ELM 理论视角 [Antecedents of reward-based crowdfunding performance\: from the ELM perspective]. J UESTC 17(1):45–50

Zhong W [钟维], Wang Y [王毅纯] (2015) 中国式股权众筹 [Chinese style of equity crowdfunding]: 法律规制与投资者保护 [The establishment of legal rights and the protection of investors] 西南政法大学学报 [J Southwest Univ Polit Sci Law] 17(2):19–26

Zhongchou.com (ed) (n.d.) 首页 [home page]. http://www.zhongchou.com/. Accessed 17 Feb 2016

Zui gao renmin fayuan [最高人民法院] (ed) (n.d.) 最高人民法院关于审理非法集资刑事案件具体应用法律若干问题的解释 [Explanation by the Highest National Court on questions regarding the correct application of the regulation on criminal proceedings of illegal cases of fundraising]. http://www.court.gov.cn/qwfb/sfjs/201101/t20110107_12908.htm. Accessed 22 Nov 2012

The manufacturer's authorised representative in the EU is Springer Nature Customer Service Centre GmbH, Europaplatz 3, 69115 Heidelberg, Germany. If you have any concerns regarding our products, please contact ProductSafety@springernature.com

Printed and bound by CPI Group (UK) Ltd, Croydon, CR0 4YY
22/09/2026
02221055-0009